Praise for *The Loves of Theodore Roosevelt*

"Edward F. O'Keefe has given us an elegant and illuminating account of the human side of one of the most consequential Americans in our history. By detailing Theodore Roosevelt's emotional connections to the women in his life, O'Keefe reminds us that leaders are made not of marble but of heart and flesh. This is a wonderful book."

—Jon Meacham, *New York Times* bestselling author of
And There Was Light

"A graceful, powerful book that lets us into the lives of the remarkable women who shaped an extraordinary man. If you want to truly understand Theodore Roosevelt, this book is an essential guide."

—Candice Millard, *New York Times* bestselling author of
River of Doubt

"With meticulous research . . . [and] perceptive insights . . . O'Keefe has performed a most valuable service by reminding us how much Theodore Roosevelt, the most virile of presidents, owed to the brilliant women in his life."

—*The New York Times*

" 'It is not only feasible but advisable to make women equal to men before the law,' Theodore Roosevelt wrote as a Harvard senior, anticipating women's suffrage by forty years. The sentiment was consonant with the life, one shaped, advised, fortified, and energized by women. O'Keefe assembles that extraordinary cast here, nimbly cataloging the strategic, transformative power of Roosevelt's mother, daughter, sisters, and wives, all of them complicit, to different and often remarkable degrees, in TR's meteoric career."

—Stacy Schiff, *New York Times* bestselling author of
The Revolutionary

"The language is beautiful . . . and seeing Theodore's life through the lens of his female family members gives it an intimacy sorely missed in many other biographies."

—*Pittsburgh Post-Gazette*

"An extraordinary portrait of the women who nurtured, advised, and propelled one of America's most compelling leaders. *The Loves of Theodore Roosevelt* is history unearthed and more fully understood, at last."

—Susan Page, *New York Times* bestselling author of *The Matriarch*

"Entertaining. . . . [O'Keefe] celebrates [these extraordinary women's] devotion, skills and accomplishments. In doing so, he leads us to a better understanding of an equally extraordinary man."

—*The Wall Street Journal*

"A brilliantly written and entertaining look at the crucial role women played in our twenty-sixth president's political career. Highly recommended!"

—Douglas Brinkley, *New York Times* bestselling author of *The Wilderness Warrior*

"O'Keefe presents a perceptive and persuasive argument that adds a sensitive dimension to the masculine persona of Theodore Roosevelt."

—*Washington Independent Review of Books*

"Forget all that Rough Rider stuff; Roosevelt was a mushy romantic at his core, and . . . also quite progressive, which is another pleasant shocker in this very fine book."

—*Yankton Daily Press & Dakotan*

"Wonderfully readable."

—*The East Hampton Star*

"A fascinating celebration of women who helped make an iconic president. . . . [O'Keefe's] prose brings vitality and nuance to his subjects."

—*Kirkus Reviews*

"Elegant . . . a charmingly intimate view."

—*Publishers Weekly*

The
LOVES *of*
THEODORE
ROOSEVELT

THE WOMEN WHO CREATED
A PRESIDENT

EDWARD F. O'KEEFE

SIMON & SCHUSTER PAPERBACKS

NEW YORK AMSTERDAM/ANTWERP LONDON
TORONTO SYDNEY/MELBOURNE NEW DELHI

Simon & Schuster Paperbacks
An Imprint of Simon & Schuster, LLC
1230 Avenue of the Americas
New York, NY 10020

Copyright © 2024 by Edward F. O'Keefe

First Simon & Schuster trade paperback edition May 2025

SIMON & SCHUSTER PAPERBACKS and colophon are
registered trademarks of Simon & Schuster, LLC

For information about special discounts for bulk purchases,
please contact Simon & Schuster Special Sales
at 1-866-506-1949 or business@simonandschuster.com.

The Simon & Schuster Speakers Bureau can bring authors to your live event.
For more information or to book an event, contact the Simon & Schuster Speakers
Bureau at 1-866-248-3049 or visit our website at www.simonspeakers.com.

Interior design by Ruth Lee-Mui

Manufactured in the United States of America

1   3   5   7   9   10   8   6   4   2

Library of Congress Cataloging-in-Publication Data has been applied for.

ISBN 978-1-9821-4568-2
ISBN 978-1-9821-4570-5 (pbk)
ISBN 978-1-9821-4571-2 (ebook)

For Allison

"No other happiness in the world is so great or so enduring as that of two lovers who remain lovers after they are married, and who never forget the tenderness and affection, the respect and the forbearance, all of which each must at times show to the other."

—Theodore Roosevelt

Contents

M y mother and I waited together during the seven hours between my father's 5 a.m. admission to the Mayo Clinic St. Mary's Hospital in Rochester, Minnesota, and the post-op report from the surgeon. It was September 2017, and the previous day, my sixty-four-year-old father had been diagnosed with follicular lymphoma. He'd had a PET and CT scan, and we sat with the gastroenterologist to review the results.

"If it's red, it's cancer," Dr. Glenn Alexander had said.

The image on the screen lit up like a Christmas tree.

In the waiting room, I reread *The Rise of Theodore Roosevelt* by Edmund Morris, and to pass the time, I tried to construct a timeline of TR's first visit to the Dakota Badlands. My mother took note of my frantic yellow highlights and scribbled notes in the margins. On stationery from the Marriott that had become our home away from home, she wrote down the dates as I called them out: "Sept 3 1883 departs NYC, 5 days train ride layover Chicago, 21 hours to St. Paul. Sept 7 1883 Bismarck."

I was born in Grand Forks, North Dakota, and I often like to joke that at birth in North Dakota you are given a choice of idols: Peggy Lee, Lawrence Welk, Roger Maris, or Theodore Roosevelt. (Contemporary North Dakotans may also choose Phil Jackson or Josh Duhamel. Those with a literary bent are occasionally allowed Louis L'Amour or Chuck Klosterman.)

I went to Red River High School, home of the Rough Riders. More than once as a kid, my family traveled six hours west across the state to Medora, to take in the famed summer Medora Musical, and on to Theodore Roosevelt National Park, home to the Elkhorn Ranch, Roosevelt's ranch, known as the "cradle of conservation."[1] No offense to Peggy, Lawrence, or Roger but I chose Theodore Roosevelt. Maybe it was because TR—the first president to be known, in his own time and ours, by his initials—made my home state feel to me like the center of the world. Maybe it was because TR's father was the center of *his* world. Either way, my interest in Roosevelt—I won't call it what it may be, an obsession—only grew as I grew.

Dr. Mark Truty emerged from surgery with grim news. The lymphoma had grown so large that it was blocking my father's digestive pathway. He returned to the surgery, and I returned to the diverting task at hand. By then, I had reached February 1884. I noted that TR spent February 8–10 in New York City and then, curiously, even though his first wife was pregnant with their first child and due any day, returned to Albany and the New York State Assembly on February 11. Alice Hathaway Lee Roosevelt gave birth to their daughter, whom they named Alice, on February 12. I noted the date was President Abraham Lincoln's birthday.

Roosevelt returned to New York City on February 13, and in the pre-dawn hours of Valentine's Day 1884, TR lost his mother and, later that day, his wife. TR's mother was forty-eight, and his wife was twenty-two. The lore follows that in his grief Theodore Roosevelt lit out again for the Badlands of North Dakota to be a ranchman and cowboy, lived what he later called "the strenuous life," charged up San Juan Heights, Cuba, and, after an anarchist assassinated President William McKinley, became the youngest president in American history. What a simple and powerful story, I thought, as my father was delivered to the recovery room, missing an eighteen-inch portion of his intestinal tract. But he'd survived.

A little over a year later, in January 2019, I found myself at Harvard University, an "entrepreneurship fellow" at the Shorenstein Center of the Harvard Kennedy School. Ostensibly, I was there to conduct new and thought-provoking research on the potential for news and nonfiction on streaming platforms. Secretly, I spent most of my time in the nineteenth and early twentieth centuries, in the Houghton Library poring over the Theodore Roosevelt Collection.

I was determined, by this time, to tell the story of Theodore Roosevelt in the Badlands: how my native state shaped one of the most consequential presidents in American history and thus the nation and the world. I wanted to share the story of TR's resilience, the story that comforted me when I thought I was about to lose my father. That still comforted me as I watched him struggle with chemotherapy and immunotherapy to keep what remained of the cancer in his body at bay. But time and again, as I turned every page of Theodore Roosevelt's letters, I encountered something unexpected: Theodore Roosevelt was not the impossibly hardy, self-made man of myth and lore. Far from it. The most masculine president in the American memory was, in fact, the product of largely unsung and certainly extraordinary women.

The Houghton Library held a small treasure trove of letters between Theodore Roosevelt and Alice Hathaway Lee Roosevelt. Alice, his first wife, whom he married at twenty-two, is written off by most TR biographers as a privileged Victorian American gamine, an intellectual lightweight who had little to no formative consequence in her husband's life. What I found in these letters was very different. Alice was a vivacious, curious, playful, and insightful woman. It was during TR's maddening two-year pursuit of her that he embraced women's suffrage and equality—including advocating for married women to keep their maiden names—a precocious cornerstone of his progressive outlook in the 1880s.

Their time together was brief but impactful. Married to Alice, TR "rose like a rocket" in the New York State Assembly. Her death hit him all at once with all one thousand natural shocks that flesh is heir to. "*Nothing whatever* else but you," Teddy, as he was known only to his wife, close friends, and family, had written to Alice on November 5, 1881, on the eve of his first-ever election. The letter took my breath away. "Oh, my sweetest true love pray for nothing but that I may be worthy of you;

you are the light and sunshine of my life, and I could never cease thanking the Good God who gave you to me; I could not live without you, my sweet mouthed, fair haired darling, and I care for *nothing whatever* else but you. . . . The canvass is getting on superbly; there seems to be a good chance of my election, but I don't care, anyway."[2]

It wasn't only his letters to and from Alice that stunned me. Martha Bulloch Roosevelt, TR's mother, forever connected to Alice in their twinned passing on that awful Valentine's Day, was nothing like the submissively dutiful Gilded Age stereotype so often depicted. Tart, sharp-tongued, and witty, Mittie's coy turns of phrase and strong personality practically leap off the page. I thought: This indeed is the mother of Theodore Roosevelt and grandmother of Eleanor!

The revelations continued as I came to better understand the influence of TR's sisters and his second wife, Edith Kermit Carow Roosevelt. Anna Roosevelt Cowles, known as Bamie, was her younger brother's key political strategist and advisor. Bamie was to TR what Robert F. Kennedy was to President John F. Kennedy. TR's eldest daughter took the analysis of her aunt a step further: "I always believed that if she had been a man, she, rather than my father, would have been President."[3] None other than Eleanor Roosevelt agreed with that assessment: "Well, I think it might easily have been so."[4]

Corinne Roosevelt Robinson, known as Conie, was TR's younger sister, confidante, and emotional outlet. She was also one of his biggest boosters, slipping stories to the press about her brother's (quite authentic) heroics in Cuba and his White House antics and adventures with his children. Conie was her brother's press secretary before there was such a thing. Her home in New York became a center of political activity, and the siblings shrewdly took advantage of the misogyny of the era. Conie silently sat in on political discussions and, afterward, secretly gave her brother advice.

"Haven't *we* had fun being governor of New York?" TR would say to Conie.[5]

Hobbled as they were by the mores of their times, Bamie and Conie lived extraordinary lives through their brother Theodore. Had they lived in another era, their names would likely be as well known as his. Instead, they purposefully hid the roles they played in TR's rise, evidently content to fuel the narrative that he alone was the "man in the arena." Fortunately, their influence was felt by all those around them, including their niece Eleanor Roosevelt, the daughter of TR's younger brother, Elliott, who would break the boundaries of her time and inspire women for generations to come.

And then, standing beside Theodore Roosevelt, from age three to his death at age sixty, was Edith Kermit Roosevelt. Edith was TR's first love and second wife, fated to marry Theodore, but always living in the shadow of a woman who would be, in her husband's memory, forever twenty-two. While two biographies of Edith—both substantial and insightful—have been written, her full significance in American history is still not understood. She was the first modern first lady. Without a template to follow, Edith defined that role at the outset of the twentieth century. Not only did she elevate the position of presidential wife to an American institution, a curator of her husband's legacy and a curator of the White House itself, she exerted an enormous political, moral, and emotional influence on her husband. Another president, Franklin D. Roosevelt, said of Edith: "She managed TR very cleverly without his being conscious of it—no slight achievement, as anyone will concede."[6] The influence of Edith could, and should, fill volumes.

This book celebrates five of the extraordinary women who surrounded TR: Martha Bulloch Roosevelt, Anna Roosevelt Cowles, Corinne Roosevelt Robinson, Edith Kermit Carow Roosevelt, and Alice Hathaway Lee Roosevelt. They are Theodore Roosevelt's remarkable mother, two sisters, and two wives—women to whom he owed an inestimable debt of gratitude, as do all of us who admire him. These women opened the door to the American Century and pushed Theodore through it, picking him up when he faltered, and relentlessly prodding him to live a life of greatness. You will also briefly meet some equally compelling women who left their mark, such as his grandmother Patsy Bulloch and aunt Anna

Bulloch Gracie, social reformer Jane Addams, author Edith Wharton, and two underappreciated icons of the American West, the delightful Patty Selmes and her groundbreaking daughter, Isabella Greenway, who will go on to become the first congresswoman in Arizona's history, founder of the famed Arizona Inn, and wife to not one but two Rough Riders. We also get a glimpse of TR's loving relationships with a younger generation of Roosevelt women, including his niece Eleanor and daughter Alice, both of whom benefited from the guidance of TR's sisters as much as he did.

I, too, owe a debt of gratitude to a pair of remarkable women. My Houghton Library research led me to read two phenomenal works: *The Roosevelt Women* by Betty Boyd Caroli and *Theodore Roosevelt: A Strenuous Life* by Dr. Kathleen Dalton. This book would not exist without the pioneering work of Betty and Kathy. Each of their volumes offers powerful and persuasive evidence that emboldened me to pursue my central argument that the women in Theodore Roosevelt's life played a much larger role in shaping his life and legacy than has yet been appreciated. I stand on their shoulders and pay respectful homage.

I once asked Kathy, who was kind enough to have me to her home outside Boston, why more hadn't been written about the women in Theodore Roosevelt's life.

"Time," she replied, without a moment's hesitation. "People weren't ready to understand TR as being anything but the product of his own will."

We are, all of us, the product of those who believed in us. Sometimes it's a brother or sister, our parents, a friend, a teacher, a mentor, or even a stranger. More often, it is a combination of some or all of these. Theodore Roosevelt's life is frequently held up as an example of resilience and willful determination, sui generis and well-nigh supernatural. I do like and admire that picture of TR, but it is mistaken. He had help, and I like Theodore Roosevelt even better knowing that he needed help from his family and friends. Mittie, Bamie, Conie, Edith, and Alice were as much a part of Theodore Roosevelt's success as his almighty autochthonous will. Maybe now the time has finally come in which we can more fully appreciate these women in the arena.

Part One

TEEDIE & EDIE

1852—1878

1

TEEDIE

"I am very thankful that I can leave the little ones with you having that implicit confidence that you will take almost a little too good care of them."

—Theodore Roosevelt Sr. to his wife, Mittie Bulloch Roosevelt

From the beginning, the survival of Theodore Roosevelt was very much in doubt.

His life, he would later say—not inaccurately—would depend on his own will. This was a centerpiece of the Theodore Roosevelt mythos: the self-built man. It was true, but it also wasn't.

He was born to Martha Bulloch Roosevelt (known to all as "Mittie") and Theodore Roosevelt Sr. (popularly known as "Thee") in the family brownstone at 28 East 20th Street, Manhattan, on October 27, 1858. It was soon obvious that the infant wasn't well. Childhood asthma, both frequent and severe, continually threatened to suffocate him, so that he was unable to sleep flat in a bed and had to prop himself on a mountain of pillows. Chronic congenital diarrhea—the family and their physicians genteelly termed it "cholera morbus"—contributed to his ghostly complexion and undersized physique, which invited comparison to a stork, especially since he developed the habit of reading while standing, the foot of one leg resting against the calf of the other. His frail frame was often assailed by high fevers and racking coughs, and his mother, more often than not, was the one who protected and cared for him.

"Mittie is quite motherly, likes to have him lying quite near her," Mittie's mother wrote a week after the birth.[1] She was not the only one devoted to the sickly boy. From the beginning Theodore Roosevelt was attended to by nurses, his mother, her mother, and Mittie's sister, Anna. A formidable corps of women cooled every fever, sat through every cough, made him eat, made him walk, and gave him strength.

Early on, physicians—the wealthy New York Knickerbocker family could afford to engage any number of them—were doubtful that the multiply afflicted child would reach his fourth year. Yet he endured. He endured patiently at first; then, as the years and ailments compounded, fiercely. In a 1921 memoir, his younger sister, Corinne (called "Conie" and pronounced "Connie"), who would become a crucial protector of her much loved brother's legacy, wrote of the irony of a man whose very "name later became the synonym of virile health and vigor," having begun life as "a fragile, patient sufferer." In the memoir, she summoned from the past an image of him "now struggling with the effort to breathe" but still "ready to weave for us long stories of animal life—stories closely resembling the jungle stories of Kipling—for Mowgli had his precursor in the brain of the little boy of seven or eight, whose knowledge of natural history even at that early age was strangely accurate, and whose imagination gave to the creatures of forest and field impersonations as vivid as those which Rudyard Kipling has made immortal for all time."[2] In Conie's always rose-colored view, Teedie was a preternaturally intelligent child eager for adventure and already able to enrapture a crowd.

To contemporary observers, the centerpiece of the Roosevelt family was its patriarch, Theodore Roosevelt Sr., who attained an almost mythical status in the oft-told story of TR's upbringing, while his mother was ushered to history's sidelines in keeping with the times. It is probably no surprise that young Theodore idolized his father, which may have compounded this problem. But Thee Roosevelt's influence on the boy was not admired by all. Dr. A. D. Rockwell, one of the many physicians who treated the sickly boy, observed to his medical partner that "the little fellow ought to make his mark in the world; but the difficulty is, he has a rich father."[3] Dr. Rockwell should have known better. Thee Roosevelt was not a father to spoil his children. Dote on them? Yes. Ensure that they knew what it meant to be a Roosevelt? Absolutely. But give them the silver spoon treatment? Not on his life. Or theirs.

Theodore Roosevelt Sr. was the son of Cornelius Van Schaack "C.V.S." Roosevelt and Margaret Barnhill Roosevelt. C.V.S. was partner in Roosevelt & Son, by the mid-nineteenth century a venerable and exceedingly successful import company and investment banking house. The family had been established in America by Claes Martenszen van Rosenvelt (1623–1659), who arrived in New Amsterdam from Tholen in Zeeland, the westernmost province of the Netherlands, sometime between 1638 and 1649. As Alice Roosevelt Longworth, Roosevelt's eldest child, gleefully snarked, the Roosevelt clan arrived "one step ahead of the bailiffs from an island in the Zuider Zee."[4] Her implication is that Claes was in flight from creditors. Not impossible, but the fact was that the Netherlands was in such political and economic upheaval at this time that the Rosenvelts were but one family of very many who emigrated from the old Netherlands in Europe to settle in America's New Netherland colony.

The Roosevelt fortune was founded on the hardware business begun in 1797 by Theodore Roosevelt's great-grandfather, James Jacobus Roosevelt (1759–1840), in lower Manhattan. This developed into Roosevelt & Son, which eventually left hardware to go into the wholesale importation of fine plate glass, much coveted by prosperous families building great homes. Thus funded, the firm branched out into investment banking. In its various iterations, Roosevelt & Son was the fountainhead of the very considerable, very old Roosevelt family money, and Theodore's father was a prominent member of the firm as well as a philanthropist, whose social consciousness was firmly rooted in the Victorian doctrine of Muscular Christianity—a notion of Christian virtue that partook of a patriotic duty to one's country, self-discipline, altruism, and a respect (bordering on worship) for strenuous athleticism and gentlemanly sportsmanship. As a movement, Muscular Christianity grew in popularity as men (especially the social elite) of the latter half of the nineteenth century searched for ways to prove a manliness compatible with turn-the-other-cheek piety. It gave rise to the Young Men's Christian Association (YMCA) and depictions of Jesus Christ that were, well, beefier. Boys learn from their fathers, and Theodore Roosevelt Sr. embraced the social progressivism of like-minded men who believed in a strong, vigorous Christ and an ethos of mens sana in corpore sano, a healthy mind in a healthy body. It is not too much to say that, for the Roosevelts, a "strenuous life" was practically a religion, not merely a virtue, as has been argued by Dr. Kathleen Dalton, the most influential TR scholar in a generation.

Of course, young TR has another parent, who was in almost every respect his father's match and just as important of an influence, but in a different manner. Where Theodore Roosevelt Sr. was a revered figure of some remove from his family, Mittie was usually in the trenches. The common view of Mittie is as a valetudinarian product of the antebellum drawing room and fainting couch. And yet, her life more frequently shows strength not weakness, especially through the Civil War. The true story of the rise of Teddy Roosevelt really begins with the woman who gave him birth, raised him, and bequeathed in him the same fiery, often indomitable, spirit.

Few husbands and wives were more opposite than Thee and Mittie Roosevelt. He was a monument to discipline and order. While his son called him unreservedly "the best man I ever knew," he also confessed that "he was the only man of whom I was ever really afraid" and characterized him as the family's "dispenser of serious punishment," which was undoubtedly physical.[5] Mittie, in contrast, was in the words of Roosevelt biographer Edmund Morris "small, vague, and feminine to the point of caricature."[6] And yet Mittie had already been, when Thee courted her, a woman with whom to be reckoned.

Family tradition has it that Thee met Mittie when he was nineteen.

He had visited, in Philadelphia, Mittie's older sister, Susan, who was married to Hillbourne West, a local physician. Susan enjoyed regaling her guests with stories of her Southern childhood, and young Thee was soon eager to see Bulloch Hall (and, presumably, Susan's younger sister) for himself.

Mittie Bulloch was a sharp-witted romantic, later rumored to be the inspiration for Scarlett O'Hara in *Gone with the Wind*. The comparison is, of course, not entirely flattering. The Bulloch family traveled with six slaves, and there were at least thirty-one adults and thirty-three children held in the bondage of slavery at Bulloch Hall, the family's 1839 Greek Revival mansion.[7] James Dunwoody Bulloch saw the fire in his young half-sister. Writing on July 11, 1849, he called the fourteen-year-old "a black haired bright eyed lassie lively in her disposition with a ready tongue" who "does everything by impulse with an air of perfect self-confidence, but she is a warm hearted little darling."[8] These words almost perfectly predict how people almost uniformly saw her son, Theodore Roosevelt: lively, impulsive, and self-confident with a ready tongue.

Thee's first meeting with Mittie was hardly auspicious—at least not from her point of view. The fifteen-year-old girl found Roosevelt rather too serious and even pedantic (he called every plant he saw by its Latin name). As for Thee, he was sufficiently impressed to send Mittie the token gift of a gold thimble after he returned to New York. It was not until three years later, in early 1853, that he conjured another invitation to the Wests' when he heard that the elusive Mittie was visiting them in Philadelphia. Now eighteen, she was far more appreciative of Thee's looks and manner. They spent much time together in Philadelphia, he invited her to New York, and the long-delayed courtship suddenly accelerated. Immediately after Mittie returned to Georgia in May, Thee wrote to her mother, asking for her hand. Steeped in her own regional prejudice, Patsy responded less than enthusiastically: "I have never interfered with the matrimonial designs of my children and never will when the object chosen is a worthy one. Therefore I refer the matter back to Mittie and yourself."[9]

Mittie, flirtatious and coy, could not resist being playful with her stern suitor. "I suppose ere this you have seen that our engagement is approved of," she wrote Thee two weeks later, on June 1. "The first day from Mittie was rather lonely, was it? I cannot tell you for fear of flattering you, how much I thought of you that day. I will say this much, you were ever nearest my heart." Mittie asked that Thee keep their engagement a secret, and asked her older sister, Anna, to wear a diamond ring to confuse gossip-prone society.[10] Anna, less than two years older than Mittie, was her closest confidante, as calm and even-keeled as Mittie was impetuous and strong-willed. The Bulloch sisters were inseparable until Mittie's marriage.

"Does it not seem strange to think we should have met [again] and become engaged, after only knowing each other time enough to create a passing interest, and then [being] separated for almost three years," Mittie remarked to Thee in another letter on June 9. "Some times when I think of it all I feel as 'tho it were ordered by some higher power."[11] The wedding took place at Bulloch Hall, just three days before Christmas of 1853. Patsy had been widowed four years earlier, and while Mittie appreciated that her mother could ill afford extravagance, she demanded it anyway. "The great fault of the present day is the excessive extravagance and fondness for show," Patsy later wrote Mittie. "I wish, my precious child, I could do all for you that my heart dictates, but I hope that you will make so good a wife that Thee will never have cause to regret his having married a girl without a fortune. It is important for your own happiness darling, and the happiness of your husband, that you should be industrious, practical, and moderate in your desires—without these qualities you would not be contended if you possessed millions—with them, you [will be] happy with what you and Anna call paltry stipends."[12] But Mittie was far from frugal and Thee would be no more successful than Patsy in restraining her. When he tried, Mittie playfully bantered that Thee was her "loving tyrant." His love language was infantilizing, calling Mittie "one of my little babies" and demanding, "Do not become a strong-minded woman."[13] She had, as ever, other ideas.

Before Thee arrived—on his bride's orders "one day before the nuptials 'and not a day sooner'"—she wrote him teasingly all about the attention local men were lavishing upon her: "My dear Thee I kiss a great many different people and always expect to," Mittie defiantly explained. "I cannot allow you a monopoly there. Why just think of what the world would be without kisses. I could not think of depriving my friends of that *pleasure.*"[14]

He could well believe it. Diminutive at five feet, Mittie had shimmering sable hair, pellucid blue eyes, and a complexion her granddaughter described as "more moonlight white than cream-white."[15] Thee was outgunned, overmastered, and outnumbered—as none of his four brothers or their families deigned to make the trip to Georgia. Only his parents, Cornelius Van Schaack Roosevelt and Margaret Barnhill Roosevelt, were in attendance for the wedding in the dining room of Bulloch Hall on December 22.

Her coquettish teasing notwithstanding, Mittie was proud of and grateful for the match she had made, telling Thee that he was the "only person who could ever suit me" and that she "put every confidence" in him.[16] Certainly, the Roosevelt family was distinguished and Thee was firmly ensconced in the venerable and prosperous family business, but Mittie was the product of a lineage rather bolder and certainly more colorful. Her people were pioneering missionary stock who made good first in South Carolina and then, from 1760 on, in Georgia. Settling on a two-thousand-acre Georgia land grant, the family produced Archibald Bulloch, who became Speaker of the Georgia Royal Assembly and, as the American Revolution approached in 1775, president of the Provincial Congress before being appointed delegate to the First Continental Congress. The Bullochs grew wealthy in the cotton trade, less as planters than as exporters.

Mittie moved with her husband to a grand townhome in New York, purchased by C.V.S. Roosevelt for the newlyweds and next door to Thee's brother and his wife. Mittie went from being surrounded by Bullochs to being surrounded by Roosevelts. Her in-laws were welcoming, but living among so many intimate strangers may have been stifling. The Victorian age demanded women of Mittie's ferocious personality be proper. No such limits would be put upon her son. He was a man, and his exuberance would be celebrated as much as Mittie's independence was disdained.

Mittie and her older sister also desperately missed one another. "It is only when I think that you are happy and therefore I ought to be that I can feel in any degree reconciled to our inevitable separation," a still single Anna wrote to Mittie in September 1854, nine months after her sister's wedding. "The idea never entered my mind that either of us could ever leave the other, that we could be anything but Anna and Mittie, inseparable, always serving, reading, walking, riding and talking incessantly together. We never confided in each other because there was never anything to confide, each always knew all about the other . . . oh Mittie I believe it would kill me if anything should happen to you."[17]

There was no particular reason for Anna to fear for her sister, other than perhaps due to the ever-present risk of childbirth—and Mittie was, in fact, five months pregnant with her first child. But there were darker undercurrents to Mittie's relationship with her husband. Mittie wrote, on July 28, 1872, in a never-published letter to her sister, "Thee has appeared at the door and not in dulcet tones ordered me to bed." Defiant of her husband's "order," Mittie continued to write to Anna, confessing, "I am afraid of Thee."[18] "Greatheart," as his son sometimes referred to him in his diary, was as stern as Mittie was indulgent. And though TR gave his father virtually all the credit for his character, Thee displayed none of the vivaciousness and infectious personality for which his son and daughters became renowned. "Darling, I will try for yours and my own sake not to be provoked, but this is a hard thing," Mittie wrote Thee a year and a half into their nearly quarter-century-long marriage, "I am very sensitive and impulsive. You know what my temperament is."[19]

Despite their very different personalities, and occasional tense moments, Mittie and Thee were devoted to one another. "I feel that our interests are so entirely united that I speak of it without reserve and this unity of feeling must continue to bind us more and more closely together," Thee wrote Mittie in May 1855. "On all subjects we must learn to feel or confide in each other. . . . You will be a companion to me, will you not dearest, in all my hopes and thoughts?" Mittie was more direct: "I love you inexpressibly dearly. . . . I want to talk to you. I want to see you. I cannot live without you."[20] Mittie, in letter after letter, unabashedly expresses her devotion, though she cannot rationally explain how these diametric opposites fell in love: "Without you, Thee, I feel as tho life would lose its charm . . . it seems to me as tho my very thought and feeling had some mysterious connection with you."[21]

Mittie and Thee's "unity of feeling" would be tested during the Civil War, which erupted eight years and three children into their marriage. Theodore Sr. was a Northerner and Unionist, whereas Mittie, born in Hartford, Connecticut, but raised in Georgia, was, in her son's words, "a sweet, gracious, beautiful Southern woman, a delightful companion and beloved by everybody" but "entirely 'unreconstructed' to the day of her death."[22] Mittie's widowed mother, Patsy, supported secession with zeal. According to some sources, Mittie went so far as to hang out the Confederate Stars and Bars battle flag after news of any major battle in which the Confederacy emerged victorious.[23] The act was defiant, bordering on dangerous, but a lack of enthusiasm for the war was not at all unusual in New York State, especially in and around New York City, where the war was seen as damaging to business. Nine-term Democratic congressman and three-term mayor of New York Fernando Wood not only led the pro-Southern delegation to the 1860 Democratic National Convention and favored compromise in the run-up to the war, he went so far as to propose that New York City secede from the Union, declare itself an independent city-state, and engage in a highly profitable commerce with both the USA and the CSA.[24] In July 1863, the city was the site of infamous draft riots, the quelling of which required several thousand Regular Army troops, including men who had just left the Gettysburg battlefield.[25]

Thee could easily have secured an officer's billet in a New York regiment. But he did no such thing. As was the case with many American families, the war was also very personal. Thee knew only too well that one of Mittie's brothers was serving in the Confederate navy and the other in the Confederate government. Irvine Stephens Bulloch had the distinction of firing what Theodore Roosevelt claimed were the last two shots of the celebrated Confederate commerce raider CSS *Alabama*, which preyed on Northern shipping. With the sinking of that vessel, he served aboard other Confederate ships. James Dunwoody Bulloch had an even more consequential career with the Confederacy, serving in Liverpool as the secession government's chief foreign agent. Thee was faced with a profound dilemma. How could he take up arms against his own kin? It was not just his brothers-in-law. Mittie had friends and former neighbors fighting for the Confederacy. In the end, he opted for a course many of his prosperous friends chose. He hired a substitute soldier to serve in his place, a perfectly legal alternative in 1861, which would be additionally codified in the Enrollment Act of 1863.

In search of a way to be of service to his country without firing upon a single Confederate soldier, Thee and two like-minded associates drew up a legislative bill to authorize the appointment of unpaid allotment commissioners, whose mission it would be to tour Union military posts and encampments to persuade the soldiers to participate in a voluntary program by which they allotted a portion of their pay to support their families, many of which were under severe hardship due to the absence of the breadwinner. The effort also appealed to Thee's puritanical bent, as the soldiers might otherwise spend their pay on unsavory distractions such as alcohol and gambling. "I would never have felt satisfied with myself after this war was over if I had done nothing and that I do feel now that I am only doing my duty," Thee wrote to Mittie in the first year of the Civil War. "I know you will not regret having me do what is right and I don't believe you will love me any less for it."[26]

Mittie did not hide her feelings: "I have felt and continue to feel too gloomy about your frequent and prolonged absences."[27] But Thee, still stinging from his decision not to fight, felt the pull of duty and longing: "Give a great many kisses to the dear little children from me. It seems such a pity to be away from them so much still I cannot help feeling that it would be my duty unless this has had [sic] turned up to be away from them altogether by joining the army."[28]

Throughout the Civil War, the Roosevelts lived in a house divided in a nation divided. Before the war, Mittie's mother, Patsy, and her sister, Anna, left their homes in the South and were welcomed to live with the Roosevelts in New York City. Thee was outnumbered three to one in his own home by Southern sympathizers. Sunday dinner at the grand mansion of C.V.S. Roosevelt was a weekly tradition—but even this tradition appears to have buckled under the strain of war. "I went there [to C.V.S. Roosevelt's home] yesterday for dinner," Mittie wrote Thee on December 15, 1861. "But Thee something occurred there which made me determined not to dine there again unless my resolutions should be accountably changed." Mittie did not recount the exchange which irreparably altered her relationship with her father-in-law, but she reported, "I felt my blood boil. . . . I made no reply whatever but I could not touch another mouthful of dinner."[29]

"I wish we sympathized together on this question of so vital moment to our country," Thee wrote to Mittie, adding, "I know you cannot understand my feelings and of course do not expect it."[30] "Good bye my dear heartless Thee," Mittie, in a foreshadowing of her son's famously sharp tongue, would sometimes sign her Civil War era letters. If Mittie called Thee "heartless" in one letter, the next was signed "Good bye my dear old warm Thee." "That first morning when I get home I look forward to an indefinite amount of affections," Thee wrote Mittie on December 10, 1861. "You must not disappoint me."[31]

Thee traveled for weeks at a time each month during the war. Meanwhile, Mittie was home with now four children, all but one under the age of five. "Little Teedie has no nurse but is such a mischiefous little rogue that he requires as much watching as any of them," Patsy wrote her daughter Susan Hillborne West, who lived in Philadelphia. "It is amusing when they are all around her in the nursey to see Mittie's perplexed look."[32] Mittie had help but was decidedly an active and involved mother. Her letters to Thee detail the splendor and exhaustion of motherhood:

"Last night [Elliott] slept still until two oclock when he awoke in the brightest possible frame of mind. After getting up many times with him, letting him eat an indefinite quantity of crackers, being very much amused at his cunning ways. When he saw Teedie asleep he would whisper, 'Teedie heep' then suddenly catching sight of Anna he cried out in the loudest possible voice, 'Allie.' Finally becoming very sleepy and tired myself, I tried to coax him to sleep which I accomplished first after a crying spell. Then he came into my bed and fell asleep while I was stroking his curls, etc. Teedie was miserably jealous about his sleeping by me."[33]

Thee acknowledged Mittie's primary role in raising the children, especially during his prolonged absences during the Civil War, writing: "I am very thankful that I can leave the little ones with you having that implicit confidence that you will take almost a little too good care of them."[34] Mittie, for her part, was thankful to have her mother and sister, not to mention a retinue of paid caretakers, to aid in raising the children. Patsy was puritanical and far more practical than her daughter. Yet the near constant presence of three Bulloch women meant Teedie and his siblings grew up in the upper echelon of the nation's most bustling Northern city surrounded by a cocoon of Southern warmth and love.

Grandchildren provided a much needed distraction for Patsy, who fretted about the fate of Irvine and James, whose letters hardly ever reached New York. Patsy desired to travel south, a trip that required a pass and would almost certainly mean she could not return north. "If I do not go to see my poor son before he dies, I should never forgive myself," Patsy wrote. Mittie asked Thee to help but felt conflicted. If Thee succeeded in obtaining a pass, Mittie might never see her mother again. "Oh dear Thee, I have heart ache," Mittie wrote her husband in Washington on February 12, 1862. "I do not feel as tho I could endure the grief of parting." Mittie need not fear: the deeds James and Irvine were accused of doing were so dastardly that Thee could not obtain a pass. Despite their differences, Patsy wrote of her son-in-law: "Thee is a good young man. I really think if anyone ever tried to do their duty he does."[35]

Ten months into the war, Thee traveled to Washington, D.C., to meet with President Abraham Lincoln. In a never-before-published letter dated December 31, 1861, he wrote to his son, then three years old:

Dear Tedie,

There is a picture of a horse made out of stone that looks a good deal like the statue opposite Grandpa's. It stands just in front of the house of the President who governs our whole country and has just told me to go round and see all the soldiers from our state. Ask your mother to read for you the writing on the stone under the horse and then learn it by heart so that you can repeat it to me when I come back to New York.

The statue printed on the stationery features Andrew Jackson astride a horse and the words: "THE FEDERAL UNION IT MUST BE PRESERVED."[36] Did Thee succeed in needling Mittie from afar?

A profoundly moral man, Thee remained clearly torn about his role in the war effort. "It is a great luxury to feel I am at last doing something tangible for the country," he wrote in a letter to Mittie. *Luxury?* He continued: "I cannot get Bammie's and Tedee's faces, as they bid me goodbye at the door, out of my mind."[37] Riding from camp to camp, serving his country even to the point of exhaustion, was, he apologetically feared, a "luxury" purchased at the expense of his family.

Mittie spoke her mind to her husband and father-in-law, and despite her own political views to the contrary and despite her mother's watchful gaze, graciously hosted federal officials throughout the Civil War. "Thee gave a party to some Federal officers & their wives on Tuesday night," Patsy wrote to her daughter in Philadelphia. "Of course I made myself scarce."[38] In another letter, dated November 29, 1862, Patsy again wrote Susan: "Mittie can't help giving those little suppers to Thee's friends. He wishes it, and you know he does not feel as we do, and it is his own house. It jars upon my feelings but of course I keep my room."[39] On January 1, 1863, President Abraham Lincoln issued the Emancipation Proclamation, and in November of that same year he delivered the Gettysburg Address.

He would face a bitter reelection in 1864, a year of uncertainty for both sides. "The coming New Year confuses me," Patsy wrote on December 30, 1863. "Mittie & Thee give a large party New Years evening. All day they will receive visitors. Just imagine how tiresome it will be."[40] Mittie, who would later live by the credo "live for the living, not the dead," had an attitude of resiliency that she would pass to her children.[41]

Mittie was certainly aware that she was mother to a precocious and unusual child.

On April 28, 1868, ten-year-old Teedie (sometimes written as "Tedie") wrote his first known (surviving) letter. It was to his mother, who was visiting family in Savannah, accompanied by Thee and Conie. (It is a testament to the strength of their marriage that the couple made the post–Civil War trip together.) Not just extraordinarily precocious in its maturity, the letter was also clearly the work of an extraordinarily creative mind and generous sensibility. Teedie complimented his mother on the length of her letter to him—"What long letters you do write. I don't see how you can write them."—and his turn of phrase was lively with physical detail: "My mouth opened wide with astonishment when I heard how many flowers were sent in to you." Marvelous! But even better is the devilishly personal twist in the follow-up sentence: "I could revel in the buggie ones." He went on to tell her how he "jumped with delight" at her account of hearing a mockingbird, and he asked of her: "get some of its feathers if you can." He turned next to sending his love to the family in Georgia and then reported that "Aunt Annie, Edith, and Ellie (Teedie's younger brother, Elliott) send theirs to you."[42] As far as we can know, this is the first time Teedie ever mentioned, in writing, the name of his playmate (and future wife) Edith Carow, who—nestled between his aunt and brother—already seemed practically one of the family.

That first letter from child to mother did not betray the amount and frequency of illness that still dogged Teedie. In fact, illness stalked all the Roosevelt children. "Biographers who marveled at TR's ability to overcome asthma and a frail childhood, should have paid due respect to the ailing health of [Bamie]," observes Roosevelt historian Michael Cullinane. "Her story of perseverance impresses as much as her brother's."[43] Her story of courage and resilience is indeed admirable, and she didn't learn it from her brother. She taught it to him. The firstborn, Bamie suffered from a congenital spinal defect that put her into a painful harness for much of her young life. "I am quite uneasy about her back," Patsy Bulloch wrote on April 29, 1856, when her granddaughter was just over a year old. "There is something wrong there. She cannot stand more than a second on her feet and then her countenance expresses pain, and she seems to crumble down."[44] Bamie endured patiently, even stoically—an example to her loving younger brother. It is likely that her condition contributed to a certain self-reliance and almost certainly delayed any thought of marriage—so long, in fact, that everyone, including she herself, considered her a confirmed spinster.

Brother Elliott, handsome and robust of physique, looked the picture of health but likely suffered from undiagnosed epilepsy, which contributed to the alcoholism that would cast his adult life in profound shadow. Conie, like Teedie, was asthmatic and afflicted by frequent headaches.

Thus every member of Mittie and Thee's family suffered from one affliction or another, but it was Teedie's health that, with ample good reason, caused the greatest anxiety. He was sick so long and so often that his development appeared somewhat stunted; he was smaller than his younger brother. In the summer of 1868, the senior Roosevelt took the family to a summer rental in Barrytown-on-Hudson, in Dutchess County, New York. He hoped that the salubrious seasonal air and the availability of outdoor activities would bring some color to his pallid son. But his anxiety also extended to his wife, Mittie, who seemed startlingly changed from the woman he'd had "implicit confidence" could manage the household in his absence just a few years before.

Her mother, Patsy, had been seriously ill much of 1864, the last full year of the Civil War. "So long a time has passed and we have suffered so much that I am too bewildered to write anything connectedly out of the chaos of thoughts that chase each other in and out of my mind,"

Anna Bulloch wrote a cousin in Savannah in January 1865. "Our beloved Mother was ill nine months long and after *such* suffering that we call last summer her passing summer." Displaying a demeanor reminiscent of her stoic grandson, Patsy endured through sheer willpower and little complaint. Anna continued, "All these long months of sickness she never uttered one impatient word what she suffered and only groaned when no human being could have endured what she suffered. One thing that overcomes me entirely is the remembrance of the longing to see poor Irvine that never left her night nor day. One night when she was extremely ill, she called me to her bedside and said, "Anna, if I should get too ill to remind you, remember that if you should hear that Irvine was dead and the South over—come never tell me, I could not hear it!"[45]

Patsy Bulloch died on October 30, 1864, three days after her eldest grandson Theodore's sixth birthday. She was buried at Green-Wood Cemetery in Brooklyn, decidedly Northern soil, where Mittie's brothers would not be able to pay their respects. The two were deemed so egregious in their activity on behalf of the Confederacy that they were among the very few singled out for exclusion from the general amnesty the U.S. government would grant to those who fought or governed for the South. It was even alleged that James Dunwoody Bulloch directed secret funds to finance the Lincoln assassination. The brothers therefore remained in permanent exile in England. James quite literally took the Confederacy's "lost cause" to his grave, inscribing "An American by Birth, An Englishman by Choice" on his headstone.[46]

Mittie, who missed her brothers desperately, just could not seem to shake the aftereffects of the Civil War. Her formidable resolve, which had kept her family afloat, finally began to falter. Increasingly nervous and unsettled, she began to fit the endearment Elliott had created for her: "Sweet little china Dresden mother."[47] She had lost her mother, contact with two brothers, and at a time when no birth control existed had given birth to four children in six years. She adored her husband, but he could be stern and unforgiving. And while the marital and family bonds continued to be strong, the passion in their marriage was doubtless strained. For the sake of their marriage, it appears Thee and Mittie set aside politics after the Civil War. But by that time, Mittie had become something of a caricature of the feckless mid-Victorian Southern belle. She was tired, worn down by life, and eager for a change. The Roosevelt children would later recall an exhausted version of their mother for good reason.

In an era when medical science was often at a loss, travel, especially distant travel that required an ocean voyage, was seized upon as a sovereign curative for all manner of vague disease and even vaguer malaise. All Mittie really wanted was to satisfy her longing to visit England, home-in-exile of her brothers. She instigated a voyage to Liverpool, where the pair founded and operated a lucrative trade as cotton importers and brokers. In obliging her, Thee vastly expanded the trip into a Grand Tour of Europe.

He wanted the expedition not merely to divert or even to cure but to educate, and he accordingly plotted out an eight-nation itinerary requiring a year's sojourn. In the mid-nineteenth century, such Grand Tours were common among the wealthy families. Even so, Thee pushed it to something of an extreme in scope and duration. Perhaps surprisingly, the prospect of the long journey did not please the adventurous and endlessly curious Teedie any more than it did his siblings. All preferred to stay in the Hudson Valley for a halcyon summer of fun unburdened by responsibility. But the senior Roosevelt was adamant.

The lack of enthusiasm may have been compounded by the intimates they'd need to leave behind. When Conie numbered herself with Teedie and Ellie, she could well have added Edith "Edie" Carow, who was Conie's earliest and closest friend. As biographer-historian Betty Boyd Caroli noted, they had been born less than two months apart and "met when they were barely toddlers."[48] The senior Roosevelt and Charles Carow, Edie's father, had been boyhood friends, and Conie later wrote of how the Carow house backed up against the 14th Street mansion of Mr. and Mrs. Cornelius Van Schaack Roosevelt. These things were "a natural factor in the relationship of the younger generation, and Edie Carow and little Corinne Roosevelt were pledged friends from the time of their birth."[49]

Conie was hardly possessive of her friend and eagerly shared her with
Teedie, who she recognized had already developed strong feelings for the
girl, with whom he would have a sometimes fraught relationship as they
progressed together into adulthood. On May 12, 1869, the day the family
embarked on the Grand Tour, the ten-year-old boy wrote in his diary
that it "was verry hard parting from our friend" and it made him cry "a
great deal." The "friend," surely, was Edie, whom Roosevelt biographer
Edmund Morris calls young Teedie's "most intimate acquaintance outside the family circle."[50]

Conie, Ellie, and Teedie were less than thrilled about the whole
Grand Tour enterprise. Years later, Conie recalled:

> On our arrival in Liverpool we were greeted by the Bulloch uncles, and
> from that time on the whole European trip was one of interest and
> delight to the "grown people." My older sister, though not quite fifteen,
> was so unusually mature and intelligent that she shared their enjoy-
> ment, but the journey was of rather mitigated pleasure to the three
> "little ones," who much preferred the nursery at 28 East 20th Street, or
> their free summer activities in wood and field, to the picture-galleries
> and museums, or even to the wonderful Swiss mountains where they
> had to be so carefully guarded.[51]

The Grand Tour bonded the already close Roosevelt siblings even
more tightly together. Away from home, they had only one another and
slowly the primary day-to-day influence on TR shifted from his mother
to his sisters. Bamie joined the adult ranks while Conie and Ellie contented themselves in talk and play with whatever children they could
find. The dynamics of the Roosevelt siblings helped to develop TR's out-
sized personality: Bamie was so mature that rather than be the leader of
the "little ones," she ceded that role to her younger brother and instead
acted like one of the adults; Conie and Ellie were delighted to revel in
their big brother's marvelous stories and join in on his adventures, happily acquiescing to his leadership.

Teedie always looked for "some expert along the line of his own interests," especially natural history. Conie noted, however, that "the writing
and receiving of home letters [stood] out more strongly than almost any
other memory of this time, and amongst those most treasured by Teedie
and myself were the little missives written by our most intimate friend,
Edith Kermit Carow." To Conie, Edie wrote on November 19 that she was
"much pleased at receiving your kind letter telling me all about Teedie's
birthday." Conie noted that Teedie "expressed always a homesick feeling
when 'Edie's' letters came. They seemed to fill him with a strong longing for his native land!"[52] As her exclamation point suggests, Conie was
keenly cognizant of her brother's feelings toward Edie though it must be
acknowledged that Conie wrote of this youthful attachment retrospectively.

Tucked away in the Theodore Roosevelt Collection at Harvard's
Houghton Library is a tiny Belgian lace Christmas keepsake hand-
painted with a pair of doves above a cross within a crown of thorns,
which is encircled by a wreath. The doves flutter on either side of an anchor, a Christian icon of the hope of heaven. Below this is the inscription
"Espérance au Ciel, Courage sur la terre"—"Hope in heaven, courage on
earth." On the back of the keepsake is written "A peace offering," and it is
signed "T.R." The little gift had been enclosed in two pieces of paper on
both of which "Don't open till Christmas" is penciled in Teedie's young
hand; one also includes the notation "From Teedie." Why he called the
little gift a "peace offering" we do not know. But he did record in his
diary on Monday, November 22, 1869, "In the evening Mama showed me
the portrait of Eidieth Carow and her face stirred up in me homesickness and longings for the past which will come again never, alack never."
Teedie's homesickness was sufficiently powerful for him to record on November 30 that he "cried for homesickness and a wish to get out of the
land where friends (or as I think of them enemies) who can not speak
my language are forced on me." What prompted him to fear he would
"never, alack never" return to Edie? Melancholy? An overexposure to the
sentiment in the Victorian novels he read? Or had they parted after some

spat? All that is certain is that Edith Carow Roosevelt treasured the keepsake lifelong.[53]

Teedie may have been growing rather moody as adolescence approached, but Conie possessed a disarming absence of self-importance, an abundance of honesty, and an engaging ability to smile at her own foibles. She recalled how Mittie earnestly tried to instill an appreciation of Michelangelo in her eight-year-old self. She was planted before what she refers to as "The Torso of the Vatican," but what must have been the fragmentary Belvedere Torso, a first- or second-century Roman work in which Michelangelo did, in fact, find instruction and inspiration:

> [W]ith the hope of arousing artistic instinct, my lovely mother said: "Now, darling, this is one of the greatest works of art in the world, and I am going to leave you here alone for five minutes, because I want you to sit very quietly and look at it, and perhaps when I come back in the five minutes you will be able to realize how beautiful it is." And then I saw my mother's slender figure vanish into another room. Having been always accustomed to obey my parents, I virtuously and steadily kept my eyes upon the legless, armless Torso, wondering how any one could think it a beautiful work of art; and when my mother, true to her words, returning in five minutes with an expectant look on her face, said, "Now, darling, what do you think of the great 'Torso'?" I replied sadly, "Well, mamma, it seems to me a little 'chumpy'!"[54]

From her recollection of this exchange, Conie turned admiringly to a letter her brother had written to Aunt Anna. "Will you send the enclosed to Edith Carow," he wrote. "In it I described our ascent of Vesuvius, and so I will describe Pompeii to you." Ever the effective publicist, Conie related that her brother entered "into an accurate description of everything connected with Pompeii, gloating with scientific delight over the seventeen skeletons found in the Street of the Tombs." Conie read his letter closely, uncovering another detail that speaks volumes about the good-humored sensibility that dwelt a little deeper within her studious brother. He fell "for one moment into a lighter vein, [tell-ing] of two little Italian boys whom my father engaged to come and sing for us the same evening at Sorrento, and whose faces were so dirty that my father and his friend Mr. Stevens washed them with 'Kissengin Water,'" medicinal mineral water from Bavaria's Bad Kissingen. "That extravagance seems to have been specially entertaining to the mind of the young letter-writer."[55]

Far from proving salubrious to Thee's or Mittie's health, the long Grand Tour brought on a veritable ration of misery. There was, to begin with, the combination seasickness and homesickness of the voyage out, though Teedie managed to enjoy conversations with a gentleman from the West Indies whose knowledge of natural history rivaled his own.

Mittie made arrangements to reunite in England with her two self-exiled brothers. The Roosevelts traveled aboard the *Scotia*, which could not dock in Liverpool at low tide, and so "James and Irvine, anxious to see their sister and her children, used a harbor tug" to reach them. Mittie was reunited with her brother James for the first time in almost eight years, although Irvine had traveled to the United States under a pseudonym two years after the war. Mittie, Anna, and Irvine had a secret meeting in Central Park after Irvine placed a personal ad in the newspaper: "If Mrs. Theodore Roosevelt and Miss Anna Bulloch will walk in Central Park up the Mall, at 3 o'clock on Thursday afternoon of this week and notice a young man standing under the third tree on the left with a red handkerchief tied around his throat, it will be of inter-est to them." Once the harbor tug reached the *Scotia*, presumably this meeting was as joyous as the previous was clandestine.[56] The Roosevelts met Irvine's fiancée, describing her as the "freshest, dewiest pink rose bud, lovely eyes, dark, her picture is exactly like her . . . blushing and affectionate."[57]

Teedie, the avid reader, loved Scotland, including a visit to Abbots-ford, Sir Walter Scott's mansion, but found the damp climate aggravat-ing to his asthma. In London, his parents called in a doctor to examine their son. No sooner did the physician announce that his lungs were clear than Teedie was besieged by a prolonged asthma attack, which prompted his parents to rush him to Hastings for a three-day dose of sea air.

In July, the family sailed down the Thames and then made a Channel crossing to Antwerp. After touring the Netherlands, the Roosevelts went to Germany and took a voyage up the Rhine, on which Teedie was again laid under asthmatic siege. When the family crossed into Switzerland, family hikes replaced museums. One day in August, "Theodore went twenty-two miles, Bamie eighteen miles, Ellie twelve, Conie three [and] Mittie, supposedly invalid, walked nine miles." Bamie's feat is worth special note, as her congenital spinal condition had neither improved nor magically disappeared. She simply got on with it. Lifelong, Conie and TR would admire Bamie's "splendid dauntless attitude toward the physical pain she suffered."[58] As later generations remarked: "She went through great agony, and her courage was perfectly amazing. Most people would have given up long, long before. I've never seen any woman . . . suffer such pain."[59] Bamie provided a stirring example of stamina, resilience, and courage for her younger siblings.

Theodore came down with a toothache, bellyache, and asthma but remained fascinated by all that he saw. Despite his ill health, he climbed an eight-thousand-foot mountain at Chamonix. While he couldn't shake his headache or diarrhea or asthma, he pressed on, thoroughly mesmerized by his surroundings. At night, he sat up in bed, the better to breathe. He drank strong, hot, black coffee to ease his asthmatic spasms. But each milestone on the journey brought a new ailment or a revisit from an all-too-familiar one. Crossing into Austria brought on cholera morbus and asthma.[60]

Mittie spent countless hours tending to her son. She took Teedie to Russian baths and massaged his aching chest and neck. "Mama's love and attention were magic. His physical need for her, the intense attachment he felt, are expressed with striking candor and frequency," historian David McCullough observes. "Whereas Papa made him drink black coffee or smoke a cigar or swallow ipecac (with "dreadful effects"), Mama

soothed, petted, 'rubbed me with her delicate fingers.'"[61] Mittie cared little for whether her son was "manly" enough, but Thee certainly did. Thee
did what he could to help relieve his son's attacks but never suggested he
yield to them. The cigar did bring some relief from the wheezing, and
the boy was able to climb the Adelsberg, a mountain in Germany, only
to fall quite ill in Vienna. After spending a day in bed, he indicated that
he felt somewhat better and found himself accompanying his father on a
tour of the Treasury, where they saw Charlemagne's crown, and then to
the Natural History Museum.

At every stop and at every site, Thee alternately challenged and re-
assured his son. But as the summer weather gave way to autumn, the
asthma attacks increased in severity and frequency. In Salzburg, the boy
recorded in his diary a nightmare in which "the devil was carrying me
away." (Might he have read a translation of Goethe's "Erl-King"?[62]) He
apparently awoke with "collerer morbos"—cholera morbus, chronic diarrhea. In Munich, he was "verry sick." In Dresden, someone (he does not
identify who but it was almost certainly Mittie) massaged his chest until
"the blood came out." In that same city, he recorded a restless night and
how, in the wee hours, he lay awake. "All was dark excep the fire. I lay
by it and listened to the wind and thought of the times at home in the
country when I lay by the fire with some hickory nuts. . . . Again I was
lying by the roaring fire (with the cold October wind shrieking outside)
in the cheerful lighted room and I turned around half expecting to see it
all again and stern reality forced itself upon me and I thought of the time
that would come never, never, never."[63]

Thus, asthma and cholera morbus mingled with intense homesickness, but that wasn't all that was on the boy's mind. Shortly after his
twelfth birthday (which was October 27) he and his parents were in
Brussels and "went to a shoe makers," where he "saw a girl . . . the most
beautiful but ferocious girl I have ever seen in my life." Three weeks
after this, now in Paris, his mother "showed me the portrait of Eidieth
Carow and her face stired up in me homesickness and longings for the
past which will come again never, alack never."[64] Mittie knew a portrait

of Edie might be more restorative than any tonic. In this instance, she perhaps understood Teedie better than Thee did. His parents' striking differences would ultimately serve TR well. Thee challenged his son, and in later years TR would benefit from his ability to project manliness. From Mittie, he learned empathy and the essential ability to connect with people.

Sick and depressed, the twelve-year-old wrote as if he were at the end rather than the beginning of his life. As an adult, we shall see, he had something of a literary passion for the works of Edgar Allan Poe. While we don't know whether he had yet dipped into Poe's poetry and prose, it is tempting to detect an echo or perhaps a premonition of the Raven's "Nevermore" in this amalgam of homesickness, sexual awakening, and poignantly abject longing. The image of Edith—Edie—is not the ferocious beauty he glimpsed in Brussels, but it stirs up profound emotion nevertheless.

The odyssey continued. In Rome, Teedie encountered Pope Pius IX in a procession through an avenue on the Pincian Hill. Conie recalled that her brother whispered to the group of American children with whom he and she were playing that "he didn't believe in popes—that no real American would"—but then, she wrote:

> as is often the case, the miracle happened, for the crowd parted, and to our excited, childish eyes something very much like a scene in a story-book took place. The Pope, who was in his sedan-chair carried by bearers in beautiful costumes, his benign face framed in white hair and the close cap which he wore, caught sight of the group of eager little children craning their necks to see him pass; and he smiled and put out one fragile, delicate hand toward us, and, lo! the late scoffer . . . fell upon his knees and kissed the delicate hand, which for a brief moment was laid upon his fair curling hair.

Up to this point, Conie's anecdote seems headed for some good-natured ribbing. But if the tableau she described says much about young

Teedie—not to mention the pope's charisma—her interpretation of the action says even more about her love and admiration for her brother:

> Whenever I think of Rome this memory comes back to me, and in a way it was so true to the character of my brother. The Pope to him had always meant what later he would have called "unwarranted superstition," but that Pope, Pio Nono, the kindly, benign old man, the moment he appeared in the flesh brought about in my brother's heart the reaction which always came when the pure, the good, or the true crossed his path.[65]

Teedie's health soon took a turn for the better. He was quite well during the rest of his stay in Rome and in his progress through Florence, Bologna, and Turin. But Paris, to which the family returned on March 10, 1870, was cold and damp, bringing on a renewed siege of asthma. Warmer weather improved his condition, and if there is any credence to the psychosomatic dimension of asthma, so did the prospect of returning, via England, to New York, where they landed early in June. The sum of the grand journey: ten months, thousands of miles, "sixty-six different hotels in eight countries."[66] The strenuous life, indeed!

The family settled in the Hudson Valley summer home to which Teedie had so longed to return. Come September, when the Roosevelts returned to East 20th Street, Thee took his son to Dr. A. D. Rockwell for a thorough physical examination. The physician was pleased by the "bright, precocious boy" but pronounced him "by no means robust." He believed that his chest was underdeveloped and did not provide sufficient room for his lungs to operate efficiently. His difficult asthmatic breathing, the doctor said, was putting a strain on his heart.[67] This diagnosis prompted Thee to have a frank talk with his son.

Conie later wrote that her mother often told her how the senior Roosevelt sat his son down. "Theodore," he said, "you have the mind, but you have not the body, and without the help of the body the mind cannot go as far as it should. You must *make* your body. It is hard drudgery to make one's body, but I know you will do it." Based on her mother's account, Conie described a gesture characteristic of her brother, who "looked up, throwing back his head . . . then with a flash of those white teeth which later in life became so well known that when he was police commissioner the story ran that any recreant cop would faint if he suddenly came face to face with a set of *false* teeth in a shop window—he vowed, '*I'll make my body.*'"[68] It is perhaps notable that there is no record that Thee gave such advice to Bamie; she would have to find her inner strength on her own.

Conie wrote that this "was his first important promise to himself . . . and for many years one of my most vivid recollections is seeing him between horizontal bars, widening his chest by regular, monotonous motion—drudgery indeed—but a drudgery which eventuated in his being not only the apostle but the exponent of the strenuous life."[69] In Conie's telling of the story years after her brother's death, this is the moment, at nearly age twelve, that began Teedie's long march to health. There is no mention that it had been Mittie, Patsy, Anna, and a number of nurses and caregivers who ensured that Teedie would survive beyond his fourth birthday. Ironically, in perpetuating the myth of her brother as a self-made man, Conie all but erases her mother's involvement. As for so many mothers before and after her, Mittie's steady consistency would relegate her essential role to an afterthought. Ever-present in her son's life, she is quite easy to overlook, while Thee's untimely death would seal his fate in his son's story as a hero.

Conie was aligned with her brother in recognizing not just that pain and suffering were inevitable, they were useful and necessary. There is no evidence that she or her brother read Friedrich Nietzsche, but both would have recognized truth in his aphorism from *Twilight of the Idols* (1889): "What does not kill me makes me stronger."[70] She wrote in her memoir of her brother of the "lovely times when we were not obliged to think of sculpture or painting—weeks in the great Swiss mountains when, in spite of frequent attacks of [Teedie's] old enemy [asthma], my father writes that 'Teedie' walked many miles and showed the pluck and perseverance which were so strikingly part of his character. . . . And so the year of exile had its joyous memories, but in spite of them never were there happier children than those who arrived home in America in the spring of 1870."[71] The America to which Teedie returned was all the more inviting for the presence of Edie Carow there. Edith would become his most trusted advisor, the caretaker of his image and legacy, the woman most often by his side and always in the arena. It was she, by circumstance and twist of fate, who would have the most profound impact on Theodore Roosevelt's life. But, like any fated lovers, the path they trod would not be easy.

2

EDIE

"I love thee, and my heart will bear
The seal which thou hast set forever."

—Edith Carow, age fourteen

*E*dith Kermit Carow came into the world with life's odds, from all appearances, stacked in her favor. But appearances are, as the adage goes, deceiving, and Edie would soon find herself clinging to the Roosevelt family for her salvation.

She was the daughter of Charles Carow, who was a partner in his wealthy family's well-established shipping firm, Kermit & Carow. Born on October 4, 1825, Charles was the seventh of eight children, the progeny of Isaac Quentin Carow and Eliza Mowatt. Charles grew up on Cortlandt Street, at the bottom tip of Manhattan, where, at the bustling seaport intersection of South Street and Maiden Lane, the warehouse of the family business stood. From their offices located over the warehouse proper, Isaac and his son-in-law Robert Kermit, who married Charles's eldest sister, could survey their company's clippers and oversee the steady stream of goods that gangs of longshoremen transferred from ship to warehouse. The vessels of Kermit & Carow sailed from New York to the West Indies and Liverpool, transporting the produce of the islands—molasses and sugar, mostly—to trade for the manufactured merchandise of Europe and the East. Shipping was one of the key American industries of the nineteenth century, and fortunes were made as well as lost in it. The business was as tempting and treacherous as the sea and the wind and as volatile as largely unregulated local, national, and global trade could make it.

Charles, the only male child who survived into adulthood, was a bookish young man. For that matter, so was his father, but while the senior Carow was a natural entrepreneur, his son had little interest in business. Eliza Mowatt Carow died when Charles was just twelve, and his father followed her to the grave thirteen years later. Thus, at twenty-five, Charles found himself thrust prematurely into a business of which he had gathered some knowledge but for which he had neither aptitude nor passion.

Judging from his having remained a bachelor until thirty-two, far beyond the customary marrying age for men of the day, Charles Carow also had little interest in fathering a family. But when he encountered Gertrude Tyler, a young Connecticut woman nine years his junior, whom he met when she was visiting the city and lodging at the upscale New York Hotel, he was at last smitten. A photograph taken when Gertrude was probably middle-aged reveals a woman with a long, hawkish nose and a mouth rather too full, by no means conventionally beautiful yet nevertheless a commanding and refined presence.

The courtship unfolded at a leisurely pace, and perhaps the geographical distance between them served him well as he pressed his suit. Handsome and rich, Charles Carow had the obvious attributes of a good catch. What Gertrude was literally not in a position to observe at first hand on a daily basis, however, was the behavior of a man who had a prodigious and growing weakness for drink, an appetite likely stimulated by the pressures of the trade that had been thrust upon him.

Yet she must have had an inkling. Edith Carow Roosevelt biographer Sylvia Morris cites a letter in which Gertrude responded to the news that

Charles had broken two bones of one arm when he fell from his rapidly moving carriage. Absentminded clumsiness? Bad luck? Gertrude rejected such explanations and instead assumed his problem was not the velocity of the vehicle but the volume of spirits he had likely consumed. She joked about this with a ferocity one would not expect from a sweetheart, telling him in a letter that he would benefit more from consulting a doctor of divinity than a doctor of medicine.

Eight months after this exchange, though it savors little enough of affection, Charles wrote to Gertrude's father, Colonel Daniel Tyler IV, a West Point graduate with a distinguished family pedigree—he was once introduced to the Marquis de Lafayette through a letter written by his cousin, Aaron Burr. Charles's note, both formal and graceful, consisted of but three sentences: "I have to ask of you the greatest favor that one man can ask of another. I have won Gertrude's heart. Will you give me her hand."[1]

A handsome and wealthy man, though already in early middle age, he did not have to ask Colonel Tyler twice.

Gertrude Tyler had married into one of New York's wealthiest families. Charles was not only a partner in a successful shipping company, but (according to the Isaac Carow will housed in New York City Surrogate Court) had inherited a one-seventh share of his father's $258,277 estate (close to $10 million in present dollars), which included $36,670 in cash and silver plate, fine furnishings, art, jewelry, vintage wines, and a portfolio of Manhattan real estate.[2] There were also certain shares in the Hudson River Railroad, the Ohio Canal, and other investments. He must surely have appeared financially unassailable.

Six months after his birth on February 26, 1860, the first child of Charles and Gertrude Carow died. Within less than a year of this misfortune, Gertrude was again with child and, as the time of her confinement neared, she returned to her parents' home in Norwich, so that she and her baby could be closely looked after. That is how Edith Kermit Carow came to be born in Connecticut on August 6, 1861.

Gertrude had made a prudent decision in seeking the asylum of the Tyler mansion. Norwich was a much less hectic place than New York City, and the infant Edith had grandparents to dote upon her. But history penetrated even this most elegant of cocoons. The fall of Fort Sumter preceded Edith's birth by five months, and the nation was in the full throes of civil war. Sixty-three-year-old Colonel Tyler, Gertrude's father, was appointed brigadier general of U.S. volunteers in March 1862 and promptly set off to join the Union's Army of the Mississippi in what was called the Western Theater of the conflict. In March 1864, long before the war was over, Edith's maternal grandmother Emily Lee Tyler died, and the quiet, stately mansion house was shuttered and broken up into apartment dwellings.

Gertrude, Charles, and Edith had left well before this, moving with the tide of New York City wealth. This time, it was to a townhouse on Livingston Place, just off 14th Street, close to Union Square, where Cornelius Van Schaack Roosevelt, grandfather of six-year-old Theodore Roosevelt Jr., had his mansion. Charles and Cornelius became close friends.

In 1928, Edith recruited her second eldest son Kermit in the compilation of historical material to commemorate her maternal ancestors. Her status as widow of the late President Roosevelt gained her the attention of Charles Scribner's Sons, which published the compilation as *American Backlogs: The Story of Gertrude Tyler and Her Family, 1660–1860*.[3] It is a valuable, if somewhat tedious, piece of what we might call micro history, but the book's most revealing detail is the terminal date given in its subtitle. The book ends the year before Edith's birth.

Why?

It is not as if nothing worth recording had happened during Edith's lifetime. Clearly, the significance of this end date is the author's desire to suppress, if not erase, the Carow-Tyler years subsequent to 1860, at least as far as history was concerned. From her intimate vantage point, they were years of precipitous and painful decline, a break with her brutal past.

Charles Carow never asked to be a shipping magnate, but the reins of Kermit & Carow fell into his hands anyway. At first, he did manage to make money, but soon he was losing much more, year after year. Perhaps his luck was bad. Perhaps his business acumen was deficient. Or perhaps he simply lacked the heart and the resilience to bounce back from the lows that almost inevitably followed the highs. Whatever the cause, as his young family grew, he apparently took to drink with more concentrated passion than he ever devoted to the shipping enterprise. As Charles descended, he leaned on Robert Kermit, his brother-in-law and deceased father's business partner, for financial assistance and, for a time, a place to live. In a story passed down orally but never written down by the Roosevelt family, the descendants of Kermit Roosevelt claim that a grateful and somewhat chagrined Charles Carow asked Robert Kermit how he could possibly repay him, financial restitution not being a viable option. Robert, who had no children and treated Charles more like a son than brother-in-law, asked that Charles and Gertrude consider naming their first-born son Kermit. They did, and when the baby Kermit Carow died not long after birth, Gertrude and Charles decided to name their second born, a girl, Edith Kermit Carow. So important was it to the Carows and Edith that the name "Kermit" be passed down that Edith took the unusual step of maintaining her middle name even after marriage and bestowing it upon her second born, often thought to be her favorite child.[4]

"Mother . . . never told us stories about her childhood at all," Edith's stepdaughter, Alice Roosevelt Longworth, wrote in 1954 to Hermann Hagedorn, TR's friend and early biographer.[5] Neither did Edith Carow Roosevelt tell such stories to anyone else, nor commit them to the pages of history, not, anyway, at any considerable length. It is unclear when the sense of shame in her family began to take hold of her. She certainly loved her father, with whom she bonded far more intimately than she did with her mother, who, perhaps in consequence of an increasingly unhappy marriage, was emotionally distant and devoted little time to her. It also may help explain the hard soul that lurked underneath Edith's well-bred façade, which would make her a challenging spouse (and sister-in-law) as the years went on.

After the birth of Edith's sister, Emily, on April 18, 1865, Gertrude turned over both girls to Mary "Mame" (pronounced "Maim") Ledwith, a down-to-earth nurse who had emigrated from famine-afflicted Ireland in the 1840s.[6] Mame Ledwith was at the very least decent, though Theodore Roosevelt described her, presumably reflecting his wife's recollection, as an "amiable and solicitous tyrant."[7] Perhaps we can conclude from the 2-to-1 ratio of Roosevelt's formulation that her approach to the children was one of friendly attention spiked with absolute authority. It must have been at least preferable to the remote presence Gertrude projected in what Edith called "the cool rooms with high ceilings, matted floors & furnishings covered with shining gay flowered chintz that was in New York."[8] If the family could not be cheerful, at least the upholstery could be. According to stories Edith later told her grandchildren, Mame Ledwith encouraged the Carow daughters to clean their plates by invoking hard times in Ireland, where, she said, the poor required "the ticket for soup and the letter for brandy."[9] Perhaps it was nothing more than the kind of thing parents and nannies have said to picky eaters since time immemorial. Or perhaps it reflected Mame's intuition about the imminent decline in the Carows' fortunes.

How early did Edith note her father's flaws and, perhaps, his suffering? Did she see and understand the effects of his alcoholism? We don't know. Charles Carow's childhood sketchbook, which Edith treasured lifelong, reveals a sensitive soul, imaginative mind, and a skilled hand. Gallant horses, gentle pastures, and majestic ships fill the pages.[10] He encouraged in Edith a passion for reading and for learning. Like the senior Roosevelt, too, Carow nurtured the athleticism of both his daughters (Edith would become a fine horsewoman) and imparted to them his avocational interest in nature and the natural sciences. Nevertheless, between the increasing severity of his alcoholism and a disposition far more inclined toward intellectual and aesthetic pursuits than business, the family's finances, prodigious as they were when Gertrude gave Charles her heart and Colonel Tyler gave him her hand, now dwindled apace.

The increasingly straitened circumstances of the Carows hardly meant Dickensian poverty. The children were still well-mannered and well-clothed. Clearly, within the elite circles in which the family still moved there must have been much talk about the slow-moving failure of Charles Carow. Doubtless, too, tongues wagged with schadenfreude. Yet appearances were kept up, facilitated by a superficially polite society that valued appearances over almost everything else. The era would soon be called the Gilded Age for that very reason, and its desire to dwell on the surface became the subject of novels by the likes of Henry James, Edith Wharton, and William Dean Howells.

In part because Edith made a positive effort to purge these years from her recollection and may have even disposed of other, more substantial forms of documentation, we don't know what the Carows' friends and associates truly felt about them during the long decline—except in one case. The Roosevelts were consistently welcoming. The two families would soon be inexorably linked.

Emily Tyler Carow was born just four days after Abraham Lincoln was shot at Ford's Theatre. One week after her birth, most of the country's long period of mourning was culminating in the meandering railroad journey of the martyr's coffined body from Washington to Springfield, Illinois, by a route that took it through Maryland, Pennsylvania, New Jersey, New York, Ohio, Indiana, and Illinois, to arrive in Springfield on May 4.

On April 24, the funeral train reached Jersey City. Lincoln's casket was removed from the special car and taken by ferry across the Hudson River to Manhattan, where it was put on public view in City Hall. The next day, on April 25, at two in the afternoon, the coffin was placed on a fourteen-foot-long funeral car drawn by a team of sixteen horses draped in long blankets. The grandly solemn procession went up Broadway to 14th Street, to Fifth Avenue, continuing as far as 34th Street, where it turned left, proceeding to Ninth Avenue and the Hudson River Railroad Depot, from which the president's mortal remains would continue to Albany.

In every city and hamlet through which the train passed, crowds congealed along the tracks. In places where the casket was transported through the streets, people jammed every conceivable vantage point, and in Manhattan, the well-publicized procession route was packed. Residents rented spaces at windows overlooking the route for as much as $100. Edith Carow had a privileged invitation to the mansion of Teedie's grandfather, Cornelius Roosevelt, which commanded a magnificent corner view of Broadway. A famous photograph from 1865 shows the Lincoln funeral cortege proceeding north on Broadway, passing below the mansion. At the upper left of the photograph, two young boys lean out from an open second-story window, the shutters flung wide. Years later, Edith identified one of these figures as her husband at age six. She knew this to be the case because she was there—not looking out the window, but present nonetheless, having been locked in a nearby closet by her rough playmate Teedie and his younger brother, Elliott.[11]

Conie and Edie had been playmates since infancy. In a rare public sharing of a childhood memory, Edith recalled in a 1933 speech to the Woman's Roosevelt Memorial Association an instance from her fourth year "when my mother came to the nursery to say that the Roosevelt children were coming to spend the day." Edith told the ladies that she remembered "hiding my old and broken toys" until Mame Ledworth—*not* Gertrude Carow—sagely intervened. "The shabbiest of all might give the visitors the most pleasure," she said.[12] It was from this time that Edith dated her relationship with Teedie, whom she invited to play house with her, explicitly excluding his younger brother, Ellie, who was then five and a half. Teedie's mother, Mittie, was soon aware that Edie and her son were forming a special intimacy. Her embrace of Edie as a playmate for her son says something about Mittie. Although she was raised in a Georgia mansion (and thus dismissed by many Knickerbockers as a stereotypical Southern belle), it seems never to have occurred to her to hold the increasingly imperiled Carows at arm's length. She encouraged a bond with Edie that came to encompass Bamie, Conie, and Ellie in addition to Teedie, so that the family came to think of Edie as a "bonus sister." Mittie went so far as to invite Edie to attend a home school version of kindergarten with Ellie and Conie in the Roosevelt home at 28 East 20th Street. Gertrude accepted eagerly. Once again, Mittie had little concern for appearances. She was doubtless pleased that Teedie, at the time an unprepossessing boy, very nearsighted, awkward, and afflicted with a combination of childhood asthma and cholera morbus, had a devoted playmate and companion. In short, Mittie was happy her precocious child had made a friend, one who would bring out in each other both their talents and flaws.

Edie must have been impressed with Mittie, a great beauty whose bearing was what one might expect from the product of a Roswell, Georgia, antebellum mansion. Bamie recalled in a 1929 letter to her son, William S. Cowles Jr., that her mother sometimes wore "an enormous crinoline and a perfectly exquisite white muslin dress over a pink silk lining with all the little ruffles at the bottom edged with real lace." There was a cloak that matched the dress, and her "bonnet tied under her chin with great pink ribbons." The hat brim was adorned with "a great big pink rose" and "perfectly realistic little green dragon flies." Mittie also carried "a parasol with a real ivory handle and the lining of pink covered with muslin and trimmed"—again—"with real lace."[13] If Mittie sought to model for her children this high-Victorian image of pampered femininity, the indoctrination did not take. Both Bamie and Conie were destined to take more active roles in their lives and the life of their brother Theodore.

Mittie had delegated the home school tutorial duties to her maiden sister, Anna, in return for room and board in the 20th Street home. The Civil War had ruined their Aunt Anna financially. But even after 1866, when she married James K. Gracie, at the time a rising New York real estate investor (and later a wealthy investment banker), she continued to teach the children beyond the kindergarten level, Edie included. "Aunt Gracie . . . was more of a mother to them than their own mother," a

Roosevelt descendant later observed.[14] The comment was perhaps less a dig at Mittie than a compliment of their shared role in raising the children. "A large part of [Theodore's] intensity was traceable to the Bulloch blood," historian Carleton Putnam observed. "Young Theodore had his mother's and his aunt's enthusiasm of response to varied stimuli, their vividness of feeling, and he was beginning to show signs of their torrential expressiveness."[15] It's difficult to know how much was nature and how much nurture. But the Bulloch sisters were certainly raising Theodore in the image of their own strong-willed expression.

Under Aunt Anna's tutelage, Edie and Teedie learned to read together. Historian Dr. Kathleen Dalton notes that in Edith, Theodore "found . . . a kindred booklover."[16] He recalled he "greatly liked the girls' stories" which he and Edith read together, though he later noted that he made this confession of his taste in books "at the cost of being deemed effeminate."[17]

Unsurprisingly, the Roosevelt children's literary taste, and Teedie's in particular, tended toward adventure: *The Boy Hunters*, Grimm's Fairy Tales, King Arthur, and Hans Christian Andersen. One series of books taught by Aunt Anna had a particularly profound impact: the McGuffey Reader series. The McGuffey Readers were a serialized set of moral tales punctuated by clever turns of phrase and memorable characters: "nervous nellies" and "mettlesome midges" learned to "speak softly and carry a big stick." Teedie also admitted to liking the more feminine stories of Louisa May Alcott, "'Pussy Willow' and 'A Summer in Leslie Goldthwaite's Life,' just as I worshipped 'Little Men' and 'Little Women' and 'An Old-Fashioned Girl.'"[18] Alcott's depiction of the March family in *Little Women* may have plucked a chord for Teedie, not just in its loving intimacy, but in the evocation of strong women like Aunt Anna, Grandma Bulloch, and later Bamie, and a noble but absent father. Mrs. March ("Marmee") and her two eldest daughters, Meg and the aspiring writer Jo, are all essential to the support of the family as Mr. March serves as a chaplain in the Union Army. The parallel with Teedie's own peripatetic father, dutifully promoting the allotment program to New York Regiment troops in their far-flung encampments, is evident. Duty calls the noble father away, the strong women in the shadows holding family and country together.

Edie must have been aware that the Roosevelts were on the prosperous rise even as her family was in decline. If she felt any envy or resentment, none was apparent. Edie's bond with Teedie, Bamie, and Conie grew stronger and stronger, even as her connections to those beyond these intimates became increasingly tenuous as her family's financial circumstances contracted her social circle. Doubtless, the growing stress in her own home and the emotional detachment of her mother fueled a natural inclination toward shyness. She recalled many years later an occasion on which Aunt Anna—whom Edie now called Mrs. Gracie—had her small collection of pupils recite aloud and in unison Longfellow's "Children's Hour." Edith felt "all eyes turned upon me, and all voices raised at the line 'Edith with golden hair,' until I was sunk in confusion and tears."[19]

Her shyness seems, over the years, to have morphed into at least the outward appearance of remoteness. Certainly, these were the attributes modeled by her mother, and perhaps Edith unconsciously adopted them as a defense against the pains of social anxiety. She confessed in a 1912 letter to her son Kermit that "the other girls used to reproach me with 'indifference,'" and while she would go on to earn well-deserved credit for inventing the role of the modern first lady, she was also notoriously described as "'almost Oriental' in her detachment." Years later, a mature Alice Roosevelt Longworth would ascribe what she called her stepmother's "withdrawn, rather parched quality" to the unhappiness of her early years.[20]

She might have been the family's bonus sister, but she had not been invited by the Roosevelts to join in the Grand Tour of 1869–1870 nor the even grander Grand Tour that followed in 1870–1872, though Conie kept her regularly apprised of their adventures.

The Roosevelt family returned to New York on November 5, 1873, and moved into their new home on 6 West 57th Street. The family business continued to churn out profits, and the Roosevelts allowed the tide of New York wealth to carry them further uptown, where there was still room to build great houses. Both Elliott and Theodore would have reason to regard the 57th Street mansion as cursed, but for the present it was the family dream home the senior Roosevelt intended it to be.

Despite their many adventures together, Teedie's parents still deemed him too delicate to be sent away to boarding school, so he, together with Ellie and Conie, continued in home school, now under the tutelage of a variety of hired instructors rather than Aunt Anna. Edie and Conie eagerly renewed their friendship, to which was added another member of their social circle, Frances "Fanny" Theodora Smith, who became one of Teedie's favorites. Conie brought home with her from Europe the inspiration for P.O.R.E., a New York–based literary club, or writers' circle, which soon evolved into an arena of remarkably deep introspection and expression for Edie. Through P.O.R.E., Edie and Conie shared their love of poetry, as did Teedie and other friends, including Fanny Smith and Grace Potter. Originally, they declared that P.O.R.E. was an acronym for "Paradise of Ravenous Eaters," but, after some three years, they changed it to the more dignified "Party of Renowned Eligibles."[21]

For Charles Carow, there was no moving uptown. His gradual yet ineluctable financial, physical, and emotional descent was suddenly accelerated following the Panic of 1873, a global economic event exacerbated in the United States by wildly exuberant investment, especially in railroad construction, which started during the Civil War and continued unabated into the early 1870s as financiers and speculators became recklessly over-leveraged. Always pursued by debt, Carow borrowed all he could and was thus among the very overleveraged.

Charles Carow's health deteriorated as the effects of the financial panic festered, and his elder daughter, who turned twelve in 1873, seems to have felt real alarm for her family's prospects. Biographer Sylvia Morris uncovered three sketches the teenaged Edith drew on the same sheet of notepaper. One depicted

a cadaverous figure in a doorway, with Cupid hovering behind panes of glass. Below is written: "Poverty coming in at the door and love flying out at the window." Another sketch is of a lady reaching to tweak a jester's cap. The caption beneath reads: "When lovely woman stoops to folly." A third has someone blowing on a wick, and the inscription: "Out, out, brief candle."[22]

Her mood had turned gloomy. And not just gloomy, angry.

As Edie and Teedie matured and play morphed into something more closely approximating courtship, the once childish arguments of the pair became harder to laugh away. With the passing years, they both emerged as dominant personalities. Teedie always sought to lead, while friends of Edie remarked that she had been "born mature." Sylvia Morris characterizes her as downright "moody."[23] Certainly, Edie's presentation to the world was always darker than Teedie's.

No mere book club, P.O.R.E. was a bona-fide writer's workshop, in which members read aloud from their original poetry, fiction, and essays, which Edie subsequently copied into notebooks that eventually ran to several volumes. Looking back as an adult, Fanny Smith dismissed the fiction as "adolescent," but she described Edie's poetry as something much more substantial. Instead of girlishly romantic themes, there were far deeper notes of loss, sadness, regret, and, yes, glimmers of hope as well. In one verse, she described the joyous birth of a child, only to deftly modulate the key from major to minor:

Soon those helpless tiny fingers
By life's thorns will wounded be
Holding close the cruel roses
Plucked from life's deceptive tree.[24]

The tree of life that would prove so cruelly "deceptive" for young Theodore Roosevelt had already revealed its fickle nature to the teenaged Edith when she wrote these lines.

In 1877, sixteen-year-old Edith contributed to P.O.R.E. a poem titled "The Four-Leaved Clover":

'Tis one of Providence's wise dispensations
That each day bringing joy and pain anew
Shall drop a curtain twixt the last day's ruins
Where lie our old pains and old pleasures too.[25]

Another of the poems she presented to her P.O.R.E. associates during this time was "My Dream Castles." She wrote that her "noble castles / In the air" are many but are closed to visitors except for "the few / Holding to my inmost feelings / Love's own clue." Through these few castles, visitors "may wander . . . at will" except that

Only one, one tiny room
Locked they find,
One thin curtain that they ne'er
Gaze behind.
There my lost ambitions sleep,
To their tear-wept slumber deep
Long consigned.
This my lonely sanctum is;
There I go
When my heart all worn by grief
Sinketh low
Where my baseless hopes do lie
There to find my peace, go I,
Sad and slow.[26]

Formerly accustomed to summering in the "country seats" of the wealthy families who no longer counted the Carows as their peers, Edith was still invited to Tranquility, the Roosevelt home at Oyster Bay. But now she also spent time on the New Jersey shore, where, as she lamented, country seats were "not many" and what resorts existed were far from fashionable, let alone exclusive. Still, she loved to swim and so made the most of her summers.[27] In July 1874, Teedie left the country seat set to visit her at Sea Bright, New Jersey, but—tellingly—wrote little about her in the notebook he kept.[28] Nevertheless, the visit resulted in his extending another invitation to Tranquility, which Edie accepted.

Edie would keep a scrapbook with her sister, Emily, from March 10, 1875, to March 17, 1878. In its pages, the sisters pasted ornate Valentines alongside their favorite poems. One page features two prominent images: one a mirthful girl, dancing with her doll, the other a similarly aged girl in tears with a tattered doll facedown on the floor. Under the images, young Edie has written in script: "Joy" and "Sorrow." There is a white-lace Valentine of roses holding behind it a secret compartment. When carefully opened, the delicate exterior folds back to reveal a hidden message:

I Love Thee.

I love thee, and my heart will bear
The seal which thou hast set forever;
Truth weaves the silken chain I wear
That death, and death alone will sever.[29]

No doubt a wordsmith as skilled as Edith appreciated the double entendre. "Thee" was one of the many pet names Edith had for Theodore. Playfully, in later life, he often signed his letters to Edith from "Thee." But even Edith's precocious maturity could not close a gap of three years. Such a difference in age is nothing in later life but everything in youth.

The relationship between the sixteen-year-old Roosevelt and fourteen-year-old Edith, which many in the Roosevelt family believed would mature into courtship proper, engagement, and marriage, now waxed and waned. Theodore loved to row out of the Tranquility dock and across Oyster Bay. Even more, these days, he loved to do this in company with local girls—the likes of Fanny Smith, Annie Murray, and Nellie Smith.

Yet on the stern of the little craft in which he rowed them was the name he had so carefully painted: *Edith*.[30]

3

ON HIS OWN

"Sometimes when I fully realize my loss I feel as if I should go wild."
—Theodore Roosevelt

Theodore Roosevelt had never been an emotionally steady young man. And as he prepared to leave the tranquility of Oyster Bay for his freshman year at Harvard, he was about to experience the first great jolt of his life.

The Oyster Bay branch of the Roosevelt family had been established by Johannes (John) Roosevelt, the 3× great-grandfather of Theodore Roosevelt, who moved out of New York City in the early eighteenth century. Conie called this bay on the North Shore of Long Island the family's "colony." From 1874 on, Oyster Bay was the Roosevelt summer retreat. Theodore Sr. "rented a country place which, much to the amusement of our friends, we named 'Tranquility.'" As Conie observed, nothing less tranquil could be imagined. "Endless young cousins and friends of both sexes and of every kind of varied interest always filled the simple rooms and shared the delightful and unconventional life which we led in that enchanted spot."¹ She recalled in particular a summer day at Plum Point on Oyster Bay, when she, Teedie, Ellie, cousin James (Jimmy) West Roosevelt, Fanny, and Edie "made up the happy six." Conie could still see, "as if it were yesterday,"

Teedie, "who loved to row in the hottest sun, over the roughest water, in the smallest boat," rowing with his "chosen" companion, Edie.[2]

If Edith Carow was the bonus sister of the Roosevelt family, Bamie qualified as its bonus mother. As Conie recalled, "My older sister, Anna [Bamie], though only four years older than my brother Theodore, was always mysteriously classed with the 'grown people,'" while her siblings were confined to the nursery. Teedie concurred: "When I put 'We 3' I mean Ellie, Conie, and I. When I put 'big people' I mean Papa, Mama, and Bamie."[3] As they aged, she supervised, insofar as anyone could, the younger children in their Oyster Bay adventures. It was a pattern of behavior she would continue throughout her life. "There is always someone in every family who keeps it together. In ours," later generations explained, "it was [Bamie]."[4] Bamie's natural tendency toward pragmatism was the inverse of Mittie's whimsy. As she grew older, Bamie naturally gravitated toward the domestic reins. Mittie, though still vivacious and capable, gladly relinquished them.

It was Bamie, substituting for Mittie, who had preceded Theodore to Cambridge, where she rented his rooms at 16 Winthrop, and "looked after every detail of furnishing her brother's apartment, which she insisted had to be on the second floor because of his asthma."[5]

On September 27, 1876, Edith celebrated Conie's fifteenth birthday as a guest at Tranquility, the very day on which Theodore left for Cambridge. No one—perhaps not even Edith—knew better than Conie just what elements of constitution and character animated Theodore, both as he left the enchanted circle to venture off to Harvard and as he went on to navigate the rising, falling, and again ascending path beyond. College, then and now, is a time of change. For the first time, he would be away from the women who had raised and supported him, yet continually drawn back into their orbit, especially when an unforeseen tragedy shook TR to his very core.

At Harvard, Theodore joined 245 others in a highly privileged first-year class. Carleton Putnam noted in his 1958 biography of TR that "only one in five thousand [men] of the national population received a bachelor's degree" at the time, and there were no women in the student body. His daily life at college soon became routine: morning chapel, two to three classes a day, and several hours of study and exercise.[6]

One word dominates descriptions of Theodore's early life at Harvard: eccentric. He smelled like formaldehyde, kept snakes as pets, and, at least in his first year, was more interested in arsenic than alcohol. So cutting were former classmates' descriptions of Roosevelt that his first major biographer hid them from public view; "freak" and "half crazy" were among the scathing reviews. Later historians, such as David McCullough, told the truth: "His voice was thin and piping, almost comical. . . . At Harvard, some classmates soon learned to goad him into an argument for the sheer fun of hearing him."[7]

Roosevelt did make one friend his first year: Henry Davis Minot, "a kindred spirit who loved science and cared more about moral purity than popularity."[8] Minot, who bonded with Roosevelt over their shared love of ornithology, struggled with his identity in an alpha male culture and was prone to depression. "I am in trouble, and want to confide my case to you," Minot wrote to his doctor in a heart-wrenching, single-spaced five-page letter during his college years, explaining that his entire life has been "a struggle against depression." He continues: "I suffered from a dislike to the rougher boyish sports and to general society from a certain timidity, and from want of manliness. But now I am becoming manly." Minot concludes: "Ought I to have a change? Had I better exert my will to keep my burden to myself, or ought I to seek sympathy?"[9] His doctor never opened the letter. He had already set sail on a six-month trip to Europe.

It is striking that Roosevelt, who would become synonymous with the concept of manliness, was best friends in college with a person who openly struggled with "becoming manly." Though he would spend most of his life epitomizing testosterone-fueled feats, the real Roosevelt was sensitive and kind, thanks to the sympathizing influence of his mother and sisters. Rather than shed that influence and embrace college culture at the first opportunity, Roosevelt chooses the harder path: to be himself. He and Minot were two naturalists amidst the hurly-burly, fast-paced lifestyle of the privileged offspring of the Gilded Age elite. But while Minot was anguished, Roosevelt was content. "He was in a world of his own," wrote McCullough. "Absorbed, bookish, happy."[10]

Still, like many off to college, both then and now, the transition required adjustment and he longed for the familiar. His letters home show how TR related to each of the women in his life. To Bamie, ever the second mother, he boasts of high marks, seeking advice and yearning for approval. Conie is TR's intimate confidante, the one to whom he shares his secrets. Mittie is infantilized, as Thee taught his son to do. Curiously, the letters he wrote home in the days after his arrival make no mention of Edith, and while he did briefly visit New York for Thanksgiving, he barely saw her until he was home for the Christmas break. He danced with her at the first party of the season and remarked to his brother, Elliott, that she "looked as pretty as a picture and was very sweet." At another party, his Aunt Anna Gracie fed supper to the young guests she hosted at her new house on East 34th Street and then invited them upstairs to look at her painting, titled *The Ancient Mariner*. By this time, Edie seems to have begun calling Teedie "Thee," and the two paired off as a couple to have what Aunt Anna called a "cosy chat" in the dimly lit morning room.[11]

In their first year at Harvard, Theodore and his new best friend were more prone to chasing birds than women. But that didn't mean Theodore had sworn off admiring them from afar. Following the Christmas 1876 break, he returned to Cambridge early in January 1877 and wrote to Bamie that classmates who had visited him in New York thought his friends (for lack of a more definitive term) Annie Murray and Edith "the prettiest girls they had met" in the city. He told his sister that "Some of the girls [he encountered in Cambridge] are very sweet and bright," adding that "a few are very pretty," then went on in a mock poetic vein: "'Still oh Anneth I remain Faithful to Thee!' (the proper name in the above beautiful rhapsody is a compound of Annie and Edith)."[12] Later, he wrote to Conie of partaking in a sleighing party of "forty girls and fellows," noting that one of the girls "looked quite like Edith—only not nearly as pretty as her

Ladyship." But he did not stop there. He appended to this assessment of Edith's looks the proviso that her beauty exceeded that of the girl on the sleigh ride only "when she dresses well and do'n't frizzle her hair."[13]

For her part, Edie seems to have entertained no illusion that Theodore was singularly devoted to her, yet she composed a love poem, a variation on the little verse she had earlier slipped into a valentine. Almost certainly it never found "publication" beyond a youthful scrapbook she and Emily shared. "Hear a Lover's prayer" repeats that archaic pronoun "thee," the diminutive she used for "Theodore":

I LOVE THEE STILL.

I love thee still—I love thee still,
As truly as when first we met,
Ere grief o'er life had breathed its chill
Or sorrow's tear my cheek had wet.
I love thee still—I love thee still,
Thy changeless constancy and truth;
Thy name yet wakens pleasures thrill,
Star of my bright and joyous youth.[14]

If Edith hid her love for Thee or Teedie or Theodore, she did not give up on him. He did not come home for Easter, but soon after that holiday, he invited his family to visit him in Cambridge, adding that they should "*make* [Cousin] Maud [, Elliott] and Edith come."[15]

Although he had not invited her directly but, rather, through his family (he would often use family members to help win his way in life), Edith eagerly accepted and arrived in Cambridge on May 25 along with the senior Theodore Roosevelt, Conie, Bamie, Elliott, and Maud. It was a three-day visit, during which Teedie and Edie spent a great deal of time talking. Edith wasted no time in sending Theodore a note on her return to New York. While the speed with which she wrote it—it is dated May 29—suggests frank warmth, the letter, though affectionate, is peculiarly formal, especially for something written to one with whom she had shared so much of childhood. Perhaps that formality, combined with her reference to the "pleasant lunch" she "shall long remember" in the rooms of another young man, was meant to provoke jealousy:

My dear Theodore,

I feel like writing immediately now that I am back in New York, to thank you for the pleasant time I had in Boston, for indeed I enjoyed to the utmost every minuite of my stay.

May I ask you to say to all your friends that I appreciate Harvard freshmen as much as Mr. Jackson does New York girls, and tell Mr. [Lamson] especially that I shall long remember that pleasant lunch in his rooms.

So with a clear recollection of what were to me at least, three perfectly happy days,

Believe me,
Most sincerely yours,

Edith K. Carow[16]

It was not until some three weeks later that Theodore wrote to Conie, "I don't think I ever saw Edith looking prettier," adding that his friends "admired her little Ladyship intensely, and she behaved as sweetly as she looked."[17]

Her Ladyship. It was a term he had used before in writing of her. It was not a title of unalloyed affection. Perhaps Theodore meant it to convey Edith's habitual reserve, which some saw as hauteur. Her youth in what had become a troubled family hardened her—though perhaps she was never very emotive. But she was reliable, and she loved Theodore, even if she was not a fount of overt and abundant affection. This is made clearer by his curious use of the verb "behaved." It is as if Theodore were going out of his way to imply that *being* sweet required Edith to deliberately act in a way that may not have come naturally to her. Nevertheless, he did make it a point to ask Conie, when she next wrote to Edie, to "tell her I enjoyed *her* visit *very* much indeed."[18] Again, Theodore used his sister as a messenger rather than communicating directly, and, despite his emphatic underscores, he did not mention Edith in his diary for the whole summer. In what would become a lifelong trait, he instead found ample distraction in the outdoors: boating, hunting, and swimming. His most significant accomplishment of the summer was the publication of his first book, *Summer Birds of the Adirondacks in Franklin County, N.Y.*, coauthored with Henry Davis Minot as the pair traipsed after ninety-seven species of birds. Their work caught the attention of Clinton Hart Merriam, head of the U.S. Biological Survey, who called the book, "By far the best of the recent lists," further commenting that it "bears prima facie evidence of . . . exact and thoroughly reliable information."[19] Minot instinctively understood Roosevelt, and he encouraged the scientific pursuits that others, including TR's father, did not entirely embrace. With Minot, Theodore could be himself.

In August 1877, Edith spent two weeks at Oyster Bay as Conie's guest and seems to have had a delightful time. Neither she nor anyone else at Tranquility took much note of the senior Roosevelt's faltering health. There was some talk of his having "strained" himself through overwork as collector of customs for the Port of New York. The office of collector was immensely lucrative and notoriously corrupt. The collector was incentivized by a compensation scheme that paid him a percentage of every dollar of duty tax he brought in. Inflation of these proceeds was common. Looking to embarrass and humble the exuberantly crooked New York senator Roscoe Conkling by forcing upon him a scrupulously honest official, President Rutherford B. Hayes appointed the senior Roosevelt. Whatever effect this had on Conkling, it produced great stress in the new collector. Intestinal cramps that began late in the summer became excruciating in December. An alarmed Theodore wrote home on December 18 to ask if the doctor thought "it is anything serious." Two days later, his father collapsed from what the physician diagnosed as acute peritonitis.[20]

Theodore came home from Harvard on December 21 and was stunned by the transformation of his father, who, although only forty-six, suddenly looked like an enfeebled old man. The arrival of Christmas, however, visibly elevated him, at least somewhat, and his son felt sufficiently encouraged by this "improvement" to spend time with his friends, including Annie Murray (whom he called "singularly sweet"), Fanny Smith ("pure religious"—whatever that meant), and Edith, to whom he attached no adjective. He referred to this feminine group as his "trio of *freundinnen*"—female friends, the emphasis on their gender implying that he saw all three girls in something of an amorous light, at least potentially.

The Christmastime improvement in Thee's condition proved but a brief reprieve. The acute peritonitis, it turned out, was not brought on by a stressful political battle but was a symptom of advanced stomach cancer. The worshipful son worried, but in him were already planted the seeds of the man who wrote a decade later, "Black care rarely sits behind a rider whose pace is fast enough."[21] Returned to Cambridge, he threw himself into his studies. The socially awkward first-year student had grown more comfortable in his sophomore year. He crammed ferociously for his semiannual examinations while also dining, partying, boxing, and wrestling with his friends. He "Boxed with little Briggs and beat him" on January 23, had a dancing class on the evening of the 26th, partied on the 29th with friends and "the two Miss Lanes. Very nice girls are the two Miss Lanes," and on the 30th was "rather beaten in a boxing match [by] Bob Bacon" but made up for it on February 1 when he "Threw back Tebbetts in a wrestling match." Then it was back to study and test-taking.[22]

An urgent telegram from New York arrived on Saturday, February 9. Theodore took the first train available, an overnighter, which got him to the family door in Manhattan on Sunday morning. He was too late. The death of Theodore Roosevelt Sr. had been ghastly. "He was so mad with pain," sixteen-year-old Elliott recorded in his diary, "that beyond groans and horrible writhes and twists he could do nothing. Oh my God my Father what agonies you suffered."[23] The suffering was palliated with ether and chloroform, which meant that the customarily dynamic and virile Roosevelt spent most of his final six weeks of life asleep. But brother Theodore had missed it all, Greatheart having died just before midnight, hours before his train pulled into Grand Central Terminal from Cambridge.

Why had Theodore not come home sooner? Did he fear acknowledging the impending awful finality? Or could it have been that Elliott had failed to convey urgency until their father's final day? If so, was this a case of poor judgment or in some degree intentional, a way for the younger brother to assert his primacy? Certainly, Theodore Roosevelt never forgave Elliott for having missed the opportunity to bid his father farewell.

The loss, of course, was crushing. All his life his father had been the centerpiece—a model of near perfection. TR never wrote such moving tributes to his mother, the woman who'd overseen his entire childhood, as he would for his father. Mittie instead encouraged, and shared, the view that her husband was the important one in the family. His loss was felt by her and all her children, but undoubtedly the hardest hit was his namesake. And it was his grief that took precedence over all others. That very night, all that the eldest son of "the greatest man I ever knew" could manage was a heavy slash drawn in blackest ink down the margin of his diary. He started to write but got only as far as "My dear Father. Born Sept. 23, 1831."[24] He could not even bring himself to record the date on which the man's life had closed. The rest of the page remained a void. He entered nothing more in the book until his father's burial on February 12 and then detailed the void with astounding clarity:

> He has just been buried. I should never forget these terrible three days;
> the hideous suspense of the ride home; the dull, inert sorrow during
> which I felt as if I had been stunned, or as if part of my life had been
> taken away; and the two moments of sharp, bitter agony, when I kissed

the dear, dead face and realized he would never again on this earth speak to me or greet me with his loving smile, and then when I heard the sound of the first clod dropping on the coffin holding the one I loved dearest on earth.[25]

But he recorded the beginning of a return as well to the here and now. His father, he wrote, "looked so calm and sweet. I feel that if it were not for the certainty, that as he himself has so often said, 'he is not dead, but gone before,' I should almost perish. With the help of my God I will try to lead such a life as he would have wished."[26]

In contrast to her brother, Conie seems to have taken her father's death more philosophically. In the vast collection at Sagamore Hill is an autograph book kept by Edie's sister, Emily Tyler Carow, but held lifelong by Edith. These were very popular in Victorian-era America, memory albums, in which friends and others inscribed some sentiment, to which they added their signature. On page four is an autograph from Conie "To Emily." It is the second stanza of "A Farewell," a popular poem by the Reverend Charles Kingsley—novelist, poet, and priest of the Church of England, who is remembered today as an apostle of Muscular Christianity:

> Be good sweet maid, and let who will be clever
> Do noble things, not dream them all day long,
> And thus make life, death, and that vast forever
> One grand, sweet song
> Corinne Roosevelt
> To Emily

Emily dated her autograph album January 30, 1877, but almost all the autographs in it are dated beginning in February of the following year. Conie's contribution bears no date, but it is likely that she inscribed "A Farewell" during or after February, the time of her father's death.[27]

There is no record of how Mittie reacted to becoming a widow at age forty-two or how Bamie dealt with the loss of her father. The eldest son's grief, however, continued unabated. The reality of loss swept over him, receded, and returned. "It seems impossible to realize I shall never see him again," he wrote on February 19, "he is such a living memory"; and, again, on February 22: "Every now and then it seems to me like a hideous dream." But he found solace, after the funeral and the initial mourning, in his return to Harvard—"all the fellows have been wonderfully kind, especially dear old Hal Minot."[28]

Minot, despite his depression, found the will and the words to comfort his friend. Just days after Thee's death, Minot wrote: "The memory of your father will be a comfort and a guide to you through life; and a better guide than his noble unselfishness you could not have."[29] Roosevelt had a friend in Minot (whom, interestingly, he said had been "simply motherly in his care over me"), a caring (if less involved) actual mother, substitute mothers in elder sister Bamie and Aunt Anna, and an emotional outlet in Conie.[30] As was so often the case in their relationship, Conie would offer comfort to Theodore but there is scant evidence of him comforting her in return. And yet despite this support system, he buried himself in work and opened the aperture of his college experience. He studied hard, hard, and harder still. On March 3, he thought about "Father all the evening" and had "a good square break down."[31] He felt the "better for" his breakdown, and while it seemed to him "brutal to go about my ordinary occupations," he knew he "must keep employed," determined as he was to keep his pounding pace fast enough to outrun black care.[32]

On April 1, Theodore threw himself into a sparring match with friend and classmate Bob Bacon, who "rather used me up," and began looking forward to his first visit home since his father's passing.[33] In Manhattan, he was greeted "with heartfelt joy by all," save Bamie, who was away in Denver, having lit out for the territory. Theodore found the homecoming "much harder than I expected; for the memories are frightfully vivid . . . I realize now the days of unalloyed happiness are now over forever." Yet "Darling little Pussie [Conie] has been just so sweet for everything," and he and his mother and Conie went off to Oyster Bay for three days. There, TR shot a duck and some muskrats, and Conie copied out for her brother a hymn, in which he found much comfort: "Large are the mansions in my Father's dwelling, / Happy the homes which sorrows never dim."[34] In subsequent years, Theodore would follow Bamie's example, fleeing from grief and oftentimes the everyday pains of domestic life to seek solace in the West. "Live for the living, not the dead" would become a common family saying, popular with Bamie in particular.[35] It was a saying her brother was about to take very much to heart. A familiar pattern would repeat throughout TR's life—he would fall to great depths of despair, only for his sisters to offer time, patience, and words of comfort to bring him out of it.

That hymn Conie gave him set off a train of thought in Theodore Roosevelt's mind. "Sometimes when I fully realize my loss I feel as if I should go wild," he wrote in the summer of 1878. "He was everything to me."[36] It was "lovely" for him to think of meeting his father in heaven, where he would be "united with the dear one who has gone before," but the comfort of that notion was quickly drowned in the realization that "I have lost the only human being, to whom I told everything, never failing to get loving advice and sweet sympathy." This, in turn, led him to the reasoning: "In return, no one but my wife, if I ever marry, will ever be able to take his place."[37] Perhaps TR could be forgiven for once again placing his father on a pedestal, but in fact, his father was *not* the only person to whom he confided everything or from whom he received loving advice. There was of course Bamie and Conie, both of whom he seemed to take for granted in the depths of his grief.

It is a striking, even strange sequence of thought, how the loss of a dear *father* would somehow be made up for by the acquisition of a *wife*, as if these two roles were interchangeable. But perhaps he was recognizing that he could find from his wife the same constancy and comfort he received from the other women in his life. Theodore, perhaps surprisingly as the family's eldest son, does not show much interest in becoming the head of household. Instead, he thinks longingly about becoming the man of his own house. "I so wonder who my wife will be!" he mused, then answered: "'A rare and radiant maiden,' I hope"—quoting a phrase from Poe's most famous poem, "The Raven," a first-person account of a "midnight dreary" in which the narrator hears a rapping at his chamber door.

> Ah, distinctly I remember it was in the bleak December;
> And each separate dying ember wrought its ghost upon the floor.
> Eagerly I wished the morrow;—vainly I had sought to borrow
> From my books surcease of sorrow—sorrow for the lost Lenore—
> For the rare and radiant maiden whom the angels name Lenore—
> Nameless here for evermore.

The night caller, it turns out, is not a person but a raven, who enters, perches on a "bust of Pallas," and, to each question the narrator asks of it, croaks out "Nevermore," a word that rhymes with "the rare and radiant maiden whom the angels name Lenore."

It is at the very least curious that young Roosevelt described his yet undiscovered and barely even imagined yet intensely wished-for future wife with the words Poe used to describe a dead lover, particularly given the accent in the poem on her being dead—extant "nevermore." This strangeness doesn't seem to have occurred to him as he pined for "one who will be as pure and innocent as she is wise." Wise. In an age when social status, beauty, and even a dowry of sorts would be important, Roosevelt longed instead for a wife would be his intellectual equal. "Thank Heaven," he wrote, "I am at least perfectly pure."[38]

Roosevelt returned to Cambridge and resumed his studies with a vengeance, "grinding," he wrote, "like a Trojan."[39] Roosevelt even tried a new look. "At last the deed is done and I have shaved off my whiskers!" he wrote to Conie on May 3. With self-deprecation, he complained "that I look like a dissolute democrat of the fourth ward" but sent along to her "some tintypes I had taken for distribution among my family and friends. The front views are pretty good; although giving me an expression of gloomy misery that I sincerely hope is not natural. The side views do not resemble me any more than they do Michelangelo."[40]

On June 6, he left Cambridge for Oyster Bay, each return to the haven of childhood being bittersweet, and each month that passed between the death of his father and the present noted in his diary. The entry for June 9, for instance, was headed "/ Four months ago /."[41] On this stay in Oyster Bay, Theodore devoted much of his time to sandpapering and varnishing his boat and building a boathouse. In mid-June, he returned to Cambridge for his sophomore year-end exams.

Once back in Oyster Bay, Theodore, on summer break from Harvard, threw himself into what, as a mature adult, he would exalt as "the strenuous life." He rowed, swam, and rode hard, but he also remembered to send Edith a "bonbonniere" on August 6, her seventeenth birthday.[42] He began spending a succession of balmy August days in her company, sailing with her on the 19th, rowing with her on the 20th—out to Lloyds Neck, not far from Oyster Bay—then picnicking and picking water lilies together at Cold Spring on the 21st. By the standards of the day, Edie had come of age, and for her to be so much in intimate company with a highly eligible Harvard man conveyed a meaning that was, in the social syntax of Victorian America, unmistakable. Engagement, it would seem, must follow, as the night the day.

Later in the afternoon on the 22nd, Roosevelt and Edie went for a sail and then attended, together, a family party. The day concluded with an ascent to Tranquility, the Roosevelt summer house, which was uphill from the water. What happened that summer evening at Tranquility was never told. Edith and Theodore took this secret to the grave.

All we know in some firsthand detail is the aftermath. Theodore's diary records that he rode off—alone—on horseback "so long and hard that I am afraid it may have injured my horse."[43] His ride—of rage or frustration—followed what was his last mention of Edith Carow for many months. On August 22, 1878, the vital connection between them seems to have snapped. Edith's cousin later claimed "it was common knowledge in the family" that Theodore proposed to Edith but that her grandfather objected "partly because Edith was too young." Edith herself told her daughter-in-law that "Theodore as a youth had proposed to her more than once and that each time she had refused him."[44] Biographer Sylvia Jukes Morris observes: "Edith never explained the estrangement herself, except to say vaguely that Theodore had "not been nice.""[45]

While the nature of their social circle was such that the two still encountered one another from time to time, perhaps even frequently, whatever happened between them that night drove Theodore into a state approaching mania. Two days after the Tranquility diary entry, he recorded that—again, while out riding—a neighbor's dog annoyed him. In response, he drew his revolver and, he noted with evident pride, shot it, "rolling it over very neatly as it ran alongside the horse."[46] Later, in a cruise up Long Island Sound with some of his cousins, he used that same revolver to shoot at anything he encountered, "from bottles or buoys to sharks and porpoises."[47]

Had he proposed and been rejected? Had he made an advance and been rejected? Was their romance over? And did it die aborning? Or was what they had ever a romance at all? The only historical hint from the two people who knew the truth came in the form of a confession from Theodore to Bamie almost a decade after the eruption: "[Edith] and I had very intimate relations; one day there came a break for both of us had, and I suppose have, tempers that were far from being the best. To no soul now living have either of us ever since spoken a word of this."[48]

In his reverie about the "rare and radiant maiden," when Theodore wondered who his wife would be, Edith's name did not come up. Did he ever expect her to fill the void left by the passing of his father? Or was she to him always the bonus sister, neither more, nor less? It is tempting to see these outbursts as the products of thwarted passion. But perhaps it was more an issue of confusion. For whatever reason, Edie could not begin to fill the emotional void left by the death of the senior Roosevelt. If TR's heart was broken, Edie proved incapable of mending it.

As both Conie and Edie neared their seventeenth birthdays, months after Thee's passing, Conie sent her friend a touchingly melancholy missive:

"how very old we are getting, quite grown up, one short year more, and the brook will be past, and that mysterious eighteen years reached." She expressed the hope that Edie's "next seventeen years . . . will be as peaceful and sheltered (I know they have not been untroubled) as those past." It was a most ambivalent sentiment, in which the parenthetical remark quite contradicted the rest of the sentence. To any outside, objective observer, the two young women led lives on courses diverging. Conie's was on the rise while Edie's arc bent relentlessly downward. Yet in this letter, Conie seems to see more hope for Edie than for herself.[49] Edie had come of age accustomed to disappointment as the baseline condition of her life. She did her best to enjoy the social forms and formalities that made up a life in which she and her family were still included even though their declining financial status no longer qualified for full admission. Their formal education, such as it was, was over, and the expectation of the age was that a debut, marriage, and a family would follow in short order.

Conie closed her twilight-tinged letter to Edie by remarking that "the future is very secretive and on the whole I am glad." Neither young woman knew then that the arcs of their lives would so dramatically recross.

In the sweep of seven months, Theodore lost his father and the woman he may have expected to marry. As he made plans to return to Harvard, he would do so without his best friend as well. On August 23, one day after Theodore and Edith hiked Tranquility to their ill-fated rendezvous, Henry Davis Minot self-committed to a sanitarium. He would not return to Harvard but remained in contact with Theodore.

Theodore spent what remained of his summer vacation tramping the Maine woods in Aroostook County with Bill Sewall, a local wilderness guide to whom he had been introduced by Arthur Cutler, a man Theodore's father had hired to tutor him and brother Elliott. It was a life altering introduction. Sewall would become Theodore's wilderness companion for more than one sojourn in Maine and would later serve as the overseer of his ranch lands in Dakota Territory.

TR returned to Harvard on September 27, where exciting news was waiting for him. The Porcellian, most select of Harvard's celebrated "final clubs" and one to which his father belonged, had chosen to offer him membership. Unfortunately, having despaired of being tapped by the Porc, he had already accepted an offer from another only somewhat less desirable "final," the A.D. TR set aside whatever regret he may have had over having chosen to settle for second best and threw himself into a nine-subject academic schedule, which required twenty hours a week of laboratory, personal taxidermy, and classroom work. Then luck, with the aid of a little alcohol, intervened. As TR explained in his diary on October 9–10:

> Last night a Porcellian and an A.D. man, both drunk, were discussing me, and in the quarrel the former let it leak out that I preferred his club. The A.D. men held a meeting and voted to give me my choice of the two clubs—as I had never been in the A.D. rooms, had not signed the constitution, possessed no voting powers and in fact was not a member. Of course by this arrangement I have to hurt somebody's feelings, and I have rarely felt as badly as I have during the last 24 hours; it is terribly hard to know what is the honorable thing to do.[50]

His crisis of gentlemanly conscience proved short-lived, as he decided the very next day to forsake A.D. for the Porcellian. Theodore's confidence was building, and he was beginning to be seen as a contemporary, not an outcast, by his equally privileged college classmates.

Dick Saltsonstall, who in the wake of Minot's struggles had quickly become one of Theodore's closest friends at Harvard, drove Theodore on Friday afternoon, October 18, from Cambridge almost six miles southwest "in a buggy to his house on Chestnut Hill, where I am now, enjoying myself to the utmost."[51] It was one of the first times Theodore had written anything purely positive since his father's death. And indeed, he was happy, for Theodore Roosevelt had just met Alice Hathaway Lee, the woman who would help recenter his life.

Part Two

SUNSHINE

1878—1884

4

"A RARE AND RADIANT MAIDEN"

"I can not imagine a fellow having a happier time than I have had since I have been in College."

—Theodore Roosevelt

heodore Roosevelt was in darkness, and he sought out new light. Chestnut Hill must have felt like a warm family reunion to Theodore, a welcome sensation just eight months after his father had died and two months after the rupture with Edith. And not just a reunion, but an image of all that he remembered home life had been and imagined it could again be—warm, bright, bustling with activity, children, and talk. There were eleven children and fifteen family members in the combined Lee and Saltonstall clans, who effectively shared one large open unfenced plot of land between their two homes. The Saltonstall patriarch, Leverett, was married to Harriett Rose, sister of George Cabot Lee. Alice Hathaway Lee, willowy, vibrant, beautiful, was the sunshine of this warm, welcoming, and intellectually stimulating solar system of mothers, fathers, siblings, and cousins.

The Lees and Saltonstalls were "too sweet to me," Theodore wrote in his diary of his very first visit to Chestnut Hill, which he described as "so homelike."[1] As Theodore grew closer to the Saltonstalls, he would discover that Chestnut Hill was a forum in which the family talked politics, and not just any politics, but reform politics. For just as the late senior Roosevelt represented the progressive wing of Knickerbocker New York, the Saltonstalls and Lees were acolytes of progressive Boston Brahminism. They would have a formative or at least affirmative effect on young Roosevelt's evolving political views. How bright, how inviting this all must have seemed to Theodore, having passed through the darkest year of his life to date. His father had left him, Edie had rejected him (or he her), and now the Lees and Saltonstalls opened their arms.

The whole of late 1878 through 1879 offers that rarest of rarities in the life of Theodore Roosevelt: a sustained picture of his emotional evolution. He penned copious diary entries and letters during these eighteen months, sometimes multiple per day, and these intimate accounts reveal a young man who, having prematurely lost his larger-than-life father, was now both cursed and blessed with an obligation and opportunity to create an identity for himself. With Greatheart gone, he sought a new North Star to direct his prodigious energies along a worthy emotional, intellectual, and vocational course. Theodore and Alice were passionate and handsome young people. Based on his diary and letters, however, we know that Roosevelt was drawn to any number of young women, and we can only assume that Alice, for her part, had interest in other young men. What brought a long and (for Roosevelt) frustrating courtship to fruition was more than sexual attraction and romantic love. For neither Theodore nor Alice can be understood apart from their families. In Alice, Roosevelt saw and felt the world of Chestnut Hill, in which he found a family much like his own and older male figures who gave him something of what his father had given him. For her part, the discerning Alice, who had no shortage of suitors, saw in Roosevelt what the other Lees and the Saltonstalls saw: a young man of compelling potential. In Alice Lee, he would find a guiding light— but not for some time. In the interim, the young man would find himself flailing, turning his prodigious energies to all sorts of misguided ends.

On his second day at Chestnut Hill, Theodore and Alice Lee had their first extended time together. He wrote of spending "the morning walking through the woods with Dick, his sister Miss Rose, and their cousin, Miss Alice Lee—a very sweet pretty girl. About midday we drove over to the Whitneys where we spent the evening dancing and singing, driving back about 11 o'clock."[2] There was that simple adjective again, "sweet," and the next day, after church in the morning, Theodore "went chestnutting with Miss Alice Lee."[3]

Theodore and Dick drove back to Cambridge on Monday morning. Six days later, TR was home again in Oyster Bay, writing in his diary on October 27, his twentieth birthday, that, "Lovely though it is to be spending it with darling Muffie [his mother], Bysie [Bamie] and Pussie [Conie], I can not help having some very sad thoughts about my beloved Father." Then he gave vent to a full flood of emotion: "Oh, Father, sometimes I feel as though I would give half my life to see you but for a moment! Oh, what loving memories I have of you!"[4]

The grief receded, and the next weekend, on Saturday, November 2, he was absorbed in his formal induction into the Porcellian. "In evening was initiated into the Porcellian Club," he wrote, "and was 'higher' with wine than I ever have been before—or will be again. Still, I could wind up my watch. Wine always makes me awfully fighty."[5] Membership in the Porc had been high on Theodore's list of aspirations, and yet his response that evening was not so much to bask in the glory as it was to get drunk, a state that makes him aggressive ("fighty") rather than happy, let alone celebratory. Moreover, in this moment of achievement, Alice Lee finds no place in his thoughts. The next morning, he paid for "last night's spree" with a hangover ("Rather under the weather") but nevertheless took up his duties teaching a Sunday school class and noted that "the scholars were all delighted to see me."[6]

It was not until Sunday, November 10, that he saw Alice Lee again. That weekend, he was the guest in Jamaica Plains of classmate Minot Weld, one of the illustrious Welds of Boston (and a distant cousin of Hal Minot). It was in the afternoon that Weld drove Roosevelt in his

tilbury—the chic and rather dangerous two-wheeled supercharged
sportscar of its day—to "Dick Saltonstalls, where we took tea and came
home at 10 oclock by moon light. Miss Alice Lee was there, as sweet and
pretty as ever; I enjoyed myself most heartily."[7] Did this second meeting
with Alice occur by chance or design?

Bamie was already proving an adept networker for her brother.
Bamie's social instincts later translated to political strategy, always
knowing with whom Theodore should (or should not) connect to get
ahead. Theodore knew he had Bamie to thank for enabling his entrée
into Boston society, writing later that night, "You do not know how
highly they all think of you; Mr. Weld, who is generally rather an impas-
sive old gentleman, said today that he had never met anyone whom he
liked so much on so short an acquaintance. You dear, sweet sister, I really
owe very much of my pleasure in college to you, for had it not been for
your knowing so many Bostonians I should not have had any of the life
'social life' (ahem!) that I have so much enjoyed."[8] The truth was Bamie
did not know many Bostonians, but she knew who she *should* know and
procured an introduction.

To Conie that same day, Theodore wrote of his and Minot Weld's
plans to "drive over to Dick Saltonstalls, where we shall go out walking
with Miss Rose Saltonstall and Miss Alice Lee"—*after* they had "walked
home from church with Miss Wheelwright and Miss Long." The rendezvous with Rose and Alice had been arranged, then, although by which
boy it's difficult to say. Was Minot Weld also interested in their friend's
pretty cousin? The letter to Conie continued, with a touch of pointed
snark: "Remember me to Annie and Fanny, and give my love to Edith—
if she's in a good humor; otherwise my respectful regards. If she seems
particularly good tempered tell her that I hope when I see her at Xmas
it will not be on what you might call one of her off days."[9] Evidently,
Edith's influence on young TR had not eroded completely. He writes
almost as if he's afraid of her. Theodore's awareness of the precarious situation of Edith's family, its patriarch sinking further into business failure
and alcoholism, did not evoke empathy for his childhood companion.

No, the downfall of Charles Carow was yet another discordant element conspicuously absent from Chestnut Hill, where "Mr. Saltonstall" was "one of the best examples of a true, simple hearted 'gentleman of the old school'" Theodore Roosevelt had ever met. It was the beginning of a lifelong pattern for Theodore Roosevelt: removing himself from any concentrated source of emotional pain. As Mittie and Bamie said, "live for the living, not the dead."[10] As for Thanksgiving, he told Conie that his Harvard workload would preclude his coming home.

In fact, Roosevelt's diary entry for November 27, Thanksgiving eve, reveals that, after he had lunch with Dick Saltonstall, the two drove "to his place (at Chestnut Hill) where I shall spend Thanksgiving. I like the whole Saltonstall family very much; I really feel almost as if I were at home when I am over there."[11]

Leverett Saltonstall, who graduated from Harvard and was admitted to the bar, was very active in Massachusetts politics. A Democrat, he ran and lost a bid for Congress, and played an active role supporting the party's unsuccessful presidential candidate in the 1876 election that saw Rutherford B. Hayes elevated to the White House. Remarkably, Saltonstall served as collector of customs for the Port of Boston, the same politically appointed role Thee had held at the Port of New York. He "was prominent as a civil service reformer," noted his obituary, which also lauded his "great interest in agricultural, political and historical affairs."[12] Politics was the family business, reform was a shared passion, and Theodore was enthralled.

Thanksgiving was the first major holiday after his father's death. Theodore must have known that having him home from college for this most family-centric of occasions would mean much to his family. Yet he preferred being in a place in which *he* felt "almost as if I were home." Chestnut Hill was the simulacrum of the home he had known through childhood, and Alice was the one who held the key.

Who was this latest girl to catch Theodore's eye? Alice Hathaway Lee had been born on July 29, 1861, in Chestnut Hill, Massachusetts, into a family

of Brahmin bankers and financiers. Her father was the banker George
Cabot Lee, her mother Caroline Watts (Haskell) Lee of Worcester, Massachusetts. Lee's firm, Lee, Higginson & Co., known popularly as "Lee
Hig," "was one of the kingpins of finance both in the U.S. and abroad,"
leading the investment of General Electric in 1892 and refinancing General Motors in 1910.[13] Lee's partner, Henry Lee Higginson, a financial
wizard and veteran of the Massachusetts Calvary in the Civil War, was
a noted philanthropist who founded the Boston Symphony Orchestra,
which would give its inaugural concert the year after Roosevelt's graduation. Writing an article entitled "A Hint for the Rich," Higginson sum-
marized his business and philanthropic philosophy with a poem:

> *What I gave; I have;*
> *What I spent; I had;*
> *What I kept; I lost.*[14]

It was a philosophy Thee Roosevelt would have seconded—and indeed Higginson, Lee, and the younger Roosevelt would go on to exchange
letters throughout their lives.

George Cabot Lee was sufficiently wealthy to set up his large
family—Alice, her four sisters, and their brother—comfortably though
not ostentatiously. The education of the girls was devoted to fitting them
out for lives as wives of men who were on par with George (or somewhat
better) in wealth and prominence. Coming of age, second-born Alice
would have practiced the proper walk, with poise and impeccable pos-
ture; genteel domestic skills, such as fine needlework; proficient on the
piano; and, typically, a conversational familiarity with French. There was
no objection, however, to athleticism; America was, after all, approaching the era of illustrator Charles Dana Gibson's "Gibson Girl," who ex-
uded outdoorsy health. Alice excelled at tennis and archery. She was as
outwardly active as Edith was inwardly focused.

The Cabot family was descended from John Cabot, who emigrated
from the Channel Island of Jersey to Salem, Massachusetts, in 1700,

where he and his son, Joseph, born in 1720, became merchant operators of a privateer fleet that carried rum, opium, and slaves. By the time of the Revolution, Joseph and his sons were among the wealthiest men in Massachusetts. George Cabot (1752–1823) was a U.S. senator, who served from 1791 to 1796, and was appointed the first secretary of the navy but declined to serve. More famously, his great-grandson, Henry Cabot Lodge (1850–1924), served as senator from Massachusetts from 1893 until his death. Lodge, who was well known to the Lees although only a distant cousin, became an intimate friend and staunch political ally of Theodore Roosevelt. As archetypal Brahmins, the Cabots were celebrated in a popular piece of doggerel called the "Boston Toast":

> And this is good old Boston,
> The home of the bean and the cod,
> Where the Lowells talk only to Cabots,
> And the Cabots talk only to God.[15]

It would be easy to equate New York's Knickerbockers with Boston's Brahmins. Both groups regarded themselves as the "first families" of their respective regions. But the realities were not so simple. Knickerbocker identifies someone as a descendant of Dutch settlers in colonial New Amsterdam before the English moved in and called it New York. The origin of the word is found in Washington Irving's tremendously popular satirical *A History of New York*, published in 1809 under the pseudonym Diedrich Knickerbocker. By 1848, it was in common use as a label for the upper-crust descendants of the city's first comers.[16] Brahmin is of late-fourteenth-century origin (from the ancient Sanskrit) as the name for India's highest priestly Hindu caste. At least one authority says that it was first applied to Boston's wealthy "first families" in 1823, and it was popularized with the publication of the novel *Elsie Venner* by Oliver Wendell Holmes Sr. in 1847.[17] Thus the New York term is the product of a tongue-in-cheek satirical history, whereas the Boston term was borrowed from the rigid caste system of India and suggests those identified by the term regard themselves as members of a holy caste far above all others. It was no mean feat, then, for a mere Knickerbocker to enter, by marriage or otherwise, the sanctified precincts of Brahmin Boston. "New York society was still a closed circle to which one either did or did not belong," author and later Roosevelt confidante Margaret Chanler observed. "Boston girls . . . are brought up to feel that 'coming out' is the all-important event, the great test of their capacity. Marriage they come to regard as something of an abdication, a settling down to the hard facts of life, a play for safety rather than a gamble for conquest."[18] To the Brahmin Lees, the Knickerbocker Roosevelt was a gamble. A Harvard pedigree coupled with Roosevelt wealth undoubtedly helped, however.

Alice Lee was by common consent of all who knew her strikingly beautiful. The few extant photographs reveal her as slim with delicate features and a long yet girlish face in which her wide, pale blue-gray eyes shine. Her hair was a dark golden blond, wavy and long, but often coiled atop her head, revealing perfectly shaped ears. Her mouth was dainty, her nose upturned ever so slightly. At five-foot-eight (some sources put this two inches shorter), she was nearly as tall as Theodore, notwithstanding his habit of calling her "little." Her family—indeed, everyone who knew or spoke of her—called her "Sunshine." Roosevelt biographers generally assume this referred to her sunny disposition, which may in part be true, but the epithet carries a stronger, more significant meaning. Judging from Theodore's relationship to her and the passion of the letters that passed between them, "Sunshine" embodied the sheer vibrance of her presence. She glowed with life.

History often remarks on the dynamic personality of Theodore Roosevelt. Sunshine, it appears, was more than a match for his passion and strong will. One does not even need to *read* the letters that passed between her and Theodore to conclude this. It is enough just to look at them. Where Roosevelt's handwriting is neat, highly legible, very controlled (if, perhaps, a bit schoolboyish), Alice's penmanship is always electric with energy. The cursive letters do not so much slant as they lean in like the acutely raked masts of an extreme clipper ship. The hand is quite legible yet spiky rather than elegant. Ascenders shoot high up while descenders dive even lower. There is a powerful pulse present in each letter of every word. Roosevelt pined for a "rare and radiant maiden," someone "as pure and innocent as she is wise." Now he stood before Alice, the Sunshine of a family fueled by politics, business, history, and adventure.

On Thanksgiving Day, November 28—at Chestnut Hill—Theodore "Spent the day with Alice and 'Rose' [Saltonstall] dancing, walking, playing lawn tennis &c. I have gotten very well acquainted with both of them; Rose is a very good pleasant girl, and as for pretty Alice Lee, I think her one of the sweetest, most ladylike girls I have ever met. They all call me by my first name now."[19] Theodore was now addressed as Saltonstalls and Lees addressed one another. The full context and implications of this transition are not recorded in his diary. Or, if they had been, they were not preserved. The page that must have contained entries for November 29 and November 30 is visibly torn out of the diary. Could that page have contained Theodore's first profession of love to Alice? We will never know, but emotion was swelling, and Theodore was on the hunt. His first letter to her was written on December 6. "Dear Alice," it begins, "I have been anxiously expecting a letter from you and Rose [Saltonstall] for the last two or three days; but none has come." He goes on to urge her: "You *must* not forget our tintype spree; I have been dexterously avoiding forming any engagements for Saturday."[20]

A "tintype spree" was a trip to the photographer to pose together for a portrait. This was not something a man and woman did casually, for it documented—published, as it were—that the subjects of the portrait regarded themselves as a couple, in courtship or at least on its threshold. Though we do not know the contents of the diary pages from November 29 and 30, 1878, the meaning of this first letter to Alice Hathaway Lee is clear. On every blank side of the tri-folded letter, the barely twenty-year-old Roosevelt drew interlaced letters: R and L for Roosevelt and Lee. He wrote "Chestnut Hill" in an elaborate cursive, spinning the "n" in a winding, loopy curve. He coyly traced "Rose Lee," the name of Alice's sister (not to be mistaken for Alice's cousin Rose, who lived next door). But he addressed the letter only to Alice.

Theodore Roosevelt was smitten. He did not entrust to the post office his first missive to Alice. Instead, he sent it to her "by Minot Weld—who knows nothing of the contents, whatever he may say." He entreated her to "Tell Rose [Saltonstall] that I never passed a pleasanter Thanksgiving than at her house" and added "Judging from the accounts I have received, the new dress for the party at New Bedford must have been a complete success." He signed it, "*Your Fellow-conspirator.*"[21] Assuming that the "conspiracy" in question was the prospective tintype spree, it was very one-sided, because the portrait session did not occur until Saturday, *May 10, 1879*, a full five months after the letter.

While Roosevelt was indeed in love, the object of his attachment was not Alice Lee alone. During the rest of December 1878, following his letter reminding Alice of the tintype spree, his thoughts turned not to her but yet again to his father: "at night especially, I get thinking about my loved Father, and then I feel very desolate and heartsore. It seems so terrible to think that he will not be with us at Christmas. . . . O, how little worthy I am of such a father," he wrote in his diary on December 11, "I feel such a hopeless sense of inferiority to him." His profound sorrow was tinged with a guilty feeling that it was somehow not profound enough.

> He was such a very large part in my life, and yet I am now so pressed and driven by work and pleasure, that I often have not even time to think of him. But perhaps it is better so, for when I do think much, I feel such a terrible, dull pain at thinking that never in this world shall I see him again. But with the help of my God I shall try to lead such a life as he would have wished, and to do nothing I would have been ashamed to confess to him.[22]

At the end of this diary passage, a sentence beginning "I am very" is obliterated by a large ink blot. As David McCullough writes in his *Mornings on Horseback*, "The next page, consisting of seven lines, has been carefully blotted out in heavy black ink. Apparently, he had gotten drunk again, or was still sorely distraught over what had happened the night of the Porcellian initiation. For under laboratory conditions, by back-lighting the page, it has been possible to determine two and a half of the seven lines he chose to censor: "angry with myself for having gotten tight when . . ." In this diary entry, sorrow followed by self-flagellation ends in an assertive superego imposing the ham-handed censorship of a great blot. As McCullough notes, Roosevelt closes with, "May God help me to live as he would have wished."[23]

On December 21, he recorded his thoughts on having gone home for Christmas: "Went on to N.Y. It is ever so pleasant to get home again; I enjoy college to the full, and yet I am always only too delighted to get home. Truly, these are the golden years of my life. I can not imagine a fellow having a happier time than I have had since I have been in College."[24] It's an astounding statement, and Roosevelt revealed his acute consciousness of the contradiction in his entry of the next day: "Although the family are all so cheerful, yet we can none of us help thinking a good deal of our dear lost one; but now the sweet is overcoming the bitter in our memories of him. I wonder if I shall ever be very miserable! In spite of the great sorrow—the greatest which could have befallen me—I have yet been very happy these last six months!"[25] On Christmas Day itself, however, he found himself forced to note: "Xmas—had rather a melancholy day. It does seem so very terrible not to have Father with us. He was the perfect life of all our enjoyments."[26]

At the same time, it was the young man's fate, in a period of grief and mourning, to be courting Alice while also flirting with others and on occasion drinking enough to leave him with a guilty hangover. His tendency to melancholy and feelings of guilt if he caught himself being too happy were compounded by the collapse of his relationship with Edie the previous August and Alice Lee's apparent reluctance to embrace him as a serious suitor. He had been to Chestnut Hill three times for a total of nine days since October, and yet his diary records hardly any mention of Alice having deigned to speak with him alone.

Certainly, Theodore Roosevelt was hardly the standard society beau. Like most young men, he was strongly driven by sex, yet girls found him eccentric, to put it mildly. Alice's sister Rose remarked that "he danced just as you thought he would dance if you knew him—he hopped."[27] His overabundance of energy was, to use a period term, uncouth, and to use a more modern term, uncool. A classmate, W. R. Thayer, was unsparing: Roosevelt was "a good deal of a joke. He had none of the charm that he developed later."[28] Worse, the career he contemplated at this stage in his education, that of naturalist, meant that his rooms overflowed with specimens, birds and reptiles in various stages of taxidermy. Nor was it unusual for him to carry a few of these small corpses in his coat pockets. An all-out advance from a hyperkinetic taxidermist could not have been entirely welcome—especially by a young woman as willful and independent as Alice Lee.

As 1878 made way for 1879, Roosevelt seemed increasingly intent on finding himself. Not that he was despairing or even moping. On Sunday, January 5, he noted a "sweet talk with Muffie" and mused, "I wonder if ever a man had two better sisters than I have."[29] Come Monday, he wrote that he had "begun studying with a will," and while he was dissatisfied with his performance on a Natural History exam, he recorded that he was both "studying hard" and "working on an article for the Finance Club (Municipal Taxation) and on a catalogue of the Birds of Oyster Bay."[30]

Next to all this, Alice has slipped to almost an aside. He recorded in his diary that at 10:30 the following Saturday, fellow classmate Harry Shaw drove him in his "cutter" (a sleigh) "to the Saltonstalls, where we found Dick and Minot Weld; Also Alice and Rose."[31] Alice at this point was relegated to an "also." The outing was "splendid." But figuring more prominently on the diary page—and perhaps in his mind—was the possibility of Dick Saltonstall joining the Porcellian.

Even as Theodore made another pilgrimage to Chestnut Hill, he commented on the object of one of his earlier romantic attractions. On January 15, 1879, he recorded in his diary arriving in New York for a wedding rehearsal and seeing there "One of my old flames, pretty Helen White," a bridesmaid and the daughter of the prominent physician Dr. Octavius A. White.[32] Ten days later, a Saturday, he took a "3 hour examination" at Harvard and then, in the afternoon, "went out to Chestnut Hill to pass Sunday." He spent "most of the evening" with his paternal stand-in, Mr. Saltonstall, "looking over his old family papers, comparing our Egyptian and Syrian experiences and talking over things in general." Subjects may have included economics, the spoils system, the unbridled expansion and consolidation of the railroads, and other progressive fare. Tom Lee, Alice's cousin, "came in and we had a grand theological discussion."[33] On Sunday the 26th, he went ice skating ("coasted on double runners"), one of a party of about twenty-five. "I never had better fun. The more I see of Rose Saltonstall and Alice Lee," he wrote, "the more I like them, especially pretty Alice." He went on to note that "the whole [Lee] family call me 'Thee' now."[34]

Alice had begun to reclaim his attention. It is interesting, certainly, that this coincided with his noting that her family addresses him as "Thee," the name by which Edie had often called him and, even more significant, perhaps, by which Mittie had called his late father. The young man effectively began trying on his father's identity. Eventually, this would culminate in the erasure of both "Sr." and "Jr." as Theodore Roosevelt Jr. became simply Theodore Roosevelt, whose first son—born in 1887—was designated Theodore Roosevelt Jr.

TR's strategy to win Alice, not surprising given his later and more celebrated efforts to charge up San Juan Heights, bust a trust, or run as a third-party independent, was simple: direct and sustained advance. What's more surprising is the manner of this advance. On March 29, he "cut the first part" of a Porcellian supper to meet her. In the middle of the week, on Wednesday, April 2, Roosevelt "gave a little lunch party in my rooms" for Alice and a dozen other male and female friends. On this occasion, TR "gave Alice [a] lynx skin, made into a rug; and Rose [a] fox." Lynx, of course, is considerably more valuable than fox, and by "rug," Roosevelt clearly meant a lap robe of the kind ladies and gentlemen used to keep lap and legs warm when traveling. Alice let it be known that she was making Thee a gift in return, a pair of slippers.[35]

It is open to debate whether a lap robe and slippers are gifts more domestic than intimate or vice versa. Edmund Morris regarded the exchange of gifts as a sign that the "relationship was moving into an intimate, more serious phase." But we must note that the very next day, April 3, found Roosevelt in New York City at his Aunt Anna's townhouse, where he noted that "Margie Tuckerman, Fanny Smith & Edith Carow were there, looking very prettily." He added, "Edith is just the same sweet little flirt as ever."[36]

Apparently, the definitive and mysterious summer house events of August 22, 1878, were neither the last meeting nor the last chance for Theodore and Edith. Theodore was, at many times, torn between Alice and Edith, even as he flirted with others. Yet it was Alice whom he now pursued most relentlessly, stalking her as if she were an exotic beast. Did Theodore suspect Edith would wait for him, return to him, if Alice gave her affections to someone else?

As his longing—punctuated by mild flirtations with others—swayed between Edith and Alice, Roosevelt decided to send for his horse, Lightfoot, and "keep him in Cambridge this Spring" at a local stable. This would make it far easier for him to travel the twelve-mile round-trip to and from Chestnut Hill. Indeed, immediately upon Lightfoot's arrival from New York, he rode the horse to that destination, where he spent the weekend. Despite heavy snow on Saturday, he wrote, "I took a long walk with pretty Alice. I spent most of the remainder of the day teaching the girls the five step and a new dance, the knickerbocker. In the evening we played whist and read ghost stories." There was another long walk on Sunday, and Thee wrote Bamie that afternoon that he liked Rose Saltonstall and Alice Lee "more and more every day—especially pretty Alice."[37]

It is telling that Roosevelt addressed this letter to Bamie, not Conie, and wrote what he had previously only confessed to his diary. Roosevelt's letters to Conie were almost always playful. To Bamie, he was typically more reserved, an attitude befitting correspondence with a sibling he regarded as something of a second mother. So, it was rather a bold step

to single out Alice—"especially pretty Alice"—for special notice, a sentiment he had previously expressed only in his private diary. Theodore
longed for "pretty Alice" but there were still few indications that Alice
reciprocated the feeling. Among the reasons for her hesitation may well
have been her age. She was not yet eighteen, perhaps a little young to
commit herself to a serious suitor. But she was at least now taking walks
with him alone. She clearly saw some potential in the young taxidermist
that few others did at the time.

Two days later, Roosevelt was on his seventh jaunt to Chestnut Hill,
where he "found (in addition to Alice, Rose [Saltonstall], and Rosy Lee)
Nana Rotch." He confessed that he "spent the afternoon with the latter,
and now my conscience reproaches me with having rather flirted with
'Nana.'" In the margin, he noted: "I sincerely wish I had not."[38] The sin-
cerity was almost certainly unfeigned, as he was acquiring an unwanted
reputation as what Nana, comparing notes with fellow Boston socialite Bessie Whitney, called a "gay deceiver." For her part, Bessie used the
milder and less sophisticated term "flirt" to describe TR. If Roosevelt intended by flirting with Nana to arouse jealousy in Alice, it did not work.

It had been nearly a half a year since he signed his first note to Alice
"Your Fellow-conspirator" and held his calendar open, hoping they might
take their picture together just after Thanksgiving. As noted, having a
formal portrait made was in this era an intermediate step toward an
engagement. Little wonder that Theodore professed himself practically
breathless with "conspiratorial" excitement. Alice, in contrast, seemed
never to have contracted his passionate urgency.

At last, on May 10, the tintype spree that had been planned five
months earlier finally took place. When the portrait was at last made,
it was not a twosome but a threesome. There were two poses. In the
first photograph, Theodore is standing, walking stick supporting his
left side, derby hat held firmly in his right hand, which barely grazes
Rose Saltonstall, who has accompanied the couple for the "spree." Rose is
seated, looking rather grim, while her cousin, Alice Lee, leans back into
her. Alice is piercing, beautiful, and angular. The picture looks almost as

though it were meant only to be of the two cousins; Theodore is so far away from the girls that he could almost be cropped out of the frame.

Imagine his frustration. Five months of waiting and this is the result?

A second photograph, however, was taken for this sitting. In this one, Theodore is seated next to Alice. The walking stick rests against his left thigh, his left hand atop the derby, which perches on his knee. Both Rose, who stands behind him, and he look off to the viewer's left, but Alice Lee, an open book lying on her lap, gazes straight into the camera, commanding the composition, even though it is Theodore who occupies dead center.

She is clearly in his peripheral vision, and his right thigh grazes her left. Theodore's right forearm, the fingers of his hand curled in a loose fist, is uneasily settled atop his own right thigh. He is almost touching Alice, almost. Their figures form a "V" vaguely reminiscent of Leonardo's *The Last Supper.* If Rose, whose hands grip the back of his chair, ever stood a chance of attracting Theodore, the photograph makes clear that there is no longer any such prospect for her.

In the second tintype, the juxtaposition of Theodore and Alice is more aspirational than intimate, but the "spree" was followed on Sunday, May 11, by an after-church walk together. On Monday, TR went off on his own, taking Lightfoot on "the longest ride I have yet taken." His steed transported him in an ecstasy of sublimated passion "through the beautiful country back of Waverly." TR remarked that the animal "has got his summer coat and is pretty well filled out, so he is looking like a little beauty. It was the best stroke I ever made, getting him on here."[39]

Lightfoot made it possible for TR to visit Chestnut Hill more spontaneously. Biographer Morris saw something more, for paying court "on horseback," he wrote, is more "in the style of a true gallant." Roosevelt's gallops to Chestnut Hill became increasingly frequent, and he himself relished his appearance in the saddle, looking "very swell, with hunting crop and beaver"—a stylish and very pricey Victorian top hat. He wrote that he could not "conceive of a fellow possibly enjoying himself more" than he was. Yet Alice would not succumb.[40]

In an episode recalling his manic, nearly horse-killing ride after the summer house breach with Edith the year before, TR's equine ecstasy went wild on Tuesday, May 13, when he galloped to the Lees' after dinner to spend the evening. "I rode like Jehu, both coming and going, and as it was pitch dark when I returned (about 10.15) we fell, while galloping down hill—a misadventure which I thoroughly deserve for being a fool." But Lightfoot deserved better. TR noted the next day that his "horse is a little lame from yesterday's exploits; so I could not go to the Saltonstalls to dinner. Spent the evening in the D.K.E. [Delta Kappa Epsilon fraternity], drowning my sorrows; I have been an awful fool to ride the horse so hard."[41]

Jehu, commander of chariots, whom God subsequently anointed king of Israel after the ruinous reign of Ahab, became proverbial to readers of the Old Testament for his hell-for-leather handling of a chariot (2 Kings 9:20). By the seventeenth century, in England, *jehu* was used as a synonym for *coachman* (especially one who was fast and reckless), and even today it is sometimes applied to reckless taxi drivers. To "ride (or drive) like Jehu" was a common phrase among churchgoing Americans in the nineteenth century.[42] Unlike the biblical Jehu, young Roosevelt's furious ride did not lead to greater things. Lightfoot was lame for weeks, during which (Morris observes) "Theodore was obliged to visit his beloved on foot—a twelve-mile [round-trip] tramp every time."[43]

With Lightfoot lamed, Roosevelt showered Alice with gifts. After dinner with Dick Saltonstall, he brought "the girls over some gold and silver charms."[44] The trinkets were doubtless welcomed but, trinkets nonetheless, were casually distributed to the girls, Alice included.

Theodore had the smarts, if not the prudence, to avoid relying solely on his dubious charm. After Thee's death, Theodore's uncles had taken over primary control of his estate. Any spending beyond the boy's allowance would have to be cleared with them. Still, as Edward P. Kohn, editor of the Roosevelt diaries, observes, "In 1879 Roosevelt spent more than double what he had in 1878: an astonishing $5200. Of that, only $320 went toward his Harvard education, with another $700 going to room and board." Kohn suggests that the difference in spending between 1878 and 1879 tells volumes about the way Roosevelt's life continued to evolve as a Harvard graduate. He now spent hundreds of dollars on club dues, more than even the cost of his education. At the beginning of his undergraduate career he had kept neither a horse nor a carriage in Cambridge. Now he kept a horse, a sporty two-wheeled "dogcart," and a wintertime sleigh, at the high cost of $650. In 1878 social "amusements" had cost Roosevelt only $32.75. The following year they cost him over $300. . . . By far, Roosevelt spent more on "presents" than any other expense, nearly $1000. Most of these were given to the young ladies of Chestnut Hill, Rose Saltonstall and Alice and Rosie Lee.[45]

In the very sentence after he mentioned these gifts, TR noted in his diary, "I am afraid I have lamed my horse hopelessly; it is very tough luck; but at least I did have royal sport for the three and half weeks I had him."[46] His tone here is nearly breathtakingly callous. Four days later, TR returned to the subject of poor Lightfoot, pronouncing him "hopelessly lame," and recording his resolve to send him back to New York. (He never did.) "I deserved it," he added and continued with a sentence whose misplaced adverb only a malevolent schoolmarm might fully appreciate: "I miss having him to ride horribly."[47]

Early June brought Theodore Roosevelt twin deliverances. He passed his first three annual examinations, and Lightfoot—miraculously, it would seem—recovered. On Saturday, June 14, he recorded that classmate "Charley Morgan got very drunk, and, not having been sober for a week, nearly had the D.T.s; I slept in his room." TR did not record his own state of relative sobriety or inebriation but did note that "walking home next morning in a dress suit nearly walked over a proctor."[48] That was bad enough, but on Sunday (his twenty-third trip to Chestnut Hill), he walked with Rose and Alice in the afternoon "and got drenched in a rain storm." By the time he drove home, "it was pitch dark, and I came within an ace of smashing up against a wagon."[49] Roosevelt's journeys to and from Chestnut Hill more often than not verged on impulsive

recklessness. Gone was the teetotaling naturalist. Ornithology with
Henry Davis Minot was replaced by excessive drinking and even fisticuffs
with the privileged men of the Porcellian. Theodore Roosevelt had found
his new North Star, but there was a certain irony to the fact that this star
was leading him further away from Greatheart. Further away from Alice,
too. For was the person he was turning into in pursuit of her—the flashy
suitor, the spendthrift, the shameless flirt—a man this discerning young
woman would really want to spend her life with?

With exams over, Theodore commenced what he called "a life of most
luxurious ease," breakfasting "in the Club about 10; my horse is there
before the door, and I ride off—generally lunching at some friends house.
It is very pleasant—but," he dutifully added, "I do not suppose it would
be healthy to continue it too long." Shaking off this brief Puritan spasm,
he continued: "When I do not stay out to tea or dinner, I generally have
some kind of spree—a 'champagne supper'—up in the club."[50] The behavior did not appeal to Alice and does not stack well with the sort of man
Theodore claimed to want to be.

The young squire made two more trips to Chestnut Hill, numbers
24 and 25. He celebrated Rose's birthday with her and Alice on June 17,
bringing the gift of a fan for each girl, and confiding to his diary, "En
passant those—2 two young ladies have cost me over $150 so far."[51] On the
18th of June, he "dined at the Lees, afterward taking Alice to a strawberry
festival at the Lowells."[52] On the 19th, he went off "to the D.K.E. strawberry night," where he allowed himself to get "into a row with a mucker
[a rough, coarse person] and knocked him down; cutting my knuckles
pretty badly against his teeth."[53] TR's diary provides no evidence of anything of import impending, but later biographers saw in the strawberry
night fight evidence of great tension, calling him "tense as a wire the
night before" Class Day. The mucker fight and a successful date with
Alice served to calm him down.[54]

"I have never passed such a pleasant day," Roosevelt said of Class
Day, June 20, 1879, in his diary. He was a Junior Class usher, lunched at

the Porcellian, danced with Alice and others and then took Alice for tea. Theodore and Alice strolled together in Harvard Yard. They sat in a window in Hollis Hall, looking out at the "lighted Yard and listening to the Glee Club."[55] Alice and Theodore danced in Memorial Hall until thirty minutes before midnight.

In a diary entry made on January 25, 1880, Roosevelt mentions that he proposed to Alice eight months earlier, which would put the proposal in June 1879.[56] If it was indeed the case that Theodore proposed and Alice rejected him on Class Day evening, she must have done so in a manner quite unlike whatever had passed between Teedie and Edie the year before. There was no rupture, permanent or even temporary. Indeed, a few days later, Theodore called on Alice at Chestnut Hill.

"Mr. + Mrs. Saltonstall are just too sweet for anything," Roosevelt wrote in his diary. "They have added so much to my happiness this year that I scarcely know how to thank them. So have the Lees. I shall be even more sorry to leave Chestnut Hill than to leave Harvard."[57] In Alice and in the Lees and Saltonstalls of Chestnut Hill, Theodore Roosevelt was finding something that Edith Carow could not give him. It was not a sisterly stand-in to fill the void left by his missing father. It was something fuller, more complete. It was a young woman, at once innocent and sexual, who was also the daughter of something Edith could not offer: a father not unlike his own—not a drunk, not a failing businessman, but the Brahmin counterpart of a Knickerbocker reformer who was also a gentleman of the old school. In Alice, Theodore Roosevelt found the promise of a certain completion, fresh, exciting, yet with a noble familiarity that felt like home. Like his many pursuits in the future, Roosevelt was all in.

If Theodore was floundering, the Lees and Saltonstalls did not see it. He continued to thrive in his studies, and the two families welcomed him back again and again. "The difference between Theodore's final two years at Harvard and the first two was enormous," remarked historian David McCullough.[58] His sister seemed to recognize something was amiss, at least in hindsight, and by his senior year, the transformation was nearly complete. "His last year at college was one of . . . growth," Conie remembered. "Although the development was not," she added mildly, "as apparent in his junior year."[59] Theodore wanted to win Alice so badly, he risked losing his sense of self in the process. Not that he seemed to notice.

"After breakfast [on June 26, 1879] I bid goodbye with most heartfelt regret, to Chestnut Hill, and rode over to Cambridge," wrote Roosevelt in his diary. Alice joined him in a special car to witness the "Great Harvard Yale Race" on the Charles River. "We did not get home till 2 a.m., and I have absolutely no voice left, thanks to the shouting. We sang during most of the return journey. I spent a large proportion of my time with Alice, who never looked prettier," he wrote.

The next day, Roosevelt left Cambridge and wrote in his diary: "So ends my Junior Year; and I can not possibly conceive of any fellow having a pleasanter time that I have had."[60] Yet Theodore Roosevelt had failed to win the hand of Alice Hathaway Lee. To do so in his senior year, he would need more than Lightfoot or trinket jewelry. He needed Mittie, Bamie, and Conie to "win his way into her family's heart" with what historian Dr. Kathleen Dalton called a "campaign by encirclement."[61] He would surround Alice with the affection and vivacity of his sisters and mother. The all-consuming pursuit would nearly break him.

5

COURTING ALICE

"It was a real case of love at first sight—and my first love too."
—Theodore Roosevelt describing Alice Hathaway Lee

There was Edith. There was Alice. And there was Teddy, torn between the two.

The birthdays of Alice and Edith were separated by a mere eight days. Alice turned eighteen on July 29, 1879, and Edith followed just over a week later on August 6. There is no record of whether TR sent Alice a gift, but to Edith he gave *Lucile*. Written by Robert, Lord Lytton under the pseudonym Owen Meredith, the book is a narrative poem about a young woman who is beloved by two bitter rivals, the English Lord Alfred Hargrave and the French Duke of Luvois. Lucile loves Alfred, but a misunderstanding separates them. Years after that separation, Alfred's son and the Duke's niece fall in love, only to be separated themselves by the old feud. Through the efforts of Lucile, they are finally reunited—the union denied in the first generation realized in the next.

Roosevelt purchased the book from the publisher James R. Osgood Co. in Boston before summer break and well in advance of Edith's August birthday. He inscribed his gift: "To Edith K. Carow on her eighteenth birthday from her sincere friend Theodore Roosevelt." It was just one year earlier, a little over two weeks after Edith's seventeenth birthday, that whatever romance Edie and Teedie had abruptly ended in the summer house Tranquility. Now, as he was courting Alice, he sent her a rhyming tale of would-be lovers torn apart by a misunderstanding and how the pain of that parting carries forth for generations.[1]

After spending a little over a month in the wilderness of Maine, Theodore Roosevelt returned to Cambridge for his senior year at Harvard on September 25. "I shall keep a dog cart + sleigh next winter," he'd determined.[2] Lightfoot was no longer enough. He was doubling down on the speed and style of a most fashionable means of transport to Chestnut Hill, a dogcart being a light, fast carriage, originally designed with sporting shooters in mind but suitable to any Victorian gentleman who wanted the nineteenth-century equivalent of a roadster. "I am keeping my horse and dogcart at Pikes Stable," he wrote in his diary the day he returned to college. "I have really got a very stylish turnout. I intend to have lovely fun this winter."[3] Graduation was nine months away, and Roosevelt wasted no time in resuming his pursuit of Alice Hathaway Lee. From the end of his junior year to the beginning of his senior year, Theodore Roosevelt had been away from Alice Lee more than they had been together. It was time to remind her of his presence.

The very next day, he rode out to Chestnut Hill in his new dogcart. "They were all so heartily glad to see me that I felt as if I had come home," he wrote. A day later, Roosevelt declared: "My cart is the greatest success of the season."[4]

Not everyone agreed. Classmate Richard Welling remarked, "Some of us were surprised, senior year, when we saw our serious friend Teddy driving a dog-cart and, between you and me, not a very stylish turnout [rig]."[5] Even his admiring modern biographer Edmund Morris has painted him as the "amorous Don Quixote, spurring Rocinante across the plain of La Mancha," so "comic a courtier" he seemed.[6]

Thomas Lee, a classmate at Harvard who graduated one year ahead of Roosevelt, was one of the many cousins counted among the Lees and Saltonstalls of Chestnut Hill. He had the rare vantage point of observing Roosevelt at both the surrogate home he so willingly embraced and at Harvard, and what he saw was a rather desperate young man: "After Roosevelt became interested in Alice he was intensely and amazingly jealous of every one of the young fellows who circled, like moths around a candle, about Miss Lee. She was a vivacious and attractive creature, and had any number of beaus, many of whom she had known all her life."[7]

For the second time in a year, Roosevelt's pursuit of Alice seems to have frustrated him so mightily that he ripped away the secret thoughts he poured into his diary. The pages are torn from Tuesday, October 14, and Wednesday, October 15. Lightfoot, a dogcart, and a cascade of gifts were not enough to win the hand of Alice Lee, not when *her* willful personality was more than a match for Theodore's own. She was not to be taken lightly or for granted. He concocted a new plan.

In a letter dated October 20, Roosevelt insisted his sisters "must come on to Boston next month if only to see Chestnut Hill."[8] Despite his increasing frustration, Theodore Roosevelt still believed he had a viable chance to win Alice Lee. In the letters they'd exchanged over the summer, he'd invited her to visit his family home in New York, and she'd accepted. Roosevelt endeared himself to the Lee and Saltonstall families by showing his most congenial self—a self very different from his recent moodiness in Cambridge. Now, at what he seemed to see as a do-or-die juncture in the courtship, he would win Alice not alone but with more Roosevelts. He realized that he needed Mittie, Bamie, and Conie to seal the deal. He needed to bring Alice to his home field, New York City, and surround her with the vitality of the Roosevelt women. In marrying TR, Alice would be marrying into the Roosevelt family, and so—especially in this era when married children often still lived with or near their parents— TR needed his mothers and sisters to show Alice that being a Roosevelt woman was great fun. Roosevelt's army of women were his best chance of winning over the recalcitrant Alice Lee.

Theodore's sisters were coming into their own. "They were always

very different people to me," Eleanor Roosevelt recalled of her aunts
Bamie and Conie. "Auntie Corinne had the greater artistic ability of expression and the greater charm. Auntie Bye had, on the other hand, the
quality of making you want to discuss problems." To "Auntie Bye you
took any problem to because you felt that she would give it her best
judgement—and it would be a good judgement."[9] The roles were clear:
Bamie was the strategic planner and wise counselor, Conie the boon companion and sympathetic ear. Theodore cherished them both. "I've never
seen a relationship between brother and sisters anywhere—or heard of
any—that was as close and absolutely adoring," remembered Helen Roosevelt Robinson (daughter of FDR's half-brother, James Roosevelt "Rosy"
Roosevelt).[10]

As for the family matriarch, Mittie's grandchildren found her "enchanting." In the wake of Thee's death, she had not recoiled from life
but in some ways seemed rejuvenated. Mittie had always been an admired hostess, and as her children grew, so, too, did her freedom. Her
renowned New York salons were touted in the *New York Times*, *Sun*, and
Observer. She was such fun to be around, an amusing conversationalist.
"[Mittie] and Aunt Gracie were the people who gave whatever humor
we have," recalled her granddaughter. She and Aunt Anna "had per-
fected a combination of competence and feminine fragility. . . . Their
smiles could wilt all but the most hostile audience, and their accents,
retaining the long vowels of their native Georgia, underlined their easy,
relaxed approach to life and their insistence on seeing the pleasures and
not the pain."[11]

Perhaps one of the biggest credits to Mittie is that she did not permit herself to outshine her daughters. "The contradiction between the
'little' Mittie that her husband and the children described and the decisive woman of her letters and actions may very well have resulted from
a conscious effort on her part," observes historian Betty Boyd Caroli.
"Her withdrawal from family competition, whether conscious or not,
served another useful purpose: it permitted her daughters to feel superior to her, to develop both wit and charm sufficient to outshine her

inordinately good looks. Plain daughters of exquisite mothers are not always so lucky."[12] Mittie let her children blossom, stepping back to allow Bamie and Conie to become confident, self-assured women in their own right, perhaps to her own detriment in the eyes of history.

Conie wrote that Mittie happily "turned over much of the management of the family home" at 6 West 57th Street to now twenty-four-year-old Bamie, who was likely thus the one making preparations for Alice's visit. Eagerly awaiting the encounter between the Lees—Alice would be traveling to New York with her parents and her cousin Rose—and his charming and brilliant mother and two sisters, Roosevelt recorded bouts of insomnia. Though it was not unusual for a college student to burn the midnight oil, insomnia became a lifelong challenge for TR—or opportunity, if you consider Roosevelt's prodigious output in multiple fields. A posthumous diagnosis is provided by noted psychologist Kay Redfield Jamison:

> Theodore Roosevelt seems to have burst into the world a full-throated exuberant. . . . Stoked by restless energy not uncommon in those with exuberant temperaments, Roosevelt drove his desolation into action. He rowed, hiked, hunted, boxed, and swam furiously during the fevered weeks that followed his father's death. . . . "He'll kill himself before he'll even say he's tired," remarked one doctor of Roosevelt's frenetic behavior. Yet through it all there remained an irrepressible sense of life: "I am of a very buoyant temper," he wrote his sister not long after his father died. It was a temper that would serve him well and ill, but mostly well.[13]

On his twenty-first birthday, October 27, Roosevelt recorded an almost pitch perfect description of what Jameson observes: "I have had so much happiness in my life so far that I feel, no matter what sorrows come, the joys will have overbalanced them. And yet on this day I can not help thinking with sadness about Father, my best and most loved and revered friend; may God help me to live as he would have wished."[14]

A week later, Sunday, November 2, the Lees arrived in New York City. A Napoleon about to send his amply prepared troops into battle, Theodore wrote: "the Roosevelts have come up to time nobly, and they have sprees on hand for every evening next week."[15] It all depended now on the strength, personality, and charm of the Roosevelt women. Theodore knew they were clever, lovely, and, in a word, magnetic. He had to trust that Alice and her parents would see them just as he did. At last, Theodore did the unthinkable for one of his exuberant personality. He leaned back, writing in his diary, "I can do nothing for them myself."[16]

"He reasoned that his best hope lay in bringing their respective families together," Edmund Morris conjectures. "Enmeshing Alice in such warm webs of mutual affection (for he was sure everybody would get along famously) that she would be powerless to break away."[17] If that was so, the plan seems to have worked. Theodore's mother and sisters likely impressed the Lees as the Lees had impressed Theodore—as simpatico in knowledge, interests, progressive leanings, and, not least, cultural and financial station. One of Roosevelt's earliest biographers wrote that "Theodore's mother seems to have been fond of Alice from the start; nor is this surprising. The young girl and the older woman had much in common."[18] There is no record of precisely what Mittie felt about Alice upon this first meeting. But the Lees were so taken by Mittie, Bamie, and Conie that they invited the Roosevelt sisters to visit Chestnut Hill later that month. Encouraged by this news, Theodore, now back in Cambridge, made his fortieth trip to Chestnut Hill on November 10, writing later that he "drove over in the afternoon to the Lees where I dined and spent a very pleasant evening, not returning till after eleven." But, in a letter to Bamie, dated the very next day, he lamented to his older sister: "Oh the changeableness of the female mind!" Had something untoward happened, had something unpleasant been said, between the 10th and the 11th? We haven't a clue, but to his diary he later confessed, "I did not think I could win [Alice] and I went nearly crazy at the mere thought of losing her." Waterloo? Not yet.[19]

Days later, Theodore returned home to New York City to retrieve his sisters and escort them to Chestnut Hill. He chose not to come home for Thanksgiving the year after his father's death but thought nothing of shuttling back and forth between Boston and New York in service of his pursuit of Alice. It may have been a mad pursuit, yet it was not entirely single-minded. Back home, he could not resist checking in on Edith, with whom he recorded having "a most delightful call," writing on November 16 that "She is the most cultivated, best read girl I know."[20]

The next day Roosevelt departed for Chestnut Hill with Bamie and Conie. The "best read girl I know" was still a friend, not yet again a potential lover or future wife. The rift of August 22 reverberated. Edie and Teedie, unlike the characters in *Lucile*, were not yet ready to make amends. Alice's Teddy was on the march to Boston.

His sisters neither stayed with him in Cambridge nor in a Boston hotel, but with the Lees and Saltonstalls at Chestnut Hill. "It seems very natural to have the girls at Chestnut Hill," Roosevelt wrote. "So natural"? Perhaps the situation recalled to him childhood days at Tranquility, in company with his sisters and his bonus sister, Edith. The week-long visit began with a festive dinner. Rainy weather did not deter Roosevelt and Dick Saltonstall from riding out. "We had the jolliest kind of time," Roosevelt wrote. "Dancing and talking . . . Just before starting back Dick took a glass of brandy which rather set him up so he insisted on galloping the horse, which of course ran away 4 or 5 times; I nearly died laughing." Two days later, despite heavy snow, Roosevelt made the twelve-mile round-trip in time for dinner.[21]

The marquee event of the week was a lunch party Roosevelt hosted on campus at the Porcellian. Alice made her first trip to Cambridge since June, when she and Theodore had shared a few magical days at the end of his junior year. If there were any question of who was courting whom, the answer is found in the visit count. By the time of Roosevelt's lunch party in November, he had called on Alice at Chestnut Hill forty-five times. The luncheon was Alice's thirteenth visit of the year to Cambridge or Boston. Thirty-four guests were seated at one long, rectangular table. TR positioned Bamie by Mrs. Lee, and Mr. Saltonstall by Conie. Roosevelt anchored one end of the table with Alice seated to his left.

Conspicuously not present was George Cabot Lee, Alice's father. Despite the absence of the person most necessary in the era to consent to his daughter's marriage, Roosevelt said of the luncheon: "It was the greatest success imaginable. Everything went off to perfection; the dinner was capital, the flowers very pretty and we had great fun with the toasts and speeches . . . all the girls looked extremely pretty, the wine was good, and the fellows all gentlemen."[22]

The next day, Sunday, November 23, the week-long campaign was over. Roosevelt drove to Chestnut Hill to bid farewell to Bamie and Conie but did not return with them to New York. Thanksgiving was the following Thursday, and for the second year in a row, he opted for Chestnut Hill over New York. He traveled back to Chestnut Hill on Wednesday, the day before Thanksgiving, writing: "I am now most thoroughly and happily at home here, and I really *love* every member of the family."[23] For the next five days, including Thanksgiving dinner, Theodore spent every moment with the two families and especially Alice. They danced and played charades and whist. "I took a long ride in the cart with Alice," Roosevelt wrote about the day after Thanksgiving. "Got caught in the rain and had to borrow an umbrella from a strange house. . . . In the evening I stayed up till all hours with dear old Mr. Saltonstall, talking poetry and theology."[24] Surely, Roosevelt's envy and anxiety intensified. He had not yet won the hand of Alice Lee and her debut was less than a week away. On Sunday, he wrote: "After Church I left the Hill, with the deepest regret that the lovely five days were over, and drove back to Cambridge."[25]

The following Tuesday, December 2, was Alice Hathaway Lee's coming-out party, her official debut in society and the traditional proclamation of her eligibility to wed. Rosebuds, the petals of the flower long associated with the Roosevelts, showered Alice and Rose, her cousin. The party was held at the home of the Wares, who were neighbors of the Lees and Saltonstalls.

In his diary, Roosevelt placidly observed the momentous event, the debut of his love into society, as though it were just another day: "Went to a party at the Wares; it was Alice's and Rose's coming out party and I was much amused at seeing all the buds."[26] In truth, Theodore was mad with jealousy. He believed that Charley Ware was a keen rival, something Alice's cousin Thomas Lee later confirmed.

"Roosevelt seemed constantly afraid that someone would run off with her, and threatened duels and everything else," Thomas Lee remarked. "On one occasion he actually sent abroad for a set of French dueling pistols, and after great difficulty got them."[27] Theodore was becoming increasingly erratic. A contemporary biographer speculated that "if Alice had known he had ordered the pistols, she might have laughed in wonderment, but his male peers understood why a duel over honor might appeal to a headstrong youth. Earlier that year a friend had asked Theodore to serve as a second in a duel, and he assented, though it never took place."[28]

Unrequited in love and, when cooler heads prevailed, unable to restore his honor in a duel with Charley Ware (whose only sin was likely nothing more than permitting his family to host Alice Lee's debut), Roosevelt resorted to what many college students, then and now, do. He drank, both spectacularly and regularly. On December 17, he made his fiftieth visit to Chestnut Hill of 1879, although a more remarkable occurrence would follow at the Hasty Pudding Club later that night.[29]

Harvard's Hasty Pudding Club is the oldest college social club in the United States, having been founded in 1795. Originally, club members entertained themselves by staging mock trials, which were eventually elaborated into the theatricals for which Hasty Pudding became famous. Sixteen-year-old Martha Cowdin, the daughter of a prominent New England shipping family, was in attendance on December 17, and later recalled that Roosevelt stormed up to her during the party and exclaimed, "See that girl? I am going to marry her. She won't have me, but I am going to have *her!*" She recalled that "the gentle Alice was alarmed by the impetuosity of the young man who had suddenly precipitated himself into the circle of more decorous beaus."[30]

The very next night, TR had a "champagne supper," went to the D.K.E. theatricals, returned to the Pudding for a "punch," and recorded in his diary having had an "awfully jolly evening." In truth, the evening concluded with a baroquely drunk and demonstratively lovelorn Roosevelt striking out into the woods around Cambridge, ranting about the illusory threat of Charley Ware. Plagued by insomnia, he refused to go to bed.[31]

Henry Davis Minot upbraided him for his behavior. The unsparingly moralistic Minot laid it on with a trowel, invoking Mittie as well as the ghost of the senior Roosevelt in a seven-page missive marked and underlined, "*Strictly Private*" that read in part:

> *Now, what disgusted me with life at Harvard, and made me willing to give up all the pleasures connected with it (except the prospective chumming with you), was the morally weakening, if not corrupting, influence of its social life, and the rarity of fellows so thoroughly upright as not to bend before it. I have had great faith in you, Teddy; and I remember distinctly two years ago, very soon after your father's death, sitting in your pleasant room by the firelight, and discussing this subject with you. I do not wish to be sentimental in my appeal, but I believe that I was near to you at that time. At any rate, we talked freely; and, after condemning worse things, you said: "Do you know, Hal, I don't mind the other fellows getting tight now and then so very much; but I should never like to be myself—I couldn't, after thinking of mother; and I can't understand how a fellow who's got such a mother as I have, can go home to her afterwards."*

To Hal Minot, a young man very different from the rest of his gregarious rather rowdy Harvard classmates, Theodore made a rare revelation about his feelings for his mother. Assuming Minot is quoting his friend accurately here, it seems that, in her way, Mittie wielded as much emotional sway over her son as the senior Roosevelt had. Both figured as powerful drivers of Theodore's conscience or even his superego. We know how strongly Greatheart inspired his son as a figure he could not bear to disappoint. Perhaps Mittie—unreconstructed Southern belle that she was, seemingly at home in crinolines and upon fainting couches—was for her son an admonitory presence not so distantly second to his father's. Mittie certainly seems to have used this power before: Thee did not take up arms against her brothers in the Civil War, and both Bamie and Conie espoused her philosophy to live in the moment, forging on through life's inevitable disappointments and losses. Mittie was, in many ways, the source of the Roosevelts greatest strength: resilience.

Hal's letter continues:

> Now, remembering clearly these words, from the time when our friendship was closest and warmest, do you suppose that I enjoyed the other night seeing you deliberately sacrifice your self-control, and yield to the silliest of all human indulgences, and hearing you talk shameful grossness before a woman whom I hope is respectable, and muddled nonsense about fighting sensible Charlie Ware with duelling pistols? I cannot say that you were alarmingly far gone, or more than too excited; but there were aggravations in your case. You were sacrificing (what most of your companions couldn't) sober refinement, cultivated reason, natural refinement (inherited refinement), and your good principles. . . . Then, you were acting on the most casuistic and miserable argument, that, as you had been faithful and steady for a certain time, you were entitled to sacrifice independence, abandon your self-restraint, and have (as you call it) "a good time." . . . Could either of us bear to think of his father as saying to himself: "I have now been faithful to my wife for twenty years; and I feel entitled to abandon my principles, excite my passions, and seek criminal indulgence, just for once" or: "I have been sober now for twenty years, and I may as well reward myself by getting drunk."? Surely, any indulgence that lowers us, is just as wrong for a mature, rational man of twenty, as for one of forty: the argument of "wild oats" is fit for only really thoughtless fools.—You have lowered yourself because you are

capable of filling a high position and of exerting high influence,—and I
am not the only person who thinks this of you.

. . . Your loving friend,

H. D. Minot.

A Happy New Year![32]

Likely via Minot, word of Theodore's drunken exploits traveled back
to the Roosevelt family in New York. Roosevelt's cousin James (Jimmy)
West Roosevelt, who was studying at Columbia Medical School, was
dispatched, very likely by Mittie or Bamie or both, from his classes to
Cambridge to bring Theodore home for Christmas to rest and recover
himself.[33] Theodore was aware of his brother Elliott's alcoholism and the
downfall of Charles Carow. He ought to have known he was careening in
a dangerous direction. Theodore was in crisis, and his family and friends
intervened—something they would try and fail to do for Elliott. For neither the first time nor the last time, Theodore's support structure would
save him.

On Christmas Eve 1879, Roosevelt called on Edith Carow. Dizzy with
disappointment from his flailing pursuit of Alice, might he have wanted
to keep the "most cultivated, best read girl I know" on standby? After
a "lovely time" on Christmas, which Roosevelt described "as pleasant
as it could be," he took Edith to lunch on December 26.[34] It had been
almost a year and a half since their explosive break and less than ten
days since Roosevelt's outburst-by-way-of-proclamation that he would
marry Alice Hathaway Lee. Yet on Christmas 1879 Roosevelt could not
know which woman was more likely to become his wife. As with most
of their relationship, whatever was said between Edith and Theodore at
lunch the day after Christmas is unknown to history. What is known is

that very evening Alice Lee arrived in New York City. Though she might have been alarmed by his erratic behavior, Alice clearly saw something in him that almost no one else, besides his sisters and Mittie, did: greatness.

"It is perfectly lovely, having the dear, sweet Chestnut Hillers with us:—and so natural," Roosevelt wrote. He played tour guide and had an "uproariously jolly time."[35] Aunt Anna Gracie threw a party for the Lees—the same contingent as had made the trip two months earlier, plus Alice's sister. Mittie, Bamie, and Conie were their hosts. They went to the music hall, sledded, and drove a buggy around Central and Riverside Parks. On New Year's Eve, Roosevelt wrote in his diary that he "took Alice out walking," and that evening the Roosevelt women threw a New Year's Eve party for their guests.[36]

Theodore closed out 1879 remarking they "danced the old year out and drank the new year in."[37] (So much for Minot's teetotaling admonitions.) He awoke in 1880 to a "beautiful" New Year's Day. Theodore, Bamie, and Conie took Alice and a host of cousins and friends on a sleigh ride and then returned home to dance the waltz, polka, and Virginia Reel.[38] The next day, Roosevelt left the group behind and "after breakfast took Alice out to drive in the Park."[39]

One of Roosevelt's earliest and most critical biographers Henry Pringle could not resist the allure of such a romantic and tumultuous courtship, writing:

Alice's last defenses had been shattered, [and she] considered Theodore wholly magnificent. The brief days between Christmas and New Year's Day in 1879 must have been high marks in Theodore's life. He saw Alice, who affected heavy white brocades to set off her fair hair and blue eyes, standing in front of the open fire after dinner; Alice being very feminine, very attentive to the conversation, very timid about taking more than a sip of wine. He saw her, demure in furs and carrying a small muff, while she skated on nearby ponds and leaned deliciously on his strong arms.[40]

Alice "was, by every surviving account, extraordinarily attractive," but she wasn't just a male fantasy.[41] "I love to talk over everything with [Alice]," Theodore later confided to his diary.[42] Conie found Alice "lovely," and presumably Bamie felt the same, for she was never one to keep thoughts to herself.[43] And, if there had been any trouble after his antics at the Hasty Pudding party, Theodore was redeemed once again by the good graces and charm of the Roosevelt women. Within the circle of his family, Theodore was clearly happy and comfortable. Seeing him among his mother and sisters, Alice could study him on his best behavior and in joyful mood. Surrounded by the Roosevelt women, Theodore was at his most charming. Time spent with Alice in their presence had a lingering effect on him. When he returned to Cambridge for the second half of his senior year, the incessant insomnia and threats of duels were bygone. His drinking abated, and he instead appeared to be readying to ask Alice, once again, for her hand in marriage.

"Darling Muffie," Roosevelt wrote his mother on Sunday, January 11, 1880, "Please send my silk hat at once," as he informed Mittie that he was "driv[ing] up to Chestnut Hill to see the girls and talk over the New York trip."[44] Bamie celebrated her twenty-fifth birthday on January 18, and two days later Theodore spent the afternoon with the Lees. He returned on Friday, January 23. This is the likeliest date on which Theodore Roosevelt asked George C. Lee and his wife, Caroline Haskell Lee, for their daughter's hand. Two days later, on January 25, Roosevelt proclaimed:

> At last everything is settled; but it seems impossible to realize it. I am so happy that I dare not trust in my own happiness. I drove over to the Lees determined to make an end of things at last; it was nearly eight months since I had first proposed to her, and I had been nearly crazy during the past year; and after much pleading [perhaps on bended knee?] my own sweet, pretty darling consented to be my wife. Oh, how bewitchingly pretty she looked! If loving her with my whole heart and soul can make her happy, she shall be happy.[45]

In this moment of triumph, Roosevelt also provides the strongest evidence we have of a first—failed—proposal in June 1879: "it was nearly eight months since I had first proposed to her." Since June 1879 was indeed eight months before January 1880, the diary entry tends to corroborate June 20, Class Day at Harvard, as the occasion of a first proposal. Additionally, the same entry mentions that "a year ago last Thanksgiving I made a vow that win her I would if it were possible," which tends to corroborate the assumption that pages Roosevelt ripped out of his diary covering Thanksgiving 1878 did in fact record his intention to marry Alice.[46]

In the end, perhaps the most that can be assumed about June 20, 1879, is that TR had proposed marriage and was not so much rejected as put off or postponed. Indeed, on January 27, 1880, he confided to his diary that he was "only just beginning to realize" she had said yes, but he confessed to still feeling "as if it would turn out, as it so often has before and that Alice will repent" of her having said yes. How many times had she changed her mind about her most aggressive suitor? On January 30, Theodore looked back with pain and even resentment "at the last four months" as he now realized "the tortures I have been through." He complained: "I have hardly had one good night's rest; and night after night I have not even gone to bed. I have been pretty nearly crazy, over my wayward, willful darling." He seemed to express relief that, likely, no "outsider suspected" his torment."[47] Of course, plenty of "outsiders" had seen his bad behavior, Henry Davis Minot the most vocal about it. Victorious, Roosevelt now freely shared his "torture." In a letter to his cousin John Roosevelt, he wrote, "The little witch led me a dance before she surrendered . . . the last six months have been perfect agony. . . . Even now, it makes me shudder to think of some of the nights I have passed."[48]

It was a full eight months later, after Alice at last said yes, that Roosevelt finally dared to present her in his diary as fulfilling for him the North Star role. He vowed to "shield her and guard her from every trial" and to "cherish my sweet queen!" For all the time, effort, emotional torment, and (for that matter) cash he lavished upon Alice, it nevertheless seemed to him that her decision to accept his proposal was explicable only as a miracle of God: "How she, so pure and sweet and beautiful can think of marrying me I can not understand, but I praise and thank God it is so."[49]

Fascinating and revealing! And yet the big bombshell is still to come, in the sentence that concludes the January 30, 1880, entry: "It was a real case of love at first sight—and my first love too."[50] For both the inquirer into the life of Theodore Roosevelt and for Roosevelt himself, this would seem to be the pure gold nugget of self-revelation at the bottom of the pan after oh so much labored panning.

Except that little or nothing in his behavior from the time of his introduction to Alice up to January 30, 1880, provides evidence of "love at first sight." What about all the other girls he flirted with? And as for Alice being his "first love," what about Edith Carow? In the making of Theodore Roosevelt, the thirtieth day of January 1880 is not the end. But it is, perhaps, the end of the beginning. Because this young woman was not the historical cipher she is so often presented as being, a figure who matters in history (if at all) only because Theodore Roosevelt, having won her, married her. No. In accepting Roosevelt, Alice significantly altered his trajectory and, therefore, history itself.

On September 1, 1878, Theodore "had a long talk with Uncle Jim [James A. Roosevelt] about my future life." Theodore confessed to his late father's older brother and the senior partner in the family business that he had "absolutely no idea what I shall do when I leave college." Through his diary, he then addressed his father: "Oh, Father, my Father, no words can tell how I shall miss your counsel and advice!"[51] Between the time Alice accepted his proposal and before his graduation, the young man chose a direction for his life, deciding against pursuing natural science and instead enrolling in law school.

Theodore was now determined to provide for Alice what his father had provided for his wife, Mittie, and the rest of the family. It clearly dawned on him that if he intended to live and provide in the manner of the senior Roosevelt, he could never do so on a naturalist's salary. His father had been a man of business as well as social causes and politics. Natural science was all well and good, but the more worldly life of a lawyer was necessary to support a wife whose father was a banker and whose world was one of Brahmin wealth. If George Lee were to bless the marriage, Roosevelt would have to demonstrate that he was a young man with great expectations.

Theodore teased Bamie with the news, writing to his big sister on January 28: "Darling Bysie, Am just in the midst of semi-annuals but am coming on next Saturday, by the 3 oclock train, to pass Sunday with you as I have a pretty important piece of information to impart."[52] Theodore traveled back to New York as promised and told his family, who "were all perfectly delighted" at the news. Mittie wrote her new daughter-in-law welcoming her to the family, and Alice replied immediately:

> My Dear Mrs. Roosevelt, I feel almost powerless to express my thanks and appreciation of your sweet note received this afternoon, full of such kind assurances of love and welcome, it is more than kind, and feeling so unworthy of such a noble man's love, makes me feel that I do not deserve it all. But I do love Theodore deeply and it will be my aim both to endear myself to those so dear to him and retain his love. How happy I am I can't begin to tell you, it seems almost like a dream. It is such pleasure to have known all his loved ones, and not to feel that I am going amongst perfect strangers . . . I just long for tomorrow to see Theodore and hear all about his visit home. I was so afraid you might be disappointed when you heard what he went on for, and I assure you my heart is full of gratitude for all your kindness. With a great deal of love, believe yours devotedly, Alice Hathaway Lee.[53]

The letters from Alice to Mittie are as rare a species as can be found. This very first exchange sets the tone: Alice will not be possessive of Theodore. For whether or not Alice knew, Mittie feared losing her oldest son. "Really you mustn't feel melancholy, sweet Motherling," Roosevelt assured Mittie shortly after the engagement. "I shall only love you all the more."[54] It must have been intriguing for the strong-willed Mittie to witness the courtship and compare it to her own experience with her Thee. Her vivacity, teasing yet unaffected, surely beguiled him, but even members of his family tended to point out the differences between them. Thee's older brother Robert Roosevelt observed, "between Mittie's liveliness and your solemnity you strike an even balance."[55] It was, perhaps, a more reasoned alternative to invoking the cliché about opposites attracting. By contrast, it was clear to practically everyone that Alice and Theodore had notably similar personalities. No one would ever describe the young Theodore Roosevelt as solemn, a word frequently ascribed to his father. Young Theodore Roosevelt longed to be his father; in truth, he was more like his humorous, storyteller mother, which makes his choice of Alice Lee, especially in contrast to Edith, even more fascinating. Historian David McCullough took note: "[Alice] is described as 'radiant,' 'bright,' 'cheerful,' 'sunny,' 'high-spirited,' 'enchanting,' 'full of life,' the same words one finds in descriptions of Mittie Bulloch at that age. She loved games, as Mittie did; she wore white; she was full of humor and flirtatious ('bewitching,' Theodore said); her birthday was in July, as was Mittie's."[56] Alice Lee was vivacious, athletic, beguiling, and beautiful. Mittie's fear of being replaced in Theodore's life is understandable; Alice Lee was decidedly like herself: fun. It is doubtful that, were her son about to marry Edith Carow, Mittie would feel herself being replaced.

Roosevelt "chose a diamond ring for my darling" at Tiffany and returned to Cambridge. It was snowing heavily but he would not be kept away from Alice. "I drove my sleigh to Chestnut Hill, the horse plunging to his belly in the great drifts, and the wind cutting my face like a knife," he wrote in his diary. Alice "was just as loveable and pretty as ever; it seems hardly possible that I can kiss her and hold her in my arms; she is so pure and so innocent, and so very, very pretty."[57]

The ring arrived on Sunday, February 8. Even Theodore Roosevelt was not strong enough to resist the intense desire to place it on his in-tended's hand immediately. "The thermometer was below zero," but he recalled this valedictory trip to Chestnut Hill as "a splendid ride." He gave Alice her engagement ring and said, "Thank heaven I am absolutely pure. I can tell Alice everything I have ever done."[58] He *could* tell, but he almost certainly withheld some things, at least.

Winning Alice only increased Theodore's already lavish spending on her, starting with $2,500 on jewelry, including not just the engagement ring but a ruby bracelet and a sapphire ring, which contributed to some $8,000 in expenditures for the year 1880, up from $5,200 in 1879. Based on such gifts and on his eye-opening exposure to the wealthy milieu Alice inhabited, we might conclude that the young Roosevelt realized that holding on to Alice demanded a change of career. He needed a first-class ticket to ride in Alice's world, and science was issuing no tickets in that class.

Such a mercenary conclusion would not be wrong, but it is incom-plete. The Theodore Roosevelt that Alice Hathaway Lee met, the youth on the verge of manhood whose attentions and proposals of marriage she turned away for some eighteen months—yet without ever rejecting him outright—was far from the dashing, chiseled Rough Rider carved into Mount Rushmore. Whether deliberately or not, Alice catalyzed the process that created the Rushmore Roosevelt. She changed him in ways never understood or appreciated by history. She could have simply re-fused him in no uncertain terms or, for that matter, embraced the bud-ding scientist. No ties of family, business, or tradition prevented Alice from simply saying no to Theodore.

So, why did she not? Her cousin Thomas Lee confirmed there was no shortage of New England scions eager to make a match with a viva-cious beauty. At seventeen, her age when Roosevelt met her, she was far from having to dread the prospect of New England spinsterhood. No, it is most likely that she saw promise in Theodore Roosevelt that practi-cally no one else, except his family and Henry Davis Minot, saw at the time. Even Edith Carow did not see what Alice Lee saw, or at least Edith did not see enough to bend her iron will. It is even more clear that Alice's immediate and extended families, the Lees and the Saltonstalls, whose houses were separated by neither fence nor wall, saw something to admire and enjoy in the Harvard undergraduate even as he found in them a set of values, a quality of intelligence, and an embrace of social progressivism as familiar and estimable as those of his own late and loved father. Alice by his side, Theodore Roosevelt prepared to embark on the rest of his life. He would approach each challenge with the same dogged determination that won Alice. But the young couple could never imagine the triumph and tragedy that lie ahead. They publicly announced their engagement on Valentine's Day.

6

"NOTHING WHATEVER
ELSE BUT YOU"

"I love to talk over everything with [Alice] from politics to poetry."
—Theodore Roosevelt to his diary

*T*heodore Roosevelt was in love.

Alice received forty-two bouquets on February 14, 1880. Elliott arrived to celebrate, and Bamie and Conie followed. George Cabot Lee, Alice's father, consented to a fall wedding only after the Roosevelt family agreed to house the couple with Mittie and his two sisters at 6 West 57th Street after their marriage. After all, Alice was still quite young, her fiancé had not yet graduated, and a summer wedding would have conflicted with the social season. The campaign victorious, Theodore prayed for foul weather and New England delivered. "Rained or snowed all day, so I was most happy, spending almost all the time with my sweet queen! Oh, how I love my little darling . . . I do'n't think there was ever any one like her."[1] So ran a typical diary entry from the weeks that followed.

Roosevelt's letters to Alice are a far cry from the intellectually lofty, albeit tender, correspondence between John and Abigail Adams. His missives are thickly sown with a mixture of infantilizing and idealizing epithets used to address and describe her. "Pretty," "sweet," "baby"—which became "baby wife" after the couple wed—alternate with "queen," "purest queen," "my pure flower," "my pearl," and "my sweet, pretty queen." He also applied the more frankly erotic "witch" and "bewitching." Such terms are fair fodder for those biographers and commentators who dismiss Alice and Theodore's marriage to her as one-dimensional, but Roosevelt's letters were never intended to be seen by anyone except her. To his diary, he was more revealing: "There is not one thing secret between us. 'Whom first we love we seldom wed'; but we shall prove exceptions to this rule."[2] One wonders whether Theodore considered Edith when he wrote these words. Certainly, she was his first love, whether he wanted to admit it or not.

During the period of his frequent visits to Chestnut Hill in 1880 and during a ten-day trip in April to New York City with Alice, Roosevelt wrote his Harvard senior thesis calling for equal rights for women. It was remarkably radical for the time, beginning with its title, "Practicability of Giving Men and Women Equal Rights." Rather than argue the morality or justice of the issue, TR effectively assumed that equal rights for women was both moral and just and summarily settled the issue of the "practicability" of acting on the matter by simply "giving" women the rights to which they were self-evidently entitled. This anticipates one of Roosevelt's most famous imperatives, which he uttered well into adulthood: "Get action; do things; be sane; don't fritter away your time; create, act, take a place where you are and be somebody; take action."[3]

"Viewed purely in the abstract," TR wrote in his senior thesis, "I think there can be no question that women should have equal rights with men.

> In the very large class of work which is purely mental . . . it is doubtful
> if women are inferior to men . . . individually many women are superior
> to the general run of men . . . if we could once thoroughly get rid of the
> feeling that an old maid is more to be looked down upon than an old

bachelor, or that woman's work, though equally good, should not be paid as well as man's, we should have taken a long stride in advance. . . . I contend that, even as the world now is, it is not only feasible but advisable to make women equal to men before the law. . . . Especially as regards the laws relating to marriage there should be the most absolute equality preserved between the two sexes. I do not think the woman should assume the man's name. The man should have no more right over the person or property of his wife than she has over the person or property of her husband. . . . I would have the word "obey" used no more by the wife than by the husband.

If this passage savors of authenticity, it is because Roosevelt wrote from experience. At twenty-five, his sister Bamie was, in the eyes of many, on her way to being an "old maid," and his Aunt Anna married rather late in life, at thirty-two. As for the assertion that many women are superior to men, Theodore had only to look at those among whom he had grown up. As for Alice, historian E. M. Halliday, the longtime editor of *American Heritage*, published in 1978 this excerpt of Roosevelt's essay in his magazine, commenting on the "indications that she [Alice Lee] was a girl of lively intellect and advanced opinions" and concluding that the views in TR's senior thesis "were largely the result of long conversations between the lovers." He calls this "an almost irresistible conclusion," noting TR's comment in his diary that "Not one thing is ever hidden between us." Halliday continues, perhaps with more certainty than is due: "it seems likely that Alice went over his essay carefully before it was handed in." Whether this was the case or not, Theodore did not need Alice's coaching. He had grown up with the evidence for his assertions. Halliday does admit, however, that the Roosevelt marriage did not put the most visible token of equality into play: "there is no evidence that when they were married in the fall [Alice] continued to go by her maiden name."[4]

"Baby wife" he might call her, but, under the law, he believed she and every other woman were a man's equal. As for input from Alice, if

Halliday's surmises are correct (an admittedly big if), it seems that Roosevelt did not scruple to take from Alice intellectual cues in a project as important as his Harvard senior thesis. It was not something he would have done for a "Baby wife." For all the infantilizing epithets he used in his letters to her during the run-up to the wedding and continuing into married life, there is no sign of inequality between the pair.

Theodore Roosevelt graduated from Harvard College, magna cum laude, with a bachelor of arts. He was twenty-first in a class of 177. However, in a letter to Henry Davis Minot, Roosevelt acknowledged what he viewed as his greatest success: his "eager, restless, passionate pursuit of one all-absorbing object"—Alice Lee.[5] "I have been in love with her for nearly two years now; and I have made everything subordinate to winning her," he confessed.[6]

That success would soon be followed by others. In his years with Alice, TR "rose like a rocket," making it the single most successful epoch of his remarkable life until his "crowded hour" that saw him rise from a presidential appointment to president in less than three years. Were it not for Alice Lee's acceptance of Roosevelt's proposal, the geeky naturalist in whose wake the odor of formaldehyde lingered and in whose pockets small dead creatures in varying states of preservation were often stuffed, may well have never metamorphosed into a confident, inspired young man in a hurry, en route to becoming a public figure of real importance. "Theodore Roosevelt was not a leader in college," classmate W. R. Thayer wrote years later. "Nobody found him fascinating." Nobody, except Alice Lee, and it was her love and faith in him, alongside the steady belief of his sisters and mother, that would give Roosevelt the confidence to find his first success. Thayer reports asking TR what he planned to do after college. "I am going to try to help the cause of better government in New York City; I don't know exactly how," said Theodore Roosevelt.[7] Not that Roosevelt was in a hurry to do so just yet. First came the honeymoon period.

As Alice celebrated her nineteenth birthday on a trip the couple took with friends to Maine, Roosevelt took to his diary to marvel: "When

I hold her in my arms there is nothing on earth left to wish for; and how infinitely blessed is my lot. If ever a man has been blessed by a merciful Providence, I am." This feeling of contented idyll would linger, but the trip wasn't a wholly happy one. His childhood afflictions resurfaced with a vengeance. On July 24, Roosevelt recorded being "Rather laid up by the cholera morbus; so stayed in the house." That same day he wrote to sister Conie of his affliction: "Very embarrassing for a lover, isn't it? So unromantic, you know; suggestive of too much unripe fruit."[8] While Teddy, as Alice and only a few close friends and family were permitted to call him, lay sick in bed, Alice, in the pink of youthful health, took first prize in the ladies' tennis tournament.

Eight days later Edith turned nineteen. Conie, who remained closest to Edith, spoke of the "shock" Edith felt "when she received a letter to say that [Theodore] was engaged to Alice Lee." It is believed the letter bringing the devastating news was sent by Theodore. Sylvia Morris, Edith Carow's biographer, surmised: "The effect of this stunning revelation upon Edith can be imagined. For sixteen years she had lived in the closest intimacy, both physical and emotional, with Theodore. She shared his education, his home life, his vacations, his dreams and desires . . . [yet] true to her lifelong practice of suppressing any intimation of her romantic feelings, she neither said nor wrote a word in reaction to Theodore's letter." This year, as opposed to last, there is also no record of a birthday gift from Theodore to Edith. Morris wryly observes Edith's reading list for February includes the book *Splendid Misery*.[9]

Alice and Theodore returned from Maine not to New York but Chestnut Hill. They read Hawthorne and Thackeray, and the poems of Longfellow and Shelley, in between carriage rides, card games, and tennis. Yet enraptured as Theodore was with Alice, he required another excursion. Lighting out for the backcountry was becoming a pattern for Roosevelt, especially when female-dominated domesticity seemed to threaten. There was something disquieting for him about the summer following his graduation and preceding his marriage. He decided to put far more distance and time between himself and his fiancée, traveling not a few miles away but far to the West and for six long weeks. On the recommendation of a doctor, he and his brother, Elliott, went hunting in the upper Midwest and to the border region straddling Minnesota and the Dakota Territory. Roosevelt may have genuinely believed that the trip was to improve his health, or perhaps that is how he chose to rationalize it to Alice. Men of the late 1800s were prescribed the "west cure" while women were prescribed the "rest cure." Men, particularly those like Roosevelt from the upper classes of society, were encouraged to "go west" for adventure, toil, and trial to cure their ailments. Women were often confined to their beds.[10]

Roosevelt wrote to Alice from Oyster Bay on August 15, the eve of his departure: "Sweet blue-eyed queen . . . remember that the more good times you have—dancing, visiting or doing anything else you like—the happier I am." In other words, the more you do without me, the better I like it! "The more attention you have the better pleased I'll be. . . . I know you love me so that you will like to get married to me—for you will always be your own mistress, and mine too." The outlook was very much in the spirit of his feminist senior thesis, yet TR used his wife's independence to rationalize his own liberation.[11]

Whatever the motivation, the pre-wedding Western adventure with Elliott proved to be anything but healthful. The pair had "hard luck," with "a constant succession of unavoidable accidents," including two broken guns and an incident where, Theodore recalled, a wagon "nearly upset over a big rock, both the driver and I being sent flying out of the wagon on our heads, but we were very little hurt."[12] Elliott drank prodigiously, and Theodore was frequently ill. In one letter, he reported: "I had to sit up most of last night with the asthma, I was so troubled with continual attacks of colic that I could hardly walk, and it rained most of the day, so I shot badly; Elliott however did splendidly. We have had pretty good fare and accommodations up here, so far, and great fun."[13] *Fun!*

Alice did not pine away at home. She went with her family to the Glades resort in Maine, walked, and played tennis. She wrote "My Dearest Teddy" on August 30:

Teddy I long for some nice quiet little evenings with you alone. It makes
me homesick to think I shall not see you for so long, for I love to be with
you so much. . . . Don't you think I am pretty good to write you every
day? I suppose you laugh and say, these funny letters, they sound just like
Alice. . . . I suppose you start today for Minnesota. Do keep well & enjoy
yourself. Good night and sweet dreams.

Your loving,

Alice[14]

Indeed, the letter reveals the real Alice: bright, light, fun, breezy, conversational, intimate, playful, sexy, flirtatious, honest, teasing.

The brothers Roosevelt took a breather in Chicago, and Roosevelt took the opportunity to write home to Conie: "Elliott revels in the change to civilization and epicurean pleasures. As soon as we got here he took some ale to get the dust out of his throat; then a milk punch [a concoction of sugar, milk, cream, vanilla, cinnamon, and bourbon] because he was thirsty; a mint julep because it was hot; a brandy mash 'to keep the cold out of his stomach,' and then sherry and bitter to give him an appetite."[15] For the first time in their long journey, the trip resembled something approximating a bachelor party. From Chicago, Theodore and Elliott ventured west again. Near Fargo, in Dakota Territory, Roosevelt recalled: "Had a lovely night; I had to sleep on the floor under a buffalo robe, the wind howling round the neat but frail little house."[16] This was Roosevelt's first experience in Dakota, the territory that would become so intertwined with his legend. He would have much to report to his future father-in-law, George C. Lee, whose Lee, Higginson & Co. was "much involved in the 'beef bonanza.' "[17]

The brothers Roosevelt returned from their adventure at the end of September, and on October 3, Roosevelt, who had spent two large slices of the summer in voluntary absence from his fiancée, recorded "with intense regret" having to go back to New York to commence law school at

Columbia, "but it will be the last separation from my darling, for three weeks from Wednesday we are married—it makes me so happy I am almost afraid."[18]

In a letter dated October 6, Alice wrote to "My own dearest Teddy" with the wish it were the day of their wedding, adding: "I just long to be with you all the time and never separate from you, even for three weeks. Teddykins, I know you can make me happy and you must never think it would have been better for me, if we had never met; I should die without you now Teddy and there is not another man I ever could have loved in this world."[19]

The love between Alice and Theodore was at once beautiful and frightful. It was intense. Sweet nothings easily pass between the lips of lovers and newlyweds but there is something foreboding in their words. "I should die without you now Teddy," Alice wrote to Theodore. "Almost afraid," TR had said of himself three days before.

In his last letter to her before the wedding, dated October 17, Roosevelt was downright plaintive in his self-abnegation: "Oh my darling, I do so hope and pray I can make you happy. I shall try very hard to be as unselfish and sunny tempered as you are, and I shall save you from every care I can. My own true love, you have made my happiness almost too great; and I feel I can do so little for you in return. I worship you so that it seems almost desecration to touch you; and yet when I am with you I can hardly let you a moment out of my arms. My purest queen, no man was worthy of your love; but I shall try very hard to serve it, at least in part."[20] His adoration of Alice made Roosevelt want to be a better man.

On October 13, 1880, Edith Carow gave a dinner party for the man everyone in their circle once believed she would marry. We cannot know what she was feeling. Whatever TR felt, his behavior betrayed nothing of the anxiety he had expressed in his diary and in at least some of his letters to Alice. Two days after the dinner party, Fanny Smith wrote in her diary that TR was "as funny and delicious as ever and wild with happiness and excitement."[21]

The wedding was set to take place at the Unitarian Church in Brookline, Massachusetts, on October 27. Edith arrived in Boston on the evening of the 25th and shared the upper floor of a two-floor suite in the Brunswick Hotel with New York friends Grace Potter and Fanny Smith, while the Roosevelts and the Gracies shared two parlors on the lower floor. Theodore had a room elsewhere in the hotel. On the 26th, members of the wedding party (in the words of Fanny Smith) "explored the city at intervals" before dining "together at a big table, and in the evening the ushers came—we had great fun." No one seemed to have more fun than Theodore, whom Fanny described as being in "wild spirits." The way his wild spirits were manifested was distinctly juvenile in nature, as TR indulged in what Fanny called "one of his favorite pastimes," namely tipping her chair so far back that she felt with terror not so much the prospect of grave injury but of involuntarily doing an embarrassing backward somersault.[22]

The next morning, Theodore Roosevelt turned twenty-two and got married. Edith drove with Fanny to the church. It was an unusual October day for New England, so sunny and so warm that the men soon shed their topcoats. As weddings among Brahmins and Knickerbockers go, the affair was modest—the "dearest little wedding," Fanny called it—noting that "Alice looked perfectly lovely and Theodore so happy." In taking his vows, Fanny wrote, he "responded in the most determined Theodore like tones." At the reception, Fanny observed, Edith Carow "danced the soles off her shoes."[23]

There was no great drama in this triumphal apotheosis of Theodore's knightly quest. He and his bride spent one night in Springfield, Massachusetts, before heading to Tranquility for two weeks. They then moved into the Roosevelts' Manhattan home at 6 West 57th Street, and Theodore spent his days at the Columbia Law School while Alice occupied hers doing what ladies of privilege did. In her case, there were tennis lessons at Drina Potter's Tennis School and afternoon tea parties she herself hosted in a parlor separated from Mittie's. We can assume that Fanny spoke for the majority in their social circle when she pronounced Alice "lovable in every way."[24] Alice blended seamlessly into the world previously ruled by Mittie, Bamie, and Conie, showing no possessiveness over her new husband. "Teddy is here; come and share him!" shouted Alice upon Theodore's arrival home.[25] But Alice felt little love from Edith, whose standoffishness toward her was sufficient to prompt her to query her new sister-in-law. Why, she asked Conie, could she make no headway with Edith?[26] A potential answer comes from the next generation. Eleanor Roosevelt recalled of her aunt and sometimes surrogate mother, "[Edith] was, in a way, a very jealous person . . . Aunt Edith wanted to excite [Theodore's] mind. She didn't want to share that!"[27]

Between Alice and Edith there was no demonstrative hostility, but neither was there any chemistry. They had been two young women with nothing in common, save for a relationship with Theodore Roosevelt, who felt no compunction about taking Edith for a "drive" just as soon as Alice had left for a visit to her parents in Chestnut Hill. Sylvia Morris speculates that their "destination was probably [Roosevelt's] favorite Riverside Park, where they could watch sailboats bobbing on the blue-green waters of the Hudson River under the sunset-pink sky. Squeezed side by side in the dogcart seat, they talked almost as they used to so many years ago. Edith missed that lost intimacy more than she cared to admit."[28]

In some ways, Edith's strongest feeling when Roosevelt became attached to Alice may well have been one of incomprehension. "When [Theodore] went off to Harvard and fell in love with Alice Lee, no one was more surprised than [Edith]," historian and Roosevelt scholar Stacy Cordery notes in her biography of Alice Roosevelt Longworth.[29] Apparently, Edith simply could not see what her Thee saw in that girl.

It is possible that the married Roosevelt missed his earlier freedom to flirt and even felt pangs of regret for having forsaken the company of Edith Carow, with whom he had grown up and, as a young adult, created a relationship enriched by intelligent conversation. But, in the case of Theodore Roosevelt, we should not rigorously quarantine the pleasures of romance from those of the hunt. Alice, the relative newcomer in his life, had been the object of a lustful pursuit. She was the prey, Theodore the hunter. Once captured, Alice held less mystery, eliciting from him a torrent of infantilizing variations on the word "baby." Further complicating matters, Theodore had always felt a deep respect for Edith, the woman mutual friends described as "born mature."

Yet there was no drama, and there were no scenes. As both Edith and Alice were close with Conie, they all three were frequently in one another's company. Still, Edith tended to shy away from the balls and other events that were the major social gatherings of Manhattan's grand families. On December 9, in a squib headed "A Brilliant Social Event," *The New York Times* reported on "Mrs. Theodore Roosevelt's Party in Honor of the 'Coming Out' of Her Second Daughter." The piece seemed to be additional ratification of Conie's ascendency in Knickerbocker circles. Some six hundred invitations were sent to people named Astor, Harriman, Vanderbilt, Gracie, and the like. The "response . . . was very general, the music, by Landers, was fine, the supper was one of Pinard's best, and the decorations in good taste." The latter were cataloged so meticulously by the anonymous reporter that they consumed some 290 out of the article's 500-plus words: tropical foliage, Japanese vines, "pink tints and roses of the same color," antique vases "with Mme. Murmet roses and lilies of the valley," a marble pedestal "on which was a basin filled with tea-roses, all of one color, and set about with maiden's hair ferns." The list of invitees then took up almost all the rest of the piece.[30]

Among the guests was Conie's oldest friend, Edith Carow, although the Carow name certainly found no place in the article. By this point in her life, Edith had come of age but her coming-out had come and gone, uncelebrated, some five months earlier. These days, she avoided the spotlight occasioned by a New York season of balls and galas, but she could not think of turning down an invitation to Conie's debut. She danced and conspicuously attended the midnight champagne supper escorted by a young man whose name is lost to history. Theodore's bride was also in attendance, wearing the wedding dress she had worn at their October nuptials.

Conie's introduction to society, delayed by the death of Theodore

Sr., was a mere formality, since she had during the summer of 1880 already met her future husband. His name was Douglas Robinson, Scots heir to a real estate fortune. He was very much in love with Conie—or at least very much coveted her—and represented what the world called a good match. Indeed, he would have been precisely that, except for the fact that, try as she might, Conie could not bring herself to love him. The mere thought of an engagement brought her to tears. Mittie could see that she was unhappy but nevertheless persistently encouraged her, and when Conie finally gave in, Mittie wrote to her sister Anna, "I hope all will be right."[31]

While Mittie hoped, Bamie, the substitute mother, acted.

"You must not retreat!" Bamie demanded of her sister only six years her junior, worried Conie would end up a spinster like her. Bamie would emphasize her determination for the match to go through by pretending to wield the "sword of Damocles" over Conie.[32] Robinson was "a man's man who got on well with Theodore, but [Conie] had misgivings about being 'forced by her family to marry a bully,'" believes historian Dr. Kathleen Dalton.[33] Conie's fiancé had a terrible temper. "Some historians attributed [Conie's] reservations to her judgement that Douglas did not measure up to her brother Theodore," observes Betty Boyd Caroli. "But there is little evidence for such a conclusion [because] at the time . . . he certainly measured up to Theodore, who had not yet done anything noteworthy or impressive."[34] There is a more logical reason for Conie's hesitation: fear of losing her independence. "I do not like the idea of being anybody's except my own," Conie wrote Douglas in a letter. To emphasize her point, Conie signed the letter "Yours" and then crossed the possessive word out.[35]

"Walking down the aisle meant renouncing her own autonomy, an idea she did not like,"[36] Caroli concludes. Bamie and Conie were, in many ways, precisely the type of woman about whom TR was writing in his eager defense of women's rights in his college thesis. Alas, TR's words were ahead of the times. Conie tried to break off the engagement and suggested Douglas marry Bamie instead. Bamie and Douglas were, after all, the same age. Elliott sided with Conie, but nevertheless, Conie, twenty, married Douglas Robinson, twenty-six, on April 29, 1882, at Fifth Avenue Presbyterian Church. Conie cried. "I married your father too young," she later confessed to one of her children.[37] Conie's prophecy was in part correct. There was no reliable contraception (Conie had witnessed her own mother's decline after four pregnancies in six years), and thus motherhood would consume her twenties. She had four children over the next seven years—Theodore (April 1883), Corinne (July 1886), Monroe (December 1887), and Stewart (March 1889). Years later their daughter recalled a playful but biting poem Conie would recite to them about their father, who managed the Astor estate among other significant real estate holdings:

> He loves you dears
> He loves you
> He roars it in your ears
> But a real estate transaction
> Is a thousand times more dear![38]

Edie, the same age as Conie, might have felt the same misgivings about marriage—a feeling she could have expressed to Teedie back on August 22, 1878, the day in which their connection tore. She would not subject herself to a loveless marriage, yet once again Edie was the odd woman out. Whatever feelings roiled within her, she wrote a sincere if ambivalent congratulatory note to her old friend when Conie formally announced the engagement in February 1881: "I know I shall like Mr. Robinson (if he will let me) . . . and I rejoice with you in your happiness my own dear little girl."[39]

Theodore and Alice spent their first two weeks of marriage together in Oyster Bay. "There is hardly an hour of the twenty-four that we are not together; I am living in dreamland," Roosevelt wrote in his diary. "How I wish it could last forever."[40] Their idyl was interrupted when Roosevelt cast his first presidential ballot for Republican James Garfield. "I love to talk over everything with Baby," Roosevelt wrote after the election. "From Politics to Poetry, and to read aloud to her, either from a History or standard novel or from the daily newspaper that forms our only intercourse with the outside world."[41] Call her "Baby" he did, but Alice was clearly a woman sufficiently mature and intelligent to discuss politics and poetry and to share an interest in both history and the daily news. She was, in short, a Lee.

But how could TR "serve"—as he'd promised the week before his wedding—his new bride's love? As winter turned to spring, Theodore dutifully assumed some of his father's philanthropic responsibilities. Elected trustee of the Orthopedic Dispensary and the New York Infant Asylum on March 18, he soon decided that the kind of charitable labor in which his father had avidly engaged was not for him.[42]

He continued to pursue the law. At the time, Columbia University Law School was lodged in a large old house in lower Manhattan at 8 Great Jones Street. Monotonously, as if intoning a formula by rote, Roosevelt recorded more than a few times "I like the law school very much"— or some variant of that sentence—in his diary.[43]

The young man's principal legal pedagogue was Professor T. W. Dwight, who, along with his other students, discovered that they had in Roosevelt "a young man who was impatient with logic, and instead of waiting for questions from on high, wished to ask his own." He was as "irrepressible as a jack-in-the-box," leaping to his feet, "glasses flashing, to argue 'for justice and against legalism,'" condemning, for instance, the doctrine of caveat emptor, which he decried as "repellant." Another classmate, Joseph A. Lawson, commented in a 1919 New York State Memorial to TR that, for the young Roosevelt, "The intricacies of the rule in Shelley's case, the study of feudal tenures as exemplified in the great work of Blackstone, were not the things upon which that avid mind must feed."[44]

Theodore never evinced a true passion for the law, but he expressed no interest whatsoever in business, though doubtless he could have entered the family organization. There is no evidence that he regarded the law as a possible entrée into politics. But the one anecdote we have, his visceral response to caveat emptor, may suggest a possible bridge between law and legislation. The Latin phrase may be translated "Let the buyer beware" and denotes the "common law doctrine that places the burden on buyers to reasonably examine property before making a purchase. A buyer who fails to meet this burden is unable to recover for defects in the product that would have been discovered had this burden been met."[45] His strong feelings against this principle would find a legislative outlet when he became a New York State assemblyman, and it was one of the informing principles of his progressivism. In short, a lawyer could do nothing but accept *caveat emptor* in law, whereas a politician could change the law of the land.

Despite Roosevelt's increasingly marked lukewarm attitude toward his legal studies, he kept at it through 1880 and 1881, noting in his diary on March 24, 1881, that he was "still working hard at law school" but adding "& at one or two unsuccessful literary projects."[46] Well, at least one was far from unsuccessful! As TR noted on May 2: "I spend most of my spare time in the Astor Library, on my 'Naval History,'" which rather rapidly evolved into Roosevelt's first major book, *The Naval War of 1812*.[47] It remained true even into the 1880s that the nation who controlled the seas ruled the world, and Roosevelt was fascinated with the politics of power. He had begun researching the War of 1812 while he was still at Harvard and had completed two chapters before enrolling in law school. While TR might have had little appetite for the "intricacies of the rule in Shelley's case," his appetite for the technical intricacies of naval warfare in the second decade of the nineteenth century proved voracious. The book is full of original and arcane research on maritime and weapons technology, naval combat tactics, the politics of war, and the life and character of those who commanded the British and American fleets. He obtained piles of primary historical materials and drew up for himself tactical diagrams and tables by which he did not merely lay out the order of the war's battles on seawater and fresh but worked to objectively demonstrate the effect of the weapons involved, especially heavy cannon versus carronades, one a long-established naval weapon, the other still relatively new in the 1812 period and extremely effective at short range. His interest was not just in unrolling a historical tale but in documenting the tactical and strategic advantage conferred by innovative versus traditional armaments. He had more than an academic interest in the naval aspects of the War of 1812. What he saw in it was a contest between the modern naval artillery of the comparatively small U.S. Navy of 1812 and the outmoded artillery of the much larger Royal Navy. He set this up as the basis of an argument for modernizing the contemporary U.S. Navy. In this motive, his Naval History of the War of 1812 became the foundation not just of a political career but of a national political career. He likely did not have such a motive in mind when he began writing the book, but the effect of the book was nonetheless as much political as it was historical.

Alice admired the literary work he was doing, though she teased him about his endless drawings of "little boats"—his method of plotting out the course of the battles he set about describing and analyzing. The American author who would be hailed as the father of the Western novel (The Virginian, 1902), Owen Wister, whose Porcellian membership was contemporary with TR's, reported in his 1930 memoir of his friendship with Roosevelt that an exasperated Alice complained one evening, "We're dining out in twenty minutes, and Teddy's drawing little ships." In a letter to her on March 29, TR wrote, "Darling Baby, I have been studying hard all day [the law]—only drawing a few 'little boats'—and did not go out driving. I felt very melancholy when I dressed with no pretty little wife to tease me till I loved her even more than ever."[48]

There was every indication that the marriage was a happy one—though it is difficult to believe that the young bride, whom her husband left to her own devices much of the time, did not feel at least somewhat neglected. Domesticity did not always sit well with Theodore. While TR worked to make a name for himself and provide for his new wife, Elliott hunted tigers and wild game in India. When Mittie read letters from Elliott aloud, Theodore (she wrote Elliott) "longs to be with you and walks up and down the room like a Caged Lynx."[49] That Huck Finn yearning to "light out for the Territories" was very much alive within him. When Alice (who was also present) observed his restless impatience, Theodore took notice and made a great demonstration of kissing her and kissing her some more, abashedly—if not persuasively—admitting that he only had fleeting moments of yearning for the wilderness and his own much used rifle.

Even as he pressed ahead on what would be a stout, rather dry, but highly regarded (and still read by naval historians today) history of the naval aspects of the War of 1812, a new temptation loomed to lure him away from his commitment to the study of law. Morton Hall, headquarters of the 21st District Republican Association, above a storefront on 59th Street at the corner of Fifth Avenue, was much closer to the 57th Street home of the Roosevelts than the Columbia University Law School downtown. TR began dropping in at this gathering place of local New York politicians and ward heelers. Roosevelt bore the hallmarks of a "swell," "dandy," or "dude"—elegant bespoke tailoring and neatly barbered side whiskers— which were looked on with suspicion in the rough-and-tumble universe of New York state and local politics. Nevertheless, he was eventually accepted into membership in the association.

Most in his family circle and numerous friends of the family regarded the membership as anything but an honor. Politics, especially urban politics, was hardly a gentleman's game. "The men I knew best were the men in the clubs of social pretension and the men of cultivated taste and easy life," Roosevelt recalled. When he had mentioned his intention of joining the local Republican Association, "these men—and the big business men and lawyers also—laughed at me, and told me that politics were 'low,'" the province of "saloon-keepers, horse-car conductors, and the like." To these gibes, Roosevelt countered "that if this were so it merely meant that the people I knew did not belong to the governing class, and that the other people did—and that I intended to be one of the governing class."[50] Men such as Roosevelt's father, his Uncle Robert, and those in the Lee and Saltonstall families endlessly discussed civil service reform, agitated for it, voted for it, and engaged in cultural philanthropy. But in America's down-and-dirty democracy, politics was a low game. Much as his distant Hyde Park cousin Franklin D. Roosevelt would do, young TR broke ranks with his class and never looked back.

What drove him? Conie's 1921 *My Brother Theodore Roosevelt* offers an answer. TR treasured his late father's letters as "talismans against evil," including one from December 16, 1877, written after the exuberantly corrupt machine politician Roscoe Conkling had won reelection as one of New York's senators.[51] Theodore Sr. had worked himself to death in opposition to the Machine which controlled appointments and many of the politicians, and he wrote of the victory that "The 'Machine politicians' have shown their colors." They were "partisan politicians who think of nothing higher than their own interests, and I feel for your future." He was addressing his son directly. "We cannot stand so corrupt a government for any great length of time."[52]

The voice of Greatheart had been stilled, yet still it echoed for Theodore Roosevelt. He had heard those echoes around the reform-minded dining table at Chestnut Hill. In the hope of providing for Alice as his father had provided for his wife and family, Theodore had shifted the trajectory of his future, shearing away from natural science to law. The contemplated shift from law to politics, perhaps inspired by his father's 1877 letter, may also have been made with Alice and a future family in mind. Roosevelt wanted to liberate politics from corruption and give to his future progeny a "more perfect union" and a stronger democracy in a nation fit to take a dominant place in the world. Roosevelt was under no illusion that politics would generate the level of income Alice and a family needed but that was a problem for solving tomorrow. However far this plan may have progressed in his mind, he began to haunt Morton Hall, gaining the merest toehold there, and then looking for a way to start climbing.

Thomas P. "Tip" O'Neill, who served for a decade as the much beloved forty-seventh Speaker of the House, took credit for having coined his favorite political axiom, but "All politics is local" originated in a 1932 newspaper column by journalist turned World War II censor turned assistant secretary general of the United Nations Byron Price.[53] There is no record of Theodore Roosevelt ever scooping both O'Neill and Price by uttering the phrase in 1881 when he decided in Morton Hall that he would enter politics by acting locally. But he certainly agreed with the sentiment.

Roosevelt had decided to champion a grassroots Street Cleaning Bill to reform the patronage-corrupted issue of urban sanitation with passage of an entirely nonpartisan law that would effectively staff New York State's urban street-cleaning forces through the civil service instead of maintaining these positions as political patronage spoils. Accordingly, he made a rousing pre-convention speech on October 24, 1881, at Morton Hall in favor of introducing the bill before the State Assembly. The speech met with an encouraging round of applause, but the end was depressingly anticlimactic: the great Republican Machine cranked up its opposition. Reform was not in the interest of the "Stalwart" incumbency, which embraced the continuation of patronage politics that kept the Machine in power. Applause or no applause, reform was not in the cards. TR's shot at the Republican primary and a possible seat in the Assembly evaporated with the last clap.

If he felt disappointed, he responded, as always, not by sulking or even regrouping but by quickening his pace to a hard-charging gallop in a different direction. At three o'clock on the afternoon of May 12, 1881, he took Alice on a delayed European honeymoon. They boarded the steamship Celtic for England. "Lots of people down to see us off," he wrote in his diary. "Hurrah! for a summer abroad with the darling little wife."[54]

Any romance in the air quickly evaporated as Alice almost immediately succumbed to seasickness. She was "sicker than the devil" on May 13, TR noted in his diary, "worse" on May 14, and "sicker than ever" on May 15. This continued straight through to the Celtic's landing at Queenstown, Ireland, when "Alice revived at once, very much." With that, the newlyweds commenced an Irish tour.[55] As he was wont to do, Roosevelt summarily shoved into a corner the voyage from hell and proclaimed to his diary, "Alice is best traveling companion I have ever known. By Jove, what luck I have had! This is the lovliest trip I ever was on."[56] England was next, and in London, among much else, came a tour of the National Gallery: "Rembrandt, Rubens, (Reynolds, Gainsborough), Murillo, Velasquez; I am very fond of Rembrandt & Murillo. Turner—idiotic."[57] They were off to Paris on June 11.[58] Then by train to Venice, "the loveliest place we have been to yet," Milan, Lake Como, and into the Alps, where TR "took Alice out donkey riding." She proved her considerable athleticism in the mountains.[59] As they traveled through Switzerland, TR recalled to his stalwart sister: "Darling Bysie . . . On Thursday we crossed the bleak Julier pass, into the Upper Engadine, and drove to [Samedan], the mere sight of the place was suggestive of sunburned nether limbs attended to by Bysie—a kind of little feminine Atlas with a small world on her shoulders; and such a squably, irritating small world at times too! At least, that component part of it formed by the present somewhat scatterbrained writer."[60] Alice was TR's "sunshine," and Bamie was his "feminine Atlas" carrying the weight of the world on her shoulders while he went out and explored it.

On August 3, Theodore—unaccompanied by Alice—set out with two guides to ascend the infamous Matterhorn. One of the loftiest summits in the Alps, a steep-faced pyramid rising more than 14,500 feet, the peak remained unconquered until 1865, a feat that cost the lives of four of the original party of seven climbers.[61] Yet Roosevelt's diary record of his ascent, over two days, is disappointingly matter-of-fact, another conquest checked off the list, with the focus not on the adventure of the climb or the awesome view from the Matterhorn summit but on his own prowess. He and his guides reached a shelter—the "Club hut"—at seven [a letter to Bamie says six o'clock] on the evening of August 3 and set off for the summit at 3:45 the next morning. "Summit at 7.00; back at Zermatt at 3.30, very laborious and rather dangerous, but I am not very tired. Am in excellent training."[62] Theodore wrote to Bamie that climbing the Matterhorn "was like going up and down enormous stairs on your hands and knees for nine hours"—not the usual activity for one's honeymoon.[63]

On September 22, Roosevelt and his bride embarked on the *Britannic* for the voyage home, which, blissfully, Alice enjoyed, unafflicted by the seasickness of the voyage out.

TR recorded on October 17 that he was "working fairly at my law, hard at politics, and hardest of all at my book ('Naval History') which I expect to publish this winter."[64] On October 28, he noted: "Much to my surprise was nominated to the Assembly from district."[65] His majority over the incumbent assemblyman William Trimble was 16 to 9, and (he recorded on November 4) "My platform is Republican, but Independent on Municipal matters."[66] As Edmund Morris sagely observed, "at the very outset of his political career, he managed to balance party loyalty with personal freedom. . . . For the next four decades he would occupy that motionless spot, while the rest of the [Republican] platform tipped giddly backward and forward, Left and Right."[67] He would toe the status quo Stalwart line until it came to dealing with city matters. Then he intended to be "independent," which is to say progressive.

Despite their continued squeamishness concerning the grubby art of politics, most of TR's family and friends were standing by him, TR records, "like trumps."[68] Roosevelt is not generally known to history as a sentimental romantic, yet he reserved tenderest words for Alice. On November 5, just three days before the election, he wrote her a letter focused first and foremost on her, telling her "I could not live without you, my sweet mouthed, fair haired darling." Aware that they had just celebrated their first anniversary a week earlier, TR framed his feelings in a most singular manner: "I care for *nothing whatever* else but you." Truly, to be the object of Theodore Roosevelt's love, as was true of many of his later pursuits, was all-consuming.

I wish for nothing but to have you to love and cherish all the days of my life, and you have been more to me than any other wife could be to

any other husband. You are all in all, my hearts darling, and I care for
nothing else; and you have given me more than I can ever repay.

With that, he took a breath, and did devote a few words to election prospects (including getting out the vote), his book, and (not uncommon for a newly married young man) financial distress:

The canvass is getting on superbly; there seems to be a good chance of
my election, but I don't care, anyway. I enclose a piece from the Evening
Post; be sure and keep all the newspaper scraps for me. My book is all
entirely finished except the remodelling of the first chapter. So everything
is getting on well except financially. I confess I am in by no means a good
condition from a monetary point of view, and in awfully bad odour with
Uncle Jim. Uncle Jimmie is standing by me like a perfect old trump. With
best love to the darling little motherling, Sweet Pussie, dearest Bysie, and
above all for your sweet self. I am

Your Ever Loving,

 Thee [69]

Romantic? Without a doubt. Yet the letter is also not without at least a trace of calculation. The virtuoso nonchalance of his transition from "nothing whatever else but you" to the election, in which he proclaims his indifference to victory or loss, would have been more sincere had he not urged Alice to save the New York *Evening Post* article he enclosed as well as "the other newspaper scraps" devoted to him. As for the "monetary point of view," we know that he ended 1880 having spent from his "Cash Account" $7,992.50. For 1881, his diary records expenditures only as far as the end of April, amounting to $1,000, and that wouldn't have included any of the expenses associated with the couple's four-month European honeymoon.[70] The newlyweds were spending lavishly—not surprising, since young Roosevelt was very free with money.

• • •

Without special flourish or exclamation of any kind, Theodore Roosevelt
recorded late on Tuesday, November 8, his election "to the Legislature
from the 21st Assembly District by a majority of 1501 over William Strew,
the Democratic candidate."[71] It was no mean feat to win one's first election. With the election behind him, he took time out to (in the following
order) drive with Alice "in the dogcart almost every day," look after his
duties at his father's charities, the "News Boys lodging house" and the
"Orthopedic," and, oh yes, finish his *Naval War of 1812* and get the manuscript into "the hands of the publishers—Putnams."[72] The span of time in
which these things were accomplished? November 8 to December 3.

He was a whirlwind—a tornado, a typhoon—entering politics and
almost immediately gaining election to the New York State Assembly
while studying law and writing a nearly six-hundred-page history, the
product almost exclusively of original research. On the face of it, these
pursuits seem disparate, almost random. And yet they were firmly rooted
in a single value over all others. Call it a zeal for *fact*, an appetite for *truth*,
a passion for *reality*.

For *The Naval War of 1812* is not a swashbuckling, flag-waving historical potboiler tale but an exercise in historical fact-finding. Historians have always approached the War of 1812 with ambivalence. The
first American war of choice rather than necessity, it has been branded
by some "the second war of American independence" and by others a
catastrophically unnecessary conflict. Because much of the land war was
incompetently fought with results mostly disastrous for the still embry-
onic American economy, the handful of stunning U.S. naval victories of
1812–1814 have been broadly romanticized. But not by Theodore Roosevelt. He used his book to explore the very nature of naval warfare in
the early nineteenth century, basing everything on thoroughly researched
fact uncolored by any political or patriotic bias. Admirers of Oliver Haz-
ard Perry and his triumph at the Battle of Lake Erie (September 10, 1813)
could take little satisfaction in Roosevelt's cold assessment of a battle in
which Perry possessed significant superiority of forces, which TR was

able to precisely quantify. As the young author saw it, Perry's achievement was not so much a victory won as a victory not lost.

Yet Roosevelt, in his exposition of the truth, did not simply give history a much needed revision. He used the naval War of 1812 to demonstrate the importance of possessing a strong and modern navy, and the book thus became a platform from which he argued for the modernization and reform of the present-day U.S. Navy. The reason for the U.S. naval victories in the War of 1812, Roosevelt explained, was that

> our navy in 1812 was the exact reverse of what our navy is now, in 1882. I am not alluding to the personnel, which still remains excellent; but, whereas we now have a large number of worthless vessels . . . we then possessed a few vessels, each unsurpassed by any foreign ship of her class. To bring up our navy to the condition in which it stood in 1812 it would not be necessary . . . to spend any more money than at present; only instead of using it to patch up a hundred antiquated hulks, it should be employed in building half a dozen ships on the most effective model. If in 1812 our ships had borne the same relation to the British ships that they do now, not all the courage and skill of our sailors would have won us a single success. . . . It is too much to hope that our political shortsightedness will ever enable us to have a navy that is first-class in point of size; but there certainly seems no reason why what ships we have should not be of the very best quality.[73]

Far from being a diversion from politics, *The Naval War of 1812* took a farseeing view of national politics and foreshadowed Theodore Roosevelt's first national office, in 1897, as assistant secretary of the navy in the first administration of President William McKinley. There, he would oversee the rise of the U.S. Navy as world-class force increasingly capable of projecting American military might on a global stage. As president, near the close of his final term, he would send the U.S. Fleet—dubbed by historians as the Great White Fleet—on circumnavigation (December 16, 1907–February 22, 1909) during which the fleet called at the ports of every major nation. It was a message to the world: America was here, and the navy had made it possible.

Roosevelt's political rise has been compared to the ascension of a rocket. In some ways, it was even faster. In the guise of a historian, looking back to the beginning of the nineteenth century, TR shot his gaze forward and thought big thoughts, beyond the local political office he had just won and toward his entrance onto the national stage and global arena.

It was not Alice or any other family member who, a month after the fact, formally celebrated TR's electoral triumph. Edith Carow—the Edie of old—threw a large party at 114 East 36th Street, the Carows' new home, humbler than their former mansion, which backed up against the grand 14th Street home of Mr. and Mrs. Cornelius Van Schaack Roosevelt. Mittie, Conie, and Alice were there. Theodore sported a brightly patterned satin waistcoat, and he led the cotillion with that gusto his sister-in-law, Rose, described as hopping.

Into the compressed span of 1880–1881, Theodore Roosevelt had squeezed three triumphs. He won, after a difficult and sometimes despairing fight, what he believed to be the woman of his dreams and his destiny. Having done so, he swore that he would make himself worthy of her. In part, this was doubtless the sentiment of a noble romantic. But in part, too, it was a recognition of just who Alice Hathaway Lee was: not the lovely but superficial being too many biographers and historians propose, but the intelligent daughter of a family very much like the one over which Theodore Roosevelt Sr. had presided. Hers was a prosperous upbringing amid a family possessed of pragmatic social consciousness. Hers was a family heritage perfectly familiar to Theodore Roosevelt Jr. For it was his own.

Having won Alice, young Roosevelt suddenly tacked away from natural science and the pursuit of specimens for taxidermy, fixing his sights instead on the law and then, more authentically, on politics. This led with astonishing swiftness to his second early victory: winning a seat in the New York State Assembly. Almost simultaneously came the third big win of 1880–1881: publication of a book that established him as a formidable historian with the unique faculty of looking, Janus-like, both backward and forward in time, settling certain facts of the past while staking out a personal future on a national and even global scale. The phrase *annus mirabilis* means literally "miraculous year," but let us take the license to apply that stirring Latin to the entire span of 1880–1881, in which Theodore Roosevelt did not merely ascend like a rocket but also, with Alice by his side, designed, built, and launched it. Now only the physics of gravity, as undeniable and inevitable as fate, could alter Theodore Roosevelt's trajectory.

Part Three

"THE LIGHT
HAS GONE OUT
OF MY LIFE"

1884—1887

7

NEVERMORE

"I do love my dear Thee *so* much. I wish I could have my little new baby soon."

—Alice Hathaway Roosevelt, February 11, 1884

Alice Lee transformed the life of Theodore Roosevelt.

He believed he had "won" her, and this victory did much to crystallize an identity he deemed worthy of his father yet all his own. It swept aside many doubts and dark moods, giving his life both a purpose and a pattern he could express passionately yet succinctly: "a year ago last Thanksgiving I made a vow that win her I would if it were possible; and now that I have done so, the aim of my whole life shall be to make her happy, and to shield her and guard her from every trial."[1]

The purpose he had found was, of course, *her*, making her happy and keeping her safe. Romantic? Yes, but also genuinely transformative. TR turned his energies and aspirations from natural science—a sincere passion, to be sure, yet, for him, more of a boyish avocation than a mature profession—to law, which, as it turned out, served as but a brief transition to politics. A polymath like Roosevelt might have been successful in any number of fields. Indeed, almost simultaneously with winning his first elective office, he published his first major book, which was both original and authoritative. But it is also the case that polymaths driven by the kind of energy Roosevelt possessed, restless and bottomless, often explode in dozens of directions without achieving greatness in any single endeavor. "Winning" Alice turned him toward politics. From then on, his myriad pursuits from writing to ranching were embarked on with a strategic purpose. They would provide him with sufficient money to support his family and the political trajectory on which he would find greatness.

"Trajectory" is the right word for Roosevelt's political start. He was launched from political novice to state assemblyman in the blink of an eye and took off and up from there. At twenty-three, he was (and remains) the youngest person elected to the New York Assembly. He arrived in Albany in the dead of winter on January 2, 1882, Alice having gone separately to Montreal with friends, planning to join him in two weeks' time. Roosevelt wanted his bride to have a major say in their Albany accommodations, so he decided to await her arrival before seeking long-term lodgings. In the interim, he took a room at the Delavan House, a favorite among the assemblymen and a place where the smoke-filled-room meetings of both parties were held.

Roosevelt quickly unpacked and took the short walk to the capitol to attend a Republican pre-session caucus for the purpose of nominating their candidate for Speaker. He made quite an entrance. Fellow assemblyman John Walsh later painted the picture:

> Suddenly our eyes, and those of everybody on the floor, became glued on a young man who was coming in through the door. His hair was parted in the center, and he had sideburns. He wore a single eye-glass, with a gold chain over his ear. He had on a cutaway coat with one button at the top, and the ends of its tails almost reached the tops of his shoes. He carried a gold-headed cane in one hand, a silk hat in the other, and he walked in the bent-over fashion that was the style with the young men of the day. His trousers were as tight as a tailor could make them, and he had a bellshaped bottom to cover his shoes. "Who's

the dude?" I asked another member, while the same question was being put in a dozen different parts of the hall. "That's Theodore Roosevelt of New York," he answered.[2]

While he made a strong first impression, it's not clear the New York State Assembly made much of an immediate impression on him. The first week of the session was quite literally uneventful. TR went to the State House, answered the roll call, and then returned to the Delavan House, there being no business before the chamber as the Democrats, divided between the Tammany Hall crowd and the "regulars," were unsurprisingly deadlocked over their choice of candidate for Speaker. The Tammany crowd was the Democratic counterpart of the Republican Stalwarts: the machine politicians, dug into the status quo. The so-called regulars operated independently of the machine and had more in common with the GOP progressive wing.

The monotony was broken when, on the second weekend of the session, Roosevelt took the train to Boston to fetch Alice and bring her to Albany. Together, they chose a suite at one of the residential hotels that served the needs of the assemblymen and their families. Isaac Hunt, a fellow Republican whom TR instinctively tapped as an ally, lodged in the same hotel. He recorded his impression of Alice as "a very charming woman . . . tall, willowy-looking" (though Theodore himself persisted in calling her "little"), adding that he "was very much taken with her."[3]

On January 24, Roosevelt delivered his maiden speech to the Assembly. If the chamber had expected oratory in keeping with his flamboyant raiment, they were in for a surprise as the young man delivered an informal, colloquial, and workmanlike discussion of the deadlock bogging down the Assembly, coming to the remarkably pragmatic conclusion that it only served the advantage of his party to let the Democrats argue among themselves as their constituents contemplated their complete absence of productivity. Early the next month, the deadlock finally broke, Democrat Charles Patterson, a regular backed by Tammany Hall, was elected Speaker, and it was he who assigned Roosevelt to the Cities

Committee. Although the chairman and most of the committee members were Democrats, Roosevelt the progressive reformer was delighted.

With the logjam broken, TR resumed ballistic velocity. In the first forty-eight-hour span following his appointment to the committee, he introduced four bills. There was a bill to purify New York City's notoriously impure water supply (an infamous source of waterborne diseases, cholera chief among them), a bill to reform New York's cumbersome and thoroughly corrupt system of aldermen and assistant aldermen by abolishing bicameral city government, a bill to purge stocks and bonds from New York City's sinking fund (intended to finance future capital expense and service long-term debt), and a bill to reform the Court of Appeals, which was hobbled by outmoded and arcane election rules. Only one of the four was eventually passed—the so-called Aldermanic Bill—and in a diluted form at that. At this 1-for-4 record, Roosevelt did not bat an eye. His principal objective had been attained. In a flash, he had shown himself incredibly productive—a stark contrast to his colleagues—and had planted his flag as a high-energy reformer.

Roosevelt came on as a battler against corruption. The targets he chose were not abstract issues of policy but high-profile miscreants. In the coming months, he went after New York Supreme Court justice Theodoric R. Westbrook and financier Jay Gould, with whom Westbrook colluded to aid the financier in his attempt to take over the Manhattan Elevated Railway Company. With Westbrook's judicial aid, Gould was able to drive down the price of the railway's stock, forcing the company into bankruptcy so that he could acquire it at a fire sale price. Roosevelt introduced a resolution creating a special Assembly committee to investigate the relationship between the financier and the judge. Although members of the committee—who may have been bribed—quashed the results of the investigation, Roosevelt had succeeded in turning over a rock under which corruption roiled like so many maggots.

In this era, the Republican Party was famously divided into "Stalwarts" and "Half-Breeds," machine politicians versus moderates and progressives. Roscoe Conkling, U.S. senator from New York, was the shameless Stalwart boss who (among much else) chaired the Senate's Committee on Commerce, which had obediently delayed approval of Theodore Roosevelt Sr.'s appointment as New York collector of customs in 1871. The assassination of President James Garfield, a progressive Republican, elevated Vice President Chester A. Arthur (who would have been replaced by the senior Roosevelt in 1871) to the presidency. Conkling and his Stalwarts had every reason to believe that Arthur would obediently shred Garfield's progressive agenda. Instead, Arthur pursued it, believing it reflected the will of the voters, and the Stalwarts were thrown into deeper division. The disarray of the Stalwarts, together with TR's new reputation as corruption fighter, propelled the rookie legislator to a high public profile and, in the election of 1882, sent him back to the Assembly with a 2-to-1 victory over his Democratic opponent—even though Democratic gubernatorial candidate Grover Cleveland was victorious in Roosevelt's district.

Roosevelt now allied himself with that new Democratic governor to win passage of a landmark civil service reform law, which significantly advanced the merit basis of the state's civil service system. It made civil service reform a hallmark of evolving TR's political career and, more immediately, helped to assure him a third term in the Assembly. He boldly sought the speakership but was soundly defeated by fellow Republican Titus Sheard, 41 to 29 in the GOP caucus. He was nevertheless given an assignment he relished, the chairmanship of the Cities Committee. To his mother, TR admitted he had some growth to do: "Darling Motherling," he wrote in a letter from the New York State Assembly on February 20, 1883, "My speech went off very well; I did not forget a word, nor was I at all embarrassed. But I doubt if it really pays to learn a speech by heart; for I felt just like a schoolboy reciting his piece. Besides I do not speak enough from the chest, so my voice is not powerful as it ought to be."[4]

While TR vaulted from one political triumph to another, Alice Lee, who gave him everything, seemed—perhaps—incapable of giving him a child.

When he married Alice in 1880, Roosevelt purchased sixty acres on Cove Neck within the hamlet of Oyster Bay. His intention was to build a summer house in which to raise a large family. But as months became years, pregnancy was not forthcoming. Roosevelt was concerned that Alice was unable to bear children. She was also prone to what her husband referred to as "nervous fits." (Though TR could be accused of the same malady.) From Albany, on April 6, 1882, in one of only two extant Albany letters from Roosevelt to Alice, he wrote: "I hope that you are getting well by this time, my poor patient darling. I wish I could be with you while you have your nervous fits, to cheer you up and soothe you."[5] This hardly suggests that Alice was still "Sunshine." The athletic Gibson Girl had been reduced to the mid-Victorian image of neurasthenic young woman, from whom her husband frequently absented himself to attend to his political duties in the state capital. And yet the reality is more complicated than that.

We have Alice Roosevelt Longworth to thank for preserving a cache of letters between her mother and father, which she bequeathed to her granddaughter, Joanna Sturm, who, in turn, gifted them to Harvard's Houghton Library. From these, it seems clear Alice relishes the tasks sometimes seen as a burden by political wives: lunches, teas, dinners, and socializing with allies and adversaries in Albany. For every "baby wife" Theodore expresses, Alice returns the favor calling him "you dear boy." Alice is vivacious and active, playing and beating men and women in tennis. (The sport was a near obsession for Theodore, as it requires skill, tenacity, focus, and talent.) Concerning a more serious matter, historian Michael Teague surmises that the young wife's health crisis referenced in the surviving letter was related to a gynecological surgery she had just undergone. Edith Roosevelt later confirmed that Alice Hathaway Roosevelt had required surgery before becoming pregnant.[6]

"You are the light and sunshine of my life," TR had written to his wife three days before his first election. He continued: "I care for *nothing whatever* else but you."[7] But after election to a second term in 1881, he wrote to "My Blessed Little Wifie" from Albany's Kenmore Hotel on New Year's Eve:

> I felt as if my heart would break when I left my own little pink dar-
> ling, with a sad look in her sweet blue eyes, and I have just longed for
> her here in this beastly Hotel. I can not say how I feel when I think of
> the cosy little room, with its pretty furniture and well stocked book
> shelves, a bright fire of soft coal in the grate, and above all my be-
> witching little mistress, with some soft, dainty dress on, to sit and play
> backgammon with.[8]

He bemoans *his* heartbreak at leaving her and the domestic pleasures associated with being in her company, but he leaves her nonetheless, de-spite his recognition of how sad this separation makes her, to pursue his political career with unparalleled vigor; in his second and third terms, he would write more bills than any other New York state legislator.

While he left her physically, TR held her in close confidence. Even in Albany, she was the repository of his innermost thoughts, fears, and strategy. On April 6, 1882, he wrote:

> I have drawn blood by my speech against the Elevated Railroad Judges,
> and have come in for any amount of both praise and abuse from the
> newspapers. It is rather the hit of the season so far, and I think I have
> made a success of it. Letters and telegrams of congratulations come
> pouring in on me from all quarters. But the fight is severe still, and
> today I got a repulse in endeavouring to call up the debate from the
> table. How it will turn out in the end no one can now tell.[9]

In an even more remarkable exchange, Roosevelt wrote Alice again from Albany, this time on March 6, 1883, using State of New York As-sembly Chamber stationery:

Darling Wifie,

I have not been doing much so far up here. All the small curs—whether on the floor of the house or in the newspapers—are now howling at me; and the hardest thing to stand is the complacent pity of the shallow demagogues who delight to see a better man than themselves stumble, or seem to stumble. I would not care a snap of my finger if they would attack me where I could hit back. Not a man has dared to say anything to my face that I have not repaid him for with interest; but it is the attacks I can not answer that I mind. Still I am rapidly getting hardened, and shall soon cease to care anything about it.[10]

"It is not the critic who counts; not the man who points out how the strong man stumbles, or where the doer of deeds could have done them better. The credit belongs to the man who is actually in the arena," Theodore Roosevelt famously declared to a Parisian audience at the Sorbonne in 1910.[11] A full twenty-seven years before delivering "Citizenship in a Republic" (more commonly known as the "in the arena speech"), he debuted its central theme to Alice, whose love fortified his resolve as he contended in the arena.

At last, in the spring of 1883, Alice announced that she was pregnant. TR was delighted and relieved. After a dinner with college friends that April, he reminisced on their courtship, writing to her that the dinner "reminded me so much of the trip we took to the Whitney's private train down to the Yale-Harvard boat race. How pretty and fascinating you were, you darling little wifie! But you are even prettier and more fascinating now."[12]

Fascinating. TR was always "fascinated" by those who could spar with him, whether intellectually or physically. No wonder the anxiously awaited arrival of Alice's pregnancy brought awe, trepidation, and perhaps his familiar psychogenic ailments. Almost immediately after she announced her pregnancy to him, Roosevelt was assailed by "black care" and his other all too familiar nemeses, cholera morbus and asthma.

On June 15, he wrote to her from Long Island telling Alice that he was "a good deal laid up, but . . . shall try to stay out here, as I like the country air, and it good for [me]." In a familiar scenario, he absented himself from his now pregnant wife, excusing his absence by reason of health. After all, it was the doctor's orders. In July, the Roosevelt family doctor prescribed fresh mountain air. But TR, now in company with his spouse, found Richfield Springs in the Catskills an awful bore. He described it to Conie as "that quintessence of abomination, a large summer hotel and watering-place for underbred and overdressed girls" in addition to what he described as "a select collection of assorted cripples and consumptives."[13]

Michael Teague suggests (with perhaps some exaggeration) that TR was suffering from "something more than boredom, an almost desperate longing to cast off the shackles of sickness, anxiety, femininity, and domesticity and to gallop off to the wilder world of the West, which offered him, then at his lowest ebb, health, freedom, masculinity, and the chance, as he simply puts it, 'to kill some large game.'"[14] Mark Twain would write about this feeling in iconic terms that were not surpassed until the early Nick Adams stories by Ernest Hemingway. At the end of *Adventures of Huckleberry Finn*—published in 1884—Huck prepares to flee the benevolent domestic tyranny of his guardian, telling the reader "I reckon I got to light out for the Territory ahead of the rest, because Aunt Sally she's going to adopt me and sivilize me, and I can't stand it. I been there before."[15]

At the start of August, Theodore surveyed the ground on which Leeholm, as he'd decide to call the summer house, would be built. On August 20, he added ninety-five more acres to what he had bought earlier. His spread now stood at 155 acres, which he trod with the architects he had hired, Lamb and Rich, showing them precisely the vistas he wanted his family mansion to command. *Leeholm*—named to honor his "pink little wife"—having been planned out, he instantly prepared to light out for the Dakota Territory.

The journey had its origin in a conversation with one Commander

H. H. Gorringe, late of the United States Navy, who admired Roosevelt's *Naval War of 1812* and its message of building a great American naval power. The two men had chatted about hunting. Gorringe revealed that he was opening a hunting ranch out west, and he suggested that Roosevelt accompany him to the Badlands, perhaps to investigate partnering in the development of former army land he had bought out there. TR's brother, Elliott, had recently returned from India bearing with him more than enough big-game trophies to make Theodore jealous. The young expectant father suddenly burned with a desire to shoot some buffalo before they were all shot to extinction. (The irony in this eluded him.) Roosevelt took Gorringe up on his proposition but delayed out of some deference to Alice's delicate condition and his own desire to get Leeholm laid out. Maternal mortality was a very real danger in late-nineteenth-century America. At the opening of the twentieth century, for every thousand live births, six to nine women died from pregnancy-related complications, and in some U.S. cities at this time a third of infants died before their first birthday.[16]

Four days before he and Gorringe were supposed to set off, the Commander backed out. Undaunted, TR wrote to his "Sweetest little wife" (who was being looked after at Chestnut Hill) on September 2, to tell her that he had "been miserably home-sick" for her "all the last forty eight hours." He was, in fact, "so homesick that I think, if it were not that I had made all my preparations, I should have given up the journey entirely. I think all the time of my little laughing, teasing beauty, and how pretty she is, and how she goes to sleep in my arms, and I could almost cry I love you so." Then he continued: "But I think the hunting will do me good; and am very anxious to kill some large game."[17]

For all his restless hankering after new adventures, Roosevelt experienced something akin to panic at every moment of personal change in his life. Time and again, his reaction to change was the same: run not to the church but instead to the cathedral of nature. With fatherhood impending, Roosevelt lit out for Dakota. When Alice and Mittie died, Roosevelt returned to the Badlands. Not to put too fine or too trivial a point on it, but when the going got tough in his personal life, Theodore Roosevelt went hunting.

He set off for the Badlands on September 3. Enduring a difficult first pregnancy, Alice could not have relished the prospect of sending her husband, only recently recovered from a bout of illness, unaccompanied into the Badlands, a vast territory mainly in what is today southwestern North and South Dakota, which he had never seen and in which he did not know a single soul. Unfolding before him in the West were 65 million years of geologic history, unspoiled and unkept, the closest to the Wild West as one could come in a rapidly industrializing and expanding America.

Amazingly, by the time his train reached Chicago, TR felt totally rejuvenated, like "a fighting cock."[18] When he arrived at the Little Missouri River in Dakota Territory, he hired a guide, "a good looking hunter named Joe Ferris,"[19] who led him to the buffalo range. He intended to be out on the range for two or three weeks, writing to Alice a succession of highly descriptive letters. In one, dated September 14, he narrated a long ride over ground "perfectly trackless, without a tree or mark of any kind by which to go." They navigated by the sun. "The only water was to be found in rank alkaline pools." TR drank and found himself "pretty sick—in fact I have only been feeling well today. The first five days I did not eat any thing but crackers, and never over six of them a day."[20]

"Finally," Theodore wrote, "we got within about a hundred twenty five yards of the great beasts"—the buffalo—"and I took a careful aim for the shoulder of the largest. As the rifle cracked the old bull plunged forward on his knees, and I heard the 'frack' of the bullet and saw the dust fly from his hide as the ounce ball crashed through his ribs; too far back, unluckily, for the wound did not disable him, and recovering himself he went off after the others, who were covering the ground pretty fast, with their lumbering gallop." Roosevelt and Ferris pursued.

The ground was pretty hard, but I went straight as an arrow over the most breakneck places, digging the spurs into the pony and gradually closing in on the wounded buffalo. . . . Ferris, better mounted than I was, finally headed the wounded bull; then I ran in, driving my spurs into the flanks of my jaded horse. I fired once but the motion made me miss; and as I urged the horse still closer—for it was very dark—the bull turned . . . and charged me; the lunge of the formidable looking brute frightened my pony, and as he went off he threw up his head and knocked the heavy rifle I was carrying against my head with such force that it gave me a pretty severe cut on the crown, from which the blood poured over my face and into my eyes so that it blinded me for the moment.

Darkness fell, and Roosevelt's horse was "played out . . . run to a regular standstill," so that the "infernal beast escaped after all!"[21] As for Theodore Roosevelt, "I am now feeling very well," he wrote, "and am enjoying the life very much. I am every day and all day long on horseback, scrambling on the almost inconceivably rocky and difficult hills of the 'bad lands' or galloping at full speed on the rolling prairie or level bottom."[22]

Exhilarating! Was Alice concerned that such restoration of health and joy seemed to require some 1,600 miles of distance between them? How did she feel about her husband's bigamist courtship with death? Galloping full out on "inconceivably rocky" ground had its hazards: "The other day while the pony was at the full run he stepped into a badger hole and turned a regular somersault, sending myself and rifle about twenty feet, but we were not hurt at all." Immediately following that tidbit of news, Roosevelt meticulously enumerated, as he so often did, his bag: "I have killed a good deal of small game—jackrabbit, sage hen, sharptailed grouse and wild duck; so I have lived very well, and the air is delightful."

"Hurrah!" begins his letter of September 20 to Alice. "The luck has turned at last. I will bring you home the head of a great buffalo bull." As a bonus, there would also be "the antlers of two superb stags." When a "rattlesnake struck at one horse and barely missed," Thee and his guide "shot him and took his rattles." As if to drive home the lethal hazards at every turn, Thee noted that this snake "was the fourth we had seen on the trip."[23]

On September 23, the rising politician wrote to Alice about his vision to provide for her, as he had promised to do since their engagement. He wrote: "During these ten days I have also been making up my mind to go into something more important than hunting. I have taken a great fancy to the three men, Merrifield and two brothers named Ferris, at whose ranch I have been staying several days, and one of whom has been with me all the time. I have also carefully examined the country, with reference to its capacity for stock raising." The more he looked and thought, he told Alice, "the more convinced I became that there was a chance to make a great deal of money, very safely, in the cattle business." Very safely! "Accordingly I have decided to go into it," adding, "very cautiously at first." He succinctly laid out his plan:

> Of course it may turn out to be a failure; but even if it does I have made my arrangements so that I do not believe I will lose the money I put in; while, if it comes out a success, as I am inclined to think that on the whole it will, it will go a long way towards solving the problem that has puzzled us both a good deal at times—how I am to make more money as our needs increase, and yet try to keep in a position from which I may be able at some future time to again go into public life, or literary life. But, my own darling, everything will be made secondary to *your* happiness, you may be sure.[24]

Theodore discussed politics and policy with Alice, and he also discussed how best to make a living. He understood that politics alone would not support a family, certainly not at the level Alice expected and he wanted to provide, and thus he might need to step away. Increasingly and despite diminishingly favorable evidence, he would become convinced that Badlands ranching could generate the income stream he needed to subsidize his political career and support his family. The Badlands of the

Dakota Territory were open range so TR never owned any land, just the cattle, and he formed a partnership with the locals he met and trusted. Unfortunately, the "arrangements" he made were founded on hopeful (if not wishful) thinking and handshake agreements. He would end up losing about half his inheritance in these ranching ventures.

Roosevelt hired Bill Merrifield and Sylvane Ferris (Joe's brother) to run the ranch. Later, he would bring in his Maine guide, Bill Sewall, to supervise. While he did not intend to abandon New York for the Badlands, he did want to stake out a vast pied-à-terre there, which might serve as his periodic wilderness retreat. Some might accuse him of being a dilettante. In fact, he was an intellectual and vocational omnivore. His political ambitions were real. He also wanted to continue writing—and he assumed that the ranch would provide ample material for new books. Maybe he would even actually take up the practice of law. And, yes, he tried hard to convince himself that ranching would yield wealth. He was a man eager to play many roles, but as one of his most insightful modern biographers, Dr. Kathleen Dalton, says of him at this time, the "role he seemed least interested in playing was husband."[25] If he exploded in a dozen directions after marrying Alice, it would be Edith who brought him back to something like center.

On his return to the East, he found his wife, who had hiked through Europe with him, "fragile but gaining some strength from short walks."[26] The mortality rate in the era was horrendous, but TR believed his wife was improving. No sooner did he return to Alice than he began to prepare for the November election, the result of which seemed assured. After that victory, he plotted how to gain passage of legislation to reform the city charter, a bill designed to substantially loosen Tammany Hall's corrupt grip on New York City politics and municipal administration. As for Alice's ongoing pregnancy, he entrusted her care to Bamie and Mittie in the Roosevelt family home at 6 West 57th Street. "Man proposes, God disposes" runs a popular nineteenth-century mantra. But TR, whose own mantra was "Get action," operated on the assumption that what he proposed would inevitably come to pass. When Alice's physician confidently predicted that she would deliver on February 14, 1884—Valentine's Day—Roosevelt took that as certainty. After all, it was the fourth anniversary of his engagement to Alice. The confluence of medical judgment and poetic logic could not be resisted. This gave him license to set about promoting the bill in Albany in full confidence that he could work right up to the eve of the impending birth.

But all was far from well in the Roosevelt family home. Alice wrote her absent husband on February 11: "Darling Thee, I hated so to leave you this afternoon," she begins, oddly framing their separation as her leaving him, when it was he who parted from her. She continues, deflecting his concern from her, but directing it toward Mittie:

> *I don't think you need feel worried about my being sick as the Dr. told me this afternoon that I would not need my nurse before Thursday [Valentine's Day]—I am feeling well tonight but am very much worried about your little Mother. Her fever is still very high and the Dr. is rather afraid of typhoid, it is not in the least catching. I will write again tomorrow and let you know just how she is—don't say any thing about it till then. I do love my dear Thee so much. I wish I could have my little new baby soon.*

> *Ever Your Loving Wifie,*

> *Alice*[27]

In this, the last known communication between Alice and Theodore Roosevelt, she expresses concern for others, not herself. She correctly diagnoses that Mittie has typhoid but, seeking to allay Theodore's possible anxiety, she expresses no fear of catching it. Roosevelt would have been keenly attuned to the prospect of typhoid. The New York City water bill he was anxious to push through the Assembly was intended to provide wholesome water for a city whose untreated water and sewage made typhoid endemic and was responsible for three major cholera epidemics, in 1832, 1849, and 1866. Could bad water have been slowly poisoning Alice, adding to the stress of undiagnosed kidney failure presumably associated with preeclampsia that developed during her pregnancy?

Anna Bulloch Gracie, Mittie's sister and Theodore's aunt, takes us inside the delivery room at 6 West 57th Street. She records that Alice Roosevelt was born on Tuesday, February 12, at 8:30 in the evening. Caroline Haskell Lee (Alice's mother), the delivering physician, a baby nurse, and Anna were present.

"Her mother said, when I took her from the Dr. 'I *love* a little *girl*,' because I said to the baby you ought to have been a little boy. I laid her all rolled up in flannel in a large arm chair & went back to the bedside," Anna wrote. When baby Alice sneezed, she continued, "her Mother said, 'Dr. don't let my baby take cold,' he said she is not taking cold, the little girl sneezed again, and her sweet Mother said, 'Dr. you must attend to my baby.' He said, 'I always attend to the mother first.' She said, 'I suppose you know best.'"[28]

This moment reveals so much about the character of Alice Hathaway Roosevelt. She is concerned only for her baby and not herself, and she rejects Aunt Anna's suggestion that her daughter ought to have been a boy. In Alice's mind, there was equality between the sexes. This is the woman who inspired Theodore to endorse suffrage forty years before its passage. And this is the woman who, had she stood by Theodore for the rest of his remarkable rocket ride, might yet have altered history.

Aunt Anna and Caroline Lee, now a grandmother, and the baby nurse attended to the newborn. They washed and bathed her, noting she weighed 8 and ¾ lbs.

"I made up the little bassinet with all the dainty, pretty little things her sweet little Mother had laid aside ready for her to sleep in. At eleven o'clock the baby's Grand Mother Lee told me, 'Alice has had her child in her arms and kissed it.'" Alice and her baby rested overnight.[29]

Theodore had left for Albany on Monday, February 11, less than twenty-four hours before Alice defied his imagined schedule by going into labor. He received a telegram from New York on the 13th that noted Alice was "only fairly well."[30] Finding nothing alarming in these three words or in Alice's letter of the 11th noting that typhoid was likely in the house, Roosevelt lit a cigar and celebrated the news of his daughter's birth on the floor of the New York State Assembly. He made no move to head home but, rather, stayed in Albany, chaired a meeting, and reported some bills out of the Cities Committee. A man remembered for rushing headlong into danger, he too often did the opposite in family matters. He ran away.

A winter fog descended on Manhattan. "Suicidal weather," *The New York Times* called the days of cold, wet misery that enveloped the city. "The fog was so thick [on February 13] that people were almost obliged to feel their way through it . . . objects 200 feet away were at times invisible." The ferryboats did not run, no vessels left port, and several in-bound steamships dropped anchor in the harbor, awaiting better visibility. The *Times* continued: "Life does not seem worth living to a sensitive person easily influenced by atmospheric conditions. There is something comfortless and unhappy in the raw and chilly air, something suggestive of death and decay in the dampness that fills the world, clings to the house door, drips from the fences, coats the street with liquid nastiness, moistens one's garments, and paints the sky lead color."[31]

Alice Lee and Mittie both took turns for the worse. The Roosevelt family, including Bamie and Elliott, gathered at 6 West 57th Street. Conie, who was vacationing with her husband, turned back. As February 13 slouched toward evening, a second telegram was dispatched to Theodore Roosevelt in Albany. The contents of that second telegram do not survive but a description of Roosevelt's reaction upon reading it hints at the telegram's dire news. It is a single word written by Roosevelt's political comrade and ally Isaac Hunt: "Ashen."[32]

Now the young assemblyman rushed to the station in Albany. The train departed. Inching through the fog, it took five and a half hours to reach Grand Central Terminal, nearly twice the normal time. We can imagine Roosevelt leaping to the platform and urging the hansom driver west on the long block from Fourth Avenue (today Park Avenue) to Fifth Avenue and north along the fifteen blocks from 42nd Street to 57th.

His brother, Elliott, opened the door. "There is a curse on this house," he told his older brother. "Mother is dying and Alice is dying too."[33] His sisters did more useful things. While Conie attended to Alice at her bedside, Bamie did all she could to ease Mittie through the final stage of typhoid fever.

Not so many years earlier, Roosevelt had rushed home on the night train from Boston when news came that his father was in extremis. By the time he arrived, his father was dead. On this occasion, however, Roosevelt reached home in time for the bedside vigils of both his mother and wife. He left his brother and ran past the quadrant of antlers in the entry hall and under the great buffalo head of the Badlands, which hung prominently over the door. He dashed past the Grecian urns and up the thick wooden staircase to the third floor. He grasped his wife desperately in his arms, refusing to let go. Alice was in and out of consciousness as the clock struck midnight. It was February 14, 1884.

At 2:30 that morning, everyone present was summoned to Mittie's bedside. The once formidable matriarch, the architect of her children's emergence into adulthood, was in her final hour. All the Roosevelt children were gathered around their mother's deathbed in the very room in which Theodore Roosevelt Sr. had died six years earlier. As he stood beside his mother's bed after she had faded away into the darkness of 3 a.m. Theodore Roosevelt repeated Elliott's pronouncement, putting a hard accent on the verb: "There is a curse on this house."[34] But there would be no fulsome tribute to Mittie by her eldest son, then or later. Her death, at forty-eight, was not as shocking to him. And perhaps quite unfairly, she had never occupied the place in his heart and mind that his father did. Soon, very soon, he would have other concerns.

With Mittie's loss, the vigil began around Alice. It extended some eleven hours until she succumbed to kidney failure, at the time called Bright's disease.

When Alice died in the broad light of afternoon, Theodore did what he had done after his father passed. He turned to a blank page of his diary. (There was no blank page for Mittie.) At his father's death, he could get no further than writing the date of Theodore Roosevelt Sr.'s birth. On this afternoon, however, Theodore managed to draw a large X on the page for February 14, 1884, and wrote a single sentence: "The light has gone out of my life."[35]

"I so wonder who my wife will be!" Theodore had mused well before he even knew Alice Hathaway Lee existed. He answered his own musing: "'A rare and radiant maiden,' I hope"—quoting from memory a phrase from Edgar Allan Poe's "The Raven." Nevermore would Theodore Roosevelt see and feel *his* rare and radiant maiden. Yet she would never leave his heart, his mind, and his memory. As Roosevelt's life went on, the memory of Alice became less like Poe's Lenore and came to resemble a far more passionate and poignant Poe lyric about a woman who shared part of her name with Alice Lee. Given TR's love of Poe, he almost assuredly was familiar with the poem.

> *It was many and many a year ago,*
> *In a kingdom by the sea,*
> *That a maiden there lived whom you may know*
> *By the name of ANNABEL LEE;*
> *And this maiden she lived with no other thought*
> *Than to love and be loved by me.*
>
> *I was a child and she was a child,*
> *In this kingdom by the sea;*
> *But we loved with a love that was more than love—*
> *I and my Annabel Lee—*
> *. . .*
> *The angels, not half so happy in heaven,*
> *Went envying her and me—*
> *Yes—that was the reason (as all men know,*
> *In this kingdom by the sea)*

That the wind came out of the cloud by night,
Chilling and killing my Annabel Lee.

But . . . neither the angels in heaven above,
Nor the demons down under the sea,
Can ever dissever my soul from the soul
Of the beautiful Annabel Lee.

For the moon never beams without bringing me dreams
Of the beautiful Annabel Lee;
And the stars never rise but I feel the bright eyes
Of the beautiful Annabel Lee;
And so, all the night-tide, I lie down by the side
Of my darling—my darling—my life and my bride,
In the sepulchre there by the sea,
In her tomb by the sounding sea.

Alice was nineteen when she married Roosevelt on his twenty-second birthday, October 27, 1880. Their plan was for a large family, although Alice did not become pregnant until the spring of 1883, two and a half years into the marriage. As of February 13, 1884, Theodore Roosevelt had been a rising political star with a loving mother who had defended his life through a multitude of illnesses, and a golden girl who changed the course of that life. As of February 14, he was an orphaned widower with a newborn daughter he would name Alice but whom he could hardly bear to look at, let alone cradle in his arms.

The idyll of Oyster Bay, where they'd spent their first two, blissful weeks as man and wife, must have on that night and day receded for Roosevelt into a time out of mind. Alice Lee was gone, along with the enchanted "kingdom by the sea" that had once harbored a loving and be-loved father and a childhood sweetheart, the one dead, the other bitterly soured. Alice Lee was lost. But was she, in fact, the woman who for Theo-dore had played the part of Annabel Lee? For it is Edith—Edie—Carow, intimate of the Roosevelt children, and for Teedie a playmate verging on precocious sweetheart, who can most clearly be pictured as the maiden in that seaside kingdom when he was a child and she was a child. Was it *they* who "loved with a love that was more than love"? Was it she who "lived with no other thought / Than to love and be loved by me"? Or were Tranquility and Oyster Bay themselves nevermore, a light gone out of a young man's life?

"HELL, WITH THE FIRES OUT"

"Cheer up, as I know you will, that wifeless & motherless boy who[se] needs must be more staggered than us all."

—Irvine Bulloch to his niece, Bamie

Teddy Roosevelt was shattered. And it was his sister who reassembled the pieces, as she always would.

Most deaths matter to few people beyond the family. In the case of Theodore Roosevelt's mother and wife, the twin tragedies were national news. The *New York Tribune* observed, "The loss of his wife and mother in a single day is a terrible affliction," adding, "it is doubtful whether he will be able to return to his labors." The New York Assembly unanimously voted to adjourn in sympathy with their bereaved member in the hope that (in the words of the resolution) this gesture will "serve to fortify him in this moment of agony and weakness." No fewer than seven of Roosevelt's fellow legislators, Republicans and Democrats, rose to eulogize their young colleague's mother and wife. Some struggled through tears to do so.[1] The *New York Herald* turned its focus from the bereavement of Theodore Roosevelt to measure the more public loss of his mother, whose leadership "of a *salon*" was the manifestation of her "brilliant power," and his wife, "famed for her beauty, as well as many graces of the heart and head."[2]

Bamie, despite having lost her mother and sister-in-law, stepped up in the moment of family crisis. She organized the funeral service and interment, and she also took receipt of the hundreds of condolence letters, many of them from the highest levels of society. "My dearest Bamie," wrote Grace H. Dodge, a social reformer and philanthropist who focused on the needs of immigrant women. "I can think of nothing but of you and your great sorrow and must send you a few lines to tell you how much I feel for you all. But what can I say to comfort you, dear Bamie, who are always such a comfort and support to anyone else in times of trial?"[3]

"When I first heard the sad news of your Mother's death, I refused to believe it," wrote Julia M. de Forest, another prominent socialite of the age. "She was so bright and full of life when I met her just before I left for the South that even now I find it difficult to realize that she is indeed gone."[4]

Bamie sent word to Mittie's brothers, still exiled in Britain. Uncle Irvine was stunned:

> Uncle Irvine cannot write much today to his two dearly beloved and bereaved nieces Bammie & Conie. You know my darlings the peace your sweet little mother held & forever will hold in my poor heart. I am broken down with sorrow, and my heart is with you in your desolate home. My mind, my thoughts, and my soul is with you too, and beside that grave you may today see the apparition of a woebegone & distracted brother to whom there is no comfort. . . . Cheer up, as I know you will, that wifeless & motherless boy who[se] needs must be more staggered than us all, my [nephew] whose mother called her "yellow-haired Laddie."[5]

"The thought of being so far away . . . is adding greatly to the pain," Irvine's wife, Ella, wrote Bamie and Conie, reserving her greatest concern and "fearful anxiety for Teddie." "We feel sure that it is around him that you *all* gather as the greatest sufferer, poor Boy," she wrote.[6] The losses Roosevelt had suffered were widely recognized and sympathized. Yet, with the light having gone out of his life, Roosevelt himself could not *see* the public nature of his grief and the fact that many were deeply touched by his loss. Edmund Morris notes that he "seemed unable to understand the condolences of friends [and] showed no interest in his baby." He closed himself in his room and paced so endlessly that his family feared he would go mad.[7]

In a remarkable letter considering his own loss, Francis W. Lee, Alice's uncle, wrote Bamie a touching letter of condolence and concern that recognizes the joy and struggles she must be experiencing caring for a motherless infant while organizing the funeral and generally keeping the family together:

> I was glad to see Teddy was so calm + strong under his terrible blow + pray that he may go on as well as he has begun + help you with your troubles which are even greater than his, as by the greatest dispensation bestowed on us, he is so stunned by his own great grief that he can scarcely realize the two. I am so glad for you both that the little one was left behind, as a present care to you, and a deep interest for Teddy later when he comes to identify her with Alice. Wishing that there was something more that I could do for you than simply feel for you.[8]

The double funeral was held on Saturday, February 16, at Fifth Avenue Presbyterian Church—the site of Conie's wedding less than two years earlier. Morris captures the emotion of the occasion, noting that the "sight of two hearses outside the door, and two rosewood coffins standing side by side at the altar, was too much for many members of the large and distinguished congregation." Sobs could be heard throughout the simple service. Even the Reverend John Hall, who led the service, "could hardly control his voice."[9] In his prayer, Hall told his God that "We come together under the pressure of a great sorrow." In his address, the preacher admitted that he had never encountered "any thing quite like" this double death. "Of one it may be said that though she was not old, yet her work may be regarded as having been done." Her husband had died, her "children had been trained and educated; they had grown up. . . . It does not seem so strange that her work being done the Master should call her away." He then turned to Alice, with whom, he said, "it was quite different. Young in years, with little experience of life, naturally full of hope and joyous anticipation with a living man of whose life she constituted so large a part, with the hopes and joys of a mother, that she should be taken away thus early . . . this does seem strange and terrible."[10]

Having summed up the horror of the situation, Reverend Hall was hard-pressed to proceed to the usual religious anodynes that they were now in a better place. No wonder he had difficulty controlling his own tears. In truth, the day before, Speaker of the New York State Assembly James W. Husted had stated the situation more meaningfully than the reverend when he introduced an Assembly resolution to express the body's sympathy: "We are here in the presence of a dreadful sorrow. . . . The poet had described the form of death, and the terrors of death, but among them all he says 'Come to the bridal chamber, Death! / Come to the mother, when she feels, / For the first time, her first-born's breath, . . . And thou art terrible!'"[11]

Morris notes that Roosevelt had to be "handled like a child at the burial ceremony in Greenwood [sic] Cemetery," Brooklyn, and quotes the young man's former tutor, Arthur Cutler, who told Bill Sewall, "He does not know what he says or does."[12] This is terrific grief. All associated with Theodore Roosevelt and his stricken family felt it. Yet Morris interprets the emotion in Roosevelt as a "cataleptic concentration" on the task of "dislodging Alice Lee from his soul."[13]

He did no such thing, nor is there compelling evidence that he tried. Before he left for the Badlands, Roosevelt wrote a brief memorial to Alice Lee, which was published for the benefit of friends and family in a small book, privately printed by the publisher of his *Naval War of 1812*, G. P. Putnam's Sons. The memorial is moving in its economy of expression, which mirrors the brevity of Alice's life and of their life together:

> She was born at Chestnut Hill, Massachusetts, on July 29, 1861; I first saw her on October 18, 1878, and loved her as soon as I saw her sweet, fair young face; we were betrothed on January 25, 1880, and married on October 27th of the same year; we spent three years of happiness such as rarely comes to man or woman; on February 12, 1884, her baby girl was born; she kissed it, and seemed perfectly well; some hours afterward she, not knowing that she was in the slightest danger, but thinking only that she was falling into a sleep, became insensible, and died at two o'clock on Thursday afternoon. . . .
>
> She was beautiful in face and form, and lovlier [sic] still in spirit; as a flower she grew, and as a fair young flower she died; her life had been always in sunshine; . . . And when my heart's dearest died, the light went from my life for ever.[14]

This is not an act of dislodgment from one's soul. In his diary, he wrote a somewhat more intimate account, in which he spoke of a happiness "greater and more unalloyed than I have ever known fall to the lot of others . . . For joy or for sorrow, my life has now been lived out."[15]

Morris dismisses both the published memorial and the memorial diary entry as the sole exceptions to Roosevelt's banishment of Alice's name. Except for these, he writes, "there is no record of Roosevelt ever mentioning her name again," a task made more difficult by the fact that she was not the only Alice in Theodore's life.[16] "And this little new daughter, who is to bear the sweet name of her sweet Mother, will she not, after a while, be some little comfort to Teddy?" proclaimed the common sentiment captured in a condolence letter.[17] And yet the young widower evaded uttering the given name of her namesake, referring to little Alice as "Baby Lee" (not "Baby Roosevelt"). Stacy A. Cordery, Alice Roosevelt Longworth's principal biographer, observes that it was "as though Theodore could not claim her." This form—or, later, just Sister or Sissy—was adopted by Roosevelt as well as his family. In letters, Roosevelt typically called her "baby," albeit with the addition of some adjective of endearment. Reportedly, as the girl grew into womanhood, her father rarely spoke to her of her mother.[18]

Morris notes that TR "wrote movingly of the joys of family life, the ardor of youth, and the love of men and women" in his *Autobiography* of 1913 but "would not acknowledge that the first Alice ever existed." Others close to him, Morris pointed out, "took on the same attitude," their hands going "methodically through his correspondence" to destroy "all love-letters between and himself and Alice."[19] It was noted that Alice Roosevelt Longworth herself preserved a significant cache of these letters, which did not come to light until 1980.[20] So, the destruction was not quite total. But it is undeniable that an effort to destroy them had been made—which is why the preservation of the most intimate and ephemeral Alice artifacts is so remarkable.

In the collection of the library at Sagamore Hill, Roosevelt's rambling Oyster Bay summer house, is a box covered with teal velvet and lined with blue silk. Inside is a silk-covered divider with two blue ribbons to lift the divider out. There is a metal clasp in the front and two metal hinges in the back. The box contains four separately cataloged specimens of Alice Lee's hair. There is a brown lock, tied with a small white cord, which was clipped from Alice Lee at the age of two weeks. Another light brown ringlet was clipped when she was a year old. A brown-blond lock is accompanied by a photo of her and a piece of paper, on which is written, "Alice Lee's hair cut when she was 8 or 9 years old." And then there is a fourth, brown hair tied with a string. It is accompanied by an encapsulated piece of paper with this on it: "The hair of my sweet wife, Alice, cut after death."[21]

Theodore Roosevelt preserved a lock of his sweet wife's hair, which he—or someone else—cut at the time of her death. We cannot say with any certainty that Roosevelt himself collected all four locks, or that he put them in the box, or that he kept the box at Sagamore Hill, although we do know—because he tells us—that he personally handled the post-mortem clipping. We cannot say definitively, in other words, that he was responsible for these keepsakes having escaped destruction. But escape it they did, and, strangely enough, no biographer or historian has taken note of these artifacts, let alone their preservation. Theodore Roosevelt did not expel Alice from his soul. On the contrary, he made certain that a token of her physical self would remain with him forever.

It was Bamie who quickly located and hired a wet nurse to care for the newborn Alice, who was sent to the home of Aunt Anna Gracie. Doubtless, Theodore Roosevelt was in no condition to handle these matters. He struggled through the double funeral on February 16 and attended Baby Lee's christening on the 17th. Then, for someone supposedly in the throes of catalepsy, TR did what he later advised all others to do. He got action. He announced that he was going back, forthwith, to Albany and the Assembly. "There is nothing left for me except to try to live so as not to dishonor the memory of those I loved who have gone before me."[22] He boarded the train for the capital on the 18th.

Care of the remaining family and its affairs fell upon Bamie's shoulders. Alice and Mittie were gone. Elliott had married and was expecting his first child, Eleanor; he talked of moving to the country full-time. The center of Theodore's life had, in a heartbeat, shifted upstate. It was clear to Bamie that neither she nor even the family as now constituted could afford to sustain life at 6 West 57th Street. She set about finding a smaller home. Her search was spurred by the rapid sale of the 57th Street mansion—less than a week after going on the market. The buyers allowed the Roosevelts until the end of April to move out. Bamie found a suitable home at 422 Madison Avenue, invitingly near Central Park.[23] Though she bore the burden well, Bamie, too, had lost her mother and father in the space of six years. She later recalled this time as a "perfect nightmare."[24] The mail provided a daily reminder of grief as word of Mittie's and Alice's deaths reached all corners of the globe. Condolence letters came from Britain, Germany, and this from Athens, Greece, a month after the funerals: "Dear dear Anna what can I say? I wept bitter tears, when I thought never again here on earth should I see or speak to your lovely Mother."[25]

From Albany, Roosevelt put on the market the Manhattan West 45th Street brownstone he and Alice had shared after the period of time they were required by George C. Lee to live with Mittie. Though they spent most of their married years at 6 West 57th Street or in Albany, Theodore could not bear the thought of returning to live alone in that house. But neither could he steel himself to move out and close it up. Once again, this arduous and depressing task fell to Bamie. She would close the place, divide the movable property, and arrange for a sale. Long accustomed to being a second mother to her siblings, she, not her brother, was now the functional head of the family. Bamie, the eldest Roosevelt, had internalized her father's message: being a Roosevelt meant something. She would not allow her brother to flail or fail. With Bamie's urging, Theodore pressed ahead with building the Oyster Bay home he had intended to call Leeholm in honor of his wife. His plan was to get it finished by summer—though he had made no set plan to move in. Indeed, he delegated Bamie to oversee the project as well.

No one more than Bamie encouraged her brother to throw himself into his work. She expected Theodore to work as hard as *she* had been made to work—after all she had devoted most of her life to being the family's "Atlas." Theodore was plagued by insomnia and restlessness after the death of his wife and mother yet he concluded what would prove to be his most productive legislative term, writing more bills in a single term than any other legislator in New York history. Among these was the Aldermanic Bill, a classic piece of progressive legislation that, at twenty-five, gained him a regional recognition throughout New York and New England. He was regarded as an emerging party leader. Ever his confidante, Bamie encouraged her brother, who habitually sought her advice, to capitalize on his growing regional reputation to become a national political figure. At this point, however, his heart was not in it. Still, he recalled his old maxim, "Black care rarely sits behind a rider whose pace is fast enough," and decided that even work without zest was better than idle misery.

The state party had several contenders for the 1884 presidential nomination. This was the issue on everyone's minds when Roosevelt returned to Albany. The favorite was Chester A. Arthur, the incumbent president whose surprising decision to carry out his predecessor's reform agenda chagrined the Stalwarts but pleased most others in the state GOP. But when failing health—he had Bright's disease (kidney failure), the very malady that had killed Alice Roosevelt—took Arthur out of serious contention, Roosevelt successfully persuaded the GOP State Convention to embrace his preferred candidate, Senator George F. Edmunds of Vermont, a solid if humdrum anti-Stalwart reformer, as the New York party's choice for presidential nominee. This victory kept Roosevelt in the limelight.

Roosevelt's third term in the legislature was phenomenally active yet not, after all, fast enough to outrun black care. His legislative comrade Isaac Hunt recalled, "You could not mention the fact that his wife and mother had been taken away . . . you could see at once that it was a grief too deep."[26] Invited by his party to run for a fourth term in the Assembly, he declined. On April 30, in a letter to the editor of the leading newspaper of the city that would host that year's New York State Republican convention, the *Utica Morning Herald*, he explained that he had "very little expectation of being able to keep on in politics," citing the "venomous hatred" of politicians, once his supporters, who had turned against him at the dictate of "masters who are influenced by political considerations that were national and not local in their scope." These were the same politicians he had recounted feuding with in letters to Alice. He continued: "I will not stay in public life unless I can do so on my own terms; and my ideal, whether lived up to or not, is rather a high one." He went on to explain that his "work this winter has been very harassing and I feel tired and restless; for the next few months I shall probably be in Dakota, and I think I shall spend the next two to three years in making shooting trips, either in the Far West or in the Northern Woods—and there will be plenty of work to writing."[27]

To the Utica editor, Roosevelt portrayed himself as a sportsman and writer, but he was very likely aware of an article that had appeared in the "Events in the Metropolis" department of *The New York Times* on February 25 under the headline "Dressed Beef in the West. The Business Enterprise of the Marquis de Mores." To an interviewer who encountered him in Manhattan's Brunswick Hotel, de Morès explained that he had gone out west eighteen months earlier to organize a dressed (partially butchered and ready for transportation) beef business on the Northern Pacific Railroad. He built slaughterhouses, established the Northern Pacific Refrigerator Car Company (based on a new technology), and claimed to have "[slaughter]houses in all the principal towns on the Northern Pacific Railroad between St. Paul and Portland." His theory was that slaughtering cattle locally and sending the beef back east was far superior to shipping livestock to be slaughtered in the Chicago stockyards; the long rail journey took a toll on live cattle, reducing their weight, quality, and value by the time they reached the distant stockyard slaughterhouses. Where the NP tracks crossed the Little Missouri River, de Morès founded a town, naming it after his wife, Medora von Hoffman, and built a ranch house there.[28]

Roosevelt had, of course, hunted along the Little Missouri before, when he left his pregnant wife for a Badlands adventure in September 1883. On the 23rd of that month, he had written Alice about his plan to buy a ranch and enter the cattle business as an immediate alternative to politics, which did not pay enough to keep him, his wife, and what he anticipated would be a growing family in style. Ranching, he wrote to Alice, would "make more money as our needs increase" while also allowing him time "to keep in a position from which I may be able at some future time to again go into public life, or literary life."[29]

Now, in the spring of 1884, his wife was dead, his grief was great, and, if anything, the prospect of again lighting off for the territory was even more compelling. Attending as a delegate-at-large from New York, he set off for Chicago and the GOP National Convention, arriving on May 31. There, on June 3, he delivered a stirring speech in support of the nomination of John R. Lynch, the Black U.S. representative from Mississippi's 6th District, as temporary chair of the convention. Lynch was a staunch champion of Roosevelt's preferred candidate, George F. Edmunds, but James G. Blaine nevertheless came to the convention seemingly in the lead, having managed to wrangle support from a combination of Edmunds's and Arthur's supporters.

The charismatic former Speaker of the House, and U.S. senator from Maine, Blaine was tainted by more than a whiff of corruption. Yet Roosevelt broke ranks with the Mugwumps—the nickname for Republican progressives who proposed to endorse Democrat Grover Cleveland for president rather than Blaine, should he secure the Republican nomination. Normally, Roosevelt might have joined the Mugwumps in supporting Cleveland, a decision that could have been consequential given that New York was an important swing state at the time and would, ultimately, decide the election for Cleveland. But Roosevelt had been stung by Cleveland's decision as New York's Democratic governor to veto several of his bills for reform and regulation in New York City. When William Hudson, a reporter for *The Brooklyn Daily Eagle*, had tipped Roosevelt off to Cleveland's intentions, the young legislator had responded as if the matter were not entirely in the hands of the governor: "He mustn't do that! I can't have that! I won't let him do it!" And then added: "I'll go up and see him at once."[30] Cleveland parried Roosevelt's protests by explaining that the reform bills were well intentioned but imprecisely and even ambiguously written. Interestingly, Roosevelt did not attempt to refute this criticism but instead argued that the "principle" embodied in the legislation was the point, not the details. In dealing with matters of lawmaking, this was a bridge too far for the governor, who was known as a close reader of legislative language. Cleveland abruptly concluded the meeting by banging his fist on his desk and announcing, "Mr. Roosevelt, I'm going to veto those bills!"[31]

Months later, at the national convention in Chicago, the stinging memory of this exchange doubtless helped propel Roosevelt away from Cleveland yet he felt no enthusiasm for Blaine. With Massachusetts senator Henry Cabot Lodge, a fellow Edmunds supporter, Roosevelt plotted to delay the nomination in the hope that Blaine's supporters would fall out with one another. But on June 6, when Chairman Lynch gaveled the call of the first ballot, Blaine led Chester A. Arthur (who, while terminally ill, had not declined candidacy) and George F. Edmunds. The second ballot garnered more votes for Blaine, but still not a majority, and the third brought him within thirty-six votes of what was needed for nomination. At this, Roosevelt kept harrowing the delegations, seeking somehow to stop the inevitable. A motion to adjourn for the night was offered in a bid to bleed off the Blaine momentum. Eager to maintain velocity, however, Blaine supporters objected to calling a vote on adjournment. Their objections were answered by Roosevelt's repeated bellow to call the roll. At last, William McKinley—at the time a rising congressman from Ohio—calmed things down. The motion to adjourn was voted on, and promptly defeated. The fourth ballot was taken forthwith, and Blaine emerged as the 1884 Republican candidate for president of the United States. McKinley, seeking a show of unity, invited Roosevelt to second a motion to make the nomination unanimous. In response, he simply shook his head no. He had lost, but a powerful political friendship had been forged between Roosevelt and Lodge.

By the time the delegates finally dribbled out of the convention hall, having spent the day and night and morning voting, it was afternoon. A reporter cornered Roosevelt, asking him about his plans. "I am going cattle-ranching in Dakota for the remainder of the summer and a part of the fall. What I shall do after that I cannot tell you," he said. To a follow-up question about whether he intended to support his party's candidate, he responded: "That question I decline to answer. It is a subject I do not care to talk about."[32]

The day burned out, but the exhausted Roosevelt was seized by insomnia. As a convention delegate from a large swing state, he was under tremendous personal, political, and moral pressure. Whatever he decided would have an impact on his political career as well as, perhaps, the course of the nation. Around midnight, he told a reporter for the New York *Evening Post* that he would support "any decent Democrat" rather than vote for Blaine in the general election. The *Post* editor did not rush to press with this comment, and a deflated Theodore Roosevelt boarded a train for the West. Hours later, as he changed trains in St. Paul, a reporter for the *Pioneer Press* insisted on knowing whether he would accept Blaine's nomination. By this time, perhaps lulled by the soothing motion of rail travel, he was more reflective. Deciding he had no viable choice but to support Blaine if he wanted to retain his prominence in the Republican Party, he replied: "I shall bolt the convention by no means. I have no personal objections to Blaine."[33] He had chosen his adjective carefully. *Personal* was not synonymous with *political*, let alone *moral*.

The reaction, however, to Roosevelt's calculated decision was decidedly personal. The Lee family was deeply disappointed. Owen Wister overheard a heated discussion between George Cabot Lee and Henry Lee, who was George's cousin. "You can tell that young whipper-snapper in New York from me that his independence was the only thing in him we cared for, and if he's gone back on that, we don't care to hear anything more about him," Henry Lee snarled at George, who until the death of Alice had been Theodore Roosevelt's father-in-law. Wister analyzed the situation: "Particularly in the eyes of all Boston Mugwumps was [Theodore] found wanting: in spite of having married into one of their best families, he had been unfaithful to what they expected of him, had not left his party and come out for Cleveland."[34] Had Alice been alive, it is easy to imagine that Theodore would have written and talked with her about this moral dilemma. He talked over "everything" with her and wrote Alice more frequently than Bamie or Conie in their brief four years of marriage. If TR first ran for office for moral reasons and not self-aggrandizement, then this is precisely the type of decision upon which he would likely ruminate with his family of unofficial advisors. Alas, Alice and the influence of the Lees and Saltonstalls was gone, and along with Alice and Mittie to the grave went 6 West 57th Street and the magical few years the Roosevelts spent there mostly all together. The "cursed"

Roosevelt mansion on 57th Street was sold and now Bamie and Aunt Anna were caring for baby Alice; Conie had her own baby; and Theodore was alone, politically and personally, and felt profoundly adrift. It would be July 19 before he issued a formal press release, giving less ambivalent voice to his support for the "Plumed Knight," as Blaine relished being called.[35]

Roosevelt's destination was the Chimney Butte Ranch, which, among locals, also went by the name of the Maltese Cross Ranch, thanks to its eight-pointed Maltese Cross brand. It was at this ranch that Roosevelt purchased, for $14,000, a primary cattle interest during his first trip to the Badlands in September 1883. Having made his escape from Chicago and the GOP convention, he arrived at Maltese Cross on June 9 and immediately set out to hunt. His diary records the usual overstuffed bag, everything from "One jack rabbit, one curlew" on his first outing on June 13, to a badger ("galloped up to him and killed him with revolver," June 16), an antelope, then several more antelope, including a "fine buck, shot through both shoulders" (June 18), a mallard drake ("shot with rifle, for [dinner]," June 25), and "One cock pintail grouse, shot with rife, to pot" (June 27), "pot" meaning for that night's dinner.[36] But when Roosevelt recalled this outing and others in his 1885 *Hunting Trips of a Ranchman*, the emphasis was less on body count than on the melancholy-tinged beauty of Badlands solitude. He wrote of the melded song of birds as "a cadence of wild sadness, inexpressibly touching" and the "sweet, sad songs" of the hermit thrush and the "soft melancholy cooing of the mourning-dove." These all contributed to his feeling that "the Bad Lands . . . somehow *look* just exactly as Poe's tales and poem *sound*."[37] In the Badlands, he may have escaped the bitter frustration of political life, but he failed to shed the grief and sense of bottomless loss the deaths of Alice and Mittie had cut into his heart.

Roosevelt returned from the hunt to the Maltese Cross Ranch on June 22. He was alone in the one-and-a-half-story cabin that his co-owners and ranch managers, Joe Ferris and Bill Merrifield, had built at his request. The pair were away in St. Paul, buying, as Roosevelt had directed, a thousand head of cattle. Nevertheless, during this time, he likely met and socialized with the Marquis de Morès and his wife in Medora, seven miles to the north. If so, he would have imbibed the entrepreneur's wildly optimistic vision of the future of Badlands beef and was perhaps heartened by the prospect of inevitable success. The concept was ranch-to-table—brilliant but a century and a half premature. Before Roosevelt left the Badlands for New York (via Medora on July 1), he selected a location for a second, private ranch, thirty-five miles north of Medora and more than forty miles north of the Maltese Cross Ranch. He would call it the Elkhorn Ranch.

Once back in New York City, Theodore took up residence with Bamie at 422 Madison Avenue, the property she had found and purchased. Bamie loved her brother and loved his daughter. Yet, perhaps acutely aware of already risking classification as a hopeless spinster, she was concerned that she and Theodore would grow too comfortable living together. Bamie had already become accustomed to being a second mother in the family. She did not want to become a second wife to her brother.

During his Dakota absences, however, Bamie was, if anything, more preoccupied with him than if he had been living with her at 422 Madison. On July 28, Theodore left for the Badlands again, accompanied by Bill Sewall and Sewall's nephew Wilmot Dow, whom he'd told to wrap up their affairs in Maine so that they could come to Dakota without further delay, where they would soon be employed to set up and run Elkhorn Ranch. Summoning her many years of practice as a stand-in mother for her siblings and no doubt recalling the love of Aunt Anna, Grandmother Bulloch, and the retinue of caretakers in her early life, Bamie now was left a full-time surrogate mother to "Baby Lee," TR and Alice's baby. She was the recipient of a weekly stream of letters from Dakota, and this volume of correspondence was not unusual in their relationship; "Thee" wrote her at this pace throughout his life.

Bamie knew better than to try to plumb her brother's depths. Instead, in deliberate and determined counterpoint to his gloomy state, she wrote chatty letters unmistakably intended to ensure that New York continued to claim a large corner of his mind and heart. She entertained him with accounts of Baby Lee's prodigiously rapid development. "I hope Mousiekins will be very cunning; I shall dearly love her," Roosevelt wrote to Bamie about the daughter he had all but abandoned. "[Bamie] was the only one I really cared about when I was a child," an adult Alice later recalled. "She was the single most important influence on my childhood."[38]

Bamie also turned to news about the progress on Leeholm and, most important, how she was fitting out his study and bedroom in the Madison Avenue townhouse. Despite her own misgivings, she wanted to send him the message that *this* was his home. "I got one the other day," TR replied from the Badlands. "Another good head for our famous hall at Leeholm." Curious and very like TR that he would describe a hall that did not yet exist as "famous," and it was "*our* famous hall" not his alone.[39]

Bamie also assiduously clipped all the pertinent political news from the New York papers and sent the clippings to her brother, accompanied by her own well-informed commentary. Her motive could not have been anything other than a desire to see him reenter politics. Bamie made sure that he knew his friends—with the notable exception of Henry Cabot Lodge—were embracing the Mugwumps and openly announcing their support for the Democrat Cleveland in preference to Blaine. Bamie surveyed the political landscape with alacrity and was impressively delicate in her diplomacy. She forwarded to him some letters that sought to persuade him to embrace Cleveland as well or—at the very least—announce openly and once and for all exactly where he stood.

It worked. In mid-August, not wanting to leave Lodge twisting in the wind, he wrote to him that "We can take part in no bolt" from the GOP, but "I do not think we need take any *active* part in the campaign."[40] At the same time, he wrote to Bamie on August 17 about how he was growing increasingly fond of his ranches and the Badlands, which "certainly has a desolate, grim beauty of its own, that has a curious fascination for me." He launched into a remarkable description: "The grassy, scantily wooded bottoms through which the winding river flows are bounded by bare, jagged buttes; their fantastic shapes and sharp, steep edges throw the most curious shadows, under the cloudless, glaring sky; and at evening I love to sit out in front of the hut and see their hard, gray outlines gradually growing soft and purple as the flaming sunset by degrees softens and dies away; while my days I spend generally alone, riding through the lonely rolling prairie and broken lands."[41] Theodore Roosevelt was a broken man in a broken land.

Twenty-one years earlier, having failed to suppress a mutiny of men under his command during the Battle of Chancellorsville on one of the bloodiest days of the Civil War, Union Brigadier General Alfred Sully narrowly evaded court-martial. Instead, he was relieved of command by his CO and exiled to fight Indians on the Great Plains. In ruthless pursuit of Lakota and Dakota "renegades" in 1864, he looked out upon the Badlands and pronounced the landscape "hell, with the fires out."[42]

Sully was a Badlands exile from Civil War glory; to Roosevelt, the Badlands were becoming something like home. For he had just passed through hell, its fires burning *him* out, his grief reducing even politics to so many ashes in his mouth. Sojourning in this landscape allowed him to project his personal hell onto the environment. There, in the real world, he could with his own eyes see hell with fires out. While in Dakota and across the West, he witnessed the degradation of mighty species like the bison. He saw the threat of rapid and untamed industrialization. And yet Roosevelt also saw the delicate balance in nature. The outdoors, as it had been since he was an asthmatic boy, was his classroom and healer.

It was not just the nature of the American West that healed TR but also the people he spent time with out there. Bill Sewall, a tall, broad-chested Maine woodsman whom TR had hired because of their formative adventures together in Maine, was decidedly out of place in Dakota. Yet Sewall was the perfect antidote to help restore Theodore after tragedy. More comfortable roaming the woods than wrangling cattle, he had a "lust for life" and in his Maine homeland "loved to shout poetry as he fought his canoe through white water or slammed his ax into shuddering pine trees."⁴³ TR biographer Edmund Morris keenly observed that Sewall was a "magnificent specimen of manhood [that] might satisfy Theodore's cravings for a father figure."⁴⁴ It was to Sewall that TR confessed "that all his hopes lay buried in the East."⁴⁵ Sewall later recorded that "Roosevelt was very melancholy at times, and, the first year we were in Dakota, very much down in spirits." In one particularly low moment of despair, Theodore told Sewall "it did not make any difference what became of him." "You have your child to live for," Sewall replied. "Her aunt [Bamie] can take care of her a good deal better than I can," Roosevelt replied. "She never would know anything about me, anyway. She would be just as well off without me." "You won't always feel as you do now," countered Sewall. "You won't always be willing to stay here and drive cattle, because when you get back to feeling differently you will want to get back among your friends and associates where you can do more and be more benefit to the world than you can here driving cattle." Roosevelt ended the conversation and "never said anything more to [Sewall] about feeling that he had nothing to live for," perhaps Sewall surmised, because Roosevelt "thought [Sewall] was not sympathetic."⁴⁶

Bill Merrifield, one of TR's ranch hands and business partners at the Maltese Cross and a frequent hunting companion, was also a widower. Merrifield recalled in his memoirs one of the few times Theodore openly reflected on Alice's death. TR confided to Merrifield his pain was "beyond any healing," and when Merrifield attempted to reassure him that life would move on, Roosevelt cut him off, "Now don't talk to me about time will make a difference—time will never change me in that respect."⁴⁷

Time may not have dulled the pain of loss, but it did still bring with it change. Late in September, Theodore again wrote to Bamie, this time from Fort McKinney, near the Big Horn Mountains of Wyoming, among which he reveled in a big-game hunt. He reported to her that he had killed three grizzly bears and six elks, trophies that were now part of a collection of a "dozen good heads," with which he intended to adorn the halls of Leeholm.⁴⁸ Was he ready, at last, to return to his old life?

Roosevelt certainly underwent something between catharsis and exorcism, and when he arrived in New York on October 9, Bamie was encouraged by the sight of her brother, thoroughly tanned, looking healthier than he had in a very long time. He even seemed eager to see Baby Lee, but what might have most delighted him was the stream of reporters who sought him, itching to discover what he intended to do next.

Alone together, Bamie and Theodore discussed his political future. He reminded her that their father had refused to play a part in any internal Republican battle. She pointed out that the elder Roosevelt was by that time ill and exhausted, whereas Theodore brimmed over with the vigor of the West. On October 11, he granted an interview with a reporter for the New York *Sun*. Inviting the man into his study—newly furnished, courtesy of Bamie—he poured out glasses of sherry and, over this genteel libation, told him that when he had started out to his ranch two months earlier he hadn't intended to actively participate in the coming presidential campaign but had now decided to address an audience of Brooklyn Young Republicans, advising them to support the regular Republican ticket. Bamie had subtly advised him to buck the pragmatic political path. It was one of the first, but not the last, times that TR went against his sister's well-informed advice.

On November 13, shortly after the general election in which Cleveland defeated Blaine by prevailing in the swing state of New York by just 1,047 votes, Roosevelt again headed west, still struggling to decide whether his life would be in the East or West or both.[49] He arrived in Medora on the 16th. What had been hell with the fires out was now transformed into a landscape of driving white snow. If Roosevelt's attraction to the works of Poe extended to the writer's only novel, the 1838 *Narrative of Arthur Gordon Pym of Nantucket*, TR might have recalled the novel's final images of Antarctic seas turned milky white, the atmosphere a rain of white ash. A cataract of foggy mist opens to accommodate the small boat in which Pym sails. The book's very last image is of a shrouded figure with skin "of the perfect whiteness of snow."[50] The novel then ends abruptly with a putative editor's note to the effect that Pym had been killed and the final chapters of his narrative lost with him.

Though the whiteout of winter gripped Dakota, Roosevelt left to bring a beef herd to the slaughterhouse in Medora, after which he pushed northward to where Sewall and Dow were now laboring to finish building the ranch house that would be the headquarters of Roosevelt's new Elkhorn Ranch. Historian Douglas Brinkley contends that "although North Dakota provided the 'romance' of his life, it was also where his worries about the depletion of America's natural resources took root. Nobody championed the conquering of the West by the U.S. Army, mountaineers, homesteaders, trappers, farmers, and ranchers more than Roosevelt . . . [but he] nevertheless worried that the United States' innate sense of opportunity had recently degenerated into exploitation. America knew how to conquer, but it was failing in the art of properly managing its hard-won resources." In time, the Elkhorn Ranch, the birthplace of Roosevelt's conservation ethos, was christened the "cradle of conservation."[51]

Theodore claimed that he chose the name Elkhorn because on or near the property of what would become the ranch he found the interlocked horns of two elk stags, who died in combat, forever intertwined, and fated to death by their conflict.[52] Despite this ominous origin story, the Elkhorn Ranch was quickly becoming a compound, not just a ranch house. Historian Rolf Sletten sets the scene:

> [TR] spent the next three days helping [Sewall and Dow] chop down the big cottonwood trees. After all the hard work, he was dismayed to overhear Dow telling a cowboy that, "Bill cut down fifty-three, I cut forty-nine, and the boss . . . he beavered down seventeen." The issue was not so much the number of trees that had been cut, in fact downing seventeen big trees was probably quite respectable considering that his production was being compared to the output of two professional lumbermen. The problem was the reference to having "beavered" down the trees. "Those who have seen the stump of a tree gnawed down by a

beaver will understand the force of comparison," observed Roosevelt, without enthusiasm. Mercifully, he was persuaded not to "help" them build the house.[53]

Two Maine lumberjacks and a dude from New York were hardly a trio of natural-born cowboys, but they did good work. Wilmot Dow, who was closer to TR's age, was according to Sewall "a better hunter, better fisherman" than his uncle "and the best shot of any man in the country."[54] The three men worked through unspeakably bitter cold, the mercury plummeting to between ten and fifty degrees below zero.

Hell with the fires out Roosevelt had survived, but the "white weather" brought on depression, which he captured in a piece of writing titled "Winter Weather." In it, he described "days . . . dwindled to their shortest," nights that "seem never-ending," the plains transformed into "an abode of iron desolation" and "clouds of blinding snow-dust, wrapping the mantle of death round every unsheltered being" as a "still, merciless, terrible cold . . . broods over the earth like the shadow of silent death."[55] Though so many family members would have welcomed him home much earlier, they shared a belief that TR's Western forays might be the best and only cure for his depression. On December 20, he finally began the trek back east to New York, which he reached on December 23, in time for Christmas with Bamie and Baby Alice.

Come spring, the ranchman headed back to his two ranches, leaving New York on April 13, 1885, and arriving in Medora three days later. He wrote to "Darling Byssie"—which alternated with "Bye" as his pet name for Bamie—on April 29 what was for him—these days—an effusive letter, beginning, "Was awfully glad to get your letter; and I felt very tenderly to think of the darling baby calling for papa. I just long to see you both." His warmth toward his daughter is evident, yet, as always, he declined to call her by name, and he did not invite Bamie and the baby for a visit. "All my men have gone east for the cattle," he wrote, "and I am now here pretty much by myself." Roosevelt continued in this revelatory letter to Bamie:

We have had very bad weather for the past ten days; though it has now cleared off beautifully, and the air is enough to give a consumptive life. I have just come in from a very rough and solitary trip of five days after two strayed horses, one of which I recovered. I had to start off at a moments notice, when forty miles from my ranch, and so was unable to take either coat or gloves, and as on two days there were heavy snow storms you may imagine that I was pretty cold; I thought my bare hands would freeze. The worst day I travelled in company with a Texan cowboy whom I happened to meet and who proved a very good fellow. The snowstorm was blinding, and we got lost for some six hours, finally have to travel entirely by compass; we were glad enough when at dusk we reached an empty hut in which we could pass the night. All through the trip the cowboy whom I met treated me first rate; I really like them as a class. The river is now up so high as to be almost impassable; yesterday I was able to cross it in but one place, and there I had to swim my horse, through the boiling, muddy current, splashing water in his face to guide him. I got pretty wet and afterwards had to strike my own line for twenty miles before I reached home and could dry myself. However it all makes me feel very healthy and strong.[56]

Some might well call Theodore's behavior foolhardy or even suicidal. Yet, for him, at this point in his life, such abandon, even courting death, seems to have been essential to restoring him to life. Roosevelt would later say that "I would never have been president if it had not been for my experiences here in North Dakota."[57] He met cowboys, farmers, and ranchers—prairie populists and strong individualists—who would become his Rough Riders and common connection to the people. But his observation was more than a political statement. TR lived in the West the life he could only imagine in the East. His Western sojourns brought him back to the wildness in his nature, simultaneously death-defying and life-giving.

In a letter on May 12, he wrote of how he had just come in from a "rather hard six days drive, taking in our cattle. The river was so high that when the cattle came in from the east I had to make a long circuit inland with them. . . . It was my first experience on the trail, but I brought the cattle through all right. . . . I was each day from ten to sixteen hours in the saddle, and in spite of its being May we had two or three days when it snowed, and on two nights the thermometer went down to zero. And it was most exhausting work. I was heartily glad to get home to the ranch." He explained that he was "now engaged in keeping the cattle on the range; and I have had so much to do that I have done but little shooting; in a week or two I shall be off on the round up." The close of the letter began with "Good bye," and then the handwriting slumped on a downward slope, "Your loving brother, Thee," as if he were trailing off into an exhausted slumber.[58] The Badlands offered a cure for Theodore Roosevelt's depression and insomnia: hard work in a hard setting.

Five days later, Thee took the focus off his own weariness, and, in a much firmer hand than that of May 12, sought to lighten the burden he had left to Bamie, who oversaw the move into Leeholm. "[Y]ou must have had a simply fiendish time moving in; now please don't bother your dear, over-bothered head about your harum-scarum brother's goods." He assured her that he could set up the library and other rooms when he got back, which he hoped would be "as near June 25th as possible." He promised he would then "stay at home about two months, leaving again sometime about the last week of August and returning the last week in September." Tellingly, he added: "unless political considerations should produce a change in the latter part of this programme, necessitating my presence in the east earlier." He expressed his hope that "you and darling little baby will have a good, healthy, quiet time where you are."[59] His mind was no longer solely on himself and his grief. Yet while he expressed loving interest in his daughter, he still dared not write her name. It had been over a year since Alice's and Mittie's deaths and Bamie would have been well within her rights to insist on him returning to New York. Yet she did not—at least not explicitly. Bamie continued to raise her brother's daughter and manage his affairs. Most critically, she continued to allow TR the room to grieve and recover on his own timeline while tantalizing his ego with the latest political scuttlebutt.

His letter from June 5 was brighter: "I look forward so much to being at home again; the darling wee daughter must be so cunning." To a modern ear, this hardly sounds like an appropriate descriptor for a proud papa to apply to his infant daughter, though we should observe that a nineteenth-century sensibility would have been willing to define "cunning" as *cute, pretty,* or *clever,* without any pejorative connotation. Regardless, "cunning" turned out to be an apt description of the woman Alice would become. TR writes of taking far more pleasure in the work of cattle ranching than he had a month before. "I have been nearly three weeks on the roundup, and have really enjoyed the work; I have done my share just exactly like the other cowboys and haven't received a favor of any kind or sort. We get up at three, have breakfast, and are in the saddle by four." The hard work, exhausting in the May 12 letter, was portrayed as curative in the June 5 missive. It relieved his chronic insomnia: "as you may imagine, I am well pleased to turn in and go to sleep when dark comes, which is about eight oclock." But as if he did not want to imply that life in the Badlands was conducive to anything like ease, he wrote also about how "One night none of us got any sleep to speak of, having to be up all the time in a driving hurricane of hail and rain to prevent the cattle from getting away." This said, he assured his sister that ranching is "certainly a most healthy life; and how a man does sleep, and how he enjoys the coarse fare."[60]

By the time he returned from a trip back east to visit Bamie, Alice, and Conie in late August, the ranch was highly domesticated. He told Bamie that "The ranche now looks quite homelike; I have a washstand, a bed (with mattress, pillow and sheets) and a looking glass in my room; and feel quite civilized." No sooner did he use the word "civilized," however, than he wrote of riding out on his "dear old" horse Manitou with Dow. The horse, he said, was "just the same intelligent, biscuit loving old pet as ever." Thee managed to bag two whitetail deer, which supplied fresh meat, "so now we have venison, grouse, milk, butter, potatoes and bread, and feel that we fare quite sumptuously."[61]

Having painted a homey picture in the August 30 letter, he wrote two days later about an elk hunt during which he camped in "a narrow valley, with a roaring log fire in front of the tent." The next day, he had the "good luck" to kill "two blacktail buck and a bull elk, shooting the latter as he leaped out of a brushwood coulee. He was large and fat and excellent eating." So much for the imagery of civilized life, but he did close with "Give best love to baby and with very much for yourself. Your loving brother, Thee."[62] On September 7, he complained mildly about having "a light calf crop" and suffering a market that offered "low prices" for beef. "I trust," he said, "it will change by next year."[63] The implication, which likely did not escape Bamie, was rather more worrisome.

Thee altogether avoided mentioning developments in his relationship with Antoine Amédée Marie Vincent de Vallambrosa, Marquis de Morès, who had founded the town of Medora. Like TR, the Marquis was possessed of a larger-than-life personality, which often impressed Roosevelt, but also created friction between the pair in two disputes over land rights and one over a cattle deal that went bad. (Roosevelt was selling his cattle to the Marquis when it came time for slaughter and they had agreed on a price of 6 cents a pound, which de Morès unilaterally reduced to 5.5 cents.) But that was nothing compared to the conflicts de Morès created with locals by aggressively fencing off land that had been used as free range for grazing. In 1883, he'd killed a man in a gunfight. The man's business partners claimed they had been ambushed—and thus that the Marquis had committed murder. The Marquis, corroborated by his men, pleaded self-defense. Nevertheless, de Morès was charged with murder—not once, but twice. Each time, the local justice of the peace dismissed the indictments for lack of proof. Two years after the fact, however, a grand jury issued a third indictment.[64]

On September 5, 1885, Roosevelt was surprised to receive a letter from the Marquis accusing Joe Ferris—the brother of Roosevelt's trusted ranch hand Sylvane Ferris—of being "instrumental in getting me indicted" by bribing witnesses. He also accused Roosevelt himself of giving to local newspapers inflammatory accounts of the disputes between them. "If you are my enemy," he wrote, "I want to know it. I am always on hand as you know, and between gentlemen it is easy to settle matters of that sort directly."[65] Roosevelt, who had no reason to think Ferris was guilty of anything, understood that he was being challenged to a duel. "Most emphatically I am not your enemy," he replied to the Marquis, adding provocatively "if I were you would know it." He closed with: "I too, as you know, am always on hand, and ever ready to hold myself accountable in any way for anything I have said or done."[66] Anticipating a duel, Roosevelt secured the services of Bill Sewall as his second, but de Morès—who was known to have dueled before—wrote back that he had intended settling the dispute as "gentlemen—*without trouble*."[67]

Though the near duel with de Morès was a matter of pride, it marked the sixth time (at least) that Theodore had risked his life in those two formative years in the Badlands. It is easy to see TR's reckless acts in the Badlands as a death wish. It is more powerful, and closer to the truth, to instead believe that from his time in Dakota forward Theodore Roosevelt had a life wish. When he was twenty, he lost his father, who was only forty-six. Five years later, his twenty-two-year-old wife and forty-eight-year-old mother were dead, too. No one was guaranteed the next sunrise; if living life on a razor's edge tempted death, it did so no more than any other aspect of being alive. Instead, for TR, it made life worth living.

The de Morès murder trial took place in Bismarck, and Roosevelt, on his way to catch an eastbound train in the first leg of his journey to speak at the Republican State Convention in Saratoga, New York, passed through Bismarck on September 16. He paused his trip long enough to visit the Marquis in his jail cell, where he found him smoking with perfect sangfroid, quite confident of acquittal. Roosevelt then continued his eastward train journey. By the time he reached New York, the papers related that the Marquis had indeed been acquitted.[68]

Theodore Roosevelt did not make headlines with anything he did or said at the GOP convention in Saratoga, but his appearance there was important, nevertheless. It marked his intention to return to politics.

By September 19, he was ensconced at 422 Madison Avenue with

Bamie, who had, through all his weeks and months in the Badlands, kept him connected to the East and the further possibilities of a political life. She had been anxious for him to return home, and not live the life of the cowboy rancher. Her dreams for her brother were perhaps at the time larger than even his own. Her presence as a surrogate mother to Alice and, in a way, to her brother, as well through her weekly letters to the Badlands, had seen him through hell with the fires out and through the Poe-like "white weather" of the bitter winter that followed.

It was sometime in early October—the precise date is not recorded, not by a biographer, historian, or the participants in the event—that Edith Kermit Carow descended the staircase from Bamie's parlor at 422 Madison Avenue a spinster, never expecting to find her childhood sweetheart, now a widower turned gentleman cowboy, standing—right there, before her—in the hallway.

What she felt at the sight of him we cannot know. Edith was twenty-four years old, a fierce intellect prone to putting poetry over politics, and with a beauty no longer girlish by the standards of the Victorian era. Her face was angular, its features finely articulated, giving her an authoritative aura of a self-assurance she almost certainly did not possess at the time. Her visit that afternoon to Bamie, her friend of years going back to childhood, had stretched out longer than planned. Whether its undue length was the result of absorbing conversation or of Bamie's deliberate stratagem has long been a subject of conjecture. We know Bamie was determined that her younger brother live up to his potential. If she had her way, he would not remain out west, a lonely author and a solitary rancher.

Whether by fate or design, Edith's descent from the parlor coincided precisely with the entrance of Theodore Roosevelt, a man now between identities, at the moment a former politician and current cowboy, but a man who had been oscillating for some time now between East and West.[69]

9

REUNITED

"She never really forgave him his first marriage."
—Alice Roosevelt Longworth on her stepmother

N either Edith Carow nor Theodore Roosevelt left any record of that day early in the fall of 1885 when, in Bamie's hallway, they suddenly found themselves face-to-face again.

They had not seen one another since the double funeral of Mittie and Alice nineteen months earlier. Since Alice's death, Theodore had shown no interest in rekindling a relationship with Edith and, in fact, had made it a point to ask Bamie to take steps to ensure that he and Edie would never cross paths at the Madison Avenue townhouse brother and sister shared. But destiny—or Bamie—intervened.

We can only speculate on their thoughts at that—what else to call it?—fateful moment. A clue to Edith's thinking may be found in a note Nancy Roosevelt Jackson, a granddaughter of Theodore, wrote to her grandmother's most important biographer. In 1976, Jackson offered this to Sylvia Morris for her *Edith Kermit Roosevelt: Portrait of a First Lady*—"[Edith] knew that someday, somehow, she would marry Theodore Roosevelt."[1]

The encounter must have launched a flutter in Edith's heart, an anxious anticipation as her premonition of marriage suddenly seemed possible once more. And yet this ecstatic moment might also have been tempered by the consciousness of having once been a first choice but now a second. "[Edith] always resented being the second choice and she never really forgave him his first marriage," Alice the daughter later observed.[2] As for Theodore's emotions, Edmund Morris imagines that Edith appeared to him as "alarmingly attractive as he had feared—even more so, perhaps, for she had matured into complex and exciting womanhood. He could not resist her."[3]

Quite possibly, as Morris further speculates, "Nor could Edith resist him." Morris accurately portrays the post-Badlands incarnation of Roosevelt as "unrecognizably different from the Teedie she knew as a child, or the Teddy of more recent years. He was a mahogany-brown stranger, slim of leg and forearm, inclining to burliness about the head and shoulders. Most changed of all was the bull-like neck, heavy with muscle and bulging out of his city collar as if about to pop its studs."[4]

TR continued to flirt with Edith after the apparent finality of the dramatic summer house breakup at Oyster Bay on August 22, 1878. But who could possibly believe that Edith Carow sustained the faith that she would "someday, somehow" marry him even after Theodore wed Alice on October 27, 1880? She certainly behaved as if she hadn't the least trouble accepting the reality of the situation. She attended the ceremony, of course, and after the wedding, she continued to keep company with both Bamie and Conie, attending Conie's debut that December, at which Mittie and Alice were also guests and "Theodore graciously did his duty handing out cigars to all and sundry."[5] Edith made the effort to ensure that she would not show up unescorted—though it is telling that the identity of her companion for the evening is unknown or, at least, unremembered. Likely, he meant little to her, and everyone around her knew that. No one took notice of the young man, whoever he was.

The fact was that Edith Carow, to all appearances having forever lost the opportunity to marry Theodore Roosevelt, had no backup plan, no alternative suitors waiting in the wings. In the United States in 1870–1880, the median age at first marriage for native-born white women was between twenty-one and twenty-two.[6] At twenty-four and without any prospects at least publicly in the offing, she was, in the eyes of upper-crust Victorian New York "society," likely into her preamble to spinsterhood. This was bad enough, but her situation was not only in social jeopardy. Her father's business continued to suffer, assailed both by the prevailing economy and his own lack of acumen and enthusiasm. Without a fortune, her marital prospects further dimmed even as marriage became a more pressing priority if only on the grounds of her increasing financial need. Various members of the extended Carow clan had reason to believe that Edith was sorely tempted to make a loveless match to any reasonably acceptable well-heeled or even adequately heeled suitor. But, in the end, it seems she took no steps to act on this impulse. Was she secretly holding out for Theodore? More likely, her strength of character kept her from making a loveless marriage strictly for the sake of financial security—and it did take strength of character. Unlike the Roosevelt women, Edith did not have a large family endowment to count on. Single women dominated the white female labor force in late-nineteenth-century America, but their career prospects were severely limited, as was their earning potential, which was often pegged to piecework.[7]

Those intimate with the Roosevelt-Carow circle were likely surprised that Teedie and Edie split up, for it was taken virtually for granted that the two were childhood sweethearts destined for one another. Yet when he married Alice Lee instead, who could have been shocked? She appeared to be the model wife for a young politician on the rise. She was charming, attractive, and, not least of all, loving. There was no reason to suspect that trouble was on the horizon.

Life expectancy in mid-nineteenth-century America was just over thirty-nine years. The five leading causes of death were pneumonia, tuberculosis, diarrhea (with which young Roosevelt was chronically afflicted), enteritis (intractable inflammation of the small intestine, usually from infection), and diphtheria. Death in the prime of life or even in youth was far from unusual.[8] But no one could have foreseen that "Sunshine" would die at twenty-two.

To all appearances, "Sunshine" was as vibrant, glowing, and outgoing as her nickname. And, as Edith well knew, she was just one week older than Edith herself. Nevertheless, brought up in the Episcopal Church, surely Edith Carow was familiar with the often quoted line from the funeral rites inscribed in the Anglican Book of Common Prayer: "In the midst of life we are in death." Even a young woman in the early prime of life could die.

Roosevelt wrote two memorials after his wife and his mother died. One he had privately published. The other he committed to his diary: "For joy or for sorrow, my life has now been lived out."[9] Edith, of course, did not see this private remark, but she could see his profound "cataleptic" despair. Perhaps she really did know "that someday, somehow, she would marry Theodore Roosevelt." In one respect, Alice's sudden, shocking death breathed a certain reality into Edith's conviction, and yet she may have wondered if Roosevelt's grief left any room for her. He was not affecting some version of Victorian melodrama or even manifesting the resignation of that most Victorian of poets, Tennyson: "'Tis better to have loved and lost than never to have loved at all." There can be no doubt that Roosevelt felt hollowed out, and we know that, after Alice's death, he went out of his way to avoid anything like a private meeting with Edith, succeeding in this effort for some nineteen months. He told Bamie to warn him if Edith came to call at the house he shared with her. He wanted to ensure that he would be absent.[10]

There is both a personal and cultural context for this avoidance. In the opening of *The Rise of Theodore Roosevelt*, Edmund Morris quotes Edith Wharton, who remarked of President Roosevelt, "I do delight in him." Indeed, she likened the memory of every encounter with TR to the glow of "a tiny morsel of radium." Another woman noted that, in his presence, the "world seemed blotted out" as she was "enveloped in an atmosphere of warmth and kindly consideration" that made her feel she was "the sole object of his interest and concern." As Morris describes a reception at which President Roosevelt shakes many hundreds of hands,

including those of adoring ladies, he notes that the man showed no indication of reciprocating any possible sexual interest: "in matters of morality he is as prudish as a dowager."[11] True, he was anything but prudish in
his intimacy with Alice, yet even this experience and acknowledgment
of intense sexual passion did not overshadow in him Victorian concepts
of romantic love between husband and wife. It had been some nineteen months since Alice was committed to the Roosevelt family tomb
at Green-Wood Cemetery alongside TR's mother, but by the standards
of "polite" New York society, any romantic involvement now could be
something of a scandal. The example of Queen Victoria herself was a
full three years of "deep mourning" for a spouse, signified by the wearing
of unadorned black. Theodore's feelings on the matter were even more
severe. He would later write to Bamie, "I utterly disbelieve in and disapprove of second marriages; I have always considered that they argued
weakness in a man's character."[12] It would not do to invite love back into
his life, not now and not ever.

But Edith's abiding stoicism was more formidable than even Theodore's irresistible force of will.

It is undeniable that Alice and Edith were different from one another,
perhaps even as different as day and night. If Alice was Sunshine, Edith
was a cloudy day—sunlight occluded by a series of storms. Certainly,
Edith's presentation to the world was darker, as was evident in the poetry she composed as a member of P.O.R.E., the literary club Conie had
founded as a teen. "My Dream Castles" (Chapter 2), about the secret
place deep within her, where she immures her deepest hurts and shame,
was written little more than three years before Theodore and Alice announced their engagement. Surely, Edith must have been disappointed
by that news, but she never showed it—or at least she seems to have
poured out her heart to no one. Instead, she locked it away deep within
her Dream Castle.

When the now married Theodore won election to the New York
State Assembly in November 1881, Edith threw a large party to celebrate

yet another victory for the sweetheart no longer hers. Eighteen months later, she was one of eight bridesmaids in attendance at the wedding of Corinne Roosevelt to Douglas Robinson. She wrote to Conie afterward about how, during the ceremony, she "kept realizing that you were leaving your old life behind, and if we live to be ninety years old we can never be two girls together again."[13] Conie's was precisely the kind of marriage of convenience that Edith spurned, and we have to wonder, considering that it was well known among the family and most intimate friends such as Edith that Conie did not wish to marry Douglas, if her remark about how "we can never be two girls together again" was in some part motivated by her disapproval.[14]

No Dream Castle was sufficiently strong or sufficiently remote to hide the fact that loss was rapidly emerging as the resounding keynote of Edith Carow's young life. One day, her father, his business long in decline and his alcoholism taking its relentless toll, fell into the hold of one of his own merchant vessels. According to family lore, he was never well—emotionally or physically—after that.[15] In March 1883, fifty-eight-year-old Charles Carow collapsed. He lingered between life and death for a full week, each minute consumed by his efforts simply to catch his breath. At last, on March 17, he died, the physicians ascribing his demise to pericarditis (cardiac inflammation), pneumonia, and "asthenia" (generalized debility). Unmentioned was the self-evident fact that these were all the effects of chronic alcoholism.

Carow's funeral was held at St. Mark's Church in-the-Bowery on March 20. Conie, eight months into pregnancy, did not attend, and Theodore, too busy with the Assembly in Albany, begged off, deputizing Alice to represent the Roosevelts. Edith was forced to decline an invitation to Alva Vanderbilt's "Ball of the Century," where she was to have danced the Star Quadrille in what would have been the premier event of her inexorably shrinking social life.

The companions of her youth moved on without her. Conie gave birth to Theodore Douglas in April, and the very next month Alice conceived what she and her husband planned as the first of many children. In

June, Elliott Roosevelt became "unofficially" engaged to Anna Rebecca Hall, eventually producing their justly celebrated offspring, Eleanor. Edith attended their December 1 wedding. All that was left now was the highly anticipated birth of Theodore and Alice's first child, which, Theodore was convinced, would come on Valentine's Day.

Edith stood by, observing it all, a passing parade in which she did not march. As she watched, perhaps she contemplated her own future as that most forlorn of all Victorian stereotypes: spinster. In her way, she was as definitively alone as the widower Roosevelt himself. Both had loved and lost, and neither, it seemed, could envision a future state in which that loss was replaced by another love.

So much in any life is mysterious, but the disruption of the relationship between Theodore and Edith may have had a straightforward cause. When he was nineteen and she was seventeen, Roosevelt seems to have taken Edith for granted. After all, she had always been there and, it must have seemed to him, would always be there. She was not elusive prey, hardly as exotic a species as Alice. In their youth, Teedie treated Edie as very nearly another sister, and it may have been a hard turn to lover. Many a splendid match envisioned by family and friends never blossoms into love because the familiarity between the couple is simply *too* strong. Not to mention that Edith was moody and prone to darkness, qualities less attractive than brilliant sunshine to a lustful nineteen-year-old youth. Edith's stepdaughter called it a "withdrawn, rather parched quality."[16]

Yet Theodore and Edith knew one another, intimately. There is a familiarity in first love. They had grown apart but grown up together. To a man, especially one who has suffered staggering loss, the familiarity that once worked against Edith now worked in her favor. There was a comfort in finding one another again, a sense of belonging they each and both desperately needed. Now, with the intervening passage of time marked by tragedy, Theodore could look at Edith not as a playmate, a child, a sister, or a crush, but as a woman who had lived a life in its way every bit as strenuous as his. Maybe even harsher, harder.

In a speech Roosevelt would deliver to the Hamilton Club in Chicago on April 10, 1899, he coined one of his most famous phrases. "I wish to preach, not the doctrine of ignoble ease," he proclaimed, "but the doctrine of the strenuous life."[17] The man Edith met in Bamie's hallway was not the same young man she had last seen sitting ashen-faced, bewildered, and dumbstruck in the front pew of a double funeral at Fifth Avenue Presbyterian. What she now beheld was a figure hardened by nineteen months on the prairie. Theodore Roosevelt had gained almost twenty-five pounds of pure muscle, his shoulders broadened, arms nearly protruding from his sleeves. Even his affected speech had been transformed. In the State Assembly, colleagues had gleefully mimicked the piercing falsetto with which he claimed the attention of the Chair: "Mistah Speeeakahhh!" Now his voice was deeper and flatter, his cadences more measured. In pace and pronunciation, he spoke more like a Midwesterner and less like one born into the height of Knickerbocker society.

"Born mature," as childhood friends said of her, Edith Carow was now characterized by a maturity deepened by the events of her life. In her quiet way, she had lived in the space of a very few years an entire lifetime of hardship over which a thin veneer of what Victorian Americans called shabby gentility was applied. Hers was the surface of a privileged life hollowed out by loss. Young Edith Carow had also lived a strenuous life, at least in an emotional sense. Yet she underwent no dramatic physical transformation. In a muted manner, she had blossomed. A little less than three years younger than Theodore, Edith was by physical nature angular and slender. In the opinion of some, these features had marked her as awkward in her teenage years but had since grown into themselves. Her thick, dark hair lessened the impression of an overly prominent nose and instead complemented her piercing yet somber eyes.

But these physical changes seemed a natural progression from her youth, and the emotional strain she endured did not transform her stoic, perhaps remote, psychological makeup so much as confirmed it. Born of his father's early urging to build his body, the "strenuous life" had transformed young Roosevelt from sickly child to strapping young man.

Edith's version of a strenuous life had merely deepened the introspection that had marked her as wise and perhaps wearied beyond her years.

Neither Teedie nor Edie—neither Thee nor Edith—recorded their emotions upon their surprise meeting in early October 1885. If they confided in others, those others never stepped forward to share those confidences. We do not even know what they said to one another at this meeting, a meeting Roosevelt had taken such pains to avoid. What we do know is that within just forty days of their reunion, they became secretly engaged.

However much Roosevelt believed that a second marriage was morally suspect if not worse, he must have almost immediately begun calling on Edith in the parlor of her house on East 36th Street where she lived with her mother and sister. We know, too, that their initial meetings were private, perhaps even confidential. Before too long, however, he and Edith were seen together in public, though neither signaled to the world any special intimacy. They were, in the weeks and months following their reunion, most discreet. In part, it may have been that they were assessing one another, cautiously feeling to distinguish the painful from the tender. In part, too, they were no longer adolescents. Both had drunk deeply of sorrow, and Roosevelt had tasted marriage to a woman he called his "own sunny faced queen."[18] For him, sexual passion no longer held the urgency of discovery. As for Edith, it seems that no one ever elicited from her the intensity of feeling she reserved for Thee. The fact is that no one in Edith's and Theodore's circles, not Conie or Bamie or anyone else, suspected the rekindling of romance between two people of long acquaintance who clearly and simply enjoyed one another's company.

The first major social event to which Roosevelt invited Edith was the Meadowbrook Hunt Ball, which was held on October 26, at the house he had built in Oyster Bay for himself and Alice. The original name he had given it, Leeholm, was in honor of Alice Lee, but he had recently renamed it Sagamore Hill, borrowing the Algonquin word for chief. The ball took place the evening after the hunt, and if Edith thought Theodore had mellowed at the expense of his sheer physical exuberance, she was very much mistaken. He engaged in the hunt with all the ferocity of a Badlands ranching man and quickly took a hard-riding lead in the chase. After about five miles, his steed fell, rolled over on him, broke his left arm, and made a bloody gash in his face. No matter. With his left arm useless but his right perfectly good, Roosevelt remounted and completed the ten-mile course, jumping five or six fences in the process, oblivious of both his dangling arm and the blood running down his face as he came in no further back than a hundred yards behind the others.

The sight of the bloody figure riding up to the stables horrified Baby Lee. As she screamed and ran, Theodore could not restrain his laughter. After a wash, some bandaging, and the setting and splinting of his arm, which was then suspended in a sling, he played lord of the manor over a tableful of diners, including Edith Carow.

"I don't grudge the broken arm a bit," he wrote to Henry Cabot Lodge. "I'm always ready to pay the piper when I've had a good dance; and every now and then I like to drink the wine of life with brandy in it."[19] Given his hell-for-leather ride during the hunt, Edith could not have been blamed had she assumed he would soon be returning to his ranch. Instead—and this was telling—he decided to remain in the East throughout the winter, for the remainder of the social season. Instead of riding the range, he went to balls, dinners, and operatic performances, venturing out during January and February every other evening, most often squiring Edith. Either those around him were extraordinarily obtuse or the couple did a supremely thorough job of looking like anything but a couple. Fanny Smith, now Fanny Smith Dana, a childhood companion of both Theodore and Edith, remarked that they seemed like brother and sister.[20]

In fact, on November 17, Theodore Roosevelt had proposed marriage to Edith Carow. Based on Edith's own remarks in later life, this may well have been at least his third proposal to her. This time, she accepted. They agreed to keep the engagement a secret. The display of decorum may or may not have been instigated by a guilt-ridden Roosevelt, but it seems to have been thoroughly endorsed by Edith, who treasured her privacy and theirs.

Between them there was an understanding that any correspondence from one to the other would be read and burned. Mostly, the pair must have observed this pact, since almost no letters survive. Edith did keep at least one, however, which she wrote to him seven months into their engagement. "You know I love you very much & would do anything in the world to please you. I wish I could be sure my letters sound as much like myself as yours do like you . . . You know all about me darling, I never could have loved anyone else. I love you with all the passion of a girl who has never loved before & please be patient with me when I cannot put my heart on paper."[21]

Theodore and Edith aimed to keep the engagement secret for at least a full year. But Edith's desire for privacy extended far beyond this. Years later, after thirty-three years of marriage, she audited the family correspondence, seeking to obscure details of their married life. History generally celebrates the second Roosevelt marriage as a union of felicity and fidelity, but one wonders what records or even hints of argument, discord, and even estrangement Edith may have committed to the flames.

By March 1886, the lure of Elkhorn Ranch at last became too strong for Theodore Roosevelt to resist. He thought of his cattle as his "backwoods babies"[22] and grew concerned that his hired men, Bill Sewall and Will Dow, might lack the stomach to endure any more of a Badlands winter without his presence to buck them up. Edith did not protest his departure. Under the pressure of the Carows' increasingly straitened finances, she had planned to accompany her mother and sister on an extended European sojourn, thus consolidating living expenses and selling off domestic assets. It was a bold, even daring decision on her part. For one thing, it demonstrated just how determined she was to maintain the secrecy of their engagement. Instead of trying to dissuade him from going out west, she decided to put even more distance between them. They would be separated not only by thousands of miles of mountains and prairies but also by thousands of miles of ocean. Perhaps she intended this as a test in response to his manifest ambivalence. Theodore had continued to share with her lingering feelings of guilt over his betrayal of the sacred memory of Alice. If he was still willing to go through with the wedding, he could, come next winter, take ship for London and marry her there.

Spring became summer, and on July 4, Roosevelt accepted an invitation to deliver an address in the little town of Dickinson, in what was then the territory of Dakota, to celebrate the 110th anniversary of American independence. He told his audience, perhaps a hundred or more people, "I am, myself, at heart as much a Westerner as an Easterner," and there was ample evidence of his emotional recovery in the buoyancy and optimism of his words: "Like all Americans, I like big things; big parades, big forests and mountains, big wheat fields, railroads—and herds of cattle too; big factories, steamboats, and everything else."[23] Theodore Roosevelt wanted a big, important life, beyond the plains and broken lands that both challenged and healed his body and soul.

After Theodore Roosevelt addressed the citizens of Dickinson, he told local newspaper editor Arthur Packard that he had been offered the post of president of the New York City Board of Health. When Packard (almost preposterously) replied that the job would lead him to the presidency of the nation, TR never thought to demur. "If your prophecy comes true," he told the editor, "I will do my part to make a good one."[24]

Though Edith likely would have considered living in Medora (and later, when under financial constraints, did), Roosevelt felt himself destined for big things. He would seize on opportunities, whether the Badlands or back east, and by force of will, he was confident he could grow them into the greatest American opportunity of all. A believer in his nation's Manifest Destiny, he applied that belief to himself. And so he confidently declined an offer from Endicott Peabody to teach at Groton.[25] He would instead seize the post of czar over the health of New Yorkers and begin fulfilling the frontier newspaperman's prophecy. The role had no obvious route to the presidency, but it would permit him to address issues of public hygiene that had a direct bearing on communicable diseases, such as the typhoid that had claimed his mother.

But no sooner did he arrive in New York than he learned that the job never really had been his for the taking. The current commissioner of public health refused to step down. TR made the best of the now unnecessary trip east by devoting three weeks in the Astor Library to research his next literary project, a biography of Missouri senator Thomas Hart Benton, commissioned from him by Houghton, Mifflin and Company for its "American Statesmen" series. Few fledgling authors refuse a commission, and, as a legendary senator from a frontier state, Benton was a larger-than-life politician who was also a man of the West. After his time in the library, Roosevelt returned to the Badlands. Arriving in Medora on August 5, he found an accumulated pile of letters from Edith. In one, she informed him that she had set their wedding for December in London. So much for determining his own course.

His political passion reawakened, so, too, was his sexual longing. That August, Patty Selmes, a Kentucky-born resident of Mandan, due east of Medora and across the Missouri River from Bismarck, caught Roosevelt's eye and mind. Patty had been living with her attorney father in St. Paul, Minnesota, when she met and married Yale graduate Tilden Selmes, who had moved west from Massachusetts in the early 1880s. In 1883, Tilden and Patty continued west to Mandan, where he became president of First National Bank and an attorney for the Northern Pacific Railroad.

TR wrote Bamie on August 11 from the Selmeses' home in Mandan, where he was trying to solve some matter to do with "boat thieves":

Do you remember "those two nice Kentucky girls"? Well, I met the husband of one of them, Selmes by name, and he insisted upon my at once taking up my abode with them; for they have a little house on the outskirts of Mandan, as well as the ranch. I have had a really charming time.... Mrs. Selmes is really to my mind a singularly attractive woman. She is, I think, very handsome, though not with regular features; and, as Madame de Mores, says she is very "seduisante"—like most Kentucky girls. She is very well read, has a delicious sense of humor, and is extremely fond of poetry—including that of my new favorite Browning.[26]

A "well read" woman with a "delicious sense of humor" who is "extremely fond of poetry" could well describe Edith, too. That he details to Bamie his attraction to this "seduisante" Kentucky girl is very nearly a confession of his secret engagement to Edith. To add to the intrigue, Patty recently returned from Kentucky, where she gave birth to her only child, Isabella Dinsmore Selmes, in March. Theodore held and played with baby Isabella in a home that must have made him think not only of his future life with Edith but also Alice, now almost two and a half. Roosevelt returned to Mandan a week later, and again stayed with the Selmeses. So close did Roosevelt and Patty become so quickly that TR confided to her his secret engagement. "I hope that [Edith] is all that is lovely," Patty wrote to her sister Julia. "He is one of the nicest men I ever knew."[27]

The serendipitous signs of domesticity were not limited to Mandan. That summer both Mary Sewall and Lizzie Dow gave birth. Mary's labor was difficult and, as historian Rolf Sletten described, "tragedy was averted only when Wilmot Dow stepped in to assist her. Dow had no experience with childbirth but he had a great deal of experience working with animals and had picked up enough practical experience to save both mother and child."[28]

Bill Sewall, a better woodsman than narrator, wrote his brother about the birth, amidst a longer commentary on cattle: "Firstly, on the morning of [August] 5th, Mary and I had a son born. He came like an Irishman's elephant but did not strike hard enough to knock his brains out and we hope he has shifted ends. He now weights seven pounds. Mary is nicely this afternoon and I think she is all right. I did not tell you before how many cattle we had. We put on 250 cows." The nonchalance might well have been a cowboy coping mechanism. In his memoirs, Sewall wrote, "My wife was terribly sick" but blessedly her "time had not come."[29] When, just one week later, Lizzie Dow gave birth to a son, "Bill Sewall went to work building a cradle large enough to hold both infants."[30]

There is no record of Roosevelt being present for either birth, the first eerily evoking the loss of Alice. He retreated to the Maltese Cross, and then on to Mandan with the Selmeses. When TR *was* present at

Elkhorn, he wasn't charmed by its sudden transformation. "The population of my ranch is increasing in a rather alarming manner," Roosevelt wrote Bamie. Two years into Theodore's sojourn west, the quiet respite of the Elkhorn Ranch became a veritable day care. Edmund Morris observes: "The squalling of these two new arrivals, not to mention the jam-smeared face of little Kitty Sewall, and Elkhorn's growing air of alien domesticity, seemed to emphasize his bachelor status and growing sense of misplacement. It was as if the house were no longer his own."[31]

Domesticity beckoning, there was only one thing left to do: hunt. Toward the end of August, he set off on an expedition in company with fellow widower and Maltese Cross ranch hand Bill Merrifield. On his return to Medora on September 18, Roosevelt perused *The New York Times* to catch up on what he had missed during the expedition. What he had missed was a gossipy report of his engagement to Edith Carow!

Bamie, without consulting Theodore, "rushed to place a sharply worded denial in the newspaper, noting that 'nothing is more common in society than to hear positive assertions constantly made regarding the engagement of persons who have been at all in each other's company, and no practice is more reprehensible.'" But the news was true. So sure was she that "her brother kept no secrets from her," she had not bothered to check with him.[32] Who leaked the story remains unknown, but a prime suspect is Aunt Anna Gracie, who had years earlier hosted a party in her East 34th Street home, where (she later reported) Teedie and Edie had a "cosy chat" in her dimly lit morning room.[33] With the cat out of the bag, Theodore had no choice but to write to Bamie. He delivered his news as swiftly as one might pull a painful splinter from one's finger: "I am engaged to Edith and before Christmas I shall cross the ocean and marry her. You are the first person to whom I have breathed a word on this subject." He then scourges himself for even contemplating let alone going through with the impending second marriage:

I utterly disbelieve in and disapprove of second marriages; I have always considered that they argued weakness in a man's character. You

could not reproach me one half as bitterly for my inconstancy and un-
faithfulness as I reproach myself. Were I sure there was a heaven my one
prayer would be I might never go there, lest I should meet those I loved
on earth who are dead.[34]

Similar sentiment can be found in any number of Victorian novels,
but its vehemence seems entirely genuine coming from Roosevelt. He
pleaded with Bamie "not to visit my sins upon poor little Edith." (This is
quite likely the only time he described *Edith* as "little.") The marriage, he
wrote, "is certainly not her fault; the entire blame rests on my shoulders."
He went on to acknowledge—but not, in fact, explain—his August 22,
1878, breakup with Edith, noting, "we both of us had, and I suppose have,
tempers that were far from being the best."[35] Painfully aware that the
marriage would upend Bamie's household, he essentially offered her Baby
Lee as something between a ward and a consolation prize.[36]

Later, after he arrived in London in the days before the wedding,
Roosevelt wrote an oddly effusive letter to his younger sister, Conie, in
which he noted: "I don't think even I had known how wonderfully good
and unselfish [Edith] was; she is naturally reserved and finds it especially
hard to express her feelings on paper."[37] Clearly, he felt the need to justify to both sisters this second marriage, especially marriage to Edie.
Whether the justification was directed more toward Conie or himself, it
is impossible to say. As abject as both letters were, they also embodied an
unabashed resolution to start a new life with a new wife from the halcyon
days of youth, when "Greatheart" and Mittie were still living, the Roosevelt children were all together, with Edie, and Alice Hathaway Lee had
yet to enter and prematurely exit this golden world. Together with Edith
and his sisters, TR had assembled the team who would guide his future
for the next several decades and craft his legacy.

"London is perfectly lovely now, everything is so bright and gay," Edith
wrote Theodore on June 8. "I do care about being pretty for you, and
every girl I see I think 'I wonder if I am as pretty as she is' or 'At any

rate I am not quite as ugly as that girl.'" Edith bared her soul, writing as desperately and guilelessly as a lovelorn adolescent. On the verge of spinsterhood, Edith became Edie again. She requested a photo of TR in his "hunting costume" and pleaded, "You must take me out west, or I shall repent all my life not having seen the place my dearest is so fond of. . . . I perfectly love your description of the life out west for I almost feel as if I could see you and know just what you are doing, and I do not think you sentimental in the least to love nature; please love me too and believe I think of you all the time and want so much to see you."[38]

Edith hoped TR would love her as much as he loved the Badlands, he loved nature, and perhaps though it went unsaid, as much as he loved Alice, too. The run-up to the wedding was fraught with emotional and financial stress. Roosevelt's ranching venture was faltering after a brutal winter. Adding to his burden, Sewall and Dow, having been unable to sell the fall beeves at a profit, announced that they wanted to end their contract and return to Maine. TR had grown close to Bill Sewall and Wilmot Dow, with whom he spent countless hours at the Elkhorn, yet he did not protest their planned departure. His plan now was to consolidate his herds at Elkhorn under Merrifield and Ferris. On October 9, Roosevelt left for New York.

Gotham's cowboy reached New York City in time for the Republican County Convention on October 15. Party leaders offered to nominate him as the GOP candidate for mayor of New York City, which came as a surprise, but a welcome one. Roosevelt accepted. On October 23, Bamie wrote the bride-to-be, Edith, who was waiting in Europe: "It is such happiness to see him at this best once more. Ever since he has been out of politics in any active form it has been a real heart-sorrow to me, for while he always made more of his life than any other man I know, still with his strong nature it was a permanent source of poignant regret that even at his early age, he should lose these years without the possibility of doing his best & most telling work." Bamie was as much telling Edith as informing her: Theodore will have a life in politics, and you ought to accept reality now, before you get married. In a rare moment of introspection (at least one preserved for history), Bamie confessed to her future sister-in-law: "Theodore is the only person who had the power (except Father who possessed it in a different way) of making me almost worship him ... I would never say, or, write this except to you, but it is very restful to feel how you care for him and how happy he is in his devotion to you."[39]

Bamie knew that victory was a very long shot, but her brother was back in the arena. "Never mind what the results," Bamie wrote Edith. "Theodore writes you of everything, still you will wish to hear what I long to write, of the wonderful enthusiasms he certainly inspires ... surely, in this case the latter to a great extent is the victory."[40] Henry George, the influential economist who proposed reducing taxation to a "single tax" on absentee, speculative landlords, was running on the United Labor Party ticket, and Roosevelt believed that George, whose views were extreme, would drive many voters to cast their ballot for the Democratic candidate, Abram Hewitt, a spoilsman between the United Labor Party on the left and the GOP on the right. Still, TR campaigned vigorously on a broad reform platform for the office but was defeated nevertheless on November 2, coming in not second to Hewitt, but third, behind third-party candidate George. After his failure to be voted Speaker of the New York Assembly, the mayoralty was the second of the three offices TR sought and lost in his lifetime. Remarkably, after the death of Alice, he would not hold an elected office for fifteen years.

Four days after the defeat, a "Mr. and Mrs. Merrifield" boarded the Cunard steamship RMS *Etruria* bound for Liverpool and an important wedding in London. The passengers were, in fact, brother and sister Theodore and Anna Roosevelt—Thee and Bamie. As if this tangentially incestuous charade were not sufficiently surreal, a young Englishman, Cecil Arthur Spring-Rice—"Springy" to his friends—had somehow discovered in advance that the two Roosevelts were taking the *Etruria*. He booked passage for himself and, also somehow, obtained a letter of introduction to Bamie. A man uncannily charming to both sexes, Springy introduced himself to the "Merrifields" on day two of the voyage out. His letter of introduction at the ready, he inquired of Bamie whether she might not be Miss Roosevelt. Well out from the New York shore, she cordially confessed, and an extraordinary shipboard friendship blossomed. As *Etruria* neared Liverpool on November 13, Theodore—impulsively, it would seem—recruited Springy to be his best man. It was just the sort of thing the impulsive Mittie might have done.

It turned out that Spring-Rice was no social climber. Quite the contrary, he was a congenital diplomat on the verge of a formal career in the British Foreign Office, and he gave Theodore Roosevelt instant entrée into the most exclusive London clubs, where TR made acquaintance with intellectuals, politicians, dukes, and lords. He even cadged an invitation to ride to the hounds.

But all that would await his meeting with Edith, who was staying at the Buckland's Hotel in Mayfair. He had decorously booked a suite for himself at the nearby Brown's. It was to these quarters that Edith repaired to free herself from the scrutiny of her mother and her sister, Emily. She and Thee had intimate conversations in his suite, having been given the time for this by Bamie, who lingered in Liverpool to visit the Bulloch relatives, including her uncles living there in permanent unreconstructed Confederate exile. Soon enough, however, she arrived in London, followed shortly afterward by Springy. It is a testament to the power of his charm that even Edith, austere as she often seemed, was quite taken by him.

And then, the atmosphere of the surreal reentered. Thursday, December 2, dawned amid a thick fog, impenetrable even by the standards of nineteenth-century coal-fired London. So dense was it that Bamie had to be led to the Buckland's by "link bearers," guide boys equipped with torches (called links). In Edie's suite, Bamie helped the bride arrange her gown. She undoubtedly experienced that morning with mixed emotions—Bamie and Conie were keen to see their brother get on with his life and return to politics. But they also knew from their many years together that the strong-willed Edith would displace, if not replace, their influence. Alice later contended that her aunts had been "rather concerned" by her father's second engagement as they "feared [Edith] would come between [TR] and the family."[41] Eleanor Roosevelt found Edith "quite extraordinary" but similarly acknowledged a strained pull for Theodore's attention that had not existed in his first marriage: "There were times, I think, when she would be annoyed with Auntie Bye—I think even Auntie Corinne, though not for quite the same reasons."[42]

While Edith dressed, best man Spring-Rice fetched Theodore at Brown's, stopping the cab en route to St. George's Church, Hanover Square, to purchase from his favorite haberdasher a pair of bright orange kid gloves for the bridegroom. This served to make Roosevelt the most luminous object in a fog that crept even into the church itself. What prompted Springy to go out of his way to gift his friend with such outlandish gloves? Remarkably, Edith's wedding corsage has been preserved by the National Park Service at Sagamore Hill. The arrangement is—orange.

The Anglican ceremony, presided over by the Canon of York, Charles E. Camidge, was intimate and brief. Emily and Spring-Rice signed the parish register as witnesses and then made way for the new Mr. and Mrs. Roosevelt to enter their names. In the register's line asking the signatories to describe their age and station, Thee called himself a "widower of twenty-eight" and listed his profession as "ranchman." Edith wrote that she was "twenty-five," a "spinster with no profession."[43] Were their tongues in their cheeks, or were they in earnest? In the Dakotas, some four thousand miles west of St. George's, the *Badlands Cowboy* published an announcement of the marriage rife with extravagant errors, which, one can only hope, must have afforded the couple and their circle more than a little amusement:

> While Mr. Theo. Roosevelt has gone to England to get him a wife, it is an American lady whom he is to marry. His prospective bride is just nineteen years old and is the youngest daughter of Governor Carroll of Maryland, a family famous for its wealth and blue blood. Her sister recently married an English nobleman. It is there that Miss Carroll is staying. The young lady is a grandchild of the late Royal Phelps and entered New York society about five years ago. Mr. Roosevelt is about thirty years old and has been a widower for two years. He is very wealthy.[44]

On their honeymoon, which began directly after the wedding, Theodore gave Edith something he had never given Alice—his undivided attention. On his first European honeymoon, Roosevelt left his bride to climb the Matterhorn. When Thee and Edie crossed the Channel to Paris, Lyon, and Marseilles, basking in midwinter on the balmy Mediterranean coast at Hyères in Provence, they did it all alone together. Thee even took time to write to Bamie a letter as different from his earlier self-castigating missive as sunshine is from darkest night. "It is delightful to idle one's days here with a clear conscience, for the time is all our own this winter and is to be spent for nothing else" than being together in a journey by private carriage down the French Riviera to the Italian Riviera town of Portovenere overlooking the Golfo dei Poeti (Gulf of Poets). Here, quite likely, their first child, Theodore Roosevelt Jr. (Ted), was conceived.

Consigned to spinsterhood by all who knew her, Edith was now on her way to becoming one of the august matriarchs of modern American history. In addition to Theodore Jr. (1887), there would be Kermit (1889), Ethel (1891), Archibald (1894), and Quentin (1897)—five live births and two, perhaps more, miscarriages—a total of seven pregnancies over the next fifteen years.

Edith also became stepmother to "Baby Lee," as Theodore still called her. Bamie had been raising Alice from birth and doing so as a single mother at that. Her brother had, in effect, given the child to her, but now, as his European honeymoon continued in Florence, a discordant note sounded. When he discussed the matter of Alice with Edith, his bride insisted that she be raised under their roof. She would not have her husband visiting her stepdaughter in the apartment of another woman, even her sister-in-law, who assuredly would have preferred to keep the child she had raised as her own. "Remember, darling," Alice later recalled Bamie telling her as a child, "if you are very unhappy you can always come back to me." Alice remembered that Bamie could be "really rather possessive about me and could be quite tough with my father on the subject . . . she protected me from my father with his guilt fetish, and from my stepmother, and even from myself."[45]

Thee did not put up a fight but wrote to Bamie from Florence: "I hardly know what to say about Baby Lee. Edith feels more strongly about her than I could have imagined possible." He waffled: "However, we can decide it all when we meet."[46] Edith's will would win out. "The only person I ever knew [Bamie] to be a little bit afraid of was [Edith]," observed Helen Roosevelt Robinson, wife of Conie's son, Theodore Douglas Robinson. "Both [Bamie] and [Conie] were a little bit afraid of her, which always amused me because they weren't afraid of anybody, ever; except that there was a little feeling about [Edith]. In other words, they were watching their p's and q's a little bit when they were with her . . . just that little feeling of watching their step a little bit."[47]

Margaret Chanler, a Washington neighbor and close friend of the Roosevelts, observed much the same: "[Edith] looked on the changing aspects of existence with a detached, intelligent curiosity; her warmth and passion lay far beneath the surface. One felt in her a great strength of character, and ineluctable will power. We used to think that Theodore, whom she adored, was a little afraid of his Edie."[48]

Edith began as a bonus sister, increasingly sidelined from society as her hapless father mismanaged the family business, the family fortune dwindled, and she fell out with Theodore. Now, however, the dynamics between the women had shifted, dramatically and permanently, in Edie's favor. She was no longer the childhood sweetheart and family outsider. She was Roosevelt's wife, pregnant with one child, and with a claim on the baby girl Bamie and Aunt Anna had cherished. Did Edith want to possess all her husband's progeny? Or was she looking to make a broken family whole?

Growing up, Edith had experienced something very close to penury, and she was painfully aware that her husband, though hardly poor, came up far short compared to the average Gilded Age tycoon. She also understood that her husband enjoyed living large and, for all his skills, was not good with money. "All my money will be turned over to Edith," TR told Bamie in a letter shortly after he wed Edith. "And I will draw from her what I need."[49] Edith therefore kept tight fingers on the purse strings and close watch on outflows.

TR permitted Edith to exert power over him—it was she who insisted on creating a blended family and personally managing the family's finances. The love between them was born of passion and respect. Theirs would be a marriage of equals. It was a power he never fully granted to Alice or Bamie or Conie—perhaps because Edith was the only one who demanded it.

Yet what, exactly, had Edith gained?

Theodore Roosevelt was a politician out of office. The promise of an appointment to lead the New York Board of Health had evaporated, and nomination as the Republican candidate for mayor resulted in ignominious defeat. Just after New Year's 1887, when Edith's mother and sister, Emily, arrived in Florence, Theodore began receiving news of climate catastrophe in the Badlands. Snow and temperatures tens of degrees below zero deprived cattle in the region of fodder. The prairie was covered to a depth of four feet and more of alternating layers of snow and ice. In low ground, cattle were sometimes buried alive. Fresh snow fell upon the frozen stuff and blew in the blizzard winds, so that the snow appeared to be so many waves, separated by weird violet-tinged shadows. Dakotans called it the Winter of the Blue Snow.

Reading the reports, Roosevelt began to think that he might have to close or even sell his new Oyster Bay home to attend to his ranch full-time for the next year or two, presumably bringing Edith with him. The cattle losses, he correctly assumed, must be horrific. Driven in part by a desire to do something about raising money, he at last allowed work to intrude upon the honeymoon. With a mixture of desperation and genuine pleasure, he worked at a half dozen long and lucrative articles for *Century* magazine, with an eye toward their forming the core of a book to be titled *Ranch Life and the Hunting Trail*. If Edith was upset by his time out for literary work, she did not show it. A woman with proven literary talent herself, she enjoyed Theodore's reading the pieces aloud to her as he finished each, and she contributed what he characterized as "most valuable" literary criticism and advice.[50] Doubtless, this was a sincere evaluation. It was Conie who had instigated the founding of the P.O.R.E. literary society when she had returned from the family's Dresden sojourn in 1873, but it was Edith who became its star author with youthful verse that was anything but juvenile. That she did not become a writer as an adult may be genuinely regrettable, but it also suggests that, married at last, she no longer had a need to put her pent-up emotions into words.

He was in many ways her alpha and omega. Bamie had explained to Alice Lee the close-knit bonds that existed between TR and his sisters. Accordingly, when her husband came home in the afternoon, Alice would call upstairs to Bamie and the rest of the family, "Teddy is here; come and share him."[51] Neither such words nor such a sentiment would ever issue from Edith. Edith saw him as destined to be a public man, and she was willing to see him in the context of that world. When he invited the public to shake his hand in front of the White House on January 1, 1907, he set a Guinness world record for "most handshakes by a head of state"—8,513—as Edith stood beside him in the reception line.[52] But in private, she guarded their privacy jealously. She would share him with the other politicians and cultural icons of the nation and the world, but with no other individual. No longer would the cry "Teddy is here; come and share him!" reverberate throughout the Roosevelt household. Bamie and Conie "worshipped [Theodore]," Helen Roosevelt Robinson observed, but "[Edith] was almost the only person who really, in a way, dominated him. He definitely paid a great deal of attention to what she thought and what her opinions were."[53] "Part of her greatness," journalist Mark Sullivan observed, "lay in the quiet check of graciousness and humor she kept upon her husband's slightly reckless exuberance."[54]

The one who most threatened her claim to Thee was dead but hardly gone. Roosevelt himself had conducted an emotional purging against the memory of his first wife, but the anguish he once expressed over what he characterized as a failure of character in having succumbed to a second marriage testifies to the power Alice Hathaway Lee Roosevelt continued to exercise. His letter to Bamie about "idl[ing] one's days here with a clear conscience" suggests he no longer felt his choice to marry Edith was an affront to his first wife's memory. But neither did that mean he had ceased to love her.

The living manifestation of Alice Hathaway Lee was, of course, the child Alice, from whom her father withheld her own name. Ostensibly, the name was too painful a reminder of its original possessor. In fact, it may well be that Roosevelt did not want it to belong to another so that it would always belong to the loved and lost.

Why did Edith desperately want this child in her home? Wasn't her presence a reminder of her mother? Or did Edith realize that bringing the child under the roof she and her husband shared would transform Baby Lee into Alice—not the incarnation of Alice Hathaway Lee but a little girl, Alice Roosevelt, Theodore's daughter and now the daughter as well of his wife, Edith. Did Edith think that to supplant Alice in Theodore's heart and mind, she needed to claim the girl for the new family they would raise together?

The Theodore Roosevelt Alice had married was soon a rapidly rising politician, who was quickly breaking records for legislative productivity in the New York State Assembly. Edith's husband's great expectations dimmed, even as he and his bride continued on their honeymoon from Florence, to Naples, to Pompeii. Thee had visited that extraordinary artifact of natural disaster seventeen years earlier, with his parents and siblings, but found in it now "the charm of almost absolute novelty."[55]

Did he feel a parallel between his precarious position—a politician and public servant with neither office nor portfolio, a rancher whose ranch and cattle were frozen in blue snow as the people of Pompeii were frozen in petrified magma? Whatever his emotions, it is clear that he was nearing a readiness for the honeymoon to end. "I had no idea that it was in me to enjoy the *dolce far niente* even as long as I have. Luckily, Edith would hate an extended stay in Europe as much as I would," he wrote to Conie on January 22.[56] But they still had two months more.

They went back to Rome to bid farewell to Edith's mother, then set off for Venice, which the couple greatly enjoyed. (As who would not?)

Toward the very end of their stay there, Venice was swept by an unusual snowstorm. Edith Roosevelt biographer Sylvia Jukes Morris remarked that it "made the city infinitely more strange and romantic than before."[57] Perhaps. But, again, one wonders if, in this, Roosevelt saw his floundering ranch.

Milan was next, where a copy of TR's just published biography of Thomas Hart Benton reached him. Its effect on him was to incite a desire to write some more substantial—and presumably more profitable—history book. The Roosevelts set off for Paris and then London, from which Thee wrote to Conie, "Edith has been feeling the reverse of brightly for some little time."[58] More heavy-handed than coy, it was his way of telling his sister that his bride was suffering the pangs of morning sickness.

If either Edie or Teedie felt any significant anxiety about their future, it was swept away—or at least held in abeyance—by the climactic event of their honeymoon journey, a meeting with Robert Browning, a poet the couple had loved since they were teenagers together. The encounter overlaid the entire sojourn with a joy that Edith expressed fourteen years later in a letter to her husband: "I love you all the time in my thoughts and think of our honeymoon days, and remember them all one by one, and hour by hour."[59] Are we mistaken to hear in this an echo of Browning's loveliest of love poems, "Two in the Campagna"?

> I wonder do you feel to-day
> As I have felt since, hand in hand,
> We sat down on the grass, to stray
> In spirit better through the land,
> This morn of Rome and May?[60]

The first quarter century of their lives had taught Edith and Theodore that the future was anything but certain. Edith had been beside Theodore in the beginning; now she would be with him until the end.

Martha Bulloch Roosevelt, known as Mittie, was described by her brother as "a black haired bright eyed lassie lively in her disposition and with a ready tongue" who "does everything by impulse and with an air of perfect self-confidence." The phrase could readily apply to her strong-willed son Theodore.

Thee Roosevelt, known as "Greatheart," and his wife were opposites in nearly every way. He was a stern disciplinarian; she was indulgent with a vivacious personality.

3

Born to a life of privilege, Teedie Roosevelt suffered debilitating asthma, which attacked his frail frame with fevers and racking coughs.

4

LINCOLN - FUNERAL The Funeral of President Lincoln, New-York, April 25th, 1865.

Lincoln's funeral procession through New York City traveled up Broadway, passing directly by the home of C.V.S. Roosevelt. A six-year-old Teedie Roosevelt and his younger brother, Elliott, watched from their grandfather's window. When Edie Carow screamed at the sight of disfigured Union soldiers, Teedie and Elliott locked her in a closet.

Edith, seen here at six years old, witnessed the slow-moving failure of her father as a child. The Roosevelts welcomed her without judgment, though she must have felt a pang of jealousy at their marvelous travels and happy home life.

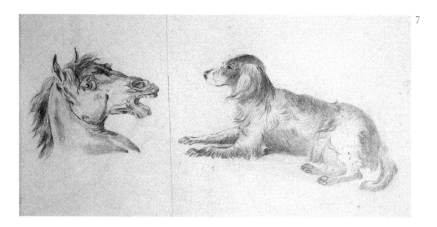

Edith cherished lifelong the watercolors painted by her father, Charles Carow. Though Charles's alcoholism weighed on the family, Edith saved the images he created of gallant horses, faithful companions,and majestic ships.

Conie Roosevelt, Theodore's younger sister, was his sympathetic ear and emotional outlet. While Bamie served as TR's political advisor and strategist, Conie was more empathetic.

Eleanor Roosevelt believed that had Bamie Roosevelt, Theodore's eldest sister, been a man that she, not TR, would have been president.

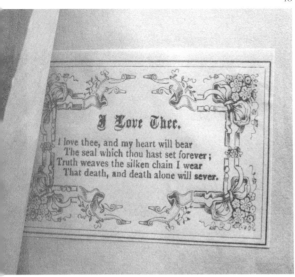

Edie Carow, at age fourteen, kept a scrapbook with her younger sister. In it, the siblings pasted ornate valentines and their favorite poems. Hidden behind a secret compartment, under the title "Joy" and "Sorrow," is a poem titled "I Love Thee."

Theodore (standing, left) stares intently at Elliott (standing, right) with Edie (seated next to Elliott) and Conie (seated on ground) in Oyster Bay. TR, seventeen, was fiercely competitive with his younger brother Elliott, fourteen, who was nearly the same age as Edie. Elliott's attempts to woo Edie from his elder brother were rebuffed. Elliott later married the beautiful but troubled Anna Hall and became the father of Eleanor Roosevelt.

1878 was a consequential year in the life and loves of Theodore Roosevelt. Midway through Harvard, and after the death of his father, Theodore broke up with Edith. Two months later, he met Alice Hathaway Lee.

The only known photograph of Alice Hathaway Roosevelt and her sisters-in-law, Conie and Bamie. To win Alice, Theodore relied on his sisters and mother to charm the Lee family. The three Roosevelt women loved one another and shared the goal of ensuring Theodore's success.

Alice Hathaway Lee was strikingly beautiful. Taller than average at five-foot-eight, Alice had pale blue-gray eyes and dark, golden blonde hair that she often wore coiled. In 1880, she inspired Theodore to pen a full-throated endorsement of women's equality, suffrage, land ownership, and equal pay for equal work.

Teddy, as he was known to Alice, desperately wanted to capture an image known as a tintype of him and Alice together. He plotted for six months to get this photograph, only to have Rose, Alice's cousin, sit between them.

Ever persistent, Teddy managed a second image, this time with Rose standing and he seated next to Alice. She leaned into her cousin but sits erect here, and Teddy's right hand is achingly close to touching Alice's arm.

Athletic and beguiling, Alice Hathaway Lee was nicknamed "Sunshine" because of the vibrancy of her presence. Teddy stares intently at the woman he called "my wayward, willful darling."

One of only three known photographs of the Roosevelt family home at 6 West 57th Street in New York City. TR's prized buffalo head adorns the parlor entrance. "There is a curse on this house! Mother is dying and Alice is dying too!" Elliott Roosevelt exclaimed.

Distraught by the deaths of Alice and Mittie on February 14, 1884, Valentine's Day, Theodore Roosevelt cut a swath of hair from his wife and wrote, "The hair of my sweet wife, Alice, cut after death." The macabre keepsake, along with photos of Alice, was kept hidden from Edith.

20

Theodore slashed his diary with an "X," writing only, "The light has gone out of my life."

Bamie, unmarried and with no children of her own when Alice Hathaway Roosevelt died on the same day as Mittie, quickly swung into action. She sold the home at 6 West 57th, oversaw the construction of Leeholm, which became Sagamore Hill, and took care of Alice for almost three years.

Theodore arrived in Dakota a "dandy," sporting a stylish deerskin hunting suit replete with an engraved knife from Tiffany.

24

Bill Sewall, a Maine woodsman and wilderness guide, helped build the Elkhorn Ranch and lived with Theodore in Dakota. Sewall was fond of poetry and helped TR live what he later called the "strenuous life."

25

Wilmot Dow, Bill Sewall's nephew, joined Theodore and his uncle in the Badlands. Sewall and Dow brought their wives from Maine to join them in Dakota and each gave birth at the Elkhorn.

26

Sylvane Ferris was hired as Theodore's hunting guide during his first trip to the Badlands in 1883. Ferris later ran a general store and caught the eye of Conie, who found him to be "the ideal cowboy of one's wildest fancy."

Alice was the eldest of six Roosevelt children and, of course, the only one not born to Edith. Here Alice is pictured with her siblings just after her sixteenth birthday—sixteen years to the day that she was baptized in Fifth Avenue Presbyterian Church, the site of her mother and grandmother's funeral one day prior.

Theodore Roosevelt was the first president of "the American Century." He was the first president to be in an automobile, airplane, and submarine—and the first to travel abroad while in office.

"Haven't *we* had fun being governor of New York?" TR would say to Conie, his younger sister. The siblings took advantage of the sexism of the age, which allowed Conie to overhear important political discussions and then talk through the options with her brother.

First Lady Edith Kermit Roosevelt read up to five newspapers a day, advised her husband every morning, and regularly sat in on critical White House meetings. "Whenever I go against her judgment, I regret it," TR admitted.

Theodore Roosevelt spoke to an audience of 2,500 women in Spokane, Washington, on September 9, 1912, and said, "The suffrage having been given to you, it is not only your right but your duty to exercise it. You are false to your duty as citizens and women if you fail to register and vote." After the speech, women rushed to register at a site one block from the theater.

33

Critics of Theodore Roosevelt's support for women's suffrage often ridiculed him. Cartoons of the era pictured TR with fanciful plumes or dressed as a woman, a purposeful jab at his carefully crafted hyper-masculine cowboy reputation.

The Progressive Party in 1912 was the first to adopt women's suffrage to its national platform. During TR's presidency (1901–1909) women had the right to vote in four states (Wyoming, Colorado, Utah, and Idaho). By 1912, five more (Washington, California, Arizona, Kansas, and Oregon) had joined the list.

One of the last photographs made of Theodore and Edith Roosevelt together in 1918. Though separated by only three years, Theodore is considerably more aged than Edith, who outlived him by three decades.

Part Four

DESTINY AND
THE REPUBLIC

1887—1901

10

"TWENTY-THREE CROSSINGS AT BREAKNECK SPEED"

"Whenever I go against [Edith's] judgment I regret it."
                                    —Theodore Roosevelt

Theodore Roosevelt was fortunate he was not the only member of his family to enjoy politics. When he and Edith set foot in New York on March 27, 1887, he renewed his friendship with Henry Cabot Lodge, to whom Edith took an instant liking. The two were omnivorous readers and shared a love for literature from the classics to poetry. Perhaps still more important, Edith believed his political influence over her husband would be invaluable. He was just the kind of astute, savvy, and strategically skilled politician-statesman that she sought out to protect and aid her husband. For his part, Lodge, like Roosevelt himself, admired Edith's judgment.

Conie, recognizing as Edith did Lodge's political and philosophical alignment, also "followed [Lodge's] career as avidly as anyone from Massachusetts," historian Betty Boyd Caroli notes. "She clipped newspaper articles on his speeches and sent them to him, and he responded with full manuscripts of his talks . . . he was pleased when she complimented him or recognized the source of some obscure quotation." Though "just how intimate Corinne became with Cabot remains unclear . . . the normally aloof senator did not reveal his emotional side to very many people."[1] Conie's pedestrian marriage to Douglas likely contributed to her need to seek intellectual, but not likely physical, fulfillment elsewhere. Conie, twenty-six years old in 1887, had been married to Douglas for five years. The marriage had by this point produced three of four children but little joy. Conie felt the constraints of her gender in this age more acutely than her older sister. She would, as the years passed and children grew, at first channel her political energy into her brother and, after his passing, carry the torch herself. "Corinne had more poetic fancy [than Bamie] and was brilliantly witty," assessed Margaret Chanler, an author and longtime friend of the Roosevelt family. "No one ever told a better story."[2]

Bamie, like her brother, had been indoctrinated by their father with the value of civic service. Unlike their father, Theodore and Bamie *enjoyed* politics. As siblings their mutual trust was unwavering and unconditional. And the unfortunate constraints of the age meant Bamie had no better vessel than her brother to channel her formidable political intellect and instinct. Chanler summed up Bamie: she was "wise and sympathetic."[3]

The unofficial brain trust—Edith, Conie, Bamie, and Lodge—now set about figuring out the best way to get TR back into politics. Bamie, Conie, Edith, and Lodge all frequently corresponded, and each would play a critical role in the reemergence of Theodore Roosevelt.

But, first, Roosevelt left for his ranch in April to ascertain for himself the impact of the terrible winter. To Bamie, he wrote, "I am bluer than indigo about the cattle. I wish I was sure I would lose no more than half the money ($80,000) I invested out here. I am planning how to get out of it." He would end up selling the cattle, though he kept the ranch itself for another decade or so. To Lodge, he wrote even more frankly: "For the first time I have been utterly unable to enjoy a visit to my ranch. I shall be glad to get home."[4] Eighty thousand 1880s dollars is about $2.25 million today.

The former Teedie and Edie moved to Sagamore Hill in May and threw themselves into the hard work of making the home theirs. Thee set up his intellectual headquarters in the library, with its southern exposure taking in the expanse of Cove Neck with Oyster Bay Cove to the west and Cold Spring Harbor to the east. Edie appropriated the room just across the hall as her personal parlor, complete with favorite books and a writing desk. The dining room down the hall was furnished with the oak table, chairs, and sideboard they had purchased in Florence.

Roosevelt plunged into his next book, a biography of Gouverneur Morris, an early senator from New York and, before that, a signatory of both the Articles of Confederation and the Constitution, to which he authored the Preamble. He was nearly unique among the founding fathers in that he made it a point to present himself *as an American* rather than as a citizen of his home state. He was thus a nationalist among federalists. This fact was key to Roosevelt's own self-conception as well as his sense of what it meant to be an American. Roosevelt had not held political office in five years—and even then, he had been a state legislator—but he was once again presenting himself as someone interested in the national political arena. He completed the new book with his customary alacrity and sent the manuscript to the publisher early in September. Edith was in the late stages of her first pregnancy, and the imminence of labor was apparent. The emotional stress of anticipation triggered a severe asthma attack that seized her husband. Almost certainly, echoes of Alice's fate reverberated in TR's memory as Edith's delivery neared. Edith went into a long and difficult labor on the evening of September 12. Theodore Jr. was born at 2:15 in the morning of September 13, eight and a half pounds, his father writing to Bamie that Edith had been "extremely plucky all through."[5]

Theodore's asthma resolved after his son had safely emerged into the world, but Edie was gripped by postpartum depression. She suffered this with the birth of each of her five children, along with two miscarriages. Meanwhile her ever-restless husband sought new diversions. Eager for a new project, TR thought big and, in March 1888, began writing *The Winning of the West*, which would grow into a four-volume saga of Manifest Destiny beginning with Daniel Boone. In June, after attending the Republican National Convention, which nominated Benjamin Harrison for president, Roosevelt eagerly stumped for him. After Harrison defeated Democratic incumbent Grover Cleveland, Henry Cabot Lodge successfully lobbied Harrison to appoint his friend to the U.S. Civil Service Commission. Intended to administer a merit-based civil service and dismantle the old spoils system, whereby most federal bureaucratic posts were jobs used by politicians to enforce loyalty among portions of the electorate, the commission remained deeply mired in political patronage. Those who served on this less-than-august body were usually in search of nothing more or less than a sinecure. As Lodge knew he would, however, Roosevelt used the role as a platform for vigorous reform in a fight against the death grip of the spoils system. His activism drew attention and returned Roosevelt to the national spotlight.

Inclusion in even the outer circle of the Harrison administration brought with it invitations to Washington society events. Introvert that she was, Edith at first resisted, but soon gave in and found a social connection with the similarly introverted historian and social philosopher Henry Adams, who (with whatever glee he could muster) noted that her husband, Theodore, stood in "abject terror" of her.[6] She was indeed becoming a quietly formidable presence in Washington. In that milieu, Edith Roosevelt met women—the wives of prominent political figures—who were both beautiful and powerful. She grew close with the wife of Henry Cabot Lodge, Anna, familiarly known as Nannie, and with Elizabeth Cameron, the wife of former Pennsylvania senator Simon Cameron. Elizabeth Cameron was a quarter century younger than her husband, a Washington insider who had survived a scandal as Abraham Lincoln's first secretary of war. Nannie and Lizzie were compelling role models, able to show Edie aspects of a wife's role in Washington politics she had never contemplated. An astute political wife served as another set of eyes and ears for her husband. Politicians would tell a sufficiently charming and intelligent woman like Edith things they would not necessarily tell Roosevelt directly. Moreover, wives were privy to the private opinions of their husbands and would share these judiciously with other political wives. The network of Washington wives existed in sympathetic parallel with the official D.C. network of who's who, and Edith grew into an increasingly formidable political asset. "[Edith]," journalist Mark Sullivan assessed, "belonged to the generation in which smiling self-control was one of the marks of good breeding." Women of the age, particularly those in the higher echelons of society and politics such as Nannie, Lizzie, Margaret, and Edith, were the hidden hands of power. "That her code kept her in the background," Sullivan continues, "deprived the public of knowing not merely one of the great women but one of the great persons of her time."[7] It helped that she was good at keeping secrets. After the successful birth of Ted Jr., Edith suffered a miscarriage in 1888. Guarding her privacy, she was reticent to confide in her sisters-in-law. "The whole thing has been most mysterious," Conie wrote to Bamie.[8]

Edith's next pregnancy was a success, and after birthing two children in a little over three years of marriage, she made Theodore promise she would not be pregnant again soon. She also made him take time out from the Civil Service Commission and work on yet another new book, a history of New York City, to do something he had promised during their secret engagement—to take her west to his beloved Badlands. Thee took Edie by way of Medora and the Elkhorn Ranch, and he brought along on the expedition Bamie and Conie, along with Conie's husband, Douglas Robinson. He also invited a twenty-two-year-old Scotsman, Bob Ferguson, who has been described as Bamie's "friend." The pair were introduced by Cecil Spring-Rice and were often seen together when Ferguson was in New York. Bamie treasured his company and wrote to him frequently when he was back in Scotland. In one letter she alluded to how people might interpret their time together—"I think with trembling of all that may be written!"—but as Betty Boyd Caroli writes in *The Roosevelt Women*, her letters to Ferguson "avoided flirtation, but only barely, and they showed a lot of concern. Whenever he became ill, she wanted him to come back and stay with her so that she could nurse him to health."[9]

Later, Bamie even arranged for Ferguson to get a job at the Astor Trust office alongside Conie's husband, Douglas Robinson.

Edith was at first dismayed by the sight of the Badlands town, which she saw at four in the morning in a relentless downpour that churned the dry earth into a "glutinous slime." Sylvane Ferris and Bill Merrifield met them all at the train station and escorted the party to the Elkhorn Ranch, where they were joined by Patty and Tilden Selmes. "I had been prepared by many tales for the charm and freedom and informal ease of life in the Bad Lands and had often dreamed of going there," Conie wrote in a remarkable account of the trip in *My Brother Theodore Roosevelt*, "but, unlike most dreams, this one came true in an even more enchanting fashion than I had dared hope."[10]

The vision of desolation during the thirty-three-mile ride to the ranch in a rough, unsprung wagon (Roosevelt rode separately on horseback) was even more disheartening, but the barren Badlands vista suddenly sharpened into one of majestic sandstone buttes, and the sky cleared to admit a glorious morning sun. Conie set the scene: "We forded the 'Little Missouri' River twenty-three times on the way to the ranch-house, and as the banks of the river were extremely steep, it was always a question as to whether we could go fast enough down one bank to get sufficient impetus to enable us to go through the river and up the very steep bank on the other side; so that either coming or going we were in imminent danger of doing a complete somersault."[11]

Historian Clay Jenkinson called Edith, Bamie, and Conie's daring introduction to the Badlands "twenty-three crossings at breakneck speed."[12] Almost two dozen times the wagons barreled their way down the hillside, perilously close to toppling over or buckling under, splashing headlong into water of an unknown depth. Despite the danger or perhaps because of it, Edith suddenly understood her husband's attraction to North Dakota, this land. She understood it because she, too, now felt it. Conie also felt an immediate connection to this mysterious place and its "almost grotesque" landscape. For her, "the mingling tints in the sunset sky . . . resulted in a quality of color and atmosphere the like of which I only remember in Egypt, and made as lasting an impression upon my memory as did the land of the Nile."¹³

Despite the presence of her husband, Conie was enchanted by one cowboy in particular. "No one was ever so typically the ideal cowboy of one's wildest fancy as was Sylvane Ferris," she wrote years after her trip to Medora. "Tall and slender, with strong fair hair and blue eyes of an almost unnatural clearness, and a splendid broad brow and aquiline nose, Sylvane looked the part. His leather chaps, his broad sombrero hat, his red hand-kerchief knotted carelessly around his strong, young, sunburned throat, all made him such a picture that one's eye invariably followed him as he rode a vicious pony, 'wrastled' a calf, roped a steer, or branded a heifer."¹⁴

Conie left a lasting impression on the cowboys, too. On the last night at Elkhorn Ranch, she surprised the camping party by "wrastling a calf." With a wordsmith's skill often exceeding that of her more renowned brother, Conie takes us fireside:

> I can feel now the mud in my boots as I floundered with agonized effort after that energetic animal. I can still sense the strain in every nerve in my body as I finally flung myself across its back, and still, as if it were only yesterday, do I remember the jellied sensation within me, as for some torturing minutes I lay across the heifer's spine, before, by a final Herculean effort, I caught that left leg with my right arm. The cries of "stay with him!" from the fence, the loud hand-clapping of the enthusiastic cowboys, the shrieks of laughter of my brother and my husband, all still ring in my ears, and when the deed was finally accomplished, when the calf, with one terrible lurch, actually "wrastled," so to speak, fell over on its head in the mud, all sensation left me and I only remember being lifted up, bruised and encased in an armor of oozing dirt, and being carried triumphantly on the shoulders of the cowboys into the ranch house.¹⁵

The Roosevelt women had proven they could keep pace with the cowboys. For Edith, her admission into the realm from which Roosevelt had hitherto sought escape from the dominion of the women who wanted to "sivilize" him strengthened her bond with Theodore.

Now in their late twenties and thirties, the Roosevelt women were coming into their own. Edith was overcoming her natural reserve to become the sort of wife she knew TR would need for a dazzling political career. Thirty-five-year-old spinster Bamie was having a scandalous almost-romance with a man fourteen years her junior. Conie was figuring out how to bring joy to her life despite a loveless marriage. They were sharpening their skills and having their fun, on their own and through TR.

Henry Adams's assessment—that TR stood in "abject terror of Edith"—is provocative and rings with at least a modicum of truth, but it does not tell the whole tale. He respected her, her judgment, and her opinions. She seems very definitely to have ruled the roost at home, but her influence wasn't limited to the domestic sphere. A wide circle around Roosevelt respected Edith's—and Bamie's—political sagacity. The journalist Mark Sullivan wrote, "Never, when he had his wife's judgment, did [TR] go wrong or suffer disappointment." Roosevelt himself later confessed, "Whenever I go against her judgment, I regret it."[16] When asked about Alice Roosevelt Longworth's comment that if Bamie had been a man, she would have been the one who was president, none other than Eleanor Roosevelt confirmed, "Well, I think it might easily have been so."[17] "She was much more calculating," Eleanor recalled. "Many women are quite able to think into the future . . . and there are women, who like Auntie Bye, are very good in making an analysis of a situation."[18] Indeed, some of the women in the arena's biggest help to TR would be in talking him *out* of impulsive and bad ideas.

Interestingly, TR didn't seem as conscious of the full extent of his wife's influence on his life and career as did subsequent generations, although he did recognize that she was "cunning." Of the woman he called his "Aunt Edith," no less a figure than Franklin Delano Roosevelt said that "she managed T.R. very cleverly without his being conscious of it— no slight achievement, as anyone will concede."[19]

Would FDR have thought the same about Alice? She did inspire Roosevelt to early achievement, but the field in which her influence operated was much narrower and husband and wife were often separated by the distance between Albany and New York City. Yet TR certainly talked politics with Alice all the time and, if she, too, had the chance to learn from the most successful political wives in Washington, her skills would likely have sharpened. The span of Alice's influence was far briefer and there are no examples of Alice, who was only twenty-two when she died, talking TR out of a bad idea. Whether seasoned by the years or more innate to her personality, Edith had no such compunction.

Early in August 1894, Congressman Lemuel Ely Quigg, a New York City Republican with a deserved reputation as the right-hand man of New York State party boss Tom Platt, sought to entice Roosevelt into taking a second swing at the New York City mayoralty race. His initial impulse was to demur, but he was also anxious to seize another opportunity for elective office to revive a flagging political career. TR had not held elected office in ten years, and his zeal for reform earned him more political enemies than accolades. Perhaps genuinely conflicted, he went to Edith—not out of terror, abject or otherwise, but for advice and, quite likely, in the hope of being talked *into* accepting Quigg's enticement.

Far from encouraging him to run, Edith firmly rejected the idea, mainly on financial grounds. She thought the family could ill afford the expense of mounting a campaign and could afford even less to give up her husband's present salary, modest though it was, as a Civil Service commissioner. Roosevelt was only too aware of the ravages the weather had wrought upon the ranch that was to have sustained him and his family. Added to this was the impact of quite possibly suffering a second defeat for the same city office. As Edith saw it, the upside of a possible victory did not outweigh the downside of running. In the end, Roosevelt turned Quigg down—and immediately felt remorse for having done so. To Henry Cabot Lodge, he explained, "I simply had not the funds to run." But he admonished his friend, "No outsider should know that I think my decision was a mistake."[20]

There is no evidence here that Edith was looking to suppress her husband's political rise. She had already spent enough time in Washington to know that she enjoyed the company of smart political minds. And she could hardly have been unmindful of the financial burdens that contributed to her father's demise. The deciding factor could have been simply the money, as her husband told Lodge. But it would not be difficult to see her steering Roosevelt away from a mayor's race as savvy political strategy, too. Just look at the historical record. Only three mayors have gone on to become president, and none of them very quickly. Andrew Johnson was mayor of Greeneville, Tennessee, some thirty years before he ascended to the presidency. Grover Cleveland's stint as mayor of Buffalo, New York, was not likely the experience that propelled him into the White House so much as his later role as that state's governor. Similarly, Calvin Coolidge was mayor of Northampton, Massachusetts, but his rise, like his "Silent Cal" persona, was slow and steady. No mayor of New York City has ever gone on to win the White House.[21] If this was part of Edith's reasoning, her political instincts were sound. Running a city did not readily translate into holding an office of national scope. Moreover, becoming mayor of a major city ran the grave risk of becoming associated with urban machine politics, the kind of disreputable politics Roosevelt, as a state legislator, had fought against. Had TR won the New York City mayoralty in 1894, it might have easily proved to be his terminal political achievement. Had he lost his second bid for city office that, too, might have proved politically fatal. It must have looked to Edith like a no-win proposition.

What is undeniable is that forgoing the New York mayoral race of 1894 put Roosevelt in a position from which he could and did accept appointment to the New York City Board of Police Commissioners, on which he served from 1895 to 1897, when he ascended to his second federal office—this one adjacent to cabinet level—as assistant secretary of the navy. The jump from one of four police commissioners on a board to president might seem even more unlikely a jump as the one from mayor to president. For a reformer, however, being one of New York's top cops was a more advantageous opportunity to build and burnish a national

reputation. As TR himself wrote in an article for *The Atlantic Monthly* in
September 1897, City Hall was still in the grip of Tammany corruption,
and the "chief centre of corruption was the police department":

> No man not intimately acquainted with both the lower and the hum-
> bler sides of New York life—for there is a wide distinction between
> the two—can realize how far this corruption extended. Except in rare
> instances, where prominent politicians made demands which could
> not be refused, both promotions and appointments towards the close
> of Tammany rule were almost solely for money, and the prices were
> discussed with cynical frankness. There was a well-recognized tariff of
> charges, ranging from two or three hundred dollars for appointment
> as a patrol-man, to twelve or fifteen thousand dollars for promotion
> to the position of captain. The money was reimbursed to those who
> paid it by an elaborate system of blackmail. . . . From top to bottom the
> New York police force was utterly demoralized by the gangrene of such
> a system, where venality and blackmail went hand in hand with the
> basest forms of low ward politics, and where the policeman, the ward
> politician, the liquor seller, and the criminal alternately preyed on one
> another and helped one another to prey on the general public.[22]

It did not take many words for Roosevelt to explain what he did to
clean up civic administration in New York City:

> In administering the police force, we found, as might be expected, that
> there was no need of genius, nor indeed of any very unusual qualities.
> What was required was the exercise of the plain, ordinary virtues, of a
> rather commonplace type, which all good citizens should be expected
> to possess. Common sense, common honesty, courage, energy, resolu-
> tion, readiness to learn, and a desire to be as pleasant with everybody
> as was compatible with a strict performance of duty, —these were the
> qualities most called for. . . .
>   Our methods for restoring order and discipline were simple, and

hardly less so were our methods for securing efficiency. We made frequent personal inspections, especially at night, going anywhere, at any time. In this way we soon got an idea of whom among our upper subordinates we could trust and whom we could not. We then proceeded to punish those who were guilty of shortcomings, and to reward those who did well, refusing to pay any heed whatever to anything except the man's own character and record. A very few promotions and dismissals sufficed to show our subordinates that at last they were dealing with superiors who meant what they said, and that the days of political pull were over while we had the power. The effect was immediate. The decent men took heart, and those who were not decent feared longer to offend. The *morale* of the entire force improved steadily.[23]

TR was building a reputation as a sensible, honorable public servant. His moral compass could not be redirected by political considerations—rare and revered, particularly among the segment of the public that read *The Atlantic Monthly*.

It was one thing for Theodore Roosevelt to personally walk officers' beats in the wee hours to confirm that they were on duty and doing their jobs diligently. The people liked that, and the politicians did not object. But when he acted to ensure uniform enforcement of New York City's Sunday Excise Law, which banned saloons from selling liquor on Sunday, Tammany Hall, party boss Tom Platt, and a sizable portion of a thirsty citizenry rose up in objection.

There is cause to consider another motivation for Roosevelt's puritanical crusade against alcohol. In August 1894, Elliott Roosevelt's long struggle with alcoholism, which perhaps exacerbated his undiagnosed and untreated epilepsy, came to a dramatic and devastating end.[24] By this point, he had had an affair and fathered a child out of wedlock, separated from his wife, and, following an accident in which he suffered a broken leg that mended very slowly, became addicted to morphine and laudanum. The siblings' reaction to Elliott's long, painful, and all-too-public decline is telling. Bamie was practical, striving always to work the problem. Theodore became increasingly frustrated with what he perceived as his brother's moral—not physical—failings. Bamie and Theodore had Elliott institutionalized.

Conie sympathized with her lost brother but was less involved in the decade-long search for solutions. She did, however, claim to have had a premonition of Elliott's death. Walking through the woods in upstate New York, Conie "suddenly . . . saw someone she identified as her brother Elliott, walking ahead of her. She never could catch up with him, and this shadowy figure she followed to the front door. When they arrived there the figure vanished through the front door. The door was then opened and she was handed a cable of a telegram or a message saying her brother Elliott had died."[25]

In a telegram and a letter he sent to Conie, her husband, Douglas Robinson, described the chaotic end of Elliott's life. Fueled by "stimulants," on Monday, August 13, Elliott "did jump out of the parlor window" of his Manhattan apartment. To all appearances, he was not seriously injured; however, "About three o'clock Tuesday afternoon the 14th the delusions came on again," Conie wrote to Bamie. "At first he was very gentle . . . then he ran upstairs and knocked at the 4th story door and asked if Miss Eleanor Roosevelt was home, and waited and then turned away and said, 'If she is out, will you tell her [that] her father is so sorry not to see her.' Soon after that he became excited and ran violently up and down stairs, suddenly stumbled and fell and stiffened and began to have one of those convulsive attacks." At ten o'clock in the evening of Tuesday, August 14, 1894, Elliott Roosevelt "breathed his last." The death certificate cites the cause of death as "alcoholism." None of his three siblings were at his bedside.[26]

Elliott Roosevelt was dead at the age of thirty-four. His wife, Anna Hall, and son, Elliott Jr., preceded him in death, Anna on December 7, 1892, from diphtheria, and Elliott Jr. on May 25, 1893, from scarlet fever. He left behind two orphans, nine-year-old Eleanor and her three-year-old brother, Hall. Bamie, Edith, and Theodore discussed adopting and even suing for custody of Eleanor, but the Hall family interceded. Still,

Eleanor would spend much of the summer with her Aunt Edith and Uncle Theodore, forever imprinted by the loss of her parents and the sharp contrast with the bustling camaraderie of Sagamore Hill.

Conie was the first of the Roosevelt siblings to view her deceased brother. "He looked like our old Elliott," she wrote Bamie. "For the terrible bloated swelled look was gone and the sweet expression around the forehead and eyes made me weep very bitter tears." Theodore arrived from Washington later that day. "[He] was more overcome than I have ever seen him," Conie told her elder sister. "[Theodore] cried like a little child for a long time" over the body of his younger brother.[27]

Finding himself the object of caricatures and other journalistic barbs, Roosevelt—his strident moral views reinforced by the death of Elliott—embraced his unpopularity as manifest evidence that he was doing the right thing. Like Henry Davis "Hal" Minot before him, Elliott served Theodore as a psychological mirror. He saw his brother's weakness as evidence of his own need for moral and physical strength.[28]

The year 1895 brought more sad news. Tilden Selmes, Patty's husband, died of cancer on August 1. For Theodore, the widowing of Patty struck a familiar nerve. "Well, we've both *had* it," Theodore wrote Patty. "We have striven, and lived, and known happiness as well as sorrow." Like TR, she had debt, not riches, from her time in the West. "You have had a hard life," his letter continued, "but you have faced it nobly and undauntedly; and there is something in that when all is said and done."[29] Roosevelt knew loss and resilience: he had lost "Greatheart," Mittie, Alice, and now Elliott, too. However comforting were his words, Theodore could not bring himself to face Patty in person. En route to the Dakotas, he failed to stop and see her and later wrote regretfully: "I could at least have given the comfort which would come from talking with one who deeply sympathizes with you, who appreciates and in some measure understands you, and who feels a very deep affection for you and for the memory of your husband." He concluded the letter, almost echoing the sadness he felt those two years in the Badlands: "I would give much if I could only help you in your time of gray sorrow."[30]

When Theodore next visited the ranch, his thoughts again turned to Patty, and almost certainly Alice. "I shall think of you very often, riding over the immense rolling plains, with their mat of short, sun scorched grass," he wrote. "For it has always seemed to me that we two *felt* those plains as no one else."[31]

For all his gloominess, TR's career was playing out as perfectly as he could have hoped. Theodore's righteous crusade was earning him national publicity. Much as they are today, many Americans were concerned about big-city crime and the inefficiency and corruption of policing. While Roosevelt's popularity in New York City plummeted, his national profile rose. There was chatter about a presidential run. Roosevelt ally Jacob Riis, the muckraking journalist and author-photographer of the epoch-making exposé of New York slum life *How the Other Half Lives*, replied to a reporter's question asking if TR was working to become president: "Of course! Teddy is bound for the Presidency!"[32] Another, more unlikely, admirer was Bram Stoker, the Irish author of *Dracula*, who met TR while on a theatrical tour of the United States. Stoker wrote of the encounter in his diary: "Must be President some day. A man you can't cajole, can't frighten, can't buy."[33] Such was the growing national—and even international—view of Theodore Roosevelt.

Bamie was garnering her own international acclaim.

After Theodore married Edith and took Alice into the new Roosevelt home, Bamie began traveling widely. In Vienna, she visited James Roosevelt Roosevelt, first secretary at the U.S. embassy. Rosy, as he was universally known, was the son of Bamie's distant cousin James. His stepmother was Sara Delano, the mother of Franklin. When Rosy married Helen Astor, Bamie served as a bridesmaid. The connection with Rosy gave her an advantage in the small universe of America's European diplomatic corps and she found herself the object of many social invitations. But her brother wanted her back home, where she could be of service to him. When she returned to New York in the autumn of 1888, she and Theodore discussed the outlook for that year's presidential elections. He "encouraged" Bamie's appointment as a member of the New York State "Board of Lady Managers" to work on the "Woman's Building" to be erected at the 1893 World's Columbian Exposition in Chicago.[34] Theodore passed on to her praise he had heard about her work, which involved arranging the loan of various objects for exhibition, including a comment that she was "really a wonder and worth all the rest of [the board members] put together." He added, "If I had your capacity, *what* a civil service commissioner I should be!"[35]

Bamie was earning a formidable reputation as a woman of parts when, shortly after returning to New York from Chicago, Rosy Roosevelt wrote to ask her for help. He had moved from Vienna to a far more demanding post of assistant secretary at the London embassy. His wife, Helen, had fallen seriously ill and, overwhelmed, he was considering resigning. Helen pleaded with him to contact Bamie before making any decision. He did, asking if she would come to London to help with official entertaining and the care of the couple's two young children. She agreed to consider it, and when he subsequently cabled with the sad news that Helen had died, she accepted.[36]

Some historians have speculated that Bamie saw Rosy as a possible husband, but there is no documentary evidence for this. Indeed, she wrote to Ferguson that she would be back in New York by the end of March—making her London sojourn no more than three months—and she committed to helping Theodore and Edith when their latest child was expected in April. And so it was that Bamie settled in at 2 Upper Belgrave Street at Christmastime.

Bamie soon became a familiar and sought-after figure in London diplomatic society. She was presented to Queen Victoria in a moment that, biographer Betty Boyd Caroli writes, "sealed her future: she was now fully recognized as a person in her own right—her name, even without a husband, would routinely appear on all the invitation lists that mattered."[37] Bamie decided to stay on with Rosy, often backchanneling economic and diplomatic information to TR and U.S. allies. The details have not come down to us, largely because when, after her brother's

death, Bamie published his letters to her, she "cut out most of the refer-
ences to her political insight or influence." But we do know that she dealt
with the likes of diplomat John Hay and Captain Alfred Mahan, the influential naval historian and strategic thinker.[38] Edith may have wrested
her husband's daughter from Bamie but she by no means supplanted her
as Theodore's most trusted counselor.

While in London, an independent woman in a foreign land, Bamie
met William Sheffield Cowles, a forty-nine-year-old divorcé and U.S.
naval officer. Bamie wrote to tell TR and the family back in the United
States that she intended to marry him. "To say that your cable and letter
surprised us is a hopelessly inadequate way of saying what we felt," TR
wrote his sister. "We were dumbfounded."[39] Henry Cabot Lodge, too, was
thunderstruck: "Why on earth should you get married? You have Theodore
and myself."[40] TR ratcheted up the hyperbole, taking Bamie's expressed
concern over Will's divorce to imply the marriage might be illegal. "In so
vital a matter, six months delay is better than a blunder which, by some
remote chance, MIGHT wreck your life," TR wrote Bamie.[41] Subtlety
was not one of TR's strengths, but he may have had a point. Divorce was
a source of social disapprobation if not scandal. Except in a few states,
adultery and insanity were the only surefire grounds, and feminists of
the era often commented that those laws made marriage something like
slavery.[42] Bamie never defined herself as a feminist, but in these matters
she sought her own counsel and deemed the threat her brother had cited
"literally infinitesimal."[43] To be fair to Bamie's genuinely concerned family, historian Caroli writes: "What these two middle-aged Americans saw
in each other remained something of an enigma to almost everyone who
knew them."[44] At forty, Bamie was thought to be well beyond her child-
bearing years. Years later, Bamie's niece concurred: "I don't think [Bamie]
was in love with him . . . I don't think that either [Bamie or Conie] were
ever really in love with any man, including their husbands." Why not?
"They were absorbed in [TR]. . . . Everything went into their brother,
everything."[45] Clearly, both Conie and Bamie loved and admired their
brother, and these emotions were great motivators for them. Yet we are

left to wonder at the emotional imbalance between TR and his sisters. They seem to have given him considerably more understanding and support than he—at least openly—gave them. Why shouldn't Bamie seek that out from someone else?

Bamie married Will but continued to focus much of her energy on her brother's success. It was to Bamie that Roosevelt wrote in the summer of 1896 about his growing discontent with the Board of Police Commissioners, calling the work on it "inconceivably arduous, disheartening, and irritating." He complained that he had to "contend with the hostility of Tammany, and the almost equal hostility of the Republican machine." Roosevelt deeply admired pragmatic reformers like the journalist Jacob Riis and Hull House founder Jane Addams, and yet he vented of feeling himself plagued by the "folly of the reformers and the indifference of decent citizens." Moreover, he told Bamie that the law governing the commission was "singularly foolish." Why foolish? If he were "a single-headed Commissioner, with absolute power," he told her, "I could in a couple of years accomplish almost all I could desire," but, as one of four commissioners, "I have to face it as best as I could, and have accomplished something."[46]

Bamie recognized that her brother was an executive trapped in a bureaucratic role. "I work and fight from dawn until dark," a dejected Theodore wrote Bamie on February 2, 1896. "And the difficulties, the opposition, the lukewarm support, I encounter give me hours of profound depression."[47] Theodore wrote Bamie again on July 26, not so subtly hinting at a possible solution: "Not since the Civil War has there been a Presidential election fraught with so much consequence to the country."[48] While TR lamented, Bamie acted. That August, at Bamie's instigation, Theodore invited Bellamy Storer, a recently retired Republican congressman from Ohio, and his wife, Maria Longworth Nichols Storer, to Sagamore Hill. Bellamy was godfather to Archibald. More importantly, the Storers were friends of GOP presidential candidate William McKinley, whom Roosevelt had not supported for the nomination, instead backing Speaker of the House Thomas B. Reed. It was a political miscalculation, but perhaps not an insurmountable one. After he rowed Maria "spasmodically and sometimes absent-mindedly" on lovely Oyster Bay, Roosevelt suddenly declared, "I should like to be Assistant Secretary of the Navy."[49] The ask was not an easy one. Though Roosevelt had come around to support McKinley, the Republican presidential nominee "was not enamored with Roosevelt."[50] Working in a partnership more akin to political strategist and candidate than older sister and younger brother, Bamie had set Theodore in motion. In turn, he kept her appraised. After the visit with Bellamy, he reported to Bamie that he had met with Mark Hanna, McKinley's most senior and trusted advisor, in early August and then, in October, with McKinley himself. "He was entirely pleasant with us, though we are not among his favorites," Theodore confessed to Bamie.[51]

Still, Theodore strategized with Bamie where he could be most helpful to McKinley. In the Coinage Act of 1873, Congress demonetized silver, leaving just the gold standard. A movement instantly grew up to reinstate silver, which would make more money more widely available. Roosevelt saw this as a dangerously inflationary act and was therefore a vigorous opponent of the free silver platform of Democratic presidential candidate William Jennings Bryan. TR made a point of vigorously supporting McKinley's anti-silver campaign, making many stump speeches on his behalf. "The Rocky Mountain states will be strong for Bryan, but on the Pacific coast and in the Dakotas we shall make a strong fight, with the chances nearly even," he wrote to Bamie.[52] Dispatched by the McKinley campaign to make a major speech in Chicago, TR played the role of "attack dog" and savaged Bryan: "Instead of a government of the people, for the people, and by the people . . . Bryan would substitute a government of the mob, by the demagogue, for the shiftless and disorderly and the criminal."[53] It worked, and Roosevelt trailed Bryan throughout a series of speeches in the swing states of the upper Midwest. The result: "Bryan had been thrown off his message and put on the defensive."[54]

After McKinley defeated Bryan, Maria Storer urged the new president to appoint Roosevelt assistant secretary of the navy. "I want peace," Maria later claimed President-elect McKinley said in response to her request. "And I am told that your friend Theodore—whom I know only slightly—is always getting into rows with everybody. I am afraid he is too pugnacious." Maria reported the conversation to Theodore, who replied that he and Edith were "deeply touched" by her efforts on their behalf. "We have read and re-read your letter, repeatedly and together," Theodore wrote Bellamy. "And it told us exactly what we wished to know . . . if [McKinley] thinks I am a hot-headed, a harum scarum, I don't think he will change his mind now."[55]

And yet he did. When Senator Henry Cabot Lodge echoed the Storers' support with McKinley, such was his reputation that McKinley appointed Roosevelt assistant secretary of the navy to John D. Long. TR's boss was sickly and something of a willing figurehead, leaving his assistant secretary to do all the heavy lifting. Roosevelt did not shrink from the task or the opportunity. He sought to put into practice what he had only written about years earlier in his *Naval War of 1812*: the expansion and modernization of the U.S. fleet. An enthusiastic champion of the naval geopolitical theorist Alfred Thayer Mahan, Roosevelt particularly called for building battleships, the vessels great nations used to project their power on a global scale before the age of naval aviation and the ascendency of the aircraft carrier.

Bamie had read the political tea leaves and pointed her brother toward the executive role that had for nearly a decade eluded him. "Auntie Bye always seemed to know just what to do," said Helen Roosevelt Robinson, expressing a sentiment common among those fortunate enough to be in Bamie's orbit.[56] The post of assistant secretary of the navy had been a highly strategic choice. Theodore and Bamie knew that a cabinet post was out of reach for someone whose federal experience had been limited to the Civil Service Commission and who hardly had a long record as a McKinley supporter. But the navy post was perfectly suited to his interests and proven expertise. It also positioned him to take a strong stand on national security. He began pressing McKinley on the importance of projecting naval power in the Pacific and the Caribbean and told a naval planner late in 1897 that it was in the American interest to push imperial Spain out of Cuba; doing so would be both a great humanitarian service to the Cuban people and a way of fulfilling President James Monroe's vision of completely, in TR's words, "freeing . . . America from European dominion."[57]

Yes, it was a strategic move, orchestrated by Bamie, but neither Bamie nor Theodore Roosevelt himself could have known just how strategic his move to assistant naval secretary would be.

11

THE CROWDED HOUR

"I have always felt that it was a shame for the cow-puncher to pass away without being given a chance to show what splendid stuff there was in him as a fighting man."

—Theodore Roosevelt to Patty Selmes

*I*t now seems a foregone conclusion that Theodore Roosevelt was destined to become a national hero, but he just as easily could have been killed in action in the Spanish-American War. There is a fine line between courage and recklessness. That either outcome was acceptable to him is what makes Theodore Roosevelt singular. His engagement in Cuba—which would be called variously brave, bold, selfish, and suicidal—would change the trajectory of his life. But it was up to the women closest to him to ensure the trajectory was a favorable one.

On February 15, 1898, the USS *Maine*—popularly called a "battleship," but more properly an armored cruiser—exploded in Havana Harbor. President McKinley had sent the *Maine* the month before for the ostensible purpose of protecting American citizens (and American investments) in Cuba as the Cuban struggle for independence from oppressive Spanish colonial rule intensified and grew more violent. American sentiment for becoming directly involved in the war on the side of the "rebels" was mounting. The growing war fever, which McKinley resisted, escalated as Cuban instability threatened U.S. agricultural investments on the island, as many Americans reflexively opposed often cruel Spanish colonial governing policies, and as many Americans also disapproved of Spanish Catholicism. With America's Western frontier largely settled, many politicians looked to Cuba as a potential new territory or even state. Finally, most of the nation's media titans—spearheaded by the "yellow journalism" of William Randolph Hearst's *New York Journal*—knew that war sells newspapers.

With the explosion of the *Maine*, the immediate loss of life was heavy, shocking, and tragic—266 of the ship's complement of 374. The sinking was what historian Clay Risen accurately labels "the worst naval disaster in American military history up to that point."[1] Roosevelt was among the many who immediately placed the blame for the explosion on Spain, a rival for power in the Caribbean, giving little thought to the possibility that it might have been the work of Cuban rebels or an accident. McKinley, who had continued Democratic predecessor Grover Cleveland's pursuit of a diplomatic solution to the conflict in Cuba, reserved judgment as did Secretary Long, Roosevelt's boss. By this point in his short-lived appointment as assistant secretary of the navy, Roosevelt had worn Long's patience and he was no longer quite so happy to stand aside and let Roosevelt have his way. "Long appreciated Roosevelt for his energy, but he would have much preferred a quietly competent career naval officer as his second," according to Risen, author of *The Crowded Hour: Theodore Roosevelt, the Rough Riders, and the Dawn of the American Century.*[2]

President McKinley authorized a naval court of inquiry into the explosion. In the meantime, without seeking the approval of Secretary Long or President McKinley, Roosevelt ordered the commanders of a number of naval vessels to prepare for war.

In the opinion of the court of inquiry, the *Maine* had been destroyed by a mine, but the officers who sat on the board were unable to reach an opinion as to whether the mine had been the work of Spain or an attempt by Cuban revolutionaries to incite the United States to war against Spain. Despite the absence of a verdict, McKinley, moved by popular political sentiment, asked Congress on April 11 to authorize an invasion. Congress not only obliged but gave the president something he hadn't asked for: a resolution recognizing Cuban independence from Spain. In response, Spain declared war on the United States on April 24.

The ambitious Roosevelt, still a young man at forty, had every incentive to remain at what was proving to be a powerful, highly visible during times of global unrest, and politically secure post. Yet the temptation to position himself for more direct action was enticing, and Theodore's impulsive nature overcame him. And the women upon whom he had depended for counsel found themselves preoccupied with other concerns. As Theodore contemplated his move, Bamie delivered a stunning announcement: she was pregnant at age forty-three. She did not find pregnancy at what was then (and now) considered an advanced maternal age a daunting prospect. Her pregnancy did, however, mean that for perhaps the first time she quite understandably had other things on her mind than helping her brother to strategize about his career. TR and Edith also now had a new son, Quentin, born on November 19, 1897. The delivery was a success "but by early January 1898, [Edith] was obviously ill . . . every day from mid-January to mid-February, Edith ran a fever of 101 degrees or higher."[3] On February 22, 1898, just over three months after the boy's birth and a week after the sinking of the *Maine*, Edith noticed an "ominous swelling" in her abdomen near her pelvis. In a panic, Roosevelt summoned no less a figure than Sir William Osler, a cofounder of Baltimore's Johns Hopkins Hospital, to examine her. The doctor pronounced Edith "critically ill" with an abscess in the psoas muscle and advised immediate surgery. And yet Roosevelt uncharacteristically avoided action, seeking second opinions from physicians of far lesser stature. Days turned into weeks, and, on March 5, Theodore at last called in a competent gynecologist, who, confirming Osler's diagnosis, operated the very next day. Theodore assured Bamie that the procedure had gone off well but that Edie's "convalescence may be a matter of months."[4] Perhaps TR was haunted by the memory of Alice, who had fallen ill and quickly died in the wake of a child's birth. Whatever the reason, it seems clear that her husband's delaying of treatment exacerbated Edith's problem.

It was early in Edith's long, slow convalescence, on March 15, while she "lay at death's door," that Theodore wrote to William Astor Chanler, a congressman from New York who was also a freelance soldier and passionately believed in fighting for the independence of colonial nations. Roosevelt proposed that Chanler raise a volunteer regiment for the war in Cuba that he felt certain would come. "I shall chafe my heart out if I am kept here" he wrote—by the side of his ailing wife—"instead of being at the front."[5]

On March 27, Edith was "terribly wasted." Yet when Theodore wrote to ten-year-old Theodore Jr., "Today I took a hard walk with Doctor [Leonard] Wood," a U.S. Army colonel and Roosevelt's personal physician, the subject of their conversation was not Edith's still precarious condition but "how we could get into the army that would go to Cuba."[6]

On April 11, President McKinley at last sent a war message to Congress, which authorized the raising of three volunteer cavalry regiments to augment the Regular Army, which was too small to go to war even on a small island nation. Following the Civil War, both Confederate and Union forces had disbanded rapidly. The U.S. Army in 1865 counted just over a million men under arms. By 1875, the zeal to demobilize after the deadliest war in U.S. history reduced the army to some 28,000 officers and men, smaller than any major army among the Western powers, essentially a force intended mainly to police recalcitrant Native Americans in the West.[7] The army was still about that size twenty-five years later.

Secretary of War Russell Alger offered Roosevelt command of one of these new volunteer regiments, but TR, in prudent deference to his own lack of military experience, asked to serve as second in command under Colonel Leonard Wood. Theodore's closest friends, including Henry Cabot Lodge, pleaded with him not to go, and President McKinley asked him, not once but twice and as a personal favor, to remain at his Navy Department post. (McKinley likely recognized Roosevelt's value given Long's weaknesses. It is also quite possible that the president feared creating a rival, anticipating the publicity Roosevelt would get in taking on a combat role.) Others sought to shame him. How could he leave his still fragile wife, not to mention his ten-year-old son, who was also ill, suffering from what physicians called "nervous exhaustion"? And, of course, there was the new baby, Quentin.

"What on earth is this report of Roosevelt's resignation?" wrote historian Henry Adams, the grandson of President John Quincy Adams and the great-grandson of President John Adams, to Elizabeth Sherman, "Washington's most fashionable hostess." "Is his wife dead? Has he quarreled with everybody? Is he quite mad?" Adams, who commented that TR lived in "abject terror" of Edith, may have imagined things going differently had Edith been well enough to give her husband a piece of her mind.[8] Theodore's decision was the talk of Washington. Winthrop Astor Chanler, known as "Wintie," wrote in a letter to his wife, Margaret Chanler, that Wintie's brother, Congressman William Astor Chanler, had been encouraging Theodore to volunteer. Wintie, however, saw the rash act of resignation as career suicide: "Theodore . . . goes to Cuba before long with a regiment of cowboys from Arizona and New Mexico. I really think he is going mad. The President has twice asked him as a personal favor to stay in the Navy Department but Theodore is wild to hack and hew. It really is sad. Of course this ends his political career for good. Even Cabot says this."[9] Though initially opposed to his enlistment, Edith of all people knew how important it was to TR to live a life of service, including the possibility of making the ultimate sacrifice for his country. "I don't want to be shot at any more than anyone else does; still less to die of yellow fever," Theodore wrote to his personal physician, Dr. Alexander Lambert. "I am altogether too fond of my wife and children."[10] For Roosevelt, the decision was a matter of honor, and on May 6, he resigned as assistant secretary of the navy.

Edith and Theodore spent time with friends and with their own children for a few days before Roosevelt, as lieutenant colonel of the 1st U.S. Volunteer Cavalry Regiment, set off for a training camp in Texas. Alice and Ted were sent to stay with Bamie, now four months pregnant, in New York. Edith, still convalescing, looked after the other four children, all under ten, herself. "Come back safe," Edith wrote her husband, "and we shall be happy, but it is quite right you should be where you are."[11]

In Texas, eight hundred volunteers—cowboys from the Badlands, a few Native Americans, Mexican Americans, Thomas Edison's brother-in-law, the first- and second-ranked professional tennis players in America, the heir to the Tabasco fortune, and some privileged adventurers from the New York and New England upper crust—assembled and drilled together. Some former "Buffalo Soldiers" (African American cavalrymen) were in segregated U.S. Army units. The Spanish-American War offered the United States the first opportunity since the Civil War for Blue and Gray to fight as red, white, and blue again. "Reconciliation between the North and South was an important, barely concealed subtext in the push for war," noted *Crowded Hour* author Clay Risen.[12] For TR, these men were the epitome of what it meant to be an American man: courageous, determined volunteers from all walks of life willing to give their lives for their country. Together, these men would manifest the destiny of the United States as a global power.

Some of the men Roosevelt himself recruited. Jesse Langdon, who grew up in Fargo, North Dakota, had first met Roosevelt as a toddler in the Badlands. At sixteen, he ran away to enlist, finding his way to Roosevelt on the steps of the recruiting office in Washington, D.C.

"Are you Mr. Roosevelt?" Langdon recalled decades later in an oral interview.

"Yes, Sir!" Roosevelt replied, and Langdon explained his connection to Dakota.

"Eh! Well, can you ride a horse?" Roosevelt asked.

"I can ride anything that wears hair," Langdon answered—and he was in.[13]

Roosevelt not only supervised the recruits' training, but he also trained in the basics of military courtesy and cavalry maneuvers right alongside them. Reveille at 6 a.m., mounted drills, target practice, and long marches filled the day. Revelry often filled the night as rank-and-file tents were within walking distance to San Antonio. The unit was officially the 1st U.S. Volunteer Cavalry, but the newspapers soon dubbed it "The Rough Riders." The name, slang for cowboys, originated in Buffalo Bill's Wild West show. At first, TR did not like the name. "Please do not call us Rough Riders," Roosevelt said to a reporter. "The name evokes a hippodrome."[14] He thought the nickname was unserious, making it sound like they were involved in some sort of stunt or performance. But TR, savvy enough to know when to fight and when to follow a trend, eventually embraced the nickname that made him famous. *The Rough Riders* even became the title of his book on the war.

When their training was as complete as it was likely to be, the regiment was packed into railcars and transferred from San Antonio to Tampa, Florida, from which it was scheduled to embark on chartered commercial vessels to Cuba. Edith summoned the strength to join her husband in Tampa, where she arrived on June 1. He had reserved a room at the Tampa Bay Hotel, which served as the U.S. Army headquarters for the invasion. He told Edith that he had secured permission from Colonel Wood to be with her, in the hotel, during each night of her stay, warning her, however, that he had to be present in camp at 4 a.m.

Whatever conflicting emotions she may have felt about her manifestly nonsoldierly husband's decision to march to war, Edith behaved very much in the spirit of a commanding officer's "lady." She met and conversed with all the subordinate officers and enthusiastically watched the cavalry at drill. During this exercise, she met Richard Harding Davis, who had established himself as a flamboyant journalist covering sensational stories, ranging from the aftermath of Pennsylvania's devastating 1889 Johnstown flood to the first judicial execution by electric chair (botched, bloody, and smoldering). It was Bamie, who during TR's time as police commissioner in New York, first brokered her brother's introduction to Davis and "cultivated" the relationship thereafter.[15] Some believed Davis had conspired with newspaper magnate William Randolph Hearst to foment war in Cuba between Spain and the United States as a means of beating rival Joseph Pulitzer in a New York City circulation war. In 1896, Hearst hired Davis to accompany the popular American artist and illustrator Frederic Remington to cover the Cuban rebellion. Davis's articles describing the Spanish summary execution of a young Cuban prisoner and the strip-search of a young Cuban woman did inflame American war fever. But this hardly constituted a "conspiracy." In fact, when Hearst printed that the strip-search had been performed by male guards, Davis abruptly resigned; he had accurately reported that the guards were female. Davis then went to work for Hearst's rival, Joseph Pulitzer, for whose New York Herald he covered the war.[16]

Introduced to TR by his charming and canny sister and encouraged by Edith, who befriended him, Davis churned out stories on Roosevelt and the Rough Riders that made both the regiment and the man instantly legendary. Such was—and remains—the power of the press. Circulation of The New York Herald was among the largest in the nation, which meant other papers across the country followed their lead and used the same tone in their coverage. "Whether Fifth Avenue millionaires or Western cowboys, they fought together and died together in Cuba for the great American principles of liberty, equality, and humanity," read one press account emblematic of how the Rough Riders were portrayed.[17] Observed historian Clay Risen on the phenomenon: "Roosevelt and the Rough Riders were everything to everyone."[18] Though the truth was embellished, the Rough Riders became a unifying symbol of what was good about America—and Theodore Roosevelt was the largest beneficiary.

"I have a horror of the people who bark but don't bite," Roosevelt wrote Conie and her husband before the war. "If I am ever to accomplish anything worth doing in politics, or ever have accomplished it, it is because I act up to what I preach."[19] Roosevelt felt he had a moral duty to fight in Cuba, but without the forbearance of Edith and the foresight of Bamie, TR might not have emerged from Cuba a national hero and global celebrity. Historian Stacy Cordery asserts that during her trip to Tampa "Edith would have had the time to assure [Theodore]—in person—that she had reconsidered her original request for him not to go to war. . . . The Tampa visit allowed TR to fight as he did—valiantly and not tentatively—because he knew then that Edith backed him fully, and that she was healthier and thus the children would not be left orphans should he die on the battlefield." The visit, Cordery contends, "strengthen[ed] their marriage."[20]

Yet the reality of the Rough Riders' career in the Spanish-American War was far from glamorous. After watching the regiment's mounted maneuvers, Edith left Tampa, and the Rough Riders boarded the SS *Yucatan*, which was to transport them to Cuba. Roosevelt had trained hard alongside his men and, when he was not in the saddle, devoured a small mountain of books on tactics and strategy. What no one in the regiment could have prepared for, however, was the near total incompetence of a U.S. military that (except for a disastrous Canadian incursion in the War of 1812) had never fielded a major expeditionary force beyond U.S. borders.

Fear that the Spanish were organizing a strong naval force to attack the chartered transport vessels delayed the departure of Roosevelt's regiment, which languished in the Florida heat on a stinking canal off Port Tampa. The decks of the *Yucatan*, like those of thirty-one other transports chartered to carry some seventeen thousand men into battle, were jammed with troops. Dysentery became a menace, as did heatstroke. Seeking to avoid the miasma on deck, Roosevelt spent six days confined to his cabin, except for a brief shore leave. He fumed over the botched embarkation and worried that it foreshadowed a failed military campaign that would, if anything, risk lives and damage his own political future.

It was not until June 14 that the transports at last began the voyage to their Cuban disembarkation point, Daiquirí, near the town of Santiago. The logistics of disembarking some seventeen thousand men and officers consumed more days as the crews and commanders struggled to unload ships in a port without a suitable pier. The concept of "combat loading," embarking and disembarking personnel so that they would be unloaded adjacent to their equipment, was unknown to the U.S. military. So, the disembarkation was even more incompetent than the embarkation had been. The total invasion force was not assembled on land until June 22. It was fortunate that the Spanish commanders were not much more capable than the Americans. Had they acted promptly and tactically, they could have bombarded and stormed the landing, quite likely driving the Americans, Roosevelt included, back into the sea.

The 1st U.S. Volunteer Cavalry together with two Regular Army units made up the 1st Cavalry Brigade, which was under the command of a brigadier general. He fell ill with yellow fever soon after the landing, and Colonel Leonard Wood was promoted to brigade command. Roosevelt received a field promotion to full colonel and thus became commanding officer of the Rough Riders.

A superb, fearless, and always hard-riding horseman, Roosevelt had crammed into his abbreviated military training as much cavalry tactics as he could. Expertly riding a horse was one thing but riding with others in a cohesive unit with the intention of forcing enemy infantry to turn away requires months of intensive drills—time the Rough Riders and TR were not afforded during their training. As it turned out, he could use none of it. One result of the blundering voyage from Tampa to Daiquirí was that almost none of the Rough Riders' horses were shipped with the men of the regiment. In consequence, the troops were obliged to march and fight as infantry. While the "Rough Riders" nickname stuck with the public, among themselves the 1st USV as well as the rest of the brigade was dubbed "Wood's Weary Walkers."[21] Though compelled to fight in a manner very different from the way he and his men had trained, Roosevelt was undaunted and even discovered in himself a genius for improvisation in combat and for leading others in what military historians call a "soldiers' battle," one in which victory depends on those in the field, not the higher officers in headquarters.

Much of the decisive action in the Spanish-American War was fought not by the army but by the U.S. Navy and much of that not in Cuba but far away in the war's Pacific theater, in the waters of the Philippines, where, under guerrilla leader Emilio Aguinaldo, Filipinos had been fighting for their independence from Spain since 1896. Indeed, with its large population (6.29 million in 1898), extensive network of plantations, and its strategic position in Southeast Asia, the Philippines loomed as a far greater prize for those with imperialist aspirations for America. Thanks to the victory at the Battle of Manila Bay (May 1, 1898) won by the U.S. Navy's Asiatic Squadron under Commodore George Dewey, the United States was positioned to gain possession of the vast archipelago.

While Dewey became a popular American hero, the Philippines were distant and Cuba was close to the U.S. mainland. The attention of most Americans was accordingly focused there, and Theodore Roosevelt led the highest-profile and critically decisive action of the land war in Cuba.

The Roosevelt family had reassembled from Bamie's care upon Edith's return. Ted Jr. prayed for his father while "eight-year-old Kermit was so upset . . . that he asked to be cuddled in his mother's arms like new baby, Quentin."[22] Fourteen-year-old Alice had to "comfort . . . her sobbing stepmother" as letters arrived from Cuba.[23] Edith might have changed her mind, supporting her husband's decision to go to war, but she still feared for his life. Conie's husband, Douglas, had given Theodore a pistol salvaged from the *Maine*. Conie sent her brother a poem to inspire his service. Theodore confided to his sister: "I loved the poem and I loved your dear letter; it made me sure that you really knew just how I felt about going. I *could not* stay; that was the sum and substance of it;— although I realize well how hard it is for Edith, and what a change for the worse it means in my after life."[24]

Before the Battle of San Juan Heights, "Roosevelt dispatched [Rough Rider] Fred Herrig, the tracker he had first encountered at Joe Ferris's general store in Medora, to find the mules that had run off with the machine gun." The gun and cannon were essential weapons for the battle to come. Herrig found the guns, and Roosevelt shouted, "Didn't I tell you? Didn't I tell you, Wood? Fred would find those guns?"[25] It was a moment of remarkable coincidence and connection between the "crowded hour"—how Roosevelt described the climactic battle that altered the trajectory of his career—and his life-altering experiences in the Badlands.

On July 1, 1898, the 1st USV's infantry charged up San Juan Heights, which was celebrated as the Battle of San Juan Hill. In this engagement, Roosevelt and the Rough Riders played the central role by storming, capturing, and holding the Heights, thus depriving the Spanish forces of tactically critical high ground, and giving the invading U.S. forces a clear path inland. For the Americans, the battle was the bloodiest land action of the Cuban war, resulting in 205 U.S. troops killed in action and 1,180 wounded. "One out of every six [Rough Riders]" were killed or injured, and though they suffered fewer casualties, 58 killed and 170 wounded, the Spanish gave up the Heights.[26]

During the combat, Roosevelt, whose horse was one of the few that found passage, rode up and down Kettle Hill, operating close-up with his men, rallying them and directing their actions in detail as they fought to dislodge the Spanish from their entrenched positions. Like Lord Nelson defiantly resplendent on the deck of HMS *Victory* at Trafalgar (October 21, 1805), Colonel Roosevelt made himself an easy target, yet, unlike the British admiral, he did not fall. Sometimes, fortune really does favor the bold. Roosevelt was one of the first to reach the principal Spanish entrenchments, and he personally killed at least one enemy soldier with the pistol given to him as a gift by Conie's husband. Fought at very close quarters, the battle was a scrum, a melee.

In hundreds of dispatches, Richard Harding Davis transformed "Teddy" Roosevelt into the Cuban conflict's single most potent avatar. There is no question that his performance at San Juan Heights was heroic. Yet, much as Andrew Jackson's stunning one-sided victory at the Battle of New Orleans (January 8, 1815) reframed, in the popular American imagination, the War of 1812 from an ill-considered pyrrhic draw into a "second War of Independence," so Roosevelt's set-piece engagement at San Juan Heights transfigured a bumbling and squalid imperialist war of choice into what John Hay (at the time U.S. ambassador to Great Britain) famously called a "splendid little war."[27] A man who now proved he knew how to fight but had always known how to dress, Roosevelt became the perfect khaki emblem of an iconic American sort of go-getting masculinity: jaunty slouch campaign hat with the left brim turned up, big-cuffed gauntlets, brass buttons on a bespoke Brooks Brothers tunic blouse with a brown choke collar and the shoulder straps of a U.S. Volunteers lieutenant colonel. Under the collar, he wore a bright blue cowboy bandana. He was the embodiment of what magazine magnate Henry Luce later called "the American Century"—a bustling, industrialized explosion of technology, culture, and prominence on the world stage. Even Roosevelt's former boss, the secretary of the navy, had to admit the gambit worked and TR was now "on the straight course to fame, to the governorship of New York and to the presidency of the United States."[28]

Colonel Roosevelt was grateful for the spotlight into which Richard Harding Davis's coverage cast him, but he was always generous in giving to his men the credit for the victory. In truth, it was Roosevelt more than any other military figure present who proposed and devised the assault on San Juan Heights. The operation was the product of his initiative, and the celebrated infantry charge, valiant as well as victorious, was made and led without orders or direction from any higher commander. During and after the battle, his Rough Riders unfailingly praised his ability to get the best out of them. In solitude, TR was often beset with self-doubt, but among others, when all were engaged in a common cause, his display of passionate confidence in himself and his companions was invariably contagious. The faith the Rough Riders inspired in him and the support they gave was similar to what Conie, Bamie, and Edith provided back home. Safely returned from battlefield and reflecting many years later, Roosevelt was callous in what can only be described as a coldhearted analysis of his decision to leave Edith and six children, not to mention a high-ranking presidential political appointment: "When the chance came for me to go to Cuba with the Rough Riders Mrs. Roosevelt was very ill and so was Teddy. It was a question if either would ultimately get well. You know what my wife and children mean to me; and yet I made up my mind that I would not allow even a death to stand in my way; that it was my one chance to do something for my country and my one chance to cut my little notch on the stick that stands as a measuring rod in every family. I know now that I would have turned from my wife's deathbed to have answered that call."[29]

In truth, Edith was recovering and never forced such a decision. She ultimately backed TR and arguably gave him the confidence to charge without remorse or regret. By any measure, Roosevelt's example was heroic, and he was duly recommended for the Medal of Honor. That he was not awarded the medal in his own lifetime may be testimony to his loyalty to his men and his intense concern for them because his advocacy for them put him at odds with the powers that be. Spain sued for peace, and hostilities were halted on August 12, less than a month and a half after TR's victory at San Juan Heights. The subsequent treaty signed in Paris on December 10, 1898, gave the United States Spain's colonies of the Philippines, Guam, and Puerto Rico. Cuba became a U.S. protectorate. Splendid indeed, but Roosevelt saw too clearly that most of the American casualties in the war were sustained *after* the shooting had stopped. Malaria, yellow fever, and other semitropical diseases were killing far more troops than bullets did as U.S. forces languished in Cuba for more than a month and a half after the Spanish forces on the island surrendered on July 17. Roosevelt led a group of fellow officers in a critical assault against the U.S. military leadership for proving as incompetent at returning its soldiers home from Cuba as it had been in getting them there. His unsparing and widely published criticism of the top army brass, including Secretary of War Russell Alger, likely spoiled any chance he had of getting a Medal of Honor, an award over which Alger had final approval.

But Roosevelt's efforts did earn him the further admiration and gratitude of his men. He spent his own money to secure them extra rations, and his agitating may have earned all the U.S. 1st Volunteers a relatively early trip home, on August 8. Perhaps even more important, it earned him self-respect. To Patty Selmes, he wrote from Cuba on July 31: "I have always felt that it was a shame for the cow-puncher to pass away without being given a chance to show what splendid stuff there was in him as a fighting man."[30] Bob Ferguson, who served alongside TR as a Rough Rider, wrote Edith: "No hunting trip so far has ever equalled it in Theodore's eyes. It makes up for the omissions of many past years . . . T. was just revelling in victory and gore . . . I really believe firmly now that they cannot kill him."[31]

The experience was, Theodore wrote to Henry Cabot Lodge, his "crowded hour"—a magical phrase born of the physical reality of men fighting furiously for a small piece of ground and the figurative reality of decisive moment crowded with danger and opportunity. He confessed to his friend, "I would rather have led that charge . . . than served three terms in the U.S. Senate."[32] But his ascent was far from over.

Theodore Roosevelt "rose like a rocket" alongside Alice Hathaway Lee, but after that meteoric rise in the New York Assembly, he held no elective office between 1884 and 1899—fifteen of his sixty years, or one quarter of all the years in his "strenuous life." Now, his admiration by the American public prompted "Easy Boss" Tom Platt to send his minion Lemuel Quigg to recruit Roosevelt as the GOP nominee for the New York gubernatorial election that fall. As the cliché has it, politics makes strange bedfellows. Roosevelt, like his father before him, had dedicated his progressive career to fighting corrupt operators like Platt and Quigg. The disdain was mutual, but Platt was first and last a pragmatist who knew better than to squander the political capital TR now had. Here was a candidate more exciting than anything either the GOP's Stalwart machine or the Democrats' Tammany Hall could field. Besides, "progressive" or not, TR was a winner. And as Lyndon Baines Johnson, master manager of political capital, would say of the unpredictable J. Edgar Hoover, "It's probably better to have him inside the tent pissing out than outside the tent pissing in."[33]

Edith, Bamie, and Conie would enthusiastically support his campaign. Mayors might not become presidents, but governors certainly did.[34]

12

A RISING TIDE

"We shall be quite private except for my sister. I always like to have her present at all my conferences. She takes so much interest in what I am doing!"

—Theodore Roosevelt to Thomas Platt,
Republican boss of New York State

t is difficult to know with certainty when TR first contemplated a bid for the presidency—there were so many times that his political career seemed to be over—but in the summer of 1898, the presidency was more conceivably in his grasp than ever before. Still, there was little consensus about how he would get there. Having two highly strategic women as your advisors could get tricky when they did not agree—with one another or with you. But for the time being, all agreed the first step was to get TR to Albany and in the governor's mansion.

Edith was downright prescient when it came to improving her husband's prospects. In mid-July 1898, days after the Battle of San Juan Heights but well before Platt sent Quigg to her husband, she cut out a letter to the editor of the New York *Sun* and sent it to her husband in Cuba. It was from three *Democrats*, recommending the nomination of TR for governor. "The crowded hour," TR had called the mortal combat atop San Juan Heights. Edith understood just how jam-packed it truly was. It contained her husband's political future.[1]

On August 8, TR and his Rough Riders sailed out of Santiago Harbor, en route to Camp Wikoff near Montauk, Long Island, for yellow fever quarantine. Tumultuous crowds greeted the ship *Miami* on its arrival. Of the sobriquets that attached to Theodore Roosevelt, two— "Teedie" and "Thee"—were sweet to him. "Teddy" was not. And yet it was *Teddy! Teddy! Teddy!* that the crowd shouted. The icon now had a name, and he would not publicly shun it.

On August 15, Edith was handed a confidential telephone message. It bade her come to Montauk. TR had found a way to pierce the quarantine so that he could see her. Long Island is indeed long, and the trip from Oyster Bay was five hours by rail. No sooner did she arrive in Montauk than she was told that an outbreak of yellow fever had tightened the quarantine. Not to be turned away, she cadged a place on an army wagon. The crusading journalist Jacob Riis, a longtime friend of Roosevelt working as a special correspondent for *The Evening Sun*, described "Mrs. Roosevelt hooded and cloaked against a threatening storm on the board seat of an army wagon bound for the Montauk hills, to receive her lover-husband back from the war."[2] She persuaded a junior officer to smuggle the colonel out of the camp for a highly unauthorized reunion. It was joyous but fleeting.

Edith did not turn back after her brief meeting with Theodore. She secured space in a Red Cross hut, passed the night there, and, come morning, found a room in a house not far away. She decided to volunteer as an assistant in the hospital, caring for sick and wounded soldiers. Cots were in short supply, as was food. When a nurse told Colonel Roosevelt that what the men needed were egg nogs, he secretly purchased a vast quantity of eggs, canned milk, sacks of sugar, and a large stock of brandy and whiskey—in addition to a case of champagne addressed to "The Red-Haired Nurse, Diet Tent, Detention Hospital, Montauk." The nurse shared the champagne with her patients, telling them it was "with Colonel Roosevelt's compliments."[3] The quarantine was not lifted until

September 13, when the Rough Riders mustered out, presenting their colonel with the gift of an authorized reproduction of Frederic Remington's celebrated *Bronco Buster* bronze. Less than a week later, from Sagamore Hill, he wrote to Henry Cabot Lodge that "Apparently," he was "going to be nominated" for governor of New York.[4]

The nomination became official on October 3, and he launched a vigorous campaign statewide. Recalling coverage of the infamous 1886 Haymarket Riot in Chicago, in which anarchist bombs killed eight and injured sixty, Edith feared exposing her husband to assassination. Writing in the New York *Sun* during TR's gubernatorial campaign, Jacob Riis observed that Edith "no sooner felt she saw [her husband] by Scylla than Charybdis loomed up."[5] The risks of combat in Cuba apparently caused her less anxiety than the fear of some unknown assassin. Her concerns were far from unfounded. Since Lincoln in 1865, twelve major American politicians had been assassinated, most prominent among them President Garfield (1881) and Chicago mayor Carter Harrison Sr. (1893). Despite this, Edith worked tirelessly—sometimes assisted by fourteen-year-old Alice—mostly sorting through massive quantities of mail and dictating responses on behalf of her husband to many of the letters.

Bamie was largely unable to participate in the campaign, much as she wanted to. She gave birth (on October 18), to ten-and-a-half-pound William Sheffield Cowles Jr. And so Conie picked up the role of unofficial publicist, a role for which she'd been practicing since the age of eight, when she sent family and friends breathless reports of her brother's antics on their first Grand Tour. She "ignored [Edith's] injunctions" about keeping TR's wartime letters private and gave "to New Jersey newspapers"[6] those he had written to her. This further fanned the flames of her brother's celebrity. If TR was bothered by this, he seems never to have voiced any objection.

On November 8, 1898, Theodore Roosevelt defeated Democratic gubernatorial candidate Augustus Van Wyck, a Brooklyn judge who had been chosen by the Democrats over William Randolph Hearst, a man "deeply jealous of the Rough Rider's fame," fame his own publishing empire had been instrumental in magnifying. During the campaign, Hearst "un-leashed the full force of his cartoonists and editorialists to ridicule Roo-sevelt as a spoiled child and political fake."[7] Frankenstein's monster was loose, in the eyes of Hearst, and the rivalry would continue for decades.

Despite Theodore's fame, the election was close. Roosevelt won by only 18,000 votes and recognized he owed victory to more than just his Republican supporters. "I shall strive to administer the office of the gov-ernor in the interests of the whole people," TR said on election night. "It is by doing so that I can best show my appreciation of the support given to me by independents and Democrats."[8]

Unlike many other politicians and their families, Edith found Al-bany—grimy and dour—quite appealing, though she had some trepida-tion about being compared to her husband's first wife, whose vivacious youth and abundant beauty had made an indelible impression on the leg-islators. As for the mansion itself, she had received numerous warnings that it was a dreary architectural dog's breakfast. What she saw, however, was solidity, comfort, and ample space for her family and guests—public housing, as it were, offering the simultaneous financial benefit of all but shuttering Sagamore Hill for most of the year.

Sworn in privately on Monday, January 2, TR attended the formal public ceremony the next day, which offered typical upstate New York winter weather with temperatures of six degrees below zero—so cold that the musicians of the governor's ceremonial military escort were unable to play their frozen bugles; the music consisted of nothing more than drums. Edith, suffering from flu, nevertheless braved the cold to witness the pub-lic swearing-in and, afterward, entertained as best she could. She held her "arms full of flowers . . . [to] avoid in a delicate manner having to shake hands with the flood of well-wishers."[9] When the day and evening were ended, she took to her bed and did not reemerge for a week. She wrote a friendly letter to her expat spinster sister, Emily, telling her that she got "a great deal of amusement out of" her new house, but when Emily, ensconced in Italy, asked if she needed her help in Albany, Edith turned a shockingly chill shoulder: "I certainly do not want you to come home, as you do not care for America and Americans and with the new responsibilities of this position on my hands I have to be selfish to attend to everything properly."[10] On the one hand, the language of the letter is rather insufferable. On the other, however, it reflects the seriousness with which Edith took her position. For her, first lady of New York State was clearly a job—and a patriotic job at that, the performance of which could brook no disagreeable spinster who professed disdain for her native country.

As for Governor Roosevelt, if Platt expected submissive gratitude, he was sorely disappointed. The two were often in conflict and, most of the time, Roosevelt prevailed. A prime example was Roosevelt's role in sponsoring the Ford Franchise Tax Bill, which provided for taxing corporations on any public franchises (such as urban street railways) they controlled. The bill was a classic instance of progressivism that would have pleased the Lees and the Saltonstalls and which appalled Easy Boss Platt, who was at the time a United States senator. Platt considered the bill a radical "shot into the heart of the business community." To get the bill passed, Roosevelt did an end run around Platt and the party by directly appealing to the people to make their voice heard. It was a tactic he would master as president. Defeated, Platt was furious—but soon decided that, boss though he was, he could not suppress the popularity of Roosevelt. From this point on, he worked with the governor, albeit grudgingly, and Roosevelt, in turn, treated him with respect, which, since he was acting from a position of victory, was easy enough to do.[11]

Roosevelt told Henry Cabot Lodge, "I do not believe that any other man has ever had as good a time as Governor of New York."[12] Yet he told his childhood playmate and lifelong friend Fanny Parsons that, for all intents and purposes, the governorship would be the end of his political life. He had "shot his last bolt," he told her.[13] Whether TR was being modest or sincere, that was not the view of his sisters, nor his wife. Nevertheless, the governor's office was where he learned the rudiments of governing as a chief executive. It was in Albany that TR shed the last vestiges of his upper-class political identity and embraced middle-class America, which he knew had put him in the governor's mansion. He reined in corporate power by endorsing legislation like the Ford Franchise Tax Bill, warning corporate moguls and political bosses alike that if corporations did not pay their fair share of taxes, the public might demand socialism by calling for the public ownership of all franchises. It was the kind of argument his kinsman FDR would frequently make.[14]

As governor, TR promoted progressivism first and foremost by the pragmatic means of appointing highly qualified, public-spirited men to policymaking positions, taking care to first secure the approval of Easy Boss Platt. This show of respect, even mild obeisance, usually mollified Platt and made him take ownership of an appointment as if it had been his idea all along. Roosevelt took no pride of authorship in the work he did, but he did not compromise his principles. As would be true for FDR, TR developed in the governor's role much that would figure as features of his presidency, especially in the areas of corporate responsibility to the public, government mediation of labor disputes, railroad rate regulation, social welfare and workers' rights, and conservation of land and natural resources. As governor, Roosevelt appealed to the public to apply pressure to compel the breakup of trusts. This established the template for his presidential trust-busting, and it also revealed to him the benefits of establishing a direct relationship between chief executive and the public— the traditional domain of the legislative branch. It was as a governor that Roosevelt came to see the executive as the tribune of the people, a conception of the office that would become the hallmark of his presidency.

TR's "sisters vied over who could be most useful to him politically" during his governorship.[15] Bamie, despite being a mother for the first time in her early forties and staying largely out of the campaign, turned her home at 689 Madison Avenue into a substitute governor's residence in New York City, to which TR (based on his diaries) would travel to almost weekly. Despite being Bamie's residence, Roosevelt spent so much time at 689 Madison that the site is today marked as the onetime home of Governor Roosevelt. When Bamie moved to Washington, D.C., one year into his term because of her husband's latest appointment, Conie picked up the substitute hostess role at 422 Madison Avenue.[16] Theodore devised inventive means to keep his sisters abreast of developments so they could offer private advice. Conie recalled:

> After breakfast was over, Mr. Platt would say in a rather stern manner, "And, now, Governor Roosevelt, I should like to have a private word with you," and my brother would answer, "Why, certainly, Mr. Platt, we will go right up to my sister's library—good-by gentlemen," turning to his other guests, and then to Mr. Platt again, "We shall be quite private except for my sister. I always like to have her present at all my conferences. She takes so much interest in what I am doing!"[17]

Roosevelt cannily used the sexism of the age to his advantage. Platt could hardly object to allowing Bamie or Conie to stay in the room for their most sensitive political discussions, for what influence, in the estimation of the Easy Boss, could the sisters Roosevelt possibly wield? Behind the scenes, Conie and Bamie peppered their brother with policy questions to sharpen his thinking. In one such response to Conie in May 1899, TR wrote: "In reference to my attitude on the bills that have not passed, there are hundreds of people to whom, if I had time, I should explain my attitude, but I have not the time. I have the gravest kind of doubts, for instance, as to the advantages to the State of our High School system, as at present carried out . . . I strongly believe that there has been a tendency amongst some of the best educators recently to divert from mechanical trades, people who ought, for their own sake, to keep in at the mechanical trades."[18] Theodore always made time for Conie and Bamie. "Haven't *we* had fun being governor of New York State?" he often greeted them.[19]

Edith took to the role of New York's first lady, though she "preferred the quiet days alone" with her husband and rarely joined him on the campaign trail or at public events, no matter how compelling the guest list.[20] "One afternoon in May [1900]," Conie recalled, "my brother telephoned me that he wanted to bring several men to dinner the following day, amongst others, Mr. Winston Churchill."[21] Churchill, at the time a young war correspondent, proved to be a notably rude guest. In a *Saturday*

Evening Post interview in 1965, Alice Roosevelt Longworth noted that Churchill "incensed his hosts by slumping in his chair, puffing on a cigar, and refusing to get up when women came into the room."[22]

Sylvia Jukes Morris observes that Edith did become "less and less reclusive as her enjoyment of the position of First Lady of State grew" and was "with him on many public occasions."[23] For someone who, in youth, had earned a reputation as reserved and remote—"born mature"—she emerged as what seems, in retrospect, a notably modern first lady. Though she proved to be a cordial hostess, she was also engaged with and informed about the governor's business and delivered informed opinions when asked. This was not traditional with governors' wives. "Her husband's larger salary, free house, and royalties from *The Rough Riders* (1899), allowed her to escape worry and duty as she never had before," and social occasions in the Executive Mansion were lively.[24] "Receptions she held as the first lady of New York received attention in papers as far away as Kansas City," and reporters began to take interest in the Roosevelt children.[25] To the surprise of many observers, she allowed four of the Roosevelt children—Ted (born in 1887), Kermit (1889), Ethel (1891), and Archie (1894)—to observe the festivities from a perch on the staircase. (Quentin, who was born 1897, was too young for the staircase, and Alice, in her early teens, was sometimes a participant with the adults.) This permissiveness was a product of Edith's parenting style and, quite likely, indicative of her instinct for publicity and public image.

Edith complained that Alice, in many ways a typically rebellious teenager, "cares neither for athletics nor good works, the two resources of youth in this town."[26] Both stepmother and father thought that Alice should be sent to Miss Spence's School in Manhattan and may have believed that the girl would prefer this to Albany. Instead, Alice warned them that she would do something "disgraceful" if they sent her off to boarding school. Next, she refused to be confirmed in the Episcopal Church. Her ultimately pragmatic parents did not make an issue of this, since they believed their children should think for themselves.

Edith did hope that Alice would be more cooperative in making her debut into society after her father was elected to a second term. Edith was far more confident that the reelection would happen than that her stepdaughter's coming-out would be in proper form. But unusually, her prediction was not correct.

On April 10, 1899, Roosevelt delivered "The Strenuous Life" speech in Chicago, extolling a life of vigor and action, and challenging Americans to embrace "not the doctrine of ignoble ease, but the doctrine of the strenuous life, the life of toil and effort, of labor and strife."[27] In June 1900, Governor Roosevelt went to Las Vegas, New Mexico, to attend the first Rough Riders reunion, where he received a greeting tumultuous in a way that unmistakably befitted a popular presidential candidate. He wrote to Lodge that his reception did cause "some talk," so he "thought it better to come out in an interview that of course I was for President McKinley's renomination."[28] This message turned the political conversation to Roosevelt as a running mate for the president's second term. Roosevelt was receptive at first, but Edith emphatically protested. She wanted a second term in Albany. She liked the Executive Mansion, and she liked her husband's $10,000 annual salary, which was $2,000 more than what a United States vice president made. Edith clearly had no desire to reprise the straitened finances that marked so much of her childhood. As TR's wife, hers was a moderately comfortable existence lived out among some of the wealthiest families in the world.

Surely, Edith also understood that the vice presidency was rarely a launching pad to the presidency. More often, like the office of mayor, it was a political dead end. She took great comfort in her conviction that the current vice president, Garret A. Hobart, would want to run again and would prevail. But her husband was increasingly uncertain about whether he wanted to run for a second two-year term as governor. He must have been aware that the heroic halo of his national fame might not endure another term in state office. He wanted to remain in the national arena, but would another hiatus from politics be even more destructive than a return to Albany? He confided to Senator Lodge that by that time "the kaleidoscope will have shaken and I shall be out of view."[29] He did have interest in a cabinet post, namely secretary of war. His experience of the army's shortcomings in executing operations beyond the American shore revealed to him a need for military reform, something the right war secretary could deliver. McKinley was not interested in tapping him for that position, however. While TR decidedly did not want to challenge McKinley in 1900, he did begin pondering a 1904 run.

As it turned out, Garret Hobart was far from being a well man. By April 1899, stories of his heart condition, complicated by a bout of influenza, were appearing in the press. Mark Hanna—the powerful Ohio senator, chairman of the Republican National Committee, and McKinley's chief political ally and bosom friend—proclaimed that, the newspaper stories notwithstanding, "nothing but death or an earthquake can stop the re-nomination of Vice President Hobart."[30]

Death it would be. At the end of October, the McKinley administration announced that the vice president was too ill to return to public service. Hobart died the next month, almost exactly one year before the 1900 election. Political pressure to tap Theodore Roosevelt as the next vice presidential candidate mounted. Edith continued to counsel against her husband's acceptance. Although Roosevelt himself felt that the vice presidency might be a very sound platform from which to launch a 1904 White House bid, he was also aware that it would take him out of much of the political action during the intervening years. Arguably, therefore, declining the offer might well have been sound advice.

Not everyone was delighted with Theodore Roosevelt. The traditional New Year's Day reception at the governor's mansion on January 1, 1900, lacked a significant guest: Easy Boss Thomas Platt. His absence sent a powerful message of disapproval of Roosevelt's plans for the new year, which included state regulation of large corporations and a requirement that they disclose their earnings to the public. To his fellow Republicans in New York and beyond, Platt recommended that Roosevelt be consigned to the vice presidency as a way to politically neuter him. Shortly before New Year's, Roosevelt himself had written Cecil Spring-Rice that he would like

to be named governor of the Philippines—a prospect that kindled the special enthusiasm of his daughter Alice, who said she pictured herself living
"among the palm trees in a 'palace' surrounded by young officers in white
uniforms."[31] To Henry Cabot Lodge, however, TR noted that Hobart's
death left a vacuum to be filled, adding that if tomorrow McKinley were to
die, he himself might be "seriously *considered* as his successor."[32]

Hobart's death deprived Edith of a key bulwark against her husband's
accepting a VP nod from McKinley. She apparently prevailed even more
insistently on her husband. Before the end of January, Roosevelt wrote to
Lodge: "The money question is a serious one with me . . . I have felt a very
keen regret that I did not have some money-making occupation, for I am
never certain when it may be necessary to sell Sagamore and completely
alter my whole style of life . . . even to live simply as Vice-President,
would be a serious drain upon me, and would cause me, and especially
would cause Edith, continual anxiety about money."[33] There is no reason
to believe that TR would be anything other than straightforward with
his closest political friend. Clearly, Edith had a powerful influence over
him, and the argument she seems to have pressed—financial need—was
both compelling and valid. Two days later, TR went on to tell Lodge
that he was going to make a public declaration of his intent to stand for
a second gubernatorial term, which, he believed, would nip in the bud
any serious attempts to recruit him for the McKinley reelection ticket.
"Edith," he added, "bids me to say that she hopes you will forgive her!"[34]

It would be simple to conclude that TR had become uxorious. The reality was almost certainly rather more complex. Yes, he did want to please
her. He may also have felt that he "owed her" for his having fled to his
great Cuban adventure when she was critically ill. But he also respected
her and sought her opinion on important matters, including those relating to his political career. Ultimately, she had supported his role in the
Spanish-American War at least in part as a political stepping-stone—and
it had paid off almost instantly by helping to make him governor of the
nation's most populous and powerful state, the center of its commercial
life, the capital of its banking industry, home to its securities industry,

cultural capital, and principal Atlantic port of entry. He must have appreciated her frequently expressed belief that the vice presidency was what Platt and received opinion deemed it to be: a political dead end.

Edith felt no conflict about her husband's plan to forestall attempts to name him the vice presidential nominee at the GOP National Convention in July. In fact, she went on vacation—with Emily but without Theodore—to the scene of her husband's triumph, Cuba. She told others that she wanted to see, for herself, just how formidable San Juan Hill was. When she and her sister arrived on March 10, Leonard Wood, now military-general of Cuba, greeted them at the gangplank, and she was given undiluted first lady treatment. She found Cuba charming but seemed unimpressed by the scene of the San Juan Heights battle. To daughter Ethel, she wrote: "It looks so quiet now, and in the trenches our soldiers have made nice little gardens of lettuce and radishes."[35]

The clock was ticking. She and Emily had spent nearly a month traveling, but she arrived back in Albany in plenty of time to accompany her husband on a four-day sojourn in Washington, D.C., in early May. At this point, the Republican National Convention was just a month and a half away, and Edith was dismayed to discover that the city was buzzing with the prospect of TR as vice president. Roosevelt knew that the state party seemed eager to have him—a popular governor still basking in the glow of San Juan Heights—run for a second term, the wishes of Easy Boss Platt notwithstanding. Accordingly, he had his eyes and ears wide open, eager now to gauge what the national party felt about a second gubernatorial term. Was he looking for confirmation that the State House was the better platform for a presidential run in 1904? Or did he seek a reason to reconsider the vice presidency? Conie summed up the situation: "Theodore Roosevelt, the loving brother, the humorous philosopher, the acute politician, was once more in the saddle. In a moment, in a masterly moment, he had sketched the situation for me: 'Yes, Platt and [Benjamin] Odell [the eventual Republican gubernatorial candidate in 1900] did want to eject him, that was true, but it wasn't only that. The West felt strongly, and the Middle West as strongly, that his name would be an asset on the presidential ticket. No, he didn't want to give up a second term as governor of New York State; he hated the thought of a vice-presidential burial-party, but what was he to do? He didn't really know himself."[36] Bamie was unambiguous. She was "livid" with those advising her brother to run for vice president. She, like Edith, worried what "comparatively inactive years" would do to him.[37] Doubtless, they feared he would fail to achieve his potential, and they may have also felt that, frustrated and bored, he would launch into who knows what wild adventure.

Edith's disdain for the vice presidency did not keep her from reserving a box at Philadelphia's convention hall—although she claimed that all she wanted to do was see a national convention for the first time. When the couple returned to Albany from their D.C. sojourn, a dinner guest, Judge Alton B. Parker, told her that she had much to look forward to at the convention, including a tumultuous "demonstration of applause" when "your husband [is] unanimously nominated for the office of Vice-President of the United States." Edith cut him off abruptly: "You disagreeable thing," she exclaimed, "I don't *want* to see him nominated for the Vice-Presidency!"[38]

When the Roosevelts checked into their hotel in Philadelphia on June 16, they were greeted with pro-Roosevelt demonstrations, including delegates roaming the hotel corridors chanting "We Want Teddy!" to the accompaniment of banging drums and shrilling fifes. Edith supervised the drafting of a statement intended to counter any TR stampede. The message was that Governor Roosevelt believed he could best serve the public interest by remaining *Governor* Roosevelt for another term. On the final day of the convention, June 21, Edith ensconced herself in the gallery box she had reserved. Her husband came onto the floor somewhat tardily. He wore a hat with a broad brim that unmistakably echoed the campaign hat he wore as colonel of the Rough Riders, an image by now very familiar to everyone in the hall.

Mark Hanna, a Stalwart, was as fearful of the progressive Roosevelt becoming the GOP vice presidential nominee as Platt was of his reelection as New York governor for another two years. Hanna famously told anyone who would listen to him, "Don't you realize that there's only one life between this madman and the White House?"[39]

Asked by the party to speak, TR ascended the rostrum to second the nomination of William McKinley for a second term. About to commence his seconding speech, he looked up at Edith in the gallery and waved to her. The picture the *New York Tribune* painted was virtually a Renaissance Annunciation, describing how, on cue, "the sun broke through an opening in the roof and its rays played for a moment like an aureole about [Roosevelt's] head. He actually flushed, but for a moment only, and then he faced the shouting throng once more. For the first time, practically, the real hero of the convention stood in full view of the admiring thousands."[40]

Not even the will of Edith Roosevelt could stop his nomination now. It was out of her hands—and out of her husband's. Platt was delighted. "Roosevelt might as well stand under Niagara Falls and try to spit the water back," he proclaimed.[41] Hanna's response was to warn McKinley: "Your *duty* to the Country is to *live* four years from next March."[42] Though TR had lingering doubts, his friend Lodge had finally persuaded him that the vice presidency was, at this point, his best route to the presidency. His fame and popular appeal were *now*. A second term as governor would end in 1902, and he himself conceded to Lodge that two years out of office was two years too long. He needed to act on his fame: "I have never known a hurrah to endure for five years."[43] McKinley did not want to appoint him secretary of war, so the vice presidency loomed as his only hope to stay in the action, relatively weak as it was. McKinley refused Hanna's pleas to publicly back another candidate for vice president. Boss Platt maneuvered behind the scenes to ensure Roosevelt's nomination, thus removing the progressive political thorn from his side in New York. When the convention finally voted, McKinley received 926 votes and Roosevelt received 925 votes—TR symbolically cast the only vote against his nomination. "The best we can do is pray fervently for the continued health of the President," said Hanna.[44] A New York *World* reporter watched Edith's reaction to the vote: "With just a little gasp of regret, Mrs. Roosevelt's face broke into smiles, as she, once for all, accepted the situation with a grace worthy of a true patriot."[45]

• • •

Roosevelt traveled over 21,000 miles in twenty-four states delivering over seven hundred speeches—much of it without Edith or the children by his side. "We can always have the night to hallow the day sweetheart . . . I love you just as I did when we were married and I count the days until you are with me once more," she wrote him.[46] Edith tended to the children, getting Ted ready for Groton School and then delivering him there in October. She also zealously collected, cut, and pasted all the TR news clippings she could garner and tended to her husband's mail, sorting it and ensuring that he saw what she considered the most important of it right away.

On Election Day, November 6, the McKinley-Roosevelt ticket handily defeated William Jennings Bryan and Adlai E. Stevenson, 7,219,193 to 6,357,698—292 electoral votes to 155. But while Roosevelt won votes, Edith lost weight, her collarbones emerging in bold relief. Far from betraying any concern over this as a sign of stress or unhappiness, TR wrote to Emily that her sister looked "prettier than ever."[47] Edith, too, wrote Emily, though with a decidedly different tone. The vice presidency was "a useless & empty position." Her husband would be "like the bridegroom at a wedding, no one even sees or thinks of him."[48]

In those days, before the Twentieth Amendment was ratified in 1933, advancing Inauguration Day from March to January, the inauguration of William McKinley and Theodore Roosevelt was constitutionally set for March 4. TR took advantage of the long interval between Election Day and Inauguration Day to do what he often did when he had time on his hands. He lit out for the territory. In February, he made a long hunting trip in the Rocky Mountains—without Edith or any other member of the family. He made it back to New York with little time to spare before the inauguration.

The train from New York to Washington bound for the inauguration collected Roosevelts along the way. Conie, her real estate broker husband, Douglas, and her four children joined in New Jersey, and Bamie, who was living in D.C. with her husband and son, met them at

Washington's Union Station. Bamie as usual took control of the proceedings and "hurried Theodore off before enough people recognized him to make a crush."[49]

"For twenty years, since he first engaged in politics in New York City, Bamie had pushed him, applauding each victory, and boasting of his competence and goodness," and now she was about to witness him take the oath of office for the second highest office in the country.[50] The usually buoyant Conie adopted a more sanguine tone about the "peculiar charm" of the inauguration. "Perhaps one felt this charm especially because of the contrast between those two happy young people [Theodore and Edith] and the more serious President, weighed down as he was with many cares, the greatest of which was his loving anxiety for his fragile little wife."[51] (Ida Saxton McKinley had suffered the deaths of two children and her own mother within a short span, leaving her "nervous" and subject to epileptic seizures.) After the swearing-in on the East Portico of the Capitol, Edith attended the postinaugural lunch and then, with her children, went off to Thompson's Drug Store at the corner of 15th Street and Pennsylvania Avenue, above which she had rented a room (for $200—nearly $6,000 in today's currency) so that she and the children could observe the Inaugural Parade. Alice, notably, offered her observation on the passing procession, declaring that the McKinleys looked like "usurping cuckoos."[52]

After a fifteen-year hiatus from electoral politics, Theodore Roosevelt had ascended to vice president following just two years in the governor's office. "Bamie had feared," after the death of Alice Hathaway Lee, that "too long out of the political arena would cripple him."[53] Now that familiar doubt crept in once more. Roosevelt's eldest daughter, Alice, later said that her father had a "melancholic streak which didn't come out very often but which was noticeable when it did."[54] Inaugurated in March, TR was grousing by April. The vice presidency, he said, "ought to be abolished."[55] He presided over the Senate for a total of five days. "My active work is over," Roosevelt confided to his childhood playmate and good friend Fanny Parsons.[56] Roosevelt tutored Conie in American history at Sagamore Hill and arranged to revive his legal education with none other than the chief justice of the United States when he returned to Washington. Convinced his career was over, Vice President Roosevelt halfheartedly allowed Bamie and her husband to begin lining up potential donors for a 1904 presidential race. Roosevelt even hosted Woodrow Wilson, "then only an obscure Princeton government professor," at a Sagamore Hill meeting on public service.[57]

As chance or fate or destiny had it, Roosevelt was vice president for just six and a half months, perhaps the least eventful span of his political career. At the end of August 1901, he embarked on a speaking tour, essentially promoting his books and himself as a public figure worth listening to. While he toured, Edith rented a cottage facing the Tahawus Club in the Adirondacks for a two-week vacation with the children. About to return from his round of speaking, Theodore promised to join Edith and Ethel at a friend's lakeside camp not far from the club. Mother and daughter left the Tahawus Club on September 7. They stopped to water their horses at a place called the Lower Works and were met there with a telephone message from Roosevelt.

He could not meet them. President McKinley had been shot.

Leon Czolgosz, an unemployed factory worker, became an anarchist after hearing a speech by the radical Emma Goldman in Cleveland weeks before the assassination. Thus inspired, he traveled to Buffalo, New York, where McKinley was scheduled to appear at a reception at the Pan-American Exposition, essentially a celebration of American commerce, industry, innovation, and economic dominance over the hemisphere. On the afternoon of September 6, Czolgosz wrapped his right hand in a white handkerchief as if it were a bandage. Concealed within the cloth was a .32-caliber Iver Johnson revolver, which he carried into the Exposition's Temple of Music. In that building, he took a place in a long line of well-wishers waiting to shake hands with President McKinley.

The line advanced rapidly, and at 4:07 p.m., Czolgosz came face-to-face with the president. He extended his "bandaged" hand. McKinley reached out to shake it. Two shots were fired. At point-blank range, both found their mark. The first round, however, was deflected by a coat button, creating no more than a graze wound. The second tore through McKinley's stomach, scraped his kidney, deeply gouged his pancreas, and then came to rest, buried in the muscles of his back. McKinley was fully conscious. Indeed, he had the presence of mind to order the men pummeling his assassin to stop their beating.

The alert demeanor of the injured president gave his doctors a reasonable expectation that the wounds would not prove fatal, but Roosevelt was nevertheless summoned to his bedside. The decision was made to operate in an effort to find and remove the bullet. It was always a judgment call as to whether it was safer to remove a bullet or leave it where it was. In this case, the surgeon probed in vain. He could not locate the bullet, though he was able to repair some of the internal damage. It soon appeared that McKinley was recovering. Perhaps the best course of action had been chosen.

On September 8, Roosevelt telegraphed Edith to tell her that the president's condition was so much improved that he had decided to join the family in the Adirondacks. Even as the president lay wounded by an attempted assassination, Roosevelt wrote to Bamie about a planned dinner with her in Washington. Should it be canceled, or should it go on? "I shall have to trust to your own knowledge."[58]

He arrived at Tahawus on September 11, and the next day he, Edith, Ethel, and four others hiked some six miles through the woods to Camp Colden. On the following day, September 13, Roosevelt and three young men who had hiked with his party the day before set off to climb nearby mile-high Mount Marcy. Edith and Ethel started walking back to the club. On the way, they encountered two men, one of whom told them they had an urgent message for the "Marcy party."[59]

It was six that evening before Roosevelt, having been reached by the messengers, returned to the club. He sent down a message to the Lower Works, asking for news of the president's health from Buffalo. No word reached him in return, so he ate and, at nine, went to bed. To Edith, he remarked, "I'm not going unless I'm really needed. I have been there once and that shows how I feel. But I will not go to stand beside those people who are suffering and anxious."[60]

He did not sleep long. Just before midnight, a messenger delivered a telegram with the news that McKinley's condition had suddenly become grave. Early in the morning of September 14, a second telegram was sent announcing his death. By then, Roosevelt was already en route by buckboard pulled by a relay of horses to the nearest railroad station, where a special train was waiting to take him to Buffalo. It was dawn when he reached the station and was told that the president was dead, having passed away at 2:15 that morning. He sent a telegram to Lower Works for delivery to Edith: "president mckinley died at 2:15 this morning. theodore roosevelt."[61]

At the railroad station in Buffalo, longtime friend and Buffalo resident Ansley Wilcox greeted Roosevelt and invited him to have lunch with him at his home at 641 Delaware Avenue. From there, he would go to the Milburn House, to which McKinley's body had been taken. Over their lunch, Wilcox brought up the subject of where he would be sworn in, expecting his question to begin a protracted discussion. Instead, Roosevelt shot back a single word: "Here."

Wilcox told him that he understood the cabinet had decided that the ceremony should be held at the Milburn House, in a room one floor below that in which McKinley's body lay.

"Don't you think it would be far better to do as the cabinet has decided?" Wilcox asked.

"No," said the new president. "It would be far worse."[62]

This brief exchange marked a powerful contrast between the inertia of the prior six and a half months and the relentless and decisive activity that would characterize the Roosevelt presidency. In rejecting the advice of a cabinet his predecessor had appointed, TR took charge. His decision was not the product of mere willfulness or ego. Roosevelt was appalled by what would today be called the "optics" of swearing in a new president quite literally under the corpse of the old one. Such a thing was not only unseemly but morbid, sending a message that the new leader saw himself in the grasp of his predecessor's dead hand. Roosevelt understood that continuity was important after a president dies in office, especially at the hands of an anarchist assassin in an era that seemed to many plagued by incipient anarchy. He himself would soon issue a statement that he intended to carry on the work of the slain president. But TR surely saw that he could not be a leader if he allowed himself to dwell in the shadow of a corpse. Theodore Roosevelt was duly sworn in as the twenty-sixth president of the United States—at the house of Ansley Wilcox. Roosevelt, at age forty-two, remains the youngest president in history. Edith had turned forty in August.

At her home in New Jersey, Conie was "inundated" with reporters.[63] But Edith made no mention of her husband's ascendency in her diary entry for September 14, 1901, noting only, as she customarily did, the whereabouts of her children and, even more meticulously, the family's daily expenses.[64]

Edith and Bamie had been correct: Roosevelt loathed the inactivity and irrelevance of the vice presidency though it is worth noting that the women who created the president very nearly came close to changing the course of American history. They could, conceivably, have prevented TR from ever becoming president had they gotten their way. Prescient as they were, neither Bamie nor Edith could foresee such an unbelievable turn of events. Though one man had: Senator Mark Hanna, and he was stricken. The violent act was personal. A lifelong friend and political ally of William McKinley, he traveled to his bedside in the exposition hospital. "Mr. President, Mr. President," Hanna called out to McKinley. "William! William! Don't you know me?"[65] Kingmaker in the Republican old guard, Hanna had exclaimed after nominating Roosevelt as his friend's running mate, "Your *duty* to the Country is to *live* for four years from next March."[66] At 2:15 in the morning of September 14, 1901, that "one life" was gone. "Now look!" Hanna moaned. "That damned cowboy is president of the United States."[67]

Yet TR had no desire to take Washington by storm and did not rush to occupy the White House. It was, after all, now the home of a grieving widow. He therefore spent his first eight days as president of the United States—from September 14 to September 22—in the Washington home of his sister Bamie, at 1733 N Street, NW, near Dupont Circle, which the press came to call the "Little White House." For over a week, the home of the sister who was so often a second mother and strategic advisor, a woman whose counsel he often sought, was the Executive Mansion. In Bamie's home began the administration of the most transformative president since Abraham Lincoln.

On September 22, Edith remained at Sagamore Hill (where they customarily summered) with the children, preparing to move back to Washington as the first family. Theodore, now President Roosevelt, asked sisters Bamie and Conie to join him for his first meal at the White House. Flowers were passed at the table for the boutonnieres of the president and his sister's husbands. The flower given to President Roosevelt was a yellow saffronia rose. Conie wrote:

> His face flushed, and he turned again and said: "Is it not strange? This is the rose we all connect with my father." My sister and I responded eagerly that many a time in the past we had seen our father pruning the rose-bush of saffronia roses with special care. He always picked one for his buttonhole from that bush, and whenever we gave him a rose, we gave him one of those. Again my brother said, with a very serious look on his face, "I think there is a blessing connected with this."[68]

Theodore Roosevelt, alongside his beloved sisters, spent his first evening in the White House. It was their father's birthday.

Part Five

THE WOMEN IN
THE ARENA

1901—1948

13

PARTNERS IN HISTORY

"I know that he often came to see her to talk out problems in Washington."

—Eleanor Roosevelt on TR and Bamie[1]

*H*ow strange it seems that I should be here in this position with your father's son," John Hay said to Bamie as they stood behind President Roosevelt at the funeral of President McKinley, a former presidential advisor speaking to a future one.[2] Hay's illustrious political career was bookended by assassinations. He began as private secretary to President Lincoln and would conclude as secretary of state to President Roosevelt. Hay had been the connection through which Theodore Sr. secured the meeting with Lincoln that resulted in passage of the law under which he became an allotment commissioner, signing up Union troops to set aside voluntary pay deductions for the support of their families. "TR was not a superstitious man . . . [b]ut he believed in talismans and good omens connected to his father," observed TR biographer Dr. Kathleen Dalton.[3] One of those good omens was the continued presence of John Hay in the White House.

"Nothing could have been harder to the temperament of Theodore Roosevelt than to have come 'through the cemetery,'" Conie later observed. "What he had achieved in the past was absolutely through his own merits. To him to come to any position through 'dead men's shoes' was particularly distasteful."[4] TR, his sister argued, was a twenty-year overnight success, not an accidental president. He would have to prove it.

"It was a mistake to nominate that wild man," Mark Hanna had said after TR joined the ticket in the VP spot. Now Hanna advised the young president, who had galloped from assistant secretary of the navy to the White House in just three years, to "go slow."[5] He and the women he surrounded himself with would do no such thing.

Edith was an adept and unapologetic "political operator" throughout her husband's administration. She was an informal counselor to the president, but "informal" did not mean casual or arbitrary. She and TR had hour-long morning meetings daily, and the couple strolled the White House grounds and rode together on horseback as often as they could, talking through the President's domestic and foreign policy challenges. Frequently, the press reported on these outings. Nor were the rides always duos. TR also liked to go riding with Henry Cabot Lodge and Elihu Root, who served as McKinley's and then Roosevelt's secretary of war and later as Roosevelt's second-term secretary of state. Edith was often invited to accompany them.

Bamie, for her part, became an essential conduit to the president. The irrepressible Cecil Spring "Springy" Rice, now a full-fledged British diplomat, prevailed upon her as a diplomatic back channel, while Whitelaw Reid, the U.S. ambassador to the Court of St. James's in London, sent her a stream of letters containing his insightful and downright gossipy observations on the British aristocracy. The president often wrote back directly to Reid, which was the ambassador's cue that the Bamie back channel was not only acceptable to him but effective and welcome. The link between President Roosevelt and Bamie was a critical part of the chain that united the U.S. and the U.K., burgeoning in their economic and political relationship at the start of what would be a consequential century for their critical alliance.

Neither Edith nor Bamie ever boasted of their importance to the administration. Far from it, both first lady and sister to the president avoided making public statements of their opinions, and Edith did not discuss presidential business in letters—which doubtless accounts for why she wrote comparatively few letters during her husband's presidency. Those within the intimate orbit of the president and first lady, however, freely expressed their opinions on her influence.

In 1906, Roosevelt appointed Henry L. Stimson, a strong supporter, as U.S. attorney for the Southern District of New York. Stimson served in this capacity until President William Howard Taft tapped him as secretary of war in 1911. He went on to serve President Calvin Coolidge as governor-general of the Philippines, Herbert Hoover as secretary of state, and Franklin Roosevelt and Harry S. Truman as secretary of war. In this last, critical role of his career, Stimson advised Truman on the use of the atomic bomb and won the respect of notable scientists such as J. Robert Oppenheimer. In the words of Oppenheimer biographers Kai Bird and Martin J. Sherman, "Stimson was a wise man who had paid careful attention to all discussions regarding the implications of nuclear weapons . . . he . . . did not regard the bomb 'as a new weapon merely but as a revolutionary change in the relationship of man to the universe.' The atomic bomb might become 'a Frankenstein which would eat us up,' or it could secure the global peace."[6] Writing in 1913, Stimson recalled of Edith:

> In many of my conversations with [Theodore Roosevelt], Mrs. Roosevelt was present. Her judgment of men was nearly always better than his. Her poise as to events in which they were both concerned was nearly always better than his. Her sagacity and discrimination as I saw it exceeded that of any other woman in public affairs whom I have met and her influence was freely exerted on him and whenever I saw it it was in the direction for good.[7]

Gifford Pinchot, first head of the U.S. Forest Service, was a member of TR's version of a kitchen cabinet—known as the "Tennis Cabinet," because they played tennis with the president while debating the major events of the day—and thus qualified as a government insider if there ever was one. He too marveled at "how much more Mrs. T.R. had to do with Government business than was commonly supposed." Pinchot cited as an example the time he heard Edith "suggest Jim Garfield" (the former president's namesake and second-eldest son, who witnessed his father's assassination) for appointment to the Civil Service Commission. "That," he wrote, is "how Jim came into T.R.'s administration. And his case by no means stood alone."[8] Margaret Chanler, a close friend to both Edith and Theodore for decades, put it simply: "Edith's compass was safer to steer by."[9]

That Edith was a better judge of character than TR might have its roots in their very different personalities. Edith was generally more cautious than her husband. He was a politician, one who needed and wanted to be liked. Edith was more detached and, like a good political advisor or ally, often able to see a situation or potential appointee more clearly than the principal. "A woman of an independent mind," James Amos, Theodore's bodyguard and personal valet, recalled. Amos, who later became one of the first Black men to serve in the FBI, working on the nation's "toughest, most important espionage, organized crime, and white collar cases," said Edith offered "opinions that very often differed from her husband's."[10] "I have heard them talking together and discussing various subjects hundreds of times," Amos testified.[11] "He was always disposed to believe that people were all right and he liked those he met if they gave him half a chance," Amos described after personally witnessing the Roosevelts interacting with one another for almost twenty years. "She managed to keep away from the center," Amos contrasted. "She contrived to keep 'out of the picture.' This was not because she was a shrinking soul with no ideas of her own. She was a woman very well able to form opinions about everything that interested her husband. Mr. Roosevelt discussed the most important matters with her. And she did not always agree with him by any means. She was very much shrewder than the President in her judgment."[12]

What TR and Edith did have in common was their high moral code, decency, and respect for the quality of a person's character. They "never utter[ed] an impatient word to each other" insisted Amos.[13] TR's ebullient nature and Edith's natural circumspection, combined with their mutual respect and deep love, made for a formidable pair. Edith pored over four newspapers daily. In part, this was to keep herself apprised of "public matters," but she also assiduously clipped and saved articles that she believed her husband needed to see.[14] Roosevelt often shared the clippings with others. Those "others" quickly learned that Edith commanded her husband's full attention, and they began to use her, too, as a back channel to sidestep the growing White House bureaucracy.

"Washington is just a big village," TR wrote Bamie during his time as Civil Service commissioner.[15] Now, as president, he relied on Bamie for intelligence on the villagers. Her home at 1733 N Street, within a ten-minute walk from the White House, served as the location of Roosevelt's first cabinet meetings and retained its role as the "Little White House" over the next seven and a half years.[16] "The President brought guests to Bamie's house when he wanted to escape press surveillance"[17] and Eleanor Roosevelt recalled that "Uncle Ted would often drop in [to Bamie's home in Washington] at tea-time and got started on interesting conversation" on matters across the political spectrum. When he could not see Bamie, he wrote her. Hundreds of letters flowed between the siblings, exchanging ideas on every issue imaginable: currency, monetary policy, cabinet appointments, suffrage, and major milestones such as the Panama Canal and the Anthracite Coal Strike.

Edith Kermit Roosevelt was in one respect fortunate. Ida Saxton McKinley, the widowed first lady who was obliged to vacate what had been the McKinley White House, had been plagued by more than her fair share of "the thousand natural shocks that flesh is heir to." She suffered the loss of her mother in 1873, when she was just twenty-six. Shortly afterward that same year, her four-month-old second daughter and namesake died. Ida McKinley was soon stricken with phlebitis (a painful inflammation of a vein, typically in one or both legs) and assailed by frequent epileptic seizures. She lived in dread that her firstborn, Katie, who had been born on Christmas 1871, would die, too. She did—succumbing to typhoid in

June 1875. The McKinleys had no other children. Years later, now in the White House but unable to carry out even the minimal social duties of a first lady, the ailing Ida receded into the background, and Jennie Tuttle Hobart, the wife and, subsequently, widow of Vice President Garret Hobart, assumed the hostess role of a first lady. In a sense, then, Edith Roosevelt found herself in a White House that was something of a blank slate. She had no one else's shoes to fill.

Of course, it cannot be easy for any first lady to enter "office" following the unexpected, let alone violent, death of a sitting president. William McKinley was a popular president, and the shocked nation was plunged into deep bipartisan grief. Among President Roosevelt's first acts was an executive proclamation of thirty days' mourning, so entertaining, the usual province of a first lady, was out of the question for at least a month. This did not stop Edith from rolling up her sleeves, taking charge, and making changes. She began not by simply firing the official White House housekeeper but by eliminating the Office of Housekeeper itself. The White House would be *her* house, and she intended to supervise it personally.

In the view of historian Louis Gould her "most important early decision" was the hiring of Isabella "Belle" Hagner as the first social secretary in the history of the White House.[18] Bamie, ever the astute networker, had introduced Belle to Edith during TR's brief time as vice president. Redeployed from the War Department, where she served as a clerk, the "discreet and efficient" Hagner "became indispensable to Edith Roosevelt and a confidante to the president's children." She controlled access to, and photographs of, the Roosevelt family and managed social invitations as well as requests for the first lady's time. Hagner's work at Edith's behest "[set] a precedent for women who followed her in the White House" and was "the envy of every socially ambitious woman in America" because of her grace, style, and competence under pressure.[19]

In keeping with her puritan streak, Edith "began holding regular meetings with the wives of cabinet members to help set up social rules." They assembled every Tuesday so Edith could gather "needed information on the ethical lapses among members of society" and "subtly [warn] women with large budgets that they should not outshine the President's wife in staging their parties." One session was used to convince a cabinet wife to end an adulterous affair. It is little wonder that the *Christian Advocate* quoted *The Presbyterian*'s assessment of Edith Roosevelt as "an aristocrat to her fingers." She came, she saw, and she made 1600 Pennsylvania Avenue her castle.²⁰

Her regal demeanor was by no means inherited. She had begun life as the daughter of a wellborn wastrel father, whose failures eroded the family's social position and caused Edith's exile from the company of some of the best families—though never from the Roosevelts. In her precociously literary girlhood, the only "castle" Edith allowed herself to imagine occupying was one that served mainly to lock away the secrets of her loneliness. Now that the most famous address in America was hers, she meant to keep a tight hold on it, making it her home as well as a home fit for the nation. James Amos called Edith the "mistress of the White House" and said, "The affairs of that great establishment were directed by her to the smallest detail . . . Mrs. Roosevelt held the threads of it all in her hands and managed it all outright, keeping it going so smoothly that no one could hear the wheels going around. And she did this without thrusting herself in the limelight."²¹

Her task, as she saw and executed it, included managing the household finances. Although the presidency paid an annual salary of $50,000 (about $1.5 million today), getting to live in the White House was hardly a no-cost fringe benefit. After the thirty-day mourning period lapsed, the Roosevelts were expected to do what every presidential couple had been expected to do: entertain both regularly and frequently. For the most part, they were obliged to pay for it all out of personal pocket and purse. Edith hired a White House caterer at $7.50 per plate but relied on Belle Hagner to birddog RSVPs to ensure they never paid for more than the guest count. She limited her clothing budget to $300 a year. "I wonder how she does it," remarked Helen Taft, cabinet wife of second-term secretary of war William Howard Taft. The wife of a railroad executive with whom TR did battle was less complimentary: "Mrs. Roosevelt dresses on $300 a year and she looks like it."²²

Nevertheless, Edith and her husband proved to be prodigious hosts. During their first social season in the White House, wrapping up early in June 1902, they entertained some forty thousand guests. As first lady, Edith was given the credit for the sheer volume of this achievement, with *The New York Times* calling it "the most remarkable social record ever made by a President's wife."²³ Not all the entertaining was for state affairs.

One of Edith's first major events was the debutante ball debut of Alice, arguably the presidential daughter's first taste of what would become global fame. Theodore sent Patty Selmes and her daughter Isabella a personal letter "all done in black a half an inch deep," reflecting the continued mourning for President McKinley, "asking me to come over and see how I liked the White House," Patty later wrote.²⁴ The former Badlands mother and daughter had moved to New York City so Isabella could attend Miss Chapin's and later Miss Spence's school. Edith invited Isabella to Alice's debutante ball, and after the party, Patty and President Roosevelt talked in the Cabinet Room. Patty grew close to Conie, too, eventually addressing her as "Beloved" in their many letters. The Roosevelts invited Patty and Isabella to any number of teas, dinners, and dances. Isabella, a noted beauty, "had a whirl in Washington." "People are wild about our child," concurred Julia Loving, Isabella's African American caretaker who was employed by the Selmes family.²⁵ Though Edith was warm to Isabella, she kept Patty at a distance from TR. "I remember Mrs. Selmes, who was a great friend of Mrs. Robinson's and great friend of Uncle Ted's," recalled Eleanor Roosevelt, who formed a lifelong friendship with Isabella. "Uncle Ted liked her very much; Aunt Edith didn't like her at all! No, not at all, because Mrs. Selmes had the quality of exciting his mind."²⁶ Forever aware of being second, and despite fifteen years of marriage, the usually confident and unshakable Edith still experienced moments of self-doubt and jealousy when it came to sharing TR's attention with other, equally formidable, and intelligent women.

Not every social occasion was warmly received by the press and public. One of Theodore Roosevelt's very first letters from September 14,

1901, in the first hours of his first day as president, was to Black rights advocate and educator Booker T. Washington, the most prominent African American of the age. From the living room of the Ansley Wilcox House in Buffalo, New York, where TR had just taken the oath of office, he dictated: "I write you at once to say that to my deep regret my visit south must now be given up. When are you coming north? I must see you as soon as possible."[27]

"As soon as possible" turned out to be October 16, just two days after the thirty-day mourning period for President McKinley elapsed. Rejecting the proclivity of many whites to avoid mixing socially with Blacks, Conie endorsed the invitation and Edith hosted the first person of color to dine at the White House since Reconstruction.[28] The uproar was immediate and incendiary. In a public speech an Alabama congressman said "no great harm would have been done the country" if a bomb had exploded under the dinner table.[29] "The action of President Roosevelt in entertaining that nigger will necessitate our killing a thousand niggers in the South before they will learn their place again," said Senator Ben Tillman, a one-eyed racist from South Carolina.[30] Tillman had supporters but some senators took umbrage with his remarks and a fight broke out on the Senate floor. Roosevelt permanently banned Tillman from the White House.

Breaking bread with a Black man in the White House had lasting political consequences: Roosevelt would never win a single state in the South and was "for a while the most unpopular president in the South since the Civil War."[31] In the North the reaction was more charitable. "Any man who is privileged to have Booker Washington to eat with him at his table should feel himself honored," said the liberal Protestant minister Charles Sheldon.[32] Edith "commented that all the southern cant about chivalry was hypocritical," but the truth is that Edith was comfortable with the racist stereotypes of her time. Her correspondence sometimes betrays a condescending and low opinion of Black Americans, and she twice chose to offer expressions of racism as entertainment to her White House guests.[33]

In fact, while she hired what she called a "good colored butler" for the White House, she also ensured that the steward, a more senior position, was white and wrote to stepdaughter Alice, "If I could have only white men, it would be so much easier." When daughter Ethel took up charitable work, teaching a class of "young negroes" in a Sunday school at St. John's Episcopal ("the church of the presidents"), Edith wrote to son Kermit that "Ethel has gone off to her little nigs." Years later, in 1910, she wrote to an anti-suffrage leader that "long ago we decided the United States was no country for a college bred negro"—a statement made all the more stunning considering her hospitality to Booker T. Washington, a college educator and the first leader of the famed Tuskegee Institute.[34] Edith's record on race is frustratingly contradictory. Her personal beliefs, expressed in private letters, belie her public actions. "In an era when restaurants, schools, and most public places in the South and a great many in the North were segregated," observes Dr. Kathleen Dalton, "the Roosevelts had entertained blacks in Albany . . . [and] overnight at Sagamore Hill."[35] Even after the Booker T. Washington controversy, the president and his wife hosted the National Association for the Advancement of Colored People or NAACP, Black church leaders, and Black artists at the White House, and they frequently appeared at integrated events. Conie likewise invited Washington to dine at her home in New York.[36] Nevertheless, as Lewis Gould explores in his groundbreaking work, "the impact of Edith Roosevelt's racism on her husband has never been explored . . . [and] tracking her bigotry as an element in the racial policies of the Theodore Roosevelt administration raises disturbing questions about the larger historical importance of this important first lady."[37]

As president, Roosevelt strongly opposed lynching and peonage but the nadir of his record on race is Brownsville. On the night of August 12, 1906, a white woman was reportedly attacked in Brownsville, Texas. A regiment of segregated Black infantry—Buffalo Soldiers—were quartered at nearby Fort Brown. White citizens in Brownsville assumed the attack had been perpetrated by a Black soldier. In response to the concerns of the townspeople, Major Charles W. Penrose, the white officer commanding the 25th Infantry Regiment, ordered his troops curfewed. The following night a local bartender was killed and a police lieutenant wounded by gunshots. Townspeople accused members of the 25th. The white commanders responded that all the Black troops had been in barracks that night. Nevertheless, the accusers remained adamant.

At the recommendation of the army's inspector general, President Roosevelt summarily ordered the dishonorable discharge of the entire regiment, 167 enlisted men, all Black, because they insisted that they had no knowledge of the shootings. No military tribunal was convened, and a civilian Texas court even cleared the soldiers. These facts notwithstanding, Roosevelt stubbornly persisted in siding with the white residents, who continued to insist on the soldiers' guilt. He did dispatch investigators to the scene, whose report, which was not issued until February 7, 1909, years after the incident, backed the civilians.

Thus, 167 soldiers lost their military careers, salaries, pensions, and any honors they may have been awarded. Roosevelt was criticized, yet he refused to back down or reconsider, let alone apologize. His action in this case may well be the only instance of seemingly deliberate injustice he authorized during his presidency. It remains difficult to account for.[38]

While there is evidence that Edith held racist views, there is no evidence that she suggested, let alone prevailed upon him, to take the action he took in the Brownsville incident, and there is no evidence that she approved of it. Indeed, it is impossible to draw any meaningful conclusions concerning the influence of Edith Roosevelt on Theodore Roosevelt's thinking about race. Theodore's views on race would evolve slowly and did not culminate until the last speech of his life—delivered on November 2, 1918—which focused on equality. W. E. B. Du Bois invited Roosevelt to speak before the Circle for Negro War Relief at Carnegie Hall. TR had agreed to serve as a trustee of Howard University and the Tuskegee Institute, spiritual center of educator, author, and orator Booker T. Washington. He was also a member of the selection committee of the NAACP to recognize African American achievement. The Carnegie Hall audience was large and racially mixed. In his speech, TR called for equal "civil and political rights" and the "right to work" for all races. He promised the audience to work "toward securing a juster and fairer treatment in this country of colored people." The speech hit its crescendo: "I will do everything I can to aid, to bring about, to bring nearer, the day when justice, the square deal, will be given as between Black and white."[39]

As historian Dr. Kathleen Dalton captures, after the speech, Madison Grant, author of the pseudoscientific theory that justified racial hierarchy (upon which eugenicists would rely for years), wrote TR claiming to have evidence that white soldiers fought harder than Black soldiers in World War I. TR called Grant "an addlepated ass."[40] The thunderous speech, far from the horrid Brownsville decision and closer to the enlightenment of inviting Booker T. Washington to dinner, tempts one to wonder what the Roosevelt record might have been on race in a third term. The arc of TR's journey on race had come so far that after his death the NAACP editorialized in its magazine The Crisis that "We have lost a friend."[41] Unfortunately, Edith's casual racism (all too typical of the era) continued long past TR's death.

The formative experience of Theodore Roosevelt's youth was the Civil War. Thee, restrained from the battlefield by his Southern-sympathizing wife, worked with and for President Lincoln. Now Thee and Mittie's son was the chief executive of the nation. Theodore Roosevelt "told me frequently that he never took any serious step or made any vital decision for his country without thinking first what position his father would take," said Conie in her memoir of her brother.[42] But Dr. Dalton notes that on the consequential decision to prosecute the Northern Securities railroad trust "he would break loose from Thee" and embrace not just reform but unprecedented executive action.[43] In doing so, he also broke loose from the far more Stalwart conservative McKinley. Clearly, the new president would lead a very different administration. TR had inherited McKinley's cabinet and many in the Republican Party were not ready to gallop at TR's speed, but he could always count on the women in his life to support him.

When Roosevelt ascended to the presidency, mogul J. P. Morgan reacted as negatively as Mark Hanna. "I'm afraid of Mr. Roosevelt because I don't know what he'll do," Morgan, the richest and most powerful person in America, told a reporter. "He's afraid of me because he does know what I'll do," Roosevelt shot back.[44] With fellow financier E. H. Harriman, Morgan had recently created the Northern Securities Company, which held the stock of both the Northern Pacific and Burlington railroads, giving Morgan and Harriman a monopoly on Northern transcontinental rail transportation and thus a stranglehold on the movement of agricultural and industrial products from the grain belt and Chicago westward. Notoriously, Morgan declared, "I owe the public nothing."[45] Roosevelt responded to the creation of the monopoly by doing exactly what Morgan feared he would. He sued under the 1890 Sherman Anti-Trust Act, which resulted in an order breaking up Northern Securities and serving as a warning shot to other consolidating railroads. "It took courage to challenge railroads. . . . Stocks fell and Wall Street accused TR of acting like a financial Rough Rider," observes Dalton. He was seen as fearless and wild, unconcerned for his own political self-preservation.[46]

As Morgan and Harriman were battling her "trust-busting" brother, Bamie ostentatiously took the president's side. She disinvited the Harrimans from her social circle and even made her son return a toy train set that had been given to him by the Harrimans. What Bamie told her son at this time is revealing. As they were riding in her carriage down Fifth Avenue, looking "at the imitation Renaissance palaces which the robber barons had built," she explained to him that "Uncle Theodore intended to discipline the newly wealthy."[47] This may sound like New York's "old money" venting its resentment of the city's nouveau riche, but Bamie intended it as a lesson in contrast. Yes, the Roosevelts and families like them were wealthy, but they believed that their money came with responsibilities toward the very public Morgan and so many of the other newly wealthy "self-made" men disdained. Bamie understood that her brother was not opposed to Americans becoming wealthy, but that he was vehemently opposed to wealth made on the backs of ordinary people through such means as monopolistic price-gouging. It was unfair, undemocratic, un-American, and he would not have it.

The U.S. government opened the case against Northern Securities in 1902. When the decision went against the company, Morgan and Harriman challenged the Sherman Anti-Trust Act as unconstitutional. In 1904, the Supreme Court ruled against the challenge in a 5–4 decision. TR's action and the high court's response set in motion antitrust prosecutions for the next century.

So much for "going slow."

Under the pounding of forty thousand guests in a single season, the White House was showing its age and was in increasingly urgent need of repair. Yet even more pressing, as Edith saw it, was a need for more significant renovation. She understood that while the building may have been an ample domicile to John Adams, its first occupant, who was chief executive of a very small newborn nation, it could not properly accommodate the chief executive of what was becoming an imperial democracy with global reach.

Edith's objective was to transform the White House into a building adequate to the needs and befitting the dignity of a great government. She instigated the hiring of Charles Follen McKim, dean of America's Gilded Age architects, to remodel the building. Like other architects of his era, McKim was strongly influenced by historical European styles, everything from Italianate *palazzi* to Norman *chateaux*. Edith was the one who hired McKim, but once again, the hidden hand of Bamie was apparent. A decade earlier, she had traveled with McKim to the World's Columbian Exposition in Chicago as an official representative of the New York State Women's Board to "help with 'Women's Building,' a display of the accomplishments of American women" in the fine and applied arts, science, home economics, and industry.[48] It is likely Bamie recommended McKim to her sister-in-law and may even have brokered an introduction.

Edith did not simply buy things and services. She acquired them thought-
fully, and while she did not want to "share Teddy" (as Alice used to say),
she welcomed advice from both Conie and Bamie.

On April 15, 1902, Edith met with McKim, and explained that the
president's house needed executive office space apart from the family's
living quarters. She wanted to create a separation between home and
office life and perhaps also give the ever-frenetic TR another place to
go to work with advisors and meet with a parade of visitors. This led
to the removal of greenhouses and stables to make way for what ultimately became the West Wing. She further called for enlargement and
modernization—mostly structural upgrading—of the building's public
spaces. These changes were primarily intended to make the White House
more functional administratively, with a clear delineation between public and private spaces. Edith went on to propose that a hallway within the
building should become a gallery for the display of portraits of the first
ladies—herself, her predecessors, and successors. In short, Edith Roosevelt kindled the creation of the modern White House—less a mansion
than the seat of the executive branch of the American government. Mc-
Kim's work on the building is a monument to her influence not merely
on her husband's administration but on the American presidency as an
institution that deserved to be nobly and efficiently housed. The West
Wing, the "gallery of First Ladies," even the redesignation of the building from "Executive Mansion" to "The White House"—all this was the
inspiration of Edith Roosevelt. The Rose Garden, the iconic jewel of the
White House which Jacqueline Kennedy would renew, was her idea as
well. Sagamore Hill was a working farm so it's not entirely surprising
she would appreciate and want the same at the White House. Edith grew
what she called a "Colonial Garden" with sweet peas, black-eyed susans,
quince, and jasmine. So fond of what she planted, Edith's official White
House portrait shows her seated on a wooden bench in the garden.[49]

It was not just the house and gardens that she "transformed," but the
life within it. The first couple did a great deal of entertaining, and Edith
resolved to address the problem of the absence of a complete set of china

for formal occasions, including state dinners. She personally assembled for the White House a 1,320-piece suite of dishes in white Wedgwood. It soon became known as the "Roosevelt set." She also undertook the task of acquiring a gallery of presidential china from collectors as well as from the families of former presidents, forming the basis of the celebrated White House China Collection, which is on display as a feature of the public White House tour.

Jacqueline Kennedy is generally credited with transforming the White House into a salon, in which some of the world's marquee classical musicians performed in East Room musicales. In fact, many earlier first ladies hosted receptions, which sometimes featured music. And it was Edith Roosevelt, not Mrs. Kennedy, who made the White House musicale a tradition. Most distinguished musicians coveted the first lady's invitation to perform, and those who did not necessarily relish an invitation nevertheless deemed her request a command performance. The Steinway Piano Company, which had advised Ida McKinley on the selection of musical artists, continued to do so at a much accelerated pace during Edith's reign. When her husband discussed the desirability of purchasing an upright piano for the Executive Mansion, George Cortelyou, a kind of chief of executive protocol, advised stepping up to a grand piano. Cortelyou's brief was to elevate the first residence of the land into an institution with processes, mostly clerical, that expedited the office of chief executive. Edith eagerly endorsed Cortelyou's recommendation, and the Steinway Company gifted the nation with the 100,000th instrument it produced, an elaborately gilded mahogany piano.[50]

During the seven and a half years that she was first lady, Edith brought a diverse and distinguished array of classical artists to the White House, world-class musicians including piano virtuoso, composer, and champion of Polish independence Ignacy Jan Paderewski; beloved Austrian American dramatic contralto Mme. Ernestine Schumann-Heink; Italian composer and pianist Ferruccio Busoni; and master cellist Pablo Casals. (The long-lived Casals would perform again in the White House East Room in 1961, this time at the invitation of First Lady Jacqueline

Kennedy.) Edith's musical taste was far more sophisticated than that of her husband—who did not have much of an ear. She inclined toward the likes of Richard Wagner but also admired the lighter touch of John Philip Sousa. During TR's second term, Edith attended a performance of Engelbert Humperdinck's children's opera, *Hansel und Gretel*, at the Metropolitan Opera to benefit the New York Legal Aid Society. She and the president invited Humperdinck to the White House. By way of thanks for the honor, the composer presented TR with a bound copy of the opera's score.

Edith's high-profile endorsement of a performance to benefit charity set the pattern for subsequent first ladies to follow. She had a charitable sewing circle, and she routinely contributed objects from her home for fundraisers. She even gifted some charities letters from TR. Edith was also willing to use her position more directly to do good. In November 1905, in response to a plea from an Indianapolis woman whose former husband had abducted her two-year-old daughter, Edith persuaded Indiana senator Albert J. Beveridge to goad the Indianapolis police into redoubling their efforts to recover the child. This, in turn, triggered a nationwide search, and in February 1906, Charles A. Bookwalter, the city's mayor, wired the first lady: "I am delighted to inform you that Skillman Baby is found in San Francisco today." The grateful mother told reporters, "I do not believe I would ever have recovered Pauline but for Mrs. Roosevelt."[51]

Edith influenced the nation and the White House on her terms. Roosevelt appraised his wife's White House renovations and innovations in more reductive terms. In a December 8, 1902, letter to Maria Storer, wife of Bellamy Storer, who aided his ascent to assistant secretary of state and now served as TR's minister to Austria-Hungary, he declared that Edith's "changes in the White House have transformed it from a shabby likeness to the ground floor of the Astor House into a simple and dignified dwelling for the head of a great republic."[52] James Amos concurred: "The White House was a very different place when the Roosevelts left it. They had completely remodeled and reorganized it."[53]

One seemingly cosmetic change had profound impact. Edith's library on the second floor of the White House was next to her husband's private office. Side by side, according to Roosevelt biographer Dr. Kathleen Dalton, "[President Roosevelt] confided in [Edith] about even the most top secret subjects." Like Bamie and Conie during his gubernatorial years, the Roosevelts took advantage of the sexism of the age. "Political associates [cabinet members and aides] noticed that Edith would knit on the sidelines while the President held political meetings and then after the guests left she would talk with him about his choices." Edith was in the room where it happened—because she designed it that way.[54]

The kind of social, aesthetic, and cultural work Edith Roosevelt contributed to the White House as well as the institution of the American presidency set the bar high for future first ladies, but her more hard-edged political influence on her husband, aided by his sisters, was exceptional and likely not eclipsed until Edith and TR's niece Eleanor Roosevelt arrived in Washington with her husband, Franklin.

Perhaps the most unique but hitherto little acknowledged role Bamie and especially Edith played was in resolving the Anthracite Coal Strike— one of the most consequential domestic policy triumphs of the Roosevelt presidency. The early twentieth century was the apogee of coal as the energy source of choice in America and, for that matter, the rest of the world. It heated houses, it drove locomotives and ships, it fired the furnaces that made steel, and it was involved in a panoply of industrial processes, from making high-carbon steel to producing cement and even various medicines. The king of coal was anthracite. Although more expensive than bituminous coal, anthracite was richer in carbon, which made it a more efficient (and cleaner) energy source. In America, the center of anthracite mining was Pennsylvania, and on May 12, 1902, a strike broke out in the eastern part of the state after the big railroads, which owned the mines there, turned their backs on union workers' demands for higher wages, a shorter workday—the basic hourly pay was $1.60 and the workday ten hours—and recognition of their union for collective bargaining. The cost of coal doubled as production plummeted. Spring became summer, and summer fall. Still, management and labor remained deadlocked. Violence was always a threat in labor disputes, but, even worse, Roosevelt understood, was the looming prospect of a winter with little or no coal.

Henry Cabot Lodge was less concerned about a cold winter than he was about an even colder November. The strike, if unresolved, threatened the Republican Party's prospects for the midterm elections. Roosevelt assiduously worked behind the scenes, communicating with labor and company leaders as well as key members of Congress, in search of a way out. The railroads and their investors warned of the dire political consequences of attempts at governmental mediation, but they nevertheless continued to oppose any compromise with labor and the unions. Labor, for its part, stood firm and expected the progressive Roosevelt to back them. As time was running out, TR undertook a speaking tour, in which the coal strike figured as a prime example of the country's need for labor reform. On September 3, as Edith was preparing to sail across Long Island Sound to meet her husband, who was about to leave the New England leg of his speaking tour, she received an urgent telegram. The president's dignified landau carriage had collided with a trolley in Pittsfield, Massachusetts. He and George Cortelyou were thrown from the carriage, as was William Craig, a favorite among the president's Secret Service protective detail. Cortelyou and Roosevelt escaped with what were thought to be minor injuries, but Craig became the first fatality in the history of the Secret Service.[55]

Edith was unimpressed by the news that her husband was not seriously hurt. Her feelings were likely much closer to those of the newspaper reporter who was traveling with TR and wrote, "No man was ever closer to death than was the President two days ago."[56] Edith rushed to Bridgeport, Connecticut, to meet her husband. She was relieved to find him with what seemed to be nothing more than a bruised cheek and a scraped leg. "My hurts were trivial," Theodore proclaimed."[57]

But Roosevelt soon took a turn for the worse. As he pressed on with the speaking tour, an abscess developed in his shin. As it grew larger and more painful, his physicians advised surgery. His recovery was protracted. On October 1, Edith wrote to their son Kermit that "Father is still in his wheeled chair," adding with knowing sarcasm, "You can't think how cheerful a patient he is." Indeed, he would never fully recover. Years later, Roosevelt himself noted, "The shock permanently damaged the bone," and for the rest of his life, when he was fatigued or misstepped, he felt a stab of pain, which he always concealed from others.[58]

Hobbled though he was, Roosevelt convened a secret meeting at Sagamore Hill on September 16 with Republican senators Nelson Aldrich, John Spooner, and William Boyd Allison (three of the Senate's redoubtable "Big Four," who dominated the chamber in the early decades of the twentieth century), together with Henry Cabot Lodge, and the fourth, Mark Hanna. Their focus was the strike and how to avert its worst impact on the November elections.

Still, his leg worsened, with Edith remarking that the limb, which periodically went numb, had become "quite helpless." Roosevelt grew feverish on September 28, and physicians made a new deep incision to drain the wound. During the procedure, the president was awake but administered a liberal dose of cocaine. Edith faithfully watched over him, amusing TR by her "air of triumph in attending me." She sometimes liked to refer to him as another of her children and seemed to enjoy taking care of him as such. As he recuperated from this new surgery, the president tried to relax by reading, but couldn't help but repeatedly confer with advisors on his legal options for spurring a settlement. Edith, for her part, was tireless in clipping anything in the daily papers she deemed of importance, whether favorable to him or not. She was especially eager to provide intelligence on the opinion of the nation.[59]

On October 3, Roosevelt summoned to the White House the presidents of the mine-owning railroads together with the union leaders. The union president made his case, to which the railroad leaders responded by asserting (as they always did) that compromise was impossible. When the conference ended with still no resolution to this difficult political problem, Roosevelt formed a commission and charged it with investigating the strike and making recommendations. Secretary of War Elihu Root (for reasons of national defense) and banker J. P. Morgan (in defense of his own financial interests) sternly persuaded the railroad men to abide by whatever the commission decided—dangling the prospect of Roosevelt temporarily nationalizing the mines if they refused. The union also agreed to accept the commission's decision. In the meantime, on October 13, Edith engaged a professional masseur to work on her husband's leg muscles.[60] Soon, TR graduated from a wheelchair to crutches.

"Darling Bye," Roosevelt wrote his sister on October 16, as the crisis neared its apex. "The situation in the coal strike has been as difficult as it well could be. I do not know that I have ever had a more puzzling or a more important problem to deal with." In a long, detailed letter, Roosevelt seeks her advice. "I could sit idly by and see one man kill another without interference because there is no statutory duty imposed upon the President to interfere in such cases."[61] But doing nothing was not in his character.

Just four days later, pursuant to a compromise proposed by the presidential commission, the union voted to end the anthracite strike. The commission's work was not finished. The following March, it recommended a 10 percent increase (half the union's demand) in miners' pay and the reduction of the workday from ten to nine hours. There were other concessions as well. True to their promises, both sides accepted these recommendations. Thus, President Roosevelt not only ended the strike but set a precedent for presidential intervention in labor disputes that were of critical importance to the welfare of the nation. This also bolstered the principle of collective bargaining, profoundly transforming relations between capital and labor in the United States. It was a triumph of his Square Deal policy and platform, essentially a legislative bundle meant to curb the predatory abuses of capital while shielding business from what he believed were the more radical excesses of labor. It stands as an example of Edith's powerful influence on her husband in conveying public sentiment and his reliance on Bamie's judgment during the most critical periods of his administration. As for the impact of the affirmation of collective bargaining precedent, its significance is measurable. At the start of 1902, membership in American trade unions was 1,375,900. At the end of 1902, it was 1,913,900, and one year later, 2,072,700.[62] Even more immediately, the public was relieved that a coal shortage had been averted and was generally impressed at a successful demonstration of TR Square Deal values in action.

"Auntie Bye is as dear as ever and oversees the entire nation," TR joked in reference to his sister's involvement in ending the strike.[63] Eleanor Roosevelt witnessed interactions between the president and his strategist up close, observing, "[Theodore] put a great deal of trust in Auntie Bye who helped him a great deal, I believe, in analyzing situations."[64] Arguably one of, if not the most, influential first ladies in American history, she learned from the example of Edith, Bamie, and Conie—and observed their differing personalities and natural tension. "A president has so little time and [Edith] would feel, I think, sometimes, that he enjoyed being with his sisters so much that it would take time, which she wanted for herself and her children," Eleanor recalled. But she also recognized that the siblings' delight in one another's company was part of what made their success possible: "They were a wonderful family because they enjoyed each other so much."[65]

Practically speaking, Conie's influence during the White House years was lessened only by geography. She was further away, raising four children in New Jersey, but she continued to play the role of unofficial press secretary, often ignoring TR's and Edith's directives to the contrary: "Details of his camping trips with his sons and nephews found their way into the newspapers, most likely fed them by Corinne," claims TR biographer Dr. Kathleen Dalton.[66] While neither Roosevelt nor his wife was above using their children as occasional props to enhance the image of the first family, Conie's publicity efforts sometimes crossed the line into an invasion of privacy since all the children, friends, and nephews, with the exception of Alice and Ted Jr., were, after all, minors. Conie knew, perhaps because of her distance from the daily activity of the White House, of the intense, almost insatiable public interest in even the most mundane details about the first family.

• • •

"Within the family, Edith was known for her tart wit and her unsparing assessment of the politicians and public figures that she encountered," historian Betty Boyd Caroli observes. She notes that "Sometimes her sharp tongue could be turned on her children and even her husband." Caroli assumes that TR "took the . . . ribbing as part of the affection that the two Roosevelts shared," but a comment to the French ambassador, Jules Jusserand, suggests that he hardly laughed it off: "people think I have a good-natured wife, but she has a humor which is more tyrannical than half the tempestuous women of Shakespeare."[67] We can only wonder what "tempestuous" Shakespearean women Roosevelt had in mind. Kate from *The Taming of the Shrew*? Rosalind in *As You Like It*? Cleopatra, perhaps? Or could it have been Lady Macbeth?

Edith was assertive but more specifically frank, blunt, and resolutely determined to suffer gladly not a single fool. She was nearly legendary for her sharp tongue and unsparing opinions. She joked that TR's legend-making book about the adventures of the Rough Riders might have been more aptly titled "Alone in Cuba."[68] William Loeb, her husband's personal secretary, tried her patience. In letters to Theodore, she would write his name as "Lo-eb" or "low ebb," a none too subtle knock on his intelligence and energy.[69]

She was stern with her children and notably undemonstrative toward them. Her relationship with Alice, her stepdaughter, was especially strained. Edith and Alice argued bitterly the day before Edith's second miscarriage, after which she was on bed rest for eleven days. Dr. Kathleen Dalton notes, "TR did not record how he felt about the pregnancy, the spat, or his wife's confinement" but undoubtedly it stressed an already frayed relationship between the two women.[70] The frugal Edith often sparred with Alice about money. In her meticulous ledgers accounting for every penny, Edith never documented any expenses for Alice, although the teen had an ample allowance from her grandparents, the well-to-do Lees. When Alice's expenses exceeded her income a note from Edith would follow: "My 'scolding' now would be both silly and useless. If you have debts, they must be paid. I can only remind you that it is neither honest nor wise to incur them."[71] In another particularly bad exchange, Edith "snapped at [Alice] that she should have been an actress"—given Alice's global fame, which began to rise commensurate with her father's presidency, this might not have stung as effectively as her stepmother intended.[72]

In spite (or perhaps because of) these challenges, Alice blossomed during these years in the White House. Yet another remarkable woman in the arena—this one the vanguard of the next generation—Alice would be the first of the Roosevelt women to live most of her years with the right to vote, yet she, too, would defiantly struggle with the constraints and expectations of the age on her gender. Edith was more willing to assert authority over Alice than her father was. He famously said he could "either run the country or control" Alice but he "could not possibly do both."[73] Father and daughter had each other pegged, and undoubtedly they had one thing in common: their uncommon wit. Over a century later, the witticisms they traded still ring in the ear. Surely in his eldest daughter Roosevelt saw something of himself: brilliant, barrier-busting, and bristling with life. Alas, as a woman, Alice's rebellion was not as welcome in the world as his.

Theodore Roosevelt must have seen in Alice—athletic, beautiful, beguiling, and possessed of an effortlessly effervescent personality—flashes of his first wife. Contrary to the impression that Edmund Morris and some others have created, Alice Hathaway Lee did not disappear from the lives of the Roosevelts on Valentine's Day 1884. The Lees were a constant in the Roosevelts' lives. Daughter Alice spent summers in Boston and frequently traveled with her grandparents. Conie recalls the scene on the day of Alice's wedding, to lawyer, politician, and future thirty-eighth Speaker of the House Nicholas Longworth III, in 1906:

Alice's Boston grandparents, Mr. and Mrs. George C. Lee, were especially welcomed by Mrs. Roosevelt, and my memory of the great morning of the wedding has a curiously "homey" quality. . . . Almost all the

morning Mrs. Roosevelt knitted peacefully at the sunny window upstairs near her secretary's desk, chatting quietly with Mrs. Lee. . . . My
husband took Mr. Lee for a walk, as the dear old gentleman was very
much excited at the prospect of his granddaughter's nuptials in the
"East Room."[74]

Caroline Lee had been at the bedside of her daughter for Alice's
birth. She was present two days later for her daughter's premature death.
Though no record of her conversation with Edith exists, it is hard to
imagine a mother not commenting on the absence of her daughter on
such a special day.

Was that why, when the ceremony was concluded, Edith "shocked
everyone" by snapping at Alice: "I want you to know that I'm glad to see
you leave. You have never been anything but trouble." Alice dismissed
the outburst. "That's all right, Mother," she said. "I'll come back in a few
weeks and you won't feel the same way."[75] In what we can only hope is
an apocryphal (though oft-repeated) story, Edith also told Ted Jr. "who
naturally repeated it to [Alice]" that had her mother lived, she "would
have driven [her father] to suicide from sheer boredom."[76] Whatever was
actually said, Alice Roosevelt Longworth lived her life believing her stepmother thought "it was just as well that my mother had died."[77]

Later in life, Alice took pains to leave a more positive picture for
posterity. "That I was the child of another marriage was a simple fact and
made a situation that had to be coped with, and Mother [while she was
alive Edith insisted Alice address her this way] coped with it with a fair-
ness and charm and intelligence which she has to a greater degree than
almost any one else I know."[78]

Doubtless, Edith Roosevelt was a formidable figure, the survivor of an
often lonely and precarious girlhood. She had a hard edge, but doubtless as well, she loved Theodore Roosevelt. For his part, Roosevelt loved
her and raised a large family with her, one modeled on what Greatheart
had produced with Mittie. He loved Edith all the more for her support,

advice, good common sense, and political savvy. "My orders came usually from Mrs. Roosevelt," James Amos acknowledged. "During those White House years, she was my real boss."[79]

Something perhaps approaching a final assessment of the indispensable roles Edith, Bamie, and Conie played in the rise of Theodore Roosevelt can be glimpsed in what happened on election night 1904. Theodore looked to the 1904 campaign and his election to the presidency in his own right as essential to establishing his legitimacy. "The one great ambition of Theodore Roosevelt's life was to be chosen President on his own merits by the people of the United States," Conie later said.[80] He had taken risks and departed sharply from McKinley's essentially conservative Stalwart course. TR was popular with the people but also made powerful and wealthy enemies. "Whether I shall be re-elected I haven't the slightest idea," Theodore wrote to Conie. "I know there is bitter opposition to me from many sources. Whether I shall have enough support to overcome the opposition, I cannot tell. I suppose few Presidents can form the slightest idea whether their policies have met with approval or not. Certainly I cannot. But as far as I can see, these policies have been right, and I hope that time will justify them. If it doesn't why I must abide the fall of the dice, and that is all there is to it."[81]

"I have no idea what the outcome will be," a nervous Roosevelt confided to Bamie as the election neared. "Come what may, I have achieved certain substantial results, have made an honorable name to leave the children, and will have completed by March 4th next pretty nearly seven years of work, (dating from the time I became lieutenant colonel of my regiment) which has been of absorbing interest and of real importance. So, while if defeated, I shall feel disappointed, yet I shall also feel that I have had far more happiness and success than fall to any but a very few men; and this aside from the infinitely more important fact that I have had the happiest home life of any man whom I have ever known."[82] The sentiment is humble, but it is hard to imagine Theodore Roosevelt, only forty-six by the time of the 1904 election, contentedly resting on his laurels. On the campaign trail, he was bold and optimistic. In private, to

Bamie and Conie, he continued to express doubts. On October 18, he wrote to Conie, "Nobody can tell anything about the outcome. At the present time, it looks rather favorable to me." Just a week later, on October 25, he wrote to her again: "As for the result, the Lord only knows what it will be. Appearances look favorable, but I have a mind steeled for any outcome!"[83]

On Election Day, Roosevelt voted in Oyster Bay, and Conie met him in Newark, New Jersey, where the two rode the train together to Philadelphia. "In his private drawing-room on the car," she recalled, "he opened his heart to me, and told me that he had never wanted anything in his life quite as much as the outward and visible sign of his country's approval of what he had done during the last three and half years. . . . His temperament was such that he wished no favor which he had not himself won. Therefore, it seemed to him a crucial moment in his life, when, on his own merit, he was judged fit or unfit to be his own successor."[84]

Conie left the presidential train in Philadelphia, returning to her family in Orange, New Jersey. Theodore continued to the White House, to Edith's and Bamie's sides. "On election night Edith intends to have members of the Cabinet around," TR wrote Bamie. "And we intend to have a little feast which can be turned into a festival of rejoicing or into a wake, as circumstances warrant!"[85] In fact, it would be something of both, combining both a victory and a retreat.

14

TRIUMPH, REGRET, AND RELIEF

"I am so glad it is all over."

—Edith Roosevelt at the end of TR's presidency

heodore Roosevelt had achieved greatness. The problem was that once he realized it, he began to act impulsively, and often without the advice of those he most trusted—the ultimate testament to their indispensable role in his political rise. TR had always been impetuous. Now he was empowered. The sway Edith, Bamie, and Conie held with him diminished, much to Roosevelt's detriment. In some of the most consequential decisions to come, TR would regret not heeding the advice of his ever faithful and often unerring women in the arena.

The 1904 election was a Roosevelt landslide. Many Democrats, including Franklin Delano Roosevelt, crossed party lines to support TR. "I felt he was a better Democrat than the Democratic candidates," FDR wryly explained, effectively laying claim to progressive politics as a Democratic attribute.[1] When incoming returns made it clear that Theodore Roosevelt was about to win a second term, the president left Edith, Bamie, and his cabinet while he drafted a message for the press. It was a pledge that he would not seek what he called a "third" term. Although his second term was the first to which he had been *elected*, he did not want to give even the impression of violating the two-term tradition established by that "Cincinnatus of the West," George Washington. Indeed, the pledge drew overwhelming praise from the press and political advisors such as Senator Lodge, but TR soon began to regret having made it, especially as March 4, 1909, drew closer and closer.

Increasingly confident in his own abilities, perhaps overly so, he had consulted neither Edith nor Bamie nor Conie—the customary recipient of his emotional exuberance—before making the pledge. It was the biggest blunder of his political life. Writing in 1930, Owen Wister was able to report that, had Edith been consulted, she would have advised her husband against ruling out a third term. Even if she had not been asked but had been present (which she most likely was not) when he made the announcement to reporters, she would have protested.[2] A close friend of Edith, who even helped him with his memoir of his friendship with TR, Wister was in a position to know her mind on this issue, as well as her whereabouts at the time of her husband's shocking declaration. However, Edith's most thorough modern biographer, Sylvia Morris, asserts that Edith *was* present, "standing nearby as he made this rash proclamation" and "was seen to flinch."[3]

Was Edith convinced that a third TR term was best for the nation? Undoubtedly. Yet her motive may also have been her consciousness that a man who so thrives on power would become listless and depressed without it—something that proved only too true. The trouble with both Wister's account and Morris's is that neither is corroborated by contemporary sources. But there can be no doubt of the universal contemporary assumption, which was that Edith believed her husband had made a terrible mistake. Historian Lewis Gould observes that the story that Edith disapproved of her husband's pledge to give up power "grew in the telling [within the Roosevelt family] as it became more and more clear that Theodore had erred."[4] What we do know for a fact is that Edith told TR

that William Howard Taft, whom he subsequently anointed his successor, was not trustworthy. Clearly, Roosevelt did not accept this assessment. It would be his second, politically fatal, mistake made without the
wise counsel of Edith, Bamie, or Conie.

An avid reader of Shakespeare, Roosevelt might well have had a thought
or two about King Lear when he realized he had so blithely pledged to
leave office four years after taking the oath of that office for the first
time as its elected occupant. Still, he could look forward to four years
won by vote of the people, and, on the eve of the 1905 inauguration,
he made clear to John Hay that he intended to use every single day of
every one of those years.[5] "The night before [the inauguration]," Conie
recalled, "Mr. John Hay sent [Theodore] a ring with part of the lock of
Abraham Lincoln's hair which John Hay himself had cut from the dead
President's forehead almost immediately after his assassination. I have
never known my brother to receive a gift for which he cared so deeply."[6]
Roosevelt wore the ring to his inaugural. Afterward, it joined Roosevelt's
most treasured personal possessions, alongside the hidden locks of Alice
Hathaway Lee.

TR had won the presidency in his own right, and it was now time to
celebrate. Conie dressed in her "best black velvet gown and 'presidential
sister' white plumes" for a receiving line at the White House. Bamie's and
Conie's place in the receiving line carried meaningful symbolism: Roosevelt's sisters were more than just siblings. "Suddenly, coming toward
me," recalled Conie, "I recognized the lithe figure of my brother's quon-
dam cowboy, Bill Merrifield." Merrifield was now marshal of Montana.
"Well, now, Mrs. Douglas, it's a sight for sore eyes to see you again," she
recalled him saying. "Why, almost the last time I laid eyes on you, you
were standing on your head in that muddy corral with your legs waving
in the air."[7] Rough Riders, newsboys, coal miners, Harvard students, and
even Geronimo marched in a "flamboyant three-hour inaugural parade of
thirty-five thousand."[8]

Conie's picture-perfect account of Inauguration Day stands in

contrast to her private letters to Bamie. In a rare social miscue or intentional slight, Edith had miscalculated the number of tickets needed for
Conie's large family, excluding her sons from the proceedings. "I know
I was very wrong to speak as excitedly as I spoke," Conie acknowledged
to Bamie in a letter sent the day after the inauguration. "But I had been
much wrought up at lunch by everybody asking me why my boys were
not in the Senate Chamber when everybody else was there and I felt
hurt to the quick that they had been so unnecessarily excluded."[9] Nannie
Lodge, wife of Senator Cabot Lodge, intervened and secured tickets, but
Conie "did not forget the episode, and years later she still smarted from
the oversight."[10]

As Eleanor Roosevelt later observed, to her, Edith and Conie "were
always very different people," no doubt a part of why the two sometimes
clashed. But the starkly different personalities of the women in the arena
enabled each to serve a different purpose to Theodore Roosevelt. Edith
was pragmatic and staunchly guarded her private time with her husband.
She would share Theodore Roosevelt with the world, but Thee was still
her husband. Their intimacy nurtured and strengthened the bond between them, and it gave the president much needed rest from the ca-
cophony of global celebrity. Bamie was the hidden hand, shunning any
contemporary or historical credit for her influence. She quite literally
locked away their secrets, storing her letters from TR in a safe in her
bedroom. Conie was an emotional outpost, the person for whom slights
would cut deeper and last longer. Lifelong, TR could count on his little
sister to match his emotional intensity. "Auntie Corinne," said Eleanor
Roosevelt, "had to a far greater extent a certain literary and artistic
charm. . . . There was something really very lovely about Auntie Corinne
that you felt the minute you came into the room with her."[11]

Conie shared this quality with her brother. American illustrator and
sculptor James Edward Kelly, who portrayed the images of over forty
Union generals after the Civil War, was commissioned to create a bronze
of TR. During several interviews, captured in Kelly's unpublished memoirs, Theodore showed his emotional side. "People have no idea what I

look like," Roosevelt said to Kelly. "No," the artist replied. "The popular idea of you is that you look like a Thanksgiving pumpkin—all eyes and teeth." Roosevelt laughed, "That's it! That's it!" before Kelly "looked at him and saw a particular sensitiveness in his mouth, especially his lower lip, which showed he was capable of great feeling." The artist asked what might be considered an unusual question to Theodore Roosevelt: "You cry easily, don't you?" TR did not answer, and Kelly twice repeated the question. "At which he turned, looked at me and nodded his head, indicating, though not saying, 'Yes.'"[12]

The pace of Roosevelt's second term matched and sometimes even exceeded his first. In *My Brother Theodore Roosevelt*, Conie described the legendary energy that fueled the family.

> I can still see the way in which my sister-in-law (she was not *born* a Roosevelt!) fell into her stateroom. I was about to follow her example (it was midnight) when my brother turned to me in the gayest possible manner and said: "Not going to bed, are you!" "Well," I replied, "I *had thought* of it." . . . He laughed, but firmly said: "Sit down right here. You will be sorry if you go to bed." . . . Finally, at 5 A.M., with a satisfied aspect, he turned to me and said: "That is all about [a history of the United States they had been discussing]." I rose feebly to my feet and said: "Good night, darling." But not at all—still gaily, as if he had just begun a day's work, instead of having reached the weary littered end of twenty-four hours, he said once more: "Don't go to bed. I must do one other piece of work. . . ." That was the way in which Theodore Roosevelt did work.[13]

The frenetic pace—the sheer exuberance—more reminiscent of the Bullochs than the Roosevelts might help explain one of the most prodigious presidencies in the history of the country. "I so thoroughly believe in reform," Theodore Roosevelt told Jane Addams, founder of the Hull House settlement house in Chicago and a frequent correspondent of the president, who admired her deeply.[14] With her encouragement, Roosevelt supported child labor laws, public education reform, urban housing codes, the nation's first pure food and drug laws, and enforcing child support.

To his conservation efforts, a centerpiece of his second term, Speaker of the House Joseph Cannon would reply: "Not one cent for scenery." Indeed, as TR biographer Dr. Kathleen Dalton put it, "Congress responded to many of his ideas with disbelief." The groundbreaking novelist of New York's Gilded Age, Edith Wharton, another frequent correspondent, and friend of the president, believed Roosevelt the exuberant reformer had a very tough hill to climb because "most people lived life as 'a succession of pitiful compromises with fate, of concessions to old tradition, old beliefs, old charities and frailties.'"[15]

Alongside Edith, Bamie, and Conie, women of the next generation of Roosevelt relatives and friends were coming into their own. Theodore and Edith offered the White House as the setting for the marriage of distant cousin Franklin to their niece, Eleanor. The couple opted for a New York wedding on March 17, St. Patrick's Day, instead. Standing in for his deceased brother, Elliott, Theodore walked the bride down the aisle. "Nothing like keeping the name in the family, eh Franklin?" the president said with a slap to the groom's back. Isabella Selmes was the only one of Eleanor's six bridesmaids who was not a family member. Four months later, Isabella, twenty, married Bob Ferguson, who was nearly twice her age at thirty-eight. Bob served alongside Theodore as a Rough Rider in the Spanish-American War and continued to serve as an advisor to the president and close friend to Bamie. Edith strongly disapproved of the May-December marriage and made it known, refusing to attend the wedding. Isabella and Bob Ferguson honeymooned at Bamie's home in Connecticut.[16]

Despite all the strong women in the family, the Roosevelts had complicated and contradictory ideas about women's suffrage, which was becoming a cultural flashpoint. The rights of women was a rare political subject on which the women in the arena did not agree. Edith supported suffrage but neither Bamie nor Conie did.[17] The theory under which the sisters labored, common in the Gilded Age, was that women's power and influence ought to be expressed in the family and one vote by the patriarchal head of the family represented them all. Bamie was unsparing, claiming suffrage would only increase the "stupid vote."[18] Bamie and Conie also personally disliked some of the suffrage leaders and found their arguments unsound. The next generation of women did not follow their mothers' example. Eleanor, of course, was a vocal proponent of women's rights. Alice Roosevelt Longworth supported suffrage, and Corinney, Conie's daughter, actively worked for the cause.

During the White House years, Edith more quietly supported suffrage so as to not create a political dilemma for her husband. Since his trailblazing Harvard feminist thesis of 1880, Theodore had lost some of his early zeal for women's equality. Remarkably, Eleanor Brooks Saltonstall, the wife of Dick Saltonstall, who introduced Theodore to Alice Lee, wrote President Roosevelt to petition for his support of suffrage. "I dislike to refuse any request of yours," the president replied personally. "But I do not want to get drawn into any controversy such as this on matters alien to my present duties. Moreover, on the women suffrage question I should have to make a long and elaborate argument to properly state my position and I simply haven't the time to prepare it." The letter to Eleanor is addressed to Chestnut Hill. "I wish I could write you more satisfactorily," Roosevelt concluded the letter to what would have been his cousin by marriage had Alice not died. "Especially as it looks as if I am not helping you when at great cost of inconvenience you are trying to do work in the public interest."[19] Shortly after Alice's death, members of the Lee family admonished Roosevelt for losing his "independence." Here again, he was falling short in the eyes of Alice's family.

Edith might have seen the issue of suffrage pragmatically, in terms of the need for votes. After all, in four states, women could now cast ballots. During his presidency, Roosevelt met with Susan B. Anthony and pledged support for what became the Nineteenth Amendment— but promised to do so only after the movement succeeded in attaining the two-thirds supermajority of states required for ratification. In other words, Roosevelt put the challenge back on Anthony and the suffragists to do the hard work. His Progressive Party in 1912 would be the first to officially adopt women's suffrage in their platform, but when he had the presidency, TR did not act with anything like all his might. One wonders how advocacy by those women closest to him might have kindled his enthusiasm earlier—or whether their lack of enthusiasm was what dampened his. One wonders, too, what influence Alice Lee might have had over TR on women's suffrage, an issue he'd passionately supported when she consented to marry him. But as TR's second term would show, there were limits to how much the men in a family would listen to its women.

When Theodore Roosevelt wrote to Eleanor Brooks Saltonstall that he considered women's equality "alien to my present duties," he was referring to his other priorities. Because with his four final years in office ticking down, there was still so much more to do including not just changing the entire nature of the American presidency, but also picking a successor who'd ensure his changes would outlast him. TR devoted his presidency to creating a personal and direct bond with the American people. This, however, was by no means the same as simply representing them. He was determined to inspire and shape the popular will. If he began as an "accidental" president, he made the most of his elevation to the office. Like President McKinley, he was a capitalist. Unlike McKinley, he was also a progressive, who was determined to reverse what he regarded as the danger that American democracy could yield to an oligarchy populated by great corporate trusts and their owners. Like John Adams, Roosevelt believed that the only check on antidemocratic power was countervailing democratic power. Perceiving that the rise of the legislative branch was increasingly fueled by corporate interests—in this era, many senators were corporate employees or leaders—TR asserted the power of the executive branch. In a manner that recalled Andrew Jackson, he defined the chief executive as the tribune of the people. In doing this, he did not believe he was usurping this role from Congress for the simple reason that Congress had relinquished it by revealing its fealty to monopolistic big business.

In the course of a most consequential presidency, Roosevelt evolved what he termed the "New Nationalism." He broadened the reach of the executive branch by creating what is sometimes today called the administrative state. Through this mechanism, he promoted and operationalized the Pure Food and Drug Act and a meat inspection law (both 1906), affording for the first time federal protection of consumer health. He leaned heavily on the Supremacy Clause (Article VI, Clause 2 of the Constitution), which establishes the general precedence of the national constitution and national laws over state constitutions and laws. Additionally, Roosevelt positioned himself to "correct" Congress through veto or executive order whenever he saw it cater to special interests at the expense of the electorate.

A keen student of history, Roosevelt turned to Federalist Alexander Hamilton for a constitutional rationale for his bolstering of the executive branch. Hamilton observed that the Constitution was explicit on the limits of presidential power but was silent on the *positive* aspects of the executive's authority. Like Hamilton, Roosevelt took this as license to exercise any governing authority not explicitly barred by the Constitution. He defended this by arguing that there was no danger from an autocrat executive but abundant clear and present danger from members of Congress in thrall to plutocrats.

It is widely believed—but nevertheless disputed—that TR coined the phrase "bully pulpit" to describe the presidency as a public platform. Roosevelt used that pulpit to push passage of legislation he favored and to influence moral, social, and political values. Most notably, he preached conservation and thereby elevated to a national imperative what is today called environmentalism. While TR was sometimes at odds with the press, he strategically cultivated it, not only by granting interviews but by writing articles for popular and influential periodicals. He created more productive relations with journalists and magazine and newspaper publishers than any chief executive before him. And it was Bamie, Edith, and Conie who taught him the importance of harnessing the power of the press dating back to his time in Cuba.

President Roosevelt was skilled at marketing his agenda, such as the Square Deal. The idea of neatly branding the presidential agenda was emulated by Woodrow Wilson in "The New Freedom," Franklin Roosevelt in "The New Deal," Harry Truman in "The Fair Deal," John F. Kennedy in "The New Frontier," and Lyndon Johnson in "The Great Society."

Even more than the Square Deal, the TR presidency was marked by Roosevelt's leadership in antitrust actions—beginning with his action against Morgan and Harriman's Northern Securities Company (1902)—and in labor relations. He was the first American president to enumerate the legal rights of labor including fair wages, safety, and reasonable work hours, and his creation of a presidential commission to mediate an end to the Anthracite Coal Strike of 1902 created a precedent for subsequent chief executives.

Yet in no field of domestic policy was Roosevelt more creative and formative than in "conservation" (environmental policy). He set out to persuade the nation that woodlands and wilderness were the great heritage of the American people. Under his administration, national parks and wilderness preserves, including 43 million acres of "national forest," were set aside from private ownership and commercial exploitation. TR was practicing what he preached since his ranching days at the Elkhorn, now known as the "cradle of conservation."[20] What he saw in Dakota changed his outlook. Roosevelt's observation of the degradation of the bison, the rapid industrialization of the nation, and the delicate balance of nature and land use put him a century ahead of his time in his thinking about conservation, the environment, and what today might be called sustainability. "It was at the Elkhorn," wrote historian Douglas Brinkley, "that Roosevelt found his voice to caution against careless growth, deforestation, wildlife depletion, and environmental degradation."[21] Congress was not always enthusiastic, and so TR's conservation program prompted him to establish yet another administrative precedent, the use of executive orders as alternatives to congressional legislation. When, for instance, Congress voted in 1908 to transfer from the president to itself the authority to create national forests in certain Western states, Roosevelt issued a series of executive orders to work around the legislation. He freely used executive orders in other fields as well, issuing in seven and a half years some 1,091 of them. This was just short of the total of 1,259 executive orders issued by all twenty-five of the presidents before him. Accused by many in Congress of usurping the power of the legislative branch, Roosevelt responded, "I did not usurp power, but I did greatly broaden the use of executive power. In other words, I acted for the public welfare, I acted for the common well-being of all our people, whenever and in whatever manner was necessary," adding as if by afterthought: "unless prevented by direct constitutional or legislative prohibition."[22] His orders created national parks and national forests, defined appropriate uses of public land, handled relations with Native Americans, and introduced various commercial regulations on everything from land policy to safety guidelines.

As much authority as President Roosevelt assumed in the domestic sphere, he was even more aggressive in foreign relations. TR was determined to make the United States first among equals on the global stage. Of course, his signature global venture was the conception and commencement of the Panama Canal. An act of geopolitical strategy more ambitious than any prior president had attempted, the canal created a vital shortcut between the Atlantic and Pacific Oceans, avoiding the necessity of using the Drake Passage (between South America's Cape Horn and the Shetland Islands of Antarctica) or the Strait of Magellan (via Tierra del Fuego). The canal was thus a boon to global trade and to the defense of the United States and the Western Hemisphere, enabling the rapid transfer of warships from the Atlantic to the Pacific. By controlling such a canal, the United States would be able to project its economic influence and military power worldwide. Roosevelt persuaded Congress to ratify the Hay-Herrán Treaty with Colombia (of which Panama was then a part) granting the United States the right to build and to control a canal across the Panamanian isthmus. When the Colombian senate

withheld ratification, Roosevelt fueled the guttering flame of a Panamanian independence movement, precipitating a brief and bloodless
revolution in which Panama (backed by the looming offshore presence
of the heavily armed U.S. Navy cruiser *Nashville*) broke with Colombia.
Instantly proclaiming recognition of the new nation, Roosevelt just as
quickly secured from Panama approval of the canal treaty Colombia had
rejected.

In the United States, popular endorsement of the Panama Canal
project was nearly unanimous. What qualms Congress had, Roosevelt
handled by taking action. As he explained in a 1911 speech, "I took the
[Panama Canal Zone], started the canal, and then left Congress—not to
debate the canal, but to debate me. But while the debate goes on the
canal does too."[23] The popular response to an especially bold stroke of the
president's diplomacy, the so-called Roosevelt Corollary to the Monroe
Doctrine, was more mixed. The corollary was occasioned by the British
and German responses to Venezuela's defaulting on debts owed to these
two nations. The U.K. and Germany set up a naval blockade of Venezuela and threatened invasion. Both in Venezuela and the United States, it
was widely assumed that TR would invoke the Monroe Doctrine of 1823,
which held that the United States would brook no foreign interference
in the affairs of the Western Hemisphere. Roosevelt did dispatch a naval
force to "observe" the blockade and stand ready to act against an invasion by any European power. Yet instead of simply siding with Venezuela
against Germany and Britain, TR asserted on December 6, 1904, the right
of the United States to intervene in the economic affairs of any Latin
American state unable or unwilling to pay its just international debts, to
promote the peaceful stability of the Western Hemisphere. While some
greeted this as an appropriate exercise of American leadership in the
hemisphere, others condemned it as blatant imperialism. Nevertheless,
the Roosevelt Corollary, like the much older Monroe Doctrine, is still
invoked as a predicate for executive action in events taking place in Central America, South America, and the Caribbean.

Theodore Roosevelt famously cited what he called an African

proverb, "Walk softly and carry a big stick," as when, in 1907, he put the might of the navy's "Great White Fleet" (as it was later unofficially called) on display by sending it on a circumnavigation of the world. TR answered accusations of belligerency and even warmongering in his 1913 *Autobiography* with a flippant exaggeration: "When I left the presidency, I finished seven and a half years of administration, during which not one shot had been fired against a foreign foe. We were at absolute peace, and there was no nation in the world . . . whom we had wronged, or from whom we had anything to fear."[24] In fact, TR had fought the Filipino insurrection movement and sent gunboats to support the Panama revolution. Nevertheless, he could validly point to his being awarded the Nobel Peace Prize in 1906 for his 1905 mediation between Russia and Japan to end the brutal Russo-Japanese War. The year in which he received the award, he successfully mediated differences between France and Germany over Morocco at the Algeciras Conference.

TR continued to rely on Bamie, Edith, and Conie for advice and support as he attempted to get these second-term initiatives off the ground in much the same way that he did during his first term. Bamie, who relished her experience in London, was a particularly good sounding board on foreign policy. Edith could be relied on for advice on domestic affairs and the operation of the White House. But, as TR's confidence and executive experience built, he was increasingly going it alone. There is also a practical matter: Edith managed the White House and six children while TR managed the nation. She could not always be there whenever Theodore needed her wise counsel. Nor did she want to be. "Come here, Theodore, and see your children," Archie Butt recalled Edith saying to her husband. "They are of far greater importance than politics or anything else."[25]

There is little reason to doubt that Theodore Roosevelt would have won a third term in 1908 had he not acted on apparent impulse in 1904 with a pledge that he would not run again. He seems to have regretted the pledge almost as soon as he made it, but, in 1908, he resisted what has been characterized as a public "outpouring of support" or even a "sweeping demand" for a third term. He seems to have been moved to honor his pledge by charges from some quarters that he saw himself as a modern Caesar or a "Bombastes Furioso."[26] Neither his wife nor his sisters, despite their disappointment, encouraged him to go back on his word.

TR considered William Howard Taft a friend, a political ally, and even a protégé of sorts. He served not only as his secretary of war from 1904 to 1908 but as governor-general of the Philippines (1901–1903) and provisional governor of Cuba (1906). Without consulting anyone, including Edith or his sisters, Roosevelt handpicked, supported, and indeed anointed Taft as his successor.

TR must have known that Edith had a low opinion of Taft. As her astute modern biographer, Sylvia Jukes Morris, relates, Edith considered Taft a "yes-man," lacking in the "fearlessness and candor" she believed her husband needed in the men surrounding him. Indeed, while TR relished a good argument, he very much liked people who agreed with him, and few of his subordinates, including Taft, were inclined to challenge him. Writing years later in *The Washington Star*, journalist Mark Sullivan commented that Edith, in contrast, did not hesitate to challenge her husband. Sullivan wrote that TR was fortunate to have a wife with "'infinitely superior insight' into character than he" and thus could "save him 'many a slip.'"[27] For whatever reasons, he did not consult her on this any more than he had before publicly pledging not to run in 1908. There is no record of Edith trying in vain to change her husband's mind about making Taft his successor after TR's intentions became known. She, much more than Theodore, was ready to leave Washington and politics behind.

Soon after Taft's election, however, Roosevelt began to see that he had chosen a man who gave lip service to progressivism but was unwilling and perhaps unable to champion it. Taft hesitated to use executive power as boldly as TR, backed corporate interests more than his predecessor, and did not consider conservation a priority. He might favor progressivism generally, but he lacked the fire, dynamism, and straightforward gumption to execute anything like a progressive agenda. In contrast to

TR, he was a plodder, and it is a wonder that Roosevelt never recognized this until it was too late. For a long time, he struggled to hide his growing disappointment with Taft. TR's irrepressibly puckish daughter Alice Roosevelt Longworth famously embroidered on a sofa pillow the motto "If you haven't got anything good to say about anyone come and sit by me."[28] More aggressively, she "buried a voodoo doll [resembling Nellie Taft, the incoming first lady] in the White House garden to jinx the Tafts" as she and the other Roosevelts ended their tenure in the residence.[29]

With the exception of Edith, the prospect of leaving the White House grated on the Roosevelt family, and as Theodore's frustration at the powerlessness of being a lame duck intensified, "he unloaded his troubles on [her]."[30] In February 1909, as Taft's inaugural day neared, Conie made one last visit to the White House. TR was preparing for an African safari and, recalling her method during TR's gubernatorial years, she "asked [her] brother if [she] might sit quietly in the corner and listen to his interviews" while she "made a few notes of the conversations." To many who visited, Conie "heard him say: 'Remember, a new man is in the saddle, and there can't be two Presidents after March 4th.'"[31]

The siblings discussed the future: "He was glad to plunge into the wilderness, so that no one could possibly think that he wanted a 'finger in the pie' of the new administration. Over and over again he would say: 'If I am where they can't get at me, and where I cannot hear what is going on, I cannot be supposed to wish to interfere with the methods of my successor.'"[32]

Before she left, TR asked Conie for a pigskin library to carry with him to Africa.

"What is a pigskin library?" she inquired.

TR described a large satchel in which he desired to carry a collection of books: the Bible, Shakespeare, Marlowe, Homer's *Iliad* and *Odyssey*, Shelley, Emerson, Tennyson, Longfellow, and, of course, *The Federalist*, among others.[33]

A week later, Conie suffered the greatest loss of her life. Her son

Stewart, away at Harvard, fell from a window and died. One of Conie's surviving sons believed "the fall resulted from an attempt to duplicate the opening scene in *War and Peace*," in which young men of privilege binge-drink from a window ledge. Historian Betty Boyd Caroli comments, "Whatever happened that night, Stewart fell to his death just days before he would have celebrated his twentieth birthday."[34] His mother was devastated. "I was stricken by a great sorrow," she said. "My brother came to me at once, and sustained me as no one else could have done, and his one idea during those next weeks was to make me realize his constant thought and love, even in the midst of those thrilling last days at the White House, when among other events he welcomed home the great fleet which had completed its circle of the world."[35] She echoed the very words her brother had written in his diary on February 14, 1884: "Everything seems to have gone out of my life."[36]

In the shadow of this tragedy, wearied by seven and a half years in the arena of the presidency, Theodore Roosevelt was both reflective and combative. "I will confess to you confidentially that I like my job," TR told William Jennings Bryan. "I have enjoyed every moment of this so-called arduous and exacting task."[37] Yet he also told a congressman that "he wished he had sixteen lions to turn loose in Congress." When the congressman "wondered if the lions might eat the wrong people," TR replied: "Not if they stayed long enough."[38] The feeling was mutual. J. P. Morgan, upon TR's departure for Africa, offered a toast: "America expects that every lion will do its duty."[39] Theodore Roosevelt had voluntarily given up power, in deference to the tradition begun by Washington. He would never get it back.

Edith was resigned and even relieved, though anxious as ever about the family finances. She wrote her confidant and political co-conspirator, Senator Henry Cabot Lodge: "I am so glad it is all over."[40]

15

LION IN WINTER

"Put it out of your mind, Theodore. You will never be President of the United States again."

—Edith to her husband

TR could not shake the feeling that his legacy would slip into irrelevance, that, under the lackluster, passive Taft, the progressive momentum would be lost forever. Seeking as he had in the past to outrun the "black care" of regret, he embarked on an African hunting expedition that spanned March 1909 to June 1910, bagging many thousands of specimens for the Smithsonian Institution. Bamie and Conie, not Edith, hosted TR's farewell. It was unusual for the former first lady to beg off such a public duty. But Edith was not happy about her husband's trip; they had just finished eight years in the White House and he already was off to Africa. While he gallivanted around the continent, Edith immediately set to work as "her husband's post-presidential staff"—no small task considering TR received between "fifteen and twenty thousand farewell letters."[1] Bamie and Conie supplied their brother with a steady stream of political news; historian Dr. Kathleen Dalton notes that "while he was in Africa, Roosevelt's closest associates were operating on his behalf, with or without his blessing, keeping the possibility of a Theodore Roosevelt return to politics top of mind."[2]

The self-imposed exile of the African safari was followed by a Grand Tour of Europe, whose populace greeted him jubilantly as the larger-than-life spirit of the New World. At the Sorbonne, TR delivered "Citizenship in a Republic," known more popularly as the "In the Arena" speech:

> It is not the critic who counts; not the man who points out how the strong man stumbles or where the doer of deeds could have done them better. The credit belongs to the man who is actually in the arena, whose face is marred by dust and sweat and blood; who strives valiantly; who errs, who comes short again and again, because there is no effort without error and shortcoming; but who does actually strive to do the deeds; who knows the great enthusiasms, the great devotions; who spends himself in a worthy cause; who at the best knows in the end the triumph of high achievement, and who at the worst, if he fails, at least fails while daring greatly, so that his place shall never be with those cold and timid souls who neither know victory nor defeat.[3]

TR might well have been speaking to himself. Out of office but not out of the limelight, he reveled in his popularity as it continued to grow. More presciently, Edith understood the distinction between mere celebrity and a public actively calling her husband back into the arena. "[The people] look upon him as Doctor cure-all," Edith said.[4] Since the very concept of a "Doctor cure-all" is fanciful mockery, her remark is ultimately derisive. No one could be all things to all people, and, in fact, TR never presented himself as such.

Buoyed by his African adventure—it was his youthful specimen collecting writ very, very large—and the affection Europe had shown him, TR returned home, wrote the bestselling *African Game Trails*, and weighed his return to politics. "Poor [Theodore] is so harassed and worried that I could almost wish him back in Africa," Edith wrote Bamie.[5] He went on "a 5,500-mile, sixteen state tour in the summer of 1910," in which "he spoke to huge, sometimes frenzied crowds, espousing ideas that he labeled 'New Nationalism.'" In the speeches, "[TR] called for workman's compensation laws, job training, a progressive income tax, a graduated and effective inheritance tax, [and] workplace protections for women and children," all of which "many observers considered tantamount to a manifesto for a new campaign."[6] A speech on August 31, 1910, at Osawatomie, Kansas, marked the apotheosis of his reentry into politics. Roosevelt, standing on a picnic table, seemed to call out his ill-chosen successor, President Taft; stating, "No man is worth his salt in public life who makes on the stump a pledge which he does not keep after election; and, if he makes such a pledge and does not keep it, hunt him out of public life."[7] The thirty-thousand-person crowd "cheered as TR warned that Americans faced a new war 'between the men who possess more than they earned and the men who have earned more than they possess.'"[8]

Historian Dr. Kathleen Dalton has deemed this "the most important speech of his political career."[9] Yet, for a year, TR resisted calls to join the 1912 race, in no small part because his wisest political advisor saw the race for what it was: a lost cause. "Put it out of your mind, Theodore," Edith said to her husband. "You will never be President of the United States again."[10] Was she simply delivering a realistic assessment, or was this declaration an extension of what she had told Cabot Lodge when she left the White House—that she was so glad it was over?

TR might have kept going full speed ahead. What could have become a political juggernaut was, however, stopped cold. TR wasn't necessarily heeding his wife's advice, but she did bring about a change of course.

In 1905, Edith had purchased a simple rough-hewn, pitched-roof cottage in a dense forest near Rapidan, Virginia. She called it Pine Knot—because its boards, inside and out, were of the knottiest knotty pine. She saw it as a retreat for her president husband, and we might even regard it as a precursor of Camp David. She relished the place so much that she named her favorite horse after it. On September 30, 1911, she went riding with her husband and their son Archie not far from Sagamore Hill. A superb horsewoman, she loved—not unlike her husband—to gallop full out. This time, however, an automobile spooked Pine Knot, who came up short and threw her. She landed on the hard macadam of the road. Theodore and Archie ran to her. She was unresponsive. When he couldn't rouse her, Roosevelt hailed a passing delivery van, which carried her home.

Edith's condition was truly alarming—desperate, even. Through thirty-six hours, she lay in a coma. It was followed by periods of consciousness and even lucidity alternating with semiconsciousness. This went on for nine days, during which Roosevelt attended her. (This was the same man who had left a critically ill Edith so that he could enlist for service in Cuba, the same man who, many years earlier, had left Alice Lee, in the last stages of pregnancy, to fend for herself so that he could devote his full attention to the New York State Assembly in Albany.) After she revived, Edith had no memory of the accident, and she discovered that she had lost her sense of taste and smell. She suffered from unremitting headaches. As her convalescence dragged on Roosevelt at last lost his patience and secured a nerve specialist and a pair of nurses to look after her. Eventually, she recovered her sense of taste, but the deficit in her sense of smell proved permanent.

In the acute phases of the emergency, Roosevelt proved both solicitous and resourceful, but as her recovery became increasingly protracted, he turned her tragedy into his opportunity. "Her always restraining hand no longer held him back from what she knew was a quixotic path . . . and in public addresses, his strongest emotions came out when he talked about protecting women," Dr. Kathleen Dalton observes.[11] Without Edith's counsel, TR resumed his unofficial campaign for the 1912 GOP presidential nomination, despite having lost valuable months toward his goal.

Conie took a decidedly different view of her brother's triumphant return. After the death of Stewart, Conie, like her brother, lit out for the territory. Determined not to let "black care" catch her, Conie and

Douglas, along with their son Monroe, went on a six-month journey around the world visiting Italy, India, China, Japan, and Korea. "I both long and dread to get home, the home which can never again be what it was," Conie wrote Henry Cabot Lodge, to whom she had become an increasingly close correspondent. When she got home she began "some of the most productive [years] in her life" . . . "com[ing] back stronger than ever before."[12] Conie published her first volume of poetry, *The Call of Brotherhood*, in which she seemed to echo TR's self-motivating call to get back "in the arena" of life and politics:

> *Have you heard it, the dominant call*
> *Of the city's great cry, and the thrall*
> *And the throb and the stir of its Strife,*
> *As, amid the dread dust and the din*
> *It wages its battle of Sin?*[13]

As Edith convalesced, Conie conspired. Her brother "had no intention of running for the presidential nomination in 1912," she later confessed, ". . . but already a swelling tide of disapproval of the Taft administration had increased in volume to such an extent that it swept over a large part of the country." Taft's inaction was magnified by the contrast with the "crowded hours" of his predecessor's reign. What had been a rocket ride was now mere drift. The American public grew impatient. "The force of this great wave [of popular discontent] culminated in a round-robin letter from seven governors in February 1912, a letter in which those same governors begged him to take, openly, the leadership of Progressive Republicanism."[14] Edith, due to her fall, was unable to come to New York. "Do you wish to have me come alone? Do exactly what you think best," TR wrote Conie. Conie, as she had done so many times when TR was governor, made the meeting happen.

She wrote: "In the library at my own house in New York City, a fateful meeting took place shortly after this last letter came. I confess to having had serious doubts as to what his answer should be to that request of the seven governors. Personally, I felt the sacrifice asked of him was almost too great. I realized perfectly the great struggle before him and all that it would probably mean, and it seemed to me that he had already given all that was required of just such service to his beloved country."[15] Still, the Call of Brotherhood once again beckoned to Conie's eldest brother.

In the White House, President Taft ruminated over how his friend had turned foe. "[Taft] is going to be greatly beloved as President," TR had told Major Archibald Willingham Butt in December 1908, shortly after Taft's election and before the Inauguration.[16] Butt, known as Archie, served as a military aide in the White House to both Presidents Roosevelt and Taft. In one of the hundreds of letters to his sister-in-law Clara, Butt wrote: "After [dinner] the President [Taft] said: 'I cannot think of a pleasanter recollection for anyone to carry with them from Washington than an evening spent on the South Portico of the White House. . . . I know Theodore loved this spot as he did no other in the White House, and his most brilliant sallies of wit were made here, and that when the world seemed to be all awry it was here that he and Mrs. Roosevelt would sit, and his tempestuous nature would receive just that influence which made him one of the greatest figures the country has ever seen.'"[17] Edith, sidelined by the accident, was this time unable to provide "just that influence" to soothe TR's "tempestuous nature" and mend his relationship with Taft. "Since her near-fatal accident in 1911, Edith had had insufficient stamina to temper her husband's public tirades. . . . TR badly needed to have his angry tongue moderated by a wise advisor."[18]

"It distresses me very deeply, more deeply than anyone can know, to think of [Roosevelt] sitting there at Oyster Bay alone and feeling himself deserted. I know just how he feels," President Taft, with a tear in his eye, confessed to Archie Butt. "The American people are strange in their attitudes toward their idols. . . . They have even led their idols on and on to cut their legs from under them and apparently make their fall all the greater."[19] Taft, sure he would prevail should Roosevelt challenge him in the Republication primary, felt both anger and empathy toward Roosevelt: "To feel everything slipping away from him, all the popularity, the power which he loved, and above all the ability to do what he thought was of real benefit to the country, to feel it all going and then be alone!" He accurately diagnosed the problem: "If he could only fight! That's what he delights in and what is denied him now."[20]

"All great souls have their hours of darkness," Butt wrote. "But it is heart-breaking to those of us who know [Roosevelt] well and who love him sincerely."[21] His allegiance torn between Taft and Roosevelt, Butt was encouraged to take a six-week respite in Europe. When he refused, Taft concocted a reason for the trip: Butt met with the pope and was to return with a message for the president. Butt visited Rome, Paris, London, and Berlin but never made it home. His return trip was on the maiden voyage of RMS *Titanic*.[22]

"Politics are hateful," Edith wrote her son Kermit, with TR on the cusp of challenging his handpicked successor.[23] Just five months after her near death accident and less than one month after the "fateful meeting" at Conie's home in New York City, TR proclaimed: "My hat is in the ring, the fight is on." Edith "said [to Kermit that] her husband's decision to run made her 'gloomy' [b]ut she did not have the strength to try and stop him."[24] Instead, Edith and Ethel left on a month-long trip to South America. Historian Geoffrey Cowan recalls the scene:

> As she boarded the ship with Ethel, her twenty-one-year-old daughter, a reporter called out a question. "What are your plans for the trip?" he asked. "You know I never, never talk," Edith responded. Keeping pace with her as she walked to her stateroom, the reporter tried again. "Is the Colonel going to join you on the isthmus?" "You had better ask him. I never, never talk," she said, trying to back away. "Never." Ethel was a bit more forthcoming. When several large hatboxes arrived in the room, the reporter asked Ethel: "Is any one of those hats to go into the ring?" "Father's hat is not among them," Ethel [very protective of Edith and active in the American Red Cross, a fine example of the rising generation of women in the arena] said tartly. "I guess he has that one with him." Edith despised this new foray into public life. "I was

forced to be away," she wrote a family friend. "In all my life I was never so unhappy."[25]

Edith, whom Bamie and Conie worried would not "share" TR, was ready to be done with politics. After Roosevelt's presidency, Edith said to Major Archie Butt that "there had been so few happy women in the White House."

"I doubt if even I was entirely happy," she confided. "For there was always that anxiety about the President when he was away from me. I never knew what would happen before he got back. I never realized what a strain I was under continuously until it was over."[26] Whether in the White House or out of power, Edith knew her husband would never really be hers alone again. "No matter how prepared she had thought she was for the transition from public to private life, the violent suddenness of it took her by surprise," historian Sylvia Jukes Morris observed. As first lady "she had been at the center of national affairs, surrounded by aides, secretaries, fashionable women and powerful men; her days had been full of business, order and dispatch. Her six children had been constantly coming and going, and her husband at his desk only a few doors away."[27] Did she want it all again? "She says she is very content and very happy and has not regretted it for a moment that they are no longer in the White House," Major Butt recorded in a letter to his sister-in-law. "[Edith] feels a deep sense of relief when she reflects that her life can now be natural and that she has to see only those persons whom she really likes and who really like her."[28]

Edith was the one who (accurately) predicted Theodore would never again be president. Perhaps she was frustrated by the futility of the 1912 race, or perhaps she was simply frustrated by being married to a restless adventurer who was either going to run for the presidency or leave her alone and lonely at Sagamore Hill.

Bamie's record for 1912 is surprisingly silent, though given her consistent support of TR's political career, it is hard to imagine she was anything but emotionally supportive and politically pragmatic. Once again,

Major Archie Butt describes the scene in a letter to his sister-in-law: "Mrs. Cowles is very deaf, so I had to talk rather loud to be heard, but it was evidently a relief to everyone when I said in a bantering way: 'We are certainly glad to have you here [at a luncheon party at the home of the French ambassador in Washington], for those of us of two administrations have had a hard time of it lately and we need a recruit.' Mrs. Cowles enjoyed the reference and said in return: 'I cannot be a recruit, for I too am under suspicion by those of us who would draw a line and make us take sides.'"[29]

The biggest shake-up was the emergence of a new advisor. Headstrong Alice Roosevelt Longworth, whose relationship with her equally headstrong father had clearly been fraught, now engaged enthusiastically with him in his campaign. "The 1912 election was a defining event in Alice's life," historian Stacy Cordery, Alice's most significant biographer, wrote of the time.[30] Having been a fascinating and popular national figure during his presidency, Alice proved to be an attractive, intelligent, and always provocative asset to his 1912 campaign. She helped the campaign by doing what her aunts, mother, and stepmother had heretofore done: listen and advise. Her relationship with candidate TR in many ways made up for her badly flawed marriage to Nicholas Longworth, who supported the incumbent president. She was unapologetic about the political—and emotional—rift that developed between her and Longworth, believing her husband "opted for expediency over integrity" when he chose Taft over her father.[31]

Whatever the family dynamics behind Alice's political support, she was also an enthusiastic champion of her father's brand of progressive politics. Her mother and her mother's family had been early progressives, and their influence had nurtured the progressive impulse in young Theodore as well. "His independence was the only thing in him we cared for," Henry Lee proclaimed when Roosevelt failed to bolt the Republican Party in 1884. Alice Hathaway Roosevelt, born a Lee, was not there to guide him.[32] Now Alice the daughter had an opportunity to support a genuine progressive politician rather than Taft's pale imitation. Had her father's bid panned out, and with Edith receding from public life, she might have been a strong right hand for her president father. Instead, she would go on to be a confidante to a number of presidents, including Hoover, Eisenhower, Kennedy, Johnson, and Nixon. Conspicuously absent are FDR and Truman, both Democrats of course, but only one was related to Alice.

The election year 1912 introduced widespread use of the presidential primary, in which all registered members of a party could vote for the nominee. Intended as a progressive, democratizing electoral innovation, the spread of the primary system was largely a state-by-state phenomenon rather than a national initiative. Roosevelt neither championed nor opposed primaries, but once they began to catch on, he proclaimed, "Let the people rule."[33] While Taft carried the Southern primaries as well as those in New York, Indiana, Michigan, Kentucky, and Massachusetts, Roosevelt won Illinois, Minnesota, Nebraska, South Dakota, California, Maryland, Pennsylvania, and, tellingly, Ohio. Each candidate lost their home state to the other and, notably, Roosevelt *and* Taft lost North Dakota to Wisconsin senator Robert M. La Follete, who had tried to coax TR to join the National Progressive Republican League, the immediate precursor to the creation of the Progressive Party, before declaring his own bid for the Republican nomination.

Despite the loss in his native New York and adopted North Dakota, historian Dr. Kathleen Dalton notes, "If presidential primaries and popular votes had been the deciding factors in 1912, TR unequivocally would have won the Republican nomination."[34] The fact was that primaries did not supersede national conventions in choosing candidates until 1972. In 1912, it was still the Republican National Committee, made up of conservative party leaders and headed by Taft as the incumbent president, that controlled the final credentials of state delegates to the GOP National Convention. The purpose of these new primaries was to wrestle power from the party machine but in the end, Taft prevailed on the first ballot. This prompted TR to cross the political Rubicon. When "bolters" from the GOP formed the Progressive Party and held their first convention two months later, in August 1912, it enthusiastically chose TR as its standard-bearer. He enthusiastically accepted. Significantly, the Progressive platform included another cause long ago embraced by Alice Lee and her family, women's suffrage. Indeed, Roosevelt's nomination by the party convention was seconded in a speech by none other than Jane Addams, social reformer and suffragist. Theodore Roosevelt was the first candidate to be seconded by a woman.

One woman who wasn't there to see it all was Alice Roosevelt Longworth. Though she "earnestly shared the convictions of her father's Bull Moose Party,"[35] as the Progressive Party was dubbed, both her husband *and* her candidate father objected to her attending the convention because Longworth was a Republican in a hard-fought election for another term as U.S. representative from Ohio's 1st District. Not usually one to be blocked, she was brought to tears and gave in.

As the general election neared, Edith became increasingly optimistic. It only helped that Roosevelt was seen not so much as the Progressive Party's candidate as the Progressive Party was seen to be Roosevelt's party. When he lost the Republican nomination, he declared that he felt as "strong as a bull moose."[36] That animal immediately became the official mascot and emblem of the party. "The campaign adopted advertising techniques popular in the suffrage movement," observes Dr. Kathleen Dalton.[37] Toy moose, pins, bandanas, and scarfs flooded the popular marketplace and "women played a more prominent role in presidential politics during the Progressive Party's brief life than they ever had before."[38] "In the future, Henry," a cartoon of the age captured, "Please do not refer to me as the 'Missus': 'Call me the moosus.'"[39] More significant than a slogan, "TR called for an equal partnership of the sexes within the Bull Moose Party, so for the first time in U.S. history women served alongside men on the national committee and on the party's state committees as delegates."[40]

Roosevelt's boast of bull moose strength was not a pose. After years of frustration over the consequences of his pledge and his profound disappointment in Taft, he was both driven and rejuvenated. He campaigned fiercely against Taft and the Democratic nominee, Woodrow Wilson. All

three candidates were, in fact, "progressive." Roosevelt could be proud
of that. They were all, to varying degrees, avatars of the progressivism
he had initially imbibed from his father and from Alice Lee's family and
their allied Saltonstall clan. Taft (as Roosevelt saw it) had gone soft, his
progressivism become severely attenuated. The professorial Wilson, a
political scientist and political theorist, intellectualized and idealized
progressivism. Roosevelt regarded himself as the movement's true, determined, and proven champion. He was the bull moose who, propelled by
pragmatic passion, would win against all odds, bull his way back into the
White House, and, from there, bull through reform so sweeping that it
would secure his legacy forever. Privately, to Edith and others, he sometimes conceded that he would probably lose. But it didn't matter. What
mattered was that he was back in the arena. Edith, too, seemed to come
around. TR is "making an uphill fight for what he believes in," she wrote.
"When I am angry or sad I remember that mountain tops are always
lonely."[41] Edith had also long feared for Theodore's life. He was by this
time the most famous man in the world, an ex-president seeking a return
to glory. One bullet could change the trajectory of their lives and the
country.

Born in Bavaria in 1876, John Flammang Schrank immigrated to the
United States with his parents when he was three years old. His mother
and father died soon after the family arrived in the New World. An uncle
took young Schrank in, and when he was old enough to work he helped
his uncle run the New York City tavern he owned. Years later, but while
he was still young, his uncle and aunt died, leaving him the tavern and an
apartment building. If fortune did not exactly smile upon Schrank, it at
least winked. The deaths of this orphan's adoptive parents did not cast
him adrift. He was left with the means of a comfortable living, and he
had a sweetheart.

Then, she died, too. With that, he lost interest in everything except
Bible study and poetry scribbling. He drifted, desperate, lost. He went
mad.

Sometime before October 14, 1912, when Theodore Roosevelt arrived in Milwaukee to give a campaign speech, the ghost of William McKinley visited John Schrank in a dream. The presidential shade, like Dickens's Ghost of Christmas Yet to Come, pointed a sepulchral finger. It directed Schrank's gaze to a photograph of Theodore Roosevelt.

"This is my murderer," the ghost commanded.[42]

No longer aimlessly drifting, John Schrank stealthily shadowed candidate Roosevelt, silently tracking him from New Orleans to Milwaukee. He picked up a local newspaper and noted that he was scheduled to attend a dinner at the Gilpatrick Hotel before being driven a short distance along Kilbourn Avenue to make a speech at Milwaukee Auditorium (still standing today as the Miller High Life Theatre).

Schrank took up his station outside the Gilpatrick and waited for his man. At length, he saw Roosevelt stride out the front doors. As the candidate paused to greet well-wishers standing beside his waiting car, Schrank stepped up to him, revolver in hand, and squeezed off one round before people in the crowd wrestled him to the ground. As when Leon Czolgosz fired on McKinley, the shot was point-blank, but Schrank aimed higher, hitting Roosevelt not in the abdomen but squarely in the chest. The round tore into flesh and muscle. It should have penetrated heart or lung or both. But its velocity was slowed by passage through the contents of the inner pocket of his frock coat. There he had deposited both his steel eyeglasses case and the twice-folded, fifty-page manuscript of his speech.

Man and boy, Theodore Roosevelt had shot animals beyond reckoning, and, at San Juan Heights, he had shot and killed at least one man. He knew very well what it was like to shoot something living. Now he knew what it was like to be shot. He knew also that the bullet was in his chest. Roosevelt seemed always to feel a certain out-of-body detachment whenever he was injured, as when, riding to the hounds at newly built Sagamore Hill in October 1885, he fell, breaking his arm badly. Remounting the horse, he finished the course with one hand on the reins, the other at the end of his arm, uselessly dangling.

Now, in Milwaukee, having been shot, TR took careful note of the fact that he was not coughing up blood, let alone foamy blood. The bullet, he therefore reasoned, had not penetrated a lung. It was in the flesh and muscle of a stout man. It was not going to go anywhere, at least not anytime soon. As bystanders piled on his assailant, Roosevelt called out to them, "Don't hurt him." TR looked hard, looked at a man who was now cowering in fear. "What did you do it for?" TR asked his would-be assassin to no reply.[43]

Had Edith been with him, he would have heeded her calm instructions to get in the car and be driven to the hospital. But she was in New York staying with a relative in her Manhattan townhouse on East 35th Street. Over the frantic objections and earnest entreaties of everyone present, TR refused to be driven to the hospital. He intended to deliver his speech.

Naturally, it was high theater. Years earlier, on Saint Patrick's Day 1905, Theodore Roosevelt had given away his orphaned niece, Eleanor, at her wedding. Alice noted that, upon her father's entrance, all eyes turned from the bride and fixed on him. Unsurprised, she later commented, "My father always has to be the bride at every wedding and the corpse at every funeral."[44] Now he had the opportunity to be the actor, the writer, and the director of the drama—not to mention both the victim and the hero.

He mounted the stage and stood before, not behind, the lectern.

"Friends, I shall ask you to be as quiet as possible. I don't know whether you fully understand that I have just been shot; but it takes more than that to kill a Bull Moose."

He took several beats to allow the audience to give full vent to their gasps, screams, groans, and shouts.

"But fortunately," he continued, "I had my manuscript, so you see I was going to make a long speech, and there is a bullet . . ." He opened his coat and waistcoat to reveal a shirtfront drenched in blood. "There is where the bullet went through," he explained, "and it [the manuscript] probably saved me from it going into my heart. The bullet is in me now, so that I cannot make a very long speech, but I will try my best."

His best, under the circumstances, was astoundingly good. He spoke for an hour and a half, pausing several times only to wave off well-meaning pleas that he stop and get himself to the hospital.

"Don't you waste any sympathy on me. I have had an A-1 time in life and I am having it now."[45]

Doubtless he was, and when he finally made an end to his remarks, ambulance attendants, already in the wings, advanced onstage with a stretcher.

"I'll not go to the hospital lying in that thing," he snapped. "I'll walk to it [the ambulance] and I'll walk from it to the hospital. I'm no weakling to be crippled by a flesh wound."[46]

It has often been observed that assassins' bullets did not kill Presidents Garfield and McKinley. Their doctors did—probing jagged wounds with septic instruments and their own dirty fingers. Roosevelt was far more fortunate than the two presidential targets before him. The physicians who attended him in the Emergency Hospital in Milwaukee generally agreed with their patient's assessment that the wound was comparatively minor. It was better to leave the bullet where it was rather than risk making the trauma worse by probing to find it and cutting to retrieve it.

As the assassination attempt unfolded, Edith was in a Manhattan theater with Laura Roosevelt, one of the many Roosevelt cousins in New York, watching a play. Beside Edith, on the aisle, was an empty seat saved for Laura's son, Oliver. He was working at Progressive Party headquarters and arrived late, after the curtain had gone up. As he sat down, Edith touched his knee in greeting. It was "shaking violently." She instinctively knew something had happened to her husband. She gripped Oliver's hand. He told her that telegram messages from Milwaukee reported that Roosevelt had been "shot at" but not hit. Edith asked Oliver to return to headquarters to make sure the news was not worse. In the meantime, she remained at the theater. When Oliver returned, he reported that he had been "scratched but had kept on with his speech." Laura told her that they should leave the theater, but Edith declined, saying, reasonably enough, that "he couldn't be hurt if he went on with his speech."[47]

When Edith left the theater—after the performance—she did so via a side entrance to evade reporters. By that time, the full story of what had happened in Milwaukee was already out. Had she encountered the reporters gathered out front, they would have told her. A waiting car took her to the Hotel Manhattan, where the Progressive Party had set up its campaign headquarters. There she learned everything that was known up to the time. After midnight, she received word that, his wound having been dressed in the Emergency Hospital, her husband was now sleeping in a train car bound for Chicago's Mercy Hospital, about ninety miles south of Milwaukee. This was a major medical center, better equipped and staffed to determine if surgery was indeed called for. TR sent Edith a personal telegram, describing his wound as "trivial . . . not a particle more serious than one of the injuries" their boys used to have.[48]

Edith decided to go to Chicago on the next day. Early that morning, she returned to campaign headquarters and was told that her husband was at Mercy Hospital, in bed, and that the wound was in fact far from "trivial." X-rays discovered that the entry wound was halfway up his right side, the bullet broke a rib, was deflected four inches to the left, and lodged a quarter of an inch from the heart. The course of treatment prescribed at this point was nothing more or less than absolute bed rest, the common cure-all of the era.[49]

The nation's newspapers, of all political stripes, praised Roosevelt's courage. *The New York Times* called that courage "indomitable." While the paper described his insistence on delivering his speech a "rash" decision, it also called it "characteristic, and the judgment of the country will be that it was magnificent." The anti-TR *Herald* observed, "We are against his politics, but we like his grit."[50]

There was no special train laid on for Edith. Instead, she boarded the regular Twentieth Century Limited in company with Ted, Ethel, and family physician Dr. Alexander Lambert. The Limited made one special concession, stopping at a suburban Chicago station at eight-thirty on the morning of the 16th, so that Edith and the others could avoid crowds and reporters. They were driven to Mercy, where Edith was provided with a room next to her husband's. There she read the outpouring of good wishes from the prominent and the common alike. Both Wilson and Taft wired their best wishes and told her what they had both announced to the press: they were suspending their campaigns until Roosevelt's recovery was ensured.

Edith's room became a command center. She kept all visitors away but for a very few deemed essential. Among the select were Jane Addams, whom Roosevelt greatly admired and with whom he enjoyed talking. As for keeping the impatient patient in line, Charles Willis Thompson of *The New York Times* declared that of all "the bosses that had gone before" Edith Roosevelt, "Quay, Platt, Hanna and Hill . . . were amateurs [compared] to her. That sedate and determined woman, from the moment of her arrival in Chicago, took charge of affairs and reduced the Colonel to pitiable subjection. Up to her advent he was throwing bombshells into his doctors . . . and directing his own medical campaign. . . . The moment she arrived a hush fell upon T.R. . . . he became as meek as Moses. Now and then the Colonel would send out secretly for somebody he knew and wanted to talk to, but every time the vigilant Mrs. Roosevelt would swoop down on the emissary. . . . No such tyrannical sway has ever been seen in the history of American politics."[51] TR himself joked: "This thing about ours being a campaign against boss rule is a fake. I never was so boss-ruled in my life as I am at this moment."[52]

As for being shot, Roosevelt wrote to Cecil Spring-Rice on December 31, 1912, "I did not care a rap for being shot. It is a trade risk, which every prominent public man ought to accept as a matter of course. For eleven years I have been prepared any day to be shot."[53] His Chicago physicians concurred with those who had initially treated him in Milwaukee: the bullet was best left where it was, a quarter inch from his heart. As for his assailant, John Schrank, he was committed to the Central State Mental Hospital in Waupun, Wisconsin, in 1914 and remained there until he died in 1943. Roosevelt appears never to have given him another thought.

· · · · ·

Edith took her husband out of the hospital on October 21. Wheelchair-bound, he was conveyed to the train station, set up in a sleeping car, and transported to New York. During the journey, he occupied himself, not surprisingly, with reading. More surprisingly, however, he read magazines, not books. He went directly to Sagamore Hill, where he celebrated his fifty-fourth year of life on the 27th.

Alice joined her father at Sagamore to help him celebrate his birthday and prepare for the critical last weeks of the campaign. Masterful in the art of high drama, TR planned to make a major address—his first since the assassination attempt—at Madison Square Garden. With her father convalescing at home, she labored with him to draft this last, great speech of a bold third-party campaign. "He would pass over the first draft of every sheet . . . as he finished writing it," Alice recalled.[54] Father and daughter looked over every word, writing and editing together.

"Alice saw 1912 as her chance—at long last—to win her father's love," historian Dr. Kathleen Dalton judged.[55] She was a political animal like her father—married, after all, to the Speaker of the House. But did she really think that this would do it? Did she actually believe that helping with a speech would make up for being the daughter whose very coming into the world ushered her father's first bride out of it? All we can answer is that it was a most extraordinary speech, and Alice clearly played a significant role in its creation.

On October 30, sixteen days after being shot a quarter inch from his heart, Theodore Roosevelt delivered the speech at a gargantuan Progressive Party rally at Madison Square Garden.[56] His audience spilled out onto the street. Before he uttered a word, applause and shouts erupted, delaying the beginning of his address by forty-one minutes. One hundred thousand people crowded the arena and the streets outside. Among the throng was Conie Roosevelt Robinson. At forty-nine now, she had lost not only her son but also her first grandchild (to whooping cough). She was also menopausal and wrote her daughter: "I know I am nervous and restless and irritable, but you must forgive me darling . . . I would gladly be more satisfactory if I had more self-control. I am trying to have it, but all doctors agree that just at this special moment in a woman's life it is the one thing one loses."[57]

As usual, Conie found great joy in the triumph of her brother. She recalled, "[We] were obliged to take our places in the cheering, laughing, singing crowd. . . . How it swayed and swung! How it throbbed with life and elation!" Conie's VIP pass had not been accepted by the ring of police guarding the Garden but standing in the crowd only added to the excitement. "Had I lived my whole life only for those fifteen minutes during which I marched toward the Garden already full to overflowing with my brother's adoring followers, I should have been content to do so. We could hardly get into the building, and indeed had to climb up the fire-escape, which we were only allowed to do after making it well known that I was the sister of the 'Colonel.' (There never was but one 'Colonel' in American history!)."[58]

When Roosevelt finally spoke, it was of uniting the cause of the Progressive Party—this third party—with every organization and public individual of goodwill joining "with them in good faith to make an effective campaign against the invisible government, against the rule of the State by two machines under the leadership of men whose activities we regard as pernicious to decency and cleanliness in public life; two machines which work together against the interests of the people, under a system which inevitably produces corruption in public affairs. I believe our platform should be short and simple, embodying just the principles for which at this crisis, in this State, we stand." He presented the elements of his vision of a Progressive platform, which was to serve the American people, who "work hard and faithfully":

> They do not wish to shirk their work. They must feel pride in the work
> for the work's sake. But there must be bread for the work. There must
> be a time for play when the men and women are young. When they
> grow old there must be certainty of rest under conditions free from
> the haunting terror of utter poverty. . . . We here in America hold in

our hands the hope of the world, the fate of the coming years, and shame and disgrace will be ours if in our eyes the light of high resolve is dimmed, if we trail in the dust the golden hopes of men.[59]

With the help of a daughter he had in so many ways forsaken, Theodore Roosevelt—having impulsively, Lear-like, thrown away the third term for which the American electorate clamored—now offered to an overflowing arena of those voters a revolution. In the future, others would dangle alternatives to the "two machines which work together against the interests of the people," but they were never really serious. The Progressive Party cast—for a time—a spell, albeit not as the Progressive Party but as the Bull Moose Party, the *Roosevelt party*.

The nation showed intense admiration for the candidate after the attempted assassination. As Edith sagely observed in a letter to Kermit, "for about ten days after Father's wound a great change in popular feeling caused many of our leaders to feel that a Progressive landslide was possible."[60] But on November 5, 1912, Theodore Roosevelt and his running mate, Hiram Johnson, received 4,120,207 votes (27.4%), garnering 88 electoral votes and carrying six states. Democrat Woodrow Wilson won 6,294,327 votes (41.8%) and 435 electoral votes, carrying forty states. The incumbent, William Howard Taft, whom Edith had long distrusted, came in at third place, with 3,486,343 votes (23.2%) for eight electoral votes. He carried just two states. His home state of Ohio was not one of them. Only the Socialist candidate, Eugene Debs, trailed him, with 900,370 votes (6%) and no electoral votes.[61] 241,783 votes (1.6%) went to none of the four major candidates. The Progressive Party split the Republican vote. Most political observers believe had the GOP nominated Roosevelt, he would have been president, and the party would have held the White House. Nevertheless, in defeating the incumbent candidate of the GOP, TR's run as a Bull Moose Progressive was and remains the most successful third-party candidacy in the history of the United States. The party made history in another way, too. Moosette Helen B. Scott was "the first woman in U.S. history to cast an electoral vote for president," doing so eight years before women won the popular franchise. Indeed, "after talking with women activists . . . TR started speaking out for one of their pet issues—moving elections away from saloons and into public schools."[62] But these small victories were not enough.

The morning after the election, "Ethel and Edith broke into sobs over breakfast."[63] The women in the arena were unaccustomed to defeat. Fittingly, Conie named the chapter on the 1912 election in her book "The Great Denial" and offered a valedictory poem:

> *Who would not be*
> *A baffled Moses with the eyes to see*
> *The far fruition of the Promised Land!*[64]

16

PUT OUT THE LIGHT

"WATCH SAGAMORE HILL FOR ----"

—Censored telegram

*T*R put on a brave face in public after his 1912 defeat, but was privately devastated. Conie confirmed the feeling—"Never before in his varied career had Theodore Roosevelt felt such a sense of loneliness"[1]—but it was almost certainly a *feeling* and not objective fact. He was surrounded by his usual retinue of Roosevelt women, all of them trying to help him heal. As for Edith, she continued to suffer the after-effects of what today would be diagnosed as a concussion with traumatic brain injury. She was lethargic but ever more concerned for TR than herself. "In the weeks after the election," Dr. Kathleen Dalton writes, "[TR] felt the loss almost as intensely as the death of someone he loved."[2] He was, perhaps for the first time since 1884, suffering a severe depression.

He plunged into the writing of a useful but disappointingly pedestrian *Autobiography* and a far more interesting collection of essays, *History as Literature and Other Essays*. Perhaps this should come as no surprise. Theodore Roosevelt was capable of projecting forward but never (at least publicly) looking backward. Not once, for instance, in the more than

200,000 words of his *Autobiography* is the name Alice Hathaway Roosevelt mentioned. Neither does he linger on the lost cattle investment, the death of Elliott, or the recent election loss. That both the *Autobiography* and the essays were published in 1913 is nevertheless evidence that his literary productivity was undiminished.

But then he set out on a spectacular and spectacularly dangerous iteration of a familiar strategy. He lit out for the territory, endeavoring as always to outrun "black care" while his wife and sisters managed his affairs at home. This time, the "territory" was outside of the nation that had failed to restore him to the White House. Under the joint sponsorship of the American Museum of Natural History and the government of Brazil, he embarked on a South American lecture tour to be followed by an expedition deep into the jungle to explore the Paraguay River, which runs some 1,675 miles through Brazil (the origin of its headwaters), Bolivia, Paraguay, and Argentina, where it joins the Apa.

It promised to be an arduous journey—"strenuous," Roosevelt might have called it—and Edith, whose own health was far from strong at this point, insisted on accompanying him on the first leg of the trip. Likely, she sensed that, vulnerable as he now was, her husband needed her, however far she could accompany him into this new arena. This first leg proved to be no leisurely vacation by the sheer volume of stops on the itinerary. They stopped briefly in Barbados before sailing on to Bahia, Brazil, where they landed on October 18.

Edith was brave and determined but hardly foolhardy. Since she could not be with Theodore, she recruited Kermit to accompany him into the interior. This venture, unlike the African safari or Roosevelt's many domestic hunts, was life-threateningly dangerous because Theodore and Kermit were headed to parts unknown. It was a significant risk, for Kermit, of course, but also for his mother, who sought to protect her husband by risking the life of her son. Edith "had felt Kermit's absence from her life" since his move to Brazil the year before. The two shared a similar temperament and outlook. He was, at times, "the envy of her other children."[3] Her decision was not, however, irrational. Kermit had been working for the Brazil Railroad and was now supervising engineer for bridge construction with the Anglo-Brazilian Iron Company. He was a seasoned hand in this part of the world. Indeed, his company gave him half a year off because management saw the expedition as an opportunity for their employee to scout the interior. "It won't be anything like our Africa trip," TR promised.[4] He had been hyper-competitive with his son in Africa, keeping meticulous count of their respective daily kills. Dr. Dalton writes: "As if to reassert that he was still the better man, he pointed out to his reading public twice in his *African Game Trails* that the porters called him in Swahili Bwana Makuba, or 'the Great Master,' but they called Kermit only Bwana Merodadi, 'the Dandy.'"[5] If this got under Kermit's skin, he did not let on, and his father "never knew that Kermit came along on his trip because Edith pleaded with him to act as her surrogate."[6]

Kermit met his family in Bahia and accompanied them southward to Rio de Janeiro. Edith was enchanted by the city but had little time to enjoy it, since she and her husband were besieged by official and social engagements—evidence that TR was hardly "shunned" and "outcast," however he might have felt. "Father needs more scope," Edith wrote Ethel, "and since he can't be President must go away from home to have it."[7] Nevertheless, she was worried, with ample reason, that this would be the last of Theodore Roosevelt's adventures.

From Rio, the Roosevelt party journeyed through southern Brazil, Uruguay, and Argentina before crossing the Andes to Santiago, Chile. There were two unanticipated romantic episodes along this first leg of the South American journey. While she was in Buenos Aires, Margaret Roosevelt, the daughter of TR's cousin Emlen who, like Edith, joined the early part of the trip as a tourist not explorer, received bouquets of white roses—daily—from Henry Hunt, a fellow SS *Vandyck* passenger outbound from New York who was smitten.[8] While in Rio, Kermit received a cable from Belle Willard, an intimate friend of his sister Ethel and the daughter of the United States ambassador to Spain. Received on November 13, the cable informed Kermit that she accepted his proposal of marriage, which had come after a courtship that began in 1912, prior to his leaving for Brazil. Edith liked Belle, whom she dubbed "The Fair One with Golden Locks," after the heroine of a fairy tale by the seventeenth-century French author Marie-Catherine d'Aulnoy. The whimsical moniker Edith bestowed on Belle betrayed Edith's considerable anxiety. She regarded her in something of the same way as she had—unfairly—Alice Hathaway Lee Roosevelt. In Edith's view, she was pretty, sociable, and shallow. Edith's fear was that Kermit would soon be bored—or perhaps worse. She once called her fair-haired son "the one with the white head and the black heart."[9]

But there was little time left to discuss the matter with Kermit or Theodore. On November 26, Edith and Margaret parted with both of them, boarding a ship for Panama and leaving father and son to face the continent's interior alone. Proving just how treacherous the journey could be, Margaret contracted typhoid fever—the same disease that killed Mittie Roosevelt. Just a little over two weeks after returning to New York, Margaret was dead.

The loss of Edith's young, healthy traveling companion could only be interpreted as an ominous sign. The most dangerous part of the journey for TR and Kermit was yet to come. As had now happened so often over the course their partnership, Edith could see the future more presciently than her husband but was unable to prevent him from charging ahead.

She was back in the United States when she received a letter her husband had written to her from Brazil on Christmas Day 1913. He announced that he had abandoned the original plan to explore the Paraguay River and instead was setting out to explore Brazil's mysterious, almost entirely unknown, Rio da Dúvida ("River of Doubt").

We do not know what impact this news had on Edith. We do know that her husband had gotten beyond her reach—taking with him her favorite son.

Roosevelt lost his bid to be the first third-party candidate to win a presidential election. Changing the objective of the South American expedition from exploring the Paraguay River, a well-traveled waterway, to charting the obscure River of Doubt gave him another chance at a first. His partner would be Marshal Cândido Mariano da Silva Rondon, a high-ranking Brazilian army officer who was already known as that nation's premier explorer. Indeed, it was he who had not only discovered but named Rio da Dúvida. Now, with Roosevelt, he would navigate it in an attempt to map its course to its confluence with the Amazon River. The challenges were literally unknown, but both men expected to face all the dangers inherent in the Amazonian interior, including impassable rapids and treacherous waterfalls. Finding their way around these would certainly require extensive overland treks through dense jungle. It would also require them to battle plagues of illness.

By the time the Roosevelt-Rondon party had negotiated perhaps one fourth of the river's downriver length, they were largely spent—yet continued to drive themselves onward. The days wore on. Everyone, except for the indestructible Rondon, was either sick or injured or both. In an effort to free two dugouts hung up on rocks, Roosevelt suffered a deep gash in the same leg, his left, that had been so badly injured when he was thrown from his carriage after it collided with a trolley in Pittsfield, Massachusetts, back in 1902. Predictably and quickly, it became infected. Already debilitated by malaria, he was brought near death by the infection, and he pleaded with Kermit to leave him. His son refused, as Edith doubtless knew he would.

Fortunately, the explorers encountered *seringueiros*, or "rubber men," who eked out their living by tapping rubber trees for the latex sap that ended up as the tires for American automobiles. These men helped the party down the last leg of the river. By the time they reached São João, Roosevelt, who had been borne in on a litter, was fifty-seven pounds lighter than when he had embarked, had a fresh leg abscess, and was running a high "blood fever": sepsis. Of the nineteen men who set out on the expedition, sixteen returned. One had been the victim of drowning—his body never retrieved from the rapids—another was murdered and buried at the scene, and the other was his murderer, whom the surviving members of the expedition abandoned in the jungle by way of punishment.

Roosevelt received treatment at Manaus, capital city of Brazil's Amazonas state. He returned to New York about three weeks later, on May 19, 1914. In hand was a wealth of information and insight, as well as a map of the river, which the government of Brazil duly renamed Rio Roosevelt—though some Brazilians, more affectionately, have always called it Rio Teodoro. When word reached Edith that TR's "last chance to be a boy" had nearly killed him she responded: "I never felt it was a wise trip but I was probably wrong."[10] Edith was not wrong, of course, and her "insistence on sending Kermit to protect TR saved his life."[11] Conie noted: "[TR] was never wholly free from recurrent attacks of the terrible jungle fever, which resulted in ill health of various kinds, and finally his death."[12]

Although greatly weakened, prematurely aged, and destined never fully to recover his vigor, Roosevelt set to work on a new book, *Through the Brazilian Wilderness*. First, however, he had to defend against those who doubted his findings. Some even challenged his assertion that he had, in fact, made the expedition. Weak and ill, Roosevelt nevertheless booked speaking engagements at the National Geographic Society in Washington and at the Royal Geographical Society in London. His presentations tamped down the accusations of his critics, but it took a new expedition, in 1927, by the British explorer George Miller Dyott to independently confirm the discoveries of the Roosevelt-Rondon Expedition. By then, Roosevelt had been eight years in the grave.

His body ravaged, the women in the arena kept TR's mind engaged. Like her mother before her, Conie organized a literary salon at her home in New York City. A youthful Robert Frost, who would later be nominated thirty-one times for a Nobel Prize in Literature, receive a Pulitzer Prize and a Congressional Gold Medal, and deliver the poem at President John F. Kennedy's inauguration, was among the guests. None other than another Pulitzer laureate, novelist Edith Wharton, had encouraged Conie to publish her first volume of poetry, which was quickly followed by a second, *One Woman to Another*, published in 1914. Betty Boyd Caroli observes that the volume's eponymous poem "was really directed to her daughter, Corinney [and] dealt with how both mother and daughter had been unable to intervene in their brothers' deaths."[13] The poem concludes:

Because he taught me what a holy thing
Is human love, and by his gentleness
He saved my vagrant and despairing soul.
Then God, who is our Father, can but save
His erring soul by love that is divine—
What! You would kiss me? Yes, I take your kiss;
We are both women, and we have both loved![14]

Conie salved her grief with words. TR preferred adventure. Yet both siblings used grief to fuel their most successful periods of life. Both refused to believe that TR's most successful days were all behind him; Conie would encourage and renew him for another fight.

Conie shared with her brother an intense dislike of the incumbent Democratic president Woodrow Wilson, who won the 1912 election in large part because Roosevelt split the Republican Party (Wilson won just 41.8 percent of the popular vote to Taft and TR's collective 50.6 percent). In a friendly note to his old friend Maine wilderness guide and Dakota ranch manager Bill Sewall, Theodore Roosevelt couldn't resist closing with this non sequitur: "What a dreadful creature Wilson is! I cannot believe our people have grown so yellow as to stand for him."[15] Although Democrat Wilson's progressivism was, if anything, more aligned with Roosevelt's than was Republican William Howard Taft's tepid stance, Wilson's refusal to join battle in the "Great War" that had begun in Europe in July 1914 was bitter evidence, as TR saw it, that America was backing out of the ultimate arena. "I asked [TR] if I could say anything from him about the War, and he simply threw up his hands in despair," Edith wrote to Conie, nine days after the war erupted in Europe. "From the beginning he said to his family," Conie explained, "what he did not feel he could state publicly, owing to the fact that he did not wish to embarrass President Wilson. Having been President himself, he knew it was possible for one in high authority to have information which he could not immediately share with all the people, and he hoped this might be the reason of President Wilson's failure to make any protest when the enemy troops invaded Belgium."[16]

Roosevelt's personal outrage could no longer be contained after German torpedoes sank the British liner *Lusitania* on May 7, 1915, killing 1,195 of the 1,953 passengers and crew on board, including 123 American citizens.[17] His outburst to Sewall came two weeks after another U-boat attack, this one against the British cross-Channel passenger ferry SS *Sussex* on March 24, 1916. Heavily damaged, *Sussex* did not sink, but at least fifty (perhaps as many as one hundred) souls lost their lives.[18]

Once unleashed, Roosevelt was relentless in his attacks against Wilson, including in his *America and the World War* (1915), even though an editorial published in *The New Republic* on November 4, 1916, three days before the general election that would return Wilson to office, made the plausible argument that Wilson's approach to the "European War" reflected the will of the American people. (Wilson ran on the slogan "He Kept Us Out of War.") This, the editors argued, was a true progressive position, "manifestly a continuation of the great work begun and abandoned by the former progressive leader [Roosevelt]."[19] Some of Roosevelt's most prominent backers, including the inventor Thomas Alva Edison, encouraged another run in 1916. "I believe [Roosevelt] is absolutely the only man that should be considered at this crucial point," Edison wrote.[20] But Conie was retrospectively sanguine on the race: "Republicans were still smarting from what they considered, I think unjustly, his betrayal of them, and they were not ready to enroll themselves under his banner."[21] In the moment, she grew passionate: "Theodore—the people wanted you. It seems terrible to me that they could not have you." TR, according to his sister, "answered with a smile that had a subtle meaning in it: 'Do not say that; if they had wanted me *hard* enough, they could have had me.'"[22]

Indeed, Roosevelt had declined the Progressive Party's nomination in 1916 and threw his support behind Republican candidate Charles Evans Hughes, even though the two had fallen out years earlier over Roosevelt's reform agenda and Hughes's more moderate views.[23] Edith was relieved. She had undergone a "severe and trying operation," which was "probably a hysterectomy," in 1915.[24] As they had feared from the moment they learned of TR's engagement to Edith, Bamie and Conie "thought [Edith] had become 'deeply possessive' and eager to keep her husband 'to herself as much as possible'"; now, that meant keeping him from the stress of another presidential run. TR wrote Bamie that Edith wanted the "privilege of growing old peacefully together."[25] To Edith he wrote that "it is a great blessing for lovers to grow old together." In letters to Kermit, oddly perhaps but also showing the evolving closeness of their father-son relationship, he wrote of Edith: "[She is] as charming and bewitching as ever; & all her ways are so attractive, & she is so interesting. Rather absurd for a fat, rheumatic, blind old man to speak this way, isn't it?" . . . "[She] looks so pretty and charming that now and then I have to get up and make love to her—which is rather absurd on the part of a gouty old man."[26] Personal valet James Amos, who continued to work with the Roosevelts after the White House, corroborates their enduring love for one another. Theodore, Amos said, was as "gentle and affectionate and attentive to his wife as a young lover."[27]

In campaigning for Hughes, Roosevelt brought the war front and center, dredging up ugly slurs against Irish Americans and German Americans for resisting American entry into the war. (Irish Americans did not want the United States to ally with Ireland's oppressor Britain, and German Americans did not want their adopted country to fight against the country of their birth or ancestry.) TR denounced both groups as "hyphenated Americans," countering that one must be "100% American" to be American. The irony here is that Woodrow Wilson, an unreconstructed racist and something of a xenophobe to boot, was likely even more intolerant of "hyphenated Americans" than Roosevelt.[28] Wilson narrowly defeated Hughes by 277–254 in the electoral college— and less than 600,000 votes nationally. There were those who believed TR certainly would have won against Wilson in 1916 had he not played spoiler in 1912.

The weeks and months wore on as more U.S. civilians were killed in attacks on merchant ships. Even under Wilson, the country edged closer to war. On May 18, 1917, Roosevelt sent a telegram to President Wilson citing the congressional legislation which had been passed authorizing Roosevelt to raise four divisions of American volunteers to fight in France and asking his permission to do so. Wilson refused. A month later, Roosevelt met with Wilson for a "surprisingly cordial forty-five-minute meeting." According to Alice, her father told him, "Mr. President, all that has gone before is as dust on a windy street," and he made a "promise not to come back" to the White House to badger Wilson for anything more if Wilson granted his one request.[29] "The President need not fear me politically. No one need fear me politically," Conie overheard her brother say. "If I am allowed to go, I could not last; I am too old to last long under such circumstances."[30] But there would be no reprise of Cuba, no "heroic ending to his life" on the Western Front.[31]

We must assume that Edith was relieved by Wilson's veto of her husband's plea to suffer what amounted to death in a trench, but she wholeheartedly concurred with TR's and Conie's assessment of Wilson: "Every morning I wake with the feeling of something wrong, and then realize that another four years must pass with this vile and hypocritical charlatan at the head of our Nation."[32] Both she and her husband had reason to feel that the Roosevelt legacy was once again in danger. Not only had Wilson kept America out of a war the Roosevelts believed the country should have been in from the beginning, but TR had run or campaigned in four elections since leaving the White House; he or the candidate he supported lost each of them.

In time of war, Roosevelt, at last accepting he'd been spurned, looked to his sons and relatives to serve. "Uncle Ted was always urging Franklin to resign," said Eleanor Roosevelt.[33] FDR, who was not yet wheelchair-bound by polio, was assistant secretary of the navy—TR's very job at the time of the outbreak of the Spanish-American War. "I'm so fond of that boy, I'd be shot for him," TR had said of FDR.[34] He wanted FDR to emulate his career—and he would, but not through the heroics of his own

San Juan Heights. TR also urged Shef, Bamie's son, to enlist, and Ted, Archie, and Quentin dutifully enrolled in the quasi-official summer officer candidate school Major General Leonard Wood (Roosevelt's wartime commander) had established in Plattsburgh, New York. Each son did his parents proud, but Edith confessed to Bamie, especially of Quentin, who was only nineteen: "I cannot be reconciled to boys of his age taking irrevocable steps."[35] Nevertheless, Edith didn't try to talk him out of enlisting.

Like their father in 1898, they all showed a flair for military service. Theodore Roosevelt personally asked General John J. Pershing, commanding officer of the American Expeditionary Forces, to allow his sons to accompany the general to Europe as privates. Pershing agreed, but given their Plattsburgh record, Ted was immediately commissioned a major, Archie was commissioned a second lieutenant, and Quentin was admitted into the Army Air Service. Kermit joined the British Army, where, as an honorary captain, he saw hard fighting in what is today Iraq. Before the Armistice, Kermit transferred to the U.S. Army in France and fought as an artillery captain in the Meuse-Argonne Offensive.

While his boys were at war, TR increasingly felt the ravages of his "strenuous life." By the beginning of 1918, "the malignant Brazilian fever, always lurking, ready to spring at his vitality, had shown itself in a peculiarly painful way, and an operation was considered necessary," Conie reported. "The rumor spread that he was dying," and his sister went to visit him in Roosevelt Hospital. Today renamed Mount Sinai West, Roosevelt Hospital was named for its founding benefactor, James Henry Roosevelt, third cousin to TR's grandfather. "I put my ear close to his lips, and these were the words which Theodore Roosevelt said to his sister, words which he fully believed would be the last he could ever say to her . . . 'I am so glad that it is not one of my boys who is dying here, for they can die for their country.'"[36]

Ted, among the first Americans to see combat in France, immediately distinguished himself. Before the war was over, he would hold the rank of lieutenant colonel in command of the 26th Regiment, First Division. He was shot in the leg, gassed, and wounded at Soissons in 1918, was awarded the Distinguished Service Cross, and after the war was made a Chevalier Légion d'honneur by the French government.[37]

Quentin Roosevelt flew with the 95th Aero Squadron. On July 14, four days after scoring his first kill, he was shot down behind German lines during the opening of the Second Battle of the Marne. No less a figure than Captain Eddie Rickenbacker, America's "Ace of Aces" in World War I, called Quentin "one of the most popular fellows in the group," who was "loved . . . for his own natural self." Rickenbacker went on to observe that he "was reckless to such a degree that his commanding officers had to caution him repeatedly about the senselessness of his lack of caution. His bravery was so notorious that we all knew he would either achieve some great spectacular success or be killed in the attempt."[38] Like father, like son.

Within hours, Theodore Roosevelt knew something was wrong. Phil Thompson, an Associated Press reporter, "noted an enigmatic telegram coming off the wires 'WATCH SAGAMORE HILL FOR ----.' The message ended at that because censors had blocked out the rest." After 11 p.m., "Thompson showed Roosevelt the telegram at Sagamore Hill and the Colonel started doing the awful arithmetic."[39] Dr. Kathleen Dalton asserts, "Roosevelt took this to mean that something had happened to one of the boys. He said nothing to Edith."[40] Perhaps it was a false report.

No. It was true. Quentin had been killed. The Germans buried him with full military honors, and the French made a posthumous award of the Croix de Guerre with Palm.

Quentin was exhumed in 1955 and reburied alongside his brother Ted in France. (Ted, a general, would die there in 1944.) He is the only casualty of World War I buried in the Normandy American Cemetery and Memorial. He was posthumously awarded the Purple Heart and a degree from Harvard, from which he would have graduated in 1919. At present, Quentin Roosevelt is the only child of a United States president to die in combat.

Roosevelt's public statement was terse: "Quentin's mother and I are very glad that he got to the front and had a chance to render some service to his country, and show the stuff that was in him before his fate befell him." Edith was more elegiac, revealing the poet in her, though some parents might find her statement breathtaking: "You cannot bring up boys as eagles and expect them to turn out sparrows."[41]

The next day, TR delivered a planned speech to the state convention in Saratoga. New York Republicans wanted TR to run for governor in November. Edith stayed at Sagamore, and Conie traveled to Saratoga to be with her brother. "Toward the end of the speech, though he never referred to his sorrow, the realization of it again gripped him with its inevitable torture, and again the people . . . sat in breathless silence," she recalled.[42] On the train back to New York City, as on the train ride back from Cambridge when his father lay dying and the train ride from Albany as his mother and wife also neared death, TR had time to contemplate. "I could see that he was not reading," Conie wrote later. "That his sombre eyes were fixed on the swiftly passing woodlands and the river, and that the book had not the power of distracting him from the all-empowering grief which had enveloped him."[43]

TR looked at his younger sister: "Corinne, I have only one fight left in me, and I think I should reserve my strength in case I am needed in 1920."[44] He still believed he might be called to run again for president. When they reached New York, Conie commented that Edith's "self-control was a lesson to all those who have had to meet the ultimate pain of life."[45] Perhaps her intention was to model sentiments appropriate to public people. After all, thousands and tens of thousands of families were losing their boys in this war. Perhaps the Roosevelts feared a personal reaction would diminish the sacrifices of other sons and parents. Or perhaps, as ever, Edith simply wished to grieve in private.

In a private letter (to a stranger no less), TR confessed: "Quentin was her baby, the last child left in the home nest; on the night before he sailed, a year ago, she did as she always had done and went upstairs to tuck him in bed—the huge, laughing, gentle-hearted boy."[46] TR went to the stables and, standing alone with Quentin's horse, wept. Offered the GOP nomination to run for New York governor, he declined it.

The day before the 1918 elections—on November 2—TR made his last public appearance. Owen Wister, the Western fiction author who had known Roosevelt since their Harvard days, was with Theodore and Edith at Sagamore Hill as he prepared for the speech. "One evening he brought in his speech finished," Wister recalled. "He was to deliver it in a few days, and now proposed that [Theodore, Owen, and Edith] go over it. . . . While we discussed the last speech that he was ever to make, his face, buoyant no longer, battered with conflict, brave to the end, grew eager over the cause he had always served, the cause of his country, the land of his faith and his passion. I listened as he dwelt upon the points he intended to drive home in Carnegie Hall."[47]

Theodore Roosevelt took the stage with W. E. B. Du Bois in front of a mixed-race audience and delivered a full-throated endorsement of equal rights for Black Americans. "He had missed the chance to remake race relations as president and again in 1912, but his views had finally changed late in life," Dr. Kathleen Dalton remarks.[48] "He was far from well on the night he made that speech," Conie wrote later. And yet: "Many in the audience told me afterward that the speech in Carnegie Hall was one of the most convincing and thrilling appeals to patriotism ever made by Theodore Roosevelt."[49] Felix Frankfurter, the future Supreme Court justice, who had been an enthusiastic supporter of the New Nationalism, later recalled a conversation in which TR said, "This country will never really demonstrate that it is a democracy in the full reach and range of that conception until we have had both a Negro and a Jewish president of the United States."[50]

When the GOP approached TR about running for president in 1920, he did not say no, but warned that the party would have to take him as he was, "without a single modification of the things that I have always stood for."[51] Bamie, Conie, and Edith would likely have supported the run, but each of them, especially Edith, knew Theodore was gravely ill. James Amos, who traveled with Theodore on many of his speaking trips, saw the wear up close: "It was becoming clear that he would have to be the Republican candidate in 1920. And I think he contemplated the outlook with a little horror." Amos knew his boss perhaps better than anyone save Edith. "I do not think he really had the appetite for the storm and fuss of another presidential term."[52]

On November 11, 1918, World War I ended, and one week later Roosevelt was back in the hospital. Bamie was not well enough to make the trip, but Conie—whose own husband died "very suddenly"[53] of a heart attack two months earlier—sat vigil with Edith. "I have kept the promise that I made myself when I was twenty-one," Theodore said to his sister. "I promised myself that I would work up to the hilt until I was sixty, and I have done it."[54]

Edith was able to have Theodore out of the hospital in time for Christmas at Sagamore Hill. As the calendar turned to 1919, Theodore Roosevelt was the leading candidate for the presidential nomination of 1920. "If we should ever go back to the White House—which heaven forbid!" Owen Wister remembered Edith saying during a discussion of politics with her and Theodore after the war and before the new year.[55] On Saturday morning, January 4, 1919, Edith called James Amos. The President was asking for his valet and friend of twenty years. "Mr. Roosevelt wouldn't have anyone else," Edith explained. Amos observed Roosevelt: "His face bore a tired expression. There was a look of weariness in his eyes. It was perfectly plain that he had suffered deeply."[56]

Another close friend, Margaret Chanler, saw Edith and Theodore "shortly before the end came" and recalled Theodore telling her, "I seem pretty low now, but I shall get better. I cannot go without having done something about that old gray skunk in the White House."[57]

On the evening of January 5, 1919, Edith sent for the doctor, who saw no need for worry. "Edith played solitaire near him as he read," and daughter Ethel wrote, "whenever [Edith] passed him she could not resist patting his dear head or kissing him," before going to bed.[58] "James, don't you think I might go to bed now?" Theodore said. "That was his way of asking for a thing," Amos recalled. "It was a winter's night and there was nothing stirring outside. The large house was very still."

"Will you please put out the light?" Theodore asked Amos, his "faithful attendant,"[59] who stayed in the room with him, though Edith returned to check on her husband twice during a restless night. At 4 a.m., on January 6, 1919, Theodore Roosevelt stopped breathing. Amos summoned Edith, who "leaned over him and called, 'Theodore darling!' But there was no answer."[60] Edith knelt by the bed and said the Lord's Prayer. The light had gone out of Theodore Roosevelt's life and soon sunshine filled the morning.

AFTERWORD

Cleared for Strange Ports

"Those born with the wanderfoot are sometimes irked by the weight of the always beloved shackles. Then the birds fly, the nest is empty, and at the feet of the knitters in the sun lies the wide world."

—Edith Roosevelt

Edith called Conie at 6 a.m. on the morning Theodore Roosevelt died: "The telephone-bell in my room rang and my sister-in-law's voice, gentle and self-controlled, though vibrant with grief, told me that he was gone, and she wanted me to come at once to Sagamore." Conie and Edie, who had known each other practically their entire lives, walked the woods and shore near Oyster Bay. Conie stood alone with her brother in the room where he died and wrote a poem entitled "Sagamore":

At Sagamore the Chief lies low—
Above the hill in circled row
The whirring airplanes dip and fly,
A guard of honor from the sky;—

Eagles to guard the Eagle.—Woe
Is on the world. The people go
With listless footstep, blind and slow;—
For one is dead—who shall not die—
At Sagamore.

Oh! Land he loved, at last you know
The son who served you well below,
The prophet voice, the visioned eye.
Hold him in ardent memory,
For one is gone—who shall not go—
From Sagamore![1]

"The old lion is dead," Archie cabled his siblings overseas. "Death had to take Roosevelt sleeping," said the sitting vice president of the United States, Thomas R. Marshall. "For if he had been awake, there would have been a fight."[2] Roosevelt died at sixty—hardly a long enough life, perhaps, but by no means premature in 1919, when the median lifespan for men was a miserly 53.6 years. Still, it seemed cruel to Edith to lose TR when "so many women could so easily spare their husbands."[3] Though Edith had known her husband was sick, she was "just stunned" at his passing, reported her daughter, Ethel. The official cause of death was a pulmonary embolism but, "Mother and I felt," wrote Ethel to her husband, "that part of his illness was due to his grief for Quentin. It took the fight from him."[4] As was customary protocol in Victorian tradition, she did not attend the funeral. She did, however, direct that Theodore be buried at Youngs Cemetery in Oyster Bay and not entombed in the Roosevelt family plot at Green-Wood Cemetery in Brooklyn alongside his grandparents, mother, father—and Alice. Edith and Theodore had been married for thirty-three years, and they would rest in eternity together. Remarkably, Edie lived for twenty-nine years after his death. With and without Theodore, Edith had more time than all the twenty-three years in the life of Alice Hathaway Lee.

"I was bothered about something & was dozing & Father stood beside the bed & kissed me," Edith wrote to Ethel of one of the dreams she had of TR for many years after his death. "I felt his scrubby moustache—and waked."[5] She went to Bamie's home to grieve in private and would escape Sagamore Hill every year around the anniversary of TR's death.

The old lion was dead, but the women in the arena had many years of making history left in them. Conie took the most visible role. Theodore Roosevelt had been the leading candidate for president in 1920, but it was Conie who took the stage at the Republican National Convention in Chicago that summer. "Her gestures, her mannerisms, the intonation of her sentences all must have recalled to the convention the man who might have been its unrivaled candidate for the Presidential nomination," reported *The New York Times*.[6] Instead, Corinne Roosevelt Robinson became the first woman in U.S. history to address one of the two major party conventions. She wrote books, lectured, and told stories on the radio. She also had arthritis and was nearly blind. No matter, she was a Roosevelt. Even her granddaughter was aware of her growing fame: "Where's your platform, Grandmother?" she asked.[7]

Not everyone was impressed. Theodore Roosevelt Jr. believed Conie was "deranged on the subject of father." Conie often supplanted, much to his chagrin, TR's namesake. "I really believe that she is more or less convinced that she is he now," Ted Jr. complained.[8] "Occasionally, she made mistakes," niece Eleanor Roosevelt assessed. "Because she had more easy wit and sometimes couldn't resist making a witty remark at the expense of someone else."[9] Oftentimes in the decade after TR's death, that someone else was Ted Jr., who considered himself the rightful heir to the Roosevelt family legacy. Conie didn't act with malicious intent. "With Auntie Corinne, the minute she'd done something she'd be very sorry. . . . Then she'd try very often to make up for it," Eleanor Roosevelt elaborated.[10] But any attention she received drew the spotlight away from Ted Jr. The resentment grew, and competition reverberated through the generations. Corinney, Conie and Douglas's only daughter, became the first Roosevelt woman elected to public office. Just four years after women got the right to vote in

Connecticut, Corinney was elected to the State House of Representatives as a Republican. She served three two-year terms over the next decade.

Conie and Bamie led several efforts to memorialize their brother. They supported the congressional passage of the Theodore Roosevelt Memorial Association Act, which later became the Theodore Roosevelt Association (TRA), a federally chartered organization established to preserve the life and legacy of Theodore Roosevelt, still thriving over a hundred years after its creation. In New York, the sisters helped with meticulous re-creation of the Roosevelt family home at 28 East 20th Street and establishing the American Museum of Natural History as New York State's official memorial to Theodore Roosevelt.

"In later years some of us felt the sisters took their brother's Presidency a trifle too seriously," remarked Margaret Chanler, a Washington neighbor, author, and sister-in-law to a New York representative in Congress. "The Roosevelt sisters were so universally beloved that one gladly forgave them their excess of zealous pride in their distinguished brother." When a life, particularly that of a president, ends, the reassessment begins. Presidents wax and wane in popularity and the public imagination; TR is no different, but the tireless efforts of Bamie and Conie ensured their brother would be enshrined in the pantheon of great presidents.[11]

Like Conie, Bamie published the (heavily edited) correspondence between her and her brother.[12] Unlike Conie, Bamie fell out with her niece Eleanor, who campaigned against her cousin Ted when he ran for New York governor in 1924. Like his father, Ted had served as assistant secretary of the navy, and both Eleanor and Franklin tried to implicate Ted in the long-developing Teapot Dome scandal over the no-bid sales of oil leases from the navy's strategic reserve to Harry F. Sinclair of Sinclair Oil, for which Archie Roosevelt was an executive.

Bamie, the eldest of the Roosevelt children, struggled with deteriorating health of the body but not the spirit. She was crippled by arthritis, her lifelong spinal injury, and poor eyesight. "Blessed Corinne," she wrote her sister, "what crimes do you suppose you and I ever perpetrated to have such curious punishments?"[13] They committed no crime other than getting old. Conie and TR had long admired Bamie's "splendid daunt-less attitude toward the physical pain she suffered."[14] Later generations remarked: "She went through great agony, and her courage was perfectly amazing. Most people would have given up long, long before. I've never seen any woman . . . suffer such pain."[15]

The 1928 election proved another political break point for Bamie, Conie, and Edith. Franklin D. Roosevelt, emulating the path of his uncle by marriage, was running for governor of New York, and Conie crossed party lines to vote for him. "[Conie] liked being the trailblazer among the Roosevelt women," historian Betty Boyd Caroli assessed.[16] "There is no one on earth like [you]," Sara Delano Roosevelt, FDR's mother, wrote Conie. "I think it is wonderful your voting for [Franklin]. I never expected it dear. . . . Some people have *minds*, others have warm *hearts*, but you have both."[17]

Bamie would not live to see Eleanor become first lady, but the two women reconciled before Bamie died on August 25, 1931, aged seventy-six, at Oldgate, her home in Connecticut. Bamie "had pushed [TR], ap-plauding each victory and boasting of his competence and goodness"[18] and she provided essential intel, networking, and advice while purpose-fully keeping herself in the background. Her legacy of service extended through the generations, but unlike her sister, she would never take her turn in the spotlight. "It is difficult to overestimate Bamie's lack of inter-est in achieving fame for herself," historian Caroli states. "To her mind, actions counted in a person's life—not the publicity surrounding them."[19]

Edith made a rare foray back into politics, endorsing Herbert Hoover for president over FDR in 1932. The move pitted the remaining Roo-sevelt women against one another, with Conie endorsing FDR, as she had done in his governor's race four years earlier. When FDR defeated the Republican incumbent Herbert Hoover in a landslide, Conie attended a victory party hosted by Eleanor Roosevelt at the Waldorf-Astoria. A month later, on February 17, 1933, less than a month before FDR's inaugu-ration, she succumbed to pneumonia at the age of seventy-one. She was preceded in death by her parents, all her siblings, her husband, and her youngest son. Conie, an accomplished author, published three volumes of her poetry and wrote the valuable though generally underrated memoir of her brother that has often been cited in this book. Like Bamie, she was a frequent counselor to her brother, but whereas Bamie, who had always been almost a second mother to Theodore, was incredibly politically astute, Conie was far more often cast in the role of intimate confidante and enthusiastic publicist. Still, it is fascinating to consider how confidently she moved forward after TR's passing after a lifetime making him the center of attention. Accomplished for her time, it is easy to imagine her even greater individual success in another age.

Alice Hathaway Lee Roosevelt and Mittie Bulloch Roosevelt, of course, preceded TR in death. This act of fate is, in part, what led to their diminished role in history. Stories are easier to tell when the characters are caricatured, but people are often more complex than they are written.

Mittie Bulloch Roosevelt, armed with a vibrant personality and cunning wit, should be better known and beloved. She was mother to Theodore Roosevelt and grandmother to Eleanor Roosevelt, one of history's most popular presidents and first ladies respectively. And if that weren't enough, she raised Bamie and Conie, who not only helped create Theodore Roosevelt but also had a profound influence on everyone in their lives. Many of TR's traits can be traced back to Mittie and the story is incomplete without rightful recognition of a remarkable woman.

The historical harm was most pernicious for Alice Hathaway Roosevelt. As Henry Pringle, the first independent biographer of Theodore Roosevelt after his subject's death, began his research, he was naturally curious about TR's first wife and reached out to Conie for comment. She had, after all, been a reliable source of information to the press for years. "During my present sister-in-law's life time," Conie wrote the author back, "I must be very careful, and I prefer not to have my name actually mentioned. You can say 'from those close to the family' or something of that sort."[20] Pringle listed Conie as Confidential Source No. 1.[21] When the Pulitzer Prize–winning book came out in 1931, Edith wrote her daughter: "On each page is a sneer or a slap at Father. . . . I should like to burn it and mail the ashes to its author."[22] Instead, Edith "proved to be a historian's nightmare"[23] and burned much of the correspondence between her and Theodore, making those relatively few items she or Ethel saved even more valuable. It is possible, though not provable, that remembrances of Alice were not spared the same treatment. Most of anything that survives related to Alice was in the possession of Alice Roosevelt Longworth, who in turn gifted them to the granddaughter she raised, Joanna Sturm.

Perhaps the greatest historical injustice to Alice is the psychic scar that runs through generations. Alice believed she was the symbol of her father's infidelity. "His *two* infidelities, in fact: infidelity to my step-mother by marrying my mother first, and to my mother by going back to my stepmother after she died. . . . I think [Edith] always resented being the second choice and she never really forgave him his first marriage."[24] Throughout her life, Alice insisted Edith had told Ted Jr. "that it was just as well that my mother had died when she did because my father would have been bored to death staying married to her." It is no wonder, pro-vided with such rich, certainly biased evidence, that some historians have so easily written off Alice Hathaway Lee.

Yet Edith Kermit Roosevelt is neither the villain nor the saint of the story. She, too, is a person and, therefore, she, too, is complex. "Mrs. Roosevelt is more difficult of access; praise does not reach or define her," wrote Margaret Chanler. "Just as the camera is focused, she steps aside to avoid the click of the shutter." Chanler, who knew the Roosevelts long before their dramatic ascendancy to the White House, during, and after the presidency continues, "She always seemed deeply detached from the external accidents of life. No 'first lady of the land' ever lived in the White House with less trepidation, with more simple dignity and inner indifference." Chanler makes a persuasive summation of Edith: "Her fam-ily life was the all-important *continuum*."[25] Edith knew who she was and did not feel it necessary to reveal that to anyone. "Being the centre of things is very interesting, yet the same proportions remain," Edith wrote. "I don't believe I have been forced into the 'first lady of the land' model of my predecessors," by which she almost surely meant the model of a shy, retiring, subordinate "good wife."[26] The remarkable Major Archie Butt said of Edith: "The seven years at the White House without ever having made a mistake will shine like a diamond tiara on her head some day."[27] She was, in fact, remarkably centered and surprisingly unmoved by the hoopla surrounding her husband and herself. She was vital to TR, competitive with Conie, often more compatible with Bamie, and perhaps at times shadowed by the ghost of Alice. She was, according to historian Dr. Kathleen Dalton, "her husband's political alter ego,"[28] and when she could no longer function as his emotional rudder, he sputtered.

With TR ever-present as the focal point of her existence, practically from age three to fifty-seven, one might think upon his death she would fade. Instead, Edith thrived. The stickers on Edith's "Roosevelt" luggage are plentiful: the Caribbean, England, South Africa, France, and Italy. On one trip she went for two months around the world, traveling to India, Vietnam, Japan, China, Siberia, and Russia. She wrote a family history with her son Kermit, and a chapter for the travel journal *Cleared for Strange Ports*. Her essay was entitled "Odyssey of a Grandmother":

> Women who marry pass their best and happiest years in giving life and fostering it, meeting and facing the problems of the next generation and helping the universe to move, and those born with the wanderfoot are sometimes irked by the weight of the always beloved shackles. Then the birds fly, the nest is empty, and at the feet of the knitters in the sun lies the wide world.[29]

Her "beloved shackles" broken, not even grandchildren could hold her back from exploring the world her husband had conquered: "I like to see their little faces," she wrote, "but I prefer to see their backs."[30]

Edith reigned at Sagamore Hill for almost thirty years after her husband's death. Ted Jr., and his wife, Eleanor, lived on the property until Ted's death in World War II. Ethel and her family lived just down the road in Oyster Bay. Edith's days were filled with friends, family, her garden and the farm, long walks, and the often uninvited visitors paying homage. She pledged to give the home to the Theodore Roosevelt

Association and somewhat grudgingly sat with Hermann Hagedorn, one of the founders of the TRA and earliest biographers of Theodore Roosevelt. Hagedorn and the TRA's work, with Edith's cooperation, contributed the essential research, oral histories, and collections on which every subsequent effort, including this one, is based.

On September 30, 1948, Edith Kermit Roosevelt died peacefully at home at the age of eighty-seven. She was preceded in death by her parents, husband, her brother- and sisters-in-law, and three of her five children. She was the last of her generation.

Measured by their sons, the strenuous Roosevelt legacy was clearly not without burdens. Their fates combined heroism, premature death, and suicide. Quentin was shot out of the sky over the Western Front in 1918. Ted Jr. enjoyed a rich and successful career in government service and business, served in both world wars, was the only general officer to lead his men onto the Normandy beach on D-Day, yet died of a heart attack a month later, at just fifty-seven. He received the Medal of Honor posthumously, as his father would many years later. They are one of only two father-and-son pairs to receive the Medal of Honor. (The other pair was Lieutenant General Arthur MacArthur Jr. and General of the Army Douglas MacArthur.)

Also a highly decorated officer, Archie, who likewise served and was injured in both world wars, lived to the age of eighty-five and died in October 1979, but had a very ugly side. He published books and pamphlets connecting Black American leaders with communism. As for Kermit, he died by his own hand at fifty-three while serving on the Aleutian Islands in World War II, a bleak, harsh, lonely, and inglorious wartime assignment that might have driven anyone into the depths of depression and despair. Edith was spared this heartache. She was not told the cause of her son's death.

On balance, the Roosevelt daughters fared better than the sons. Ethel had a long and distinguished career with the American Red Cross, supported scholarly research about her father and family, and continued the work started by her grandfather with the American Museum of Natural History. Alice Roosevelt Longworth, unlike her mother, lived a most ample life, dying in 1980 at the age of ninety-six. On her ninetieth birthday, Alice was interviewed on *60 Minutes*. "I am a showman," she proudly proclaimed. "I'm a showoff, basically . . . my father was that sort of thing."[31] Her home near Dupont Circle was perhaps the most important salon in Washington for well over fifty years. A pillow in the living room was embroidered with an unmistakable message: "If you haven't got anything good to say about anyone come and sit by me."[32] Alice was a true Washington power broker. She served on the board of directors of the National Symphony Orchestra Association, visited Ezra Pound during his 1940s confinement, and met every president from her father to Gerald Ford. Alice concluded the rollicking *60 Minutes* interview with a coy smile: "I can't help laughing. I laugh at myself, too. You know, and see how funny we all are here in Washington." She was called, mostly with affection, "the second Washington Monument."[33]

History gives the women who created Theodore Roosevelt—Mittie, Bamie, Conie, Edith, and Alice (mother and daughter)—little credit, if any at all, for their contributions. To be sure, late-nineteenth- and early-twentieth-century America did not make it easy for women to leave an enduring mark on national and world affairs. The relative obscurity of the Roosevelt women is compounded by the fact that Bamie, Conie, and Edith did so much to efface or even erase the roles they (and their mother) played in the rise of Theodore Roosevelt.[34]

And yet it is clear from what evidence remains that the self-made man is a myth. Roosevelt had, in modern parlance, a support system, one that would care for and cajole, comfort and indulge, advise and listen, inspire and encourage him his entire life. His family, especially these incredible women, informed his career path and his values. When he made mistakes, they were there to mitigate the damage and when he triumphed, they knew just how to ensure he reaped the full benefits of that success. Despite their best efforts to obscure their role in history, these women in the arena prove no person is self-made, perhaps especially the great ones.

There is no doubt about Theodore's love for his mother. "The mother is the real Atlas, who bears aloft in her strong and tender arms, the destiny of the world," Theodore wrote in 1910.[35] Mittie held in her arms a sickly young boy who lived to change the world. Without Mittie, it is doubtful young Teedie would have survived. As he grew older and stronger, he learned from the example of Mittie and Thee that even unconditional love is tested by the trials of life.

"I not only believe in love matches, but I thoroughly disbelieve in every other kind of match," Theodore wrote to Theodore Douglas Robinson, Conie's eldest son, upon his engagement in 1902. "No other happiness in the world is so great or so enduring as that of two lovers who remain lovers after they are married, and who never forget the tenderness and affection, the respect and the forbearance, all of which each must at times show to the other."[36] This is the love Theodore had with both Alice and Edith. Each marriage—one brief and one long—was a love match filled with passion and dedication until parted by death.

Then there is the indispensable Bamie and Conie. "I wonder if ever a man had two better sisters than I have," Theodore wrote in his college diary.[37] It is common to hear about politicians and other people of influence benefiting from powerful fathers or being supported by tireless spouses, but perhaps siblings are the real underappreciated secret to success. In this case, it is hard to imagine anyone having more love, more support, more than was given selflessly by the loves of Theodore Roosevelt.

Acknowledgments

Writing is supposed to be lonely but I was hardly alone in the making of this book. Gratitude feels insufficient to express my thanks to the many individuals who believed in and encouraged me along the way. There are many women in the arena for me. The foremost is Allison Davis O'Keefe, my wife and partner. Allison, you patiently ride the waves of my ideas, and never waver in your love and support. This book would simply not exist without you. This book would also not exist without those who came before me. In particular, there is a quartet of women who wrote remarkable histories of Theodore Roosevelt and the women in the arena for him.

Dr. Kathleen Dalton authored *Theodore Roosevelt: A Strenuous Life.* "What is the best biography of Theodore Roosevelt?" I am asked near daily, and I always reply with the title of her book. It is a marvel, prescient and detailed. Every word is a morsel of goodness, the product of forty years of scholarship and a lifetime labor of love. Thank you, Kathy, for your pioneering work and for welcoming me into your home (along with Tony!), for sharing your knowledge and research, and for answering the many thousands of questions these past few years.

Similarly, and not long before Dr. Dalton completed her influential work, *The Roosevelt Women* by Betty Boyd Caroli was published. Leaning on my journalistic know-how, I tracked down Betty, who lives in New York City. She was kind enough to meet me at a coffee shop where I unloaded at least ninety questions in sixty minutes. We corresponded by email and met up again. Finally, whether it was out of pity or self-preservation, Betty said to me that she had photocopied her research and I was welcome to it. When the pandemic arrived, and I was unable to visit the research facilities at Sagamore Hill or the Houghton Library at Harvard, these notes saved the day. Betty's work is brilliant, and *The Roosevelt Women* is an incomparable guide to each one of these fascinating women in the arena and far more than I could cover in this book.

I also owe an enormous debt to a woman I hardly knew, Sylvia Jukes Morris. Remarkably, and sadly, Sylvia is still the only author to write a major biography of Edith Kermit Roosevelt. I corresponded with Sylvia and her husband, Edmund Morris, who of course wrote the definitive Roosevelt trilogy. They each wrote their first books on Roosevelt, she writing *Edith Kermit Roosevelt* and he writing *The Rise of Theodore Roosevelt*, around the same time. I imagine them writing and editing together, sharing notes (and maybe sometimes not), and the thrill of excitement that must have accompanied each new discovery. Their work paved the path for so many others and reignited a generation of passion for TR and the Roosevelt family.

Through my work as the CEO of the Theodore Roosevelt Presidential Library Foundation, I met the executor of the Morris estate and curiously found myself in the Morris basement on Saturday, November 7, 2020, the day the election was projected for Joe Biden. Sylvia and Edmund, thank you for your beautiful lives and beautiful words.

I never met Corinne Roosevelt Robinson, but I feel like I know her. Conie, your life and legacy is so much more than Theodore Roosevelt but thank you for capturing the story for generations to read and know in *My Brother Theodore Roosevelt*.

In the East, you can feel Theodore Roosevelt's ghost. In the West, you can feel Theodore Roosevelt's spirit. In researching and writing this book, I have worked both East and West and met innumerable experts and friends along the way. Christine Jacobson is the person at Harvard who first showed me the bounty that is the Theodore Roosevelt Collection at the Houghton Library. Thousands of questions followed, and

Christine answered each one patiently and professionally. I was told of
the legend of Wallace F. Dailey. By the time I reached Cambridge, he had
retired, and I hunted Wallace with a passion akin to TR. He exists, and
his depth of knowledge, courtesy, and remarkable recall is a gift to any
aspiring Roosevelt author or scholar.

Thank you to Nicco Mele, Setti Warren, and Nancy Gibbs for giving
me the chance to be an entrepreneurship fellow at the Harvard Kennedy
School, which finally gave me the time to begin my book research. To
Miguel Head and Rob Smith, my Cambridge and now forever friends,
thank you for your encouragement and support from the very beginning.
Sharon Kilzer, the longtime curator of the Theodore Roosevelt Center
at Dickinson State University and organizer of the annual symposium,
thank you for your many years of service to TR's legacy. North Dakota,
and legions of scholars and writers, have benefited from your work. What
you and Clay Jenkinson started has sparked curiosity, knowledge, and
passion—which are three of the world's greatest forces. Chris O'Brien,
you marched forward with gusto.

Sue Sarna, the curator at Sagamore Hill for nearly thirty years, your
wit and wisdom is invaluable. I am glad Edith has not yet succeeded in
seeking her vengeance. Danny Prebutt, who has dedicated a good part of
his life to protecting the boyhood home of Theodore Roosevelt, thank
you for your service to our country and for the passion you bring to every
conversation. Laura Cinturati, who was with me the day we discovered
the long-lost hair of Alice Hathaway Lee, you have become a true friend.
Thank you for spending days looking through every book on the book-
shelf and honoring Robert Caro by (literally) turning every page. Dave
Welky, thank you for your camaraderie. Darrin Lunde, your generosity is
equaled only by your depth of knowledge.

"It is the ambition of the New Yorker to live upon Fifth Avenue, to take
his airings in the [Central] Park, and to sleep with his [forebears] at Green-
Wood," said Henry Raymond, cofounder of *The New York Times*. (Jeffrey I.
Richman, *Brooklyn's Green-Wood Cemetery: New York's Buried Treasure* [New
York: The Green-Wood Historic Fund, 2008], ix.) If you are in Manhattan,

cross the bridge into Brooklyn and visit Green-Wood Cemetery, and if you are really lucky, your tour will be organized by Jeff Richman, historian and archivist at this storied and beautiful place. Joe Wiegand, thanks to you and the Theodore Roosevelt Medora Foundation for keeping TR with us in Medora and beyond. My eternal gratitude to Rolf Sletten and Doug Ellison for sharing their knowledge and porch for short sips and long talks. When, not if, you come to Medora and the Badlands, may you be so fortunate as to be led on a hike by Joe, have a chat with Doug at the Western Edge, and a visit to the Elkhorn and Maltese Cross with Rolf. To Emily Walter and Rolf, thank you for being such good friends. (And sorry about interrupting Japan for a Bamie letter, but it's in the book!)

To my phenomenal researchers, Heather Merrill in Boston, and Prem Thakker, in North Dakota and New York City, thank you for your tireless attention to detail and encouragement when I needed it. Thank you also to Brian Rosenwald for his early newspaper sleuthing. Alan Axelrod, you know the essential role you played. It was not an easy task organizing the brain of a first-time author. Thank you for your patience, skill, and exceptional attitude. Robin Sproul, you believed in me when I needed it most. I will never forget your belief and good spirit. Thank you for introducing me to Matt Latimer, who is more than an agent. Matt, yours is the hidden hand that has moved this book from idea to reality, and I can't thank you, Keith Urbahn, Frank Schembari, Bridget Lewis, and the team at Javelin enough for your good work. I first met Priscilla Painton at a dinner party hosted by Amy Entelis. Who knew then that Priscilla and I would embark on this journey together? To Priscilla and Megan Hogan, thank you for not just your work as editors but your belief in the power and potential of this idea. You are fearless women in the arena, and I am so proud to work alongside you. My profound thanks to copyeditors Fred Chase and Phil Metcalf, who smoothed the edges and made a good thing much better. If you are reading this, it is due in great part to the good work of Brianna Scharfenberg, Elizabeth Venere, and Tyanni Niles of the Simon & Schuster publicity and marketing team. My thanks to Ruth Lee-Mui for the beautiful interior design and Jackie Seow for the alluring jacket design. My thanks to the phenomenal audio book team, Karen Pearlman, Sydney Fuqua, and Alyssa Morales. Jonathan Karp, thank you for taking a leap of faith on me.

I wish I had the space to thank each of the authors who preceded me, but Michael Cullinane deserves special praise. His scholarship in *Theodore Roosevelt's Ghost* and *Remembering Theodore Roosevelt* was essential to this project. Thank you for sharing your knowledge. Stacy A. Cordery, author of the exceptional *Alice*, is a force equal to her subject. Your words have meant so much to me and thank you for not only introducing me to the idea of the women in the arena, but also for pointing me to Lewis L. Gould, whose work on first ladies and Edith in particular is groundbreaking. Geoffrey Cowan, thank you for your example. Hermann Hagedorn, where would any of us be without you? Douglas Brinkley and John Avlon, it was not as easy as you said it would be. Jon Meacham gave the prayer at our wedding, and I have often thought I should have asked him to pray for me during the writing of this book. Thank you to Jon, Doug, Stacy Schiff, Candice Millard, Susan Page, and Doris Kearns Goodwin for taking the time to read and reflect on the manuscript. David Burnett, thank you for adding me to your life in pictures.

It's better to be lucky than good, and I was lucky enough to see the publication of a series of incredibly helpful resources during my research and writing. Connie M. Huddleston and Gwendolyn I. Koehler at the Friends of Bulloch, Inc., in Roswell, Georgia, published three volumes of letters between Mittie and Thee. They caretake not only the history at Bulloch Hall but have also done a great service to researchers and writers everywhere.

Edward P. Kohn edited *The Diaries of Theodore Roosevelt, 1877–1886*—a gift from heaven, especially during the Covid-19 pandemic lockdown. Heather G. Cole had left Harvard by the time I began my project, but her publication of *Theodore Roosevelt: A Descriptive Bibliography* is the most thorough examination of TR's voluminous productivity in existence. The aforementioned Michael Cullinane and Danny Prebutt digitized and transcribed the oral interviews of several Roosevelt family members. They were magnanimous enough to share and you can see the result of their kindness in these pages. My thanks to friends at the White House Historical Association, especially Stewart McLaurin and Matthew Costello, and the CBS News Archives for unearthing two spectacular *60 Minutes* profiles of Alice Roosevelt Longworth on her eighty-fifth and ninetieth birthdays. I also have to take a moment to thank Delta Airlines and apologize to all of the passengers next to whom I was seated during the writing of this book. My day job often has me crisscrossing the nation, and too often this book was written on the fly, literally. (That is where Priscilla, Megan, Fred, and Phil come in!)

There are a great many institutions at which I conducted research: the Houghton Library at Harvard College, the Theodore Roosevelt Center at Dickinson State University, the Library of Congress, the National Archives, the Smithsonian Museum of Natural History, the Smithsonian Museum of American History, the National Historic Site at Sagamore Hill and the Boyhood Home of Theodore Roosevelt, Green-Wood Cemetery, the Theodore Roosevelt Institute at Long Island University, the Massachusetts Historical Society, the Franklin Delano Roosevelt Presidential Library, Pine Knot, and the Tabasco Museum on Avery Island. Long hikes in Theodore Roosevelt National Park in TR's beloved North Dakota Badlands cleared the mind and cleansed the soul. Last but certainly not least, my eternal gratitude to the Theodore Roosevelt Association. Thank you to Vice Admiral David Architzel, USN (Ret.), Professor Howard Ehrlich, Lieutenant Colonel Gregory Wynn, USMC (Ret.), the entire leadership of the TRA, and posthumously to John Gable. You have kept the flame of TR's legacy burning for over a hundred years and will for centuries more. If you are reading this book, you should be a member of the TRA.

Did the book or the presidential library come first? (For the record, it was the book.) I often joke I might be the only author ever to build a library for his book rather than simply write a book for the library. Secretary Doug Burgum and Kathryn Burgum, thank you for the opportunity to make history together in North Dakota. Thank you to the trustees of the Theodore Roosevelt Presidential Library Foundation for your trust and faith. To my TR Library team, thank you for support (and for respecting the headphones!). Sarah Schulz, you truly are the director of details. Robbie, thank you for getting me into this, and Dory, thank you for being a friend.

Thank you to the many members of the Roosevelt family who sat with me for formal interviews or friendly conversation: Theodore Roosevelt IV (T4) and Connie Roosevelt, Kermit Roosevelt Jr., Priscilla Roosevelt, Professor Kermit "Kim" Roosevelt, Simon Roosevelt, Professor Tweed Roosevelt, Dick Williams and Mary Kongsgaard. Joanna Sturm, thank you for trusting me. I hope I got it right. Theodore Roosevelt V (T5) and Serena Torrey Roosevelt, we have been tried and tested, and Allison and I are honored to call you our friends.

I met Linda Douglass on 9/11. Even in moments of great tragedy there is grace if we let the light shine through. Thank you is insufficient for all you and John have done. Up, up, and away to my friend and one of the best storytellers of all time, Charles Melcher. Thank you for your friendship and advice, Charlie. Nitya Chambers, the psychic was right. Allison and I treasure our friendship with you and Mark, and you will always be the person I turn to for better judgment and counsel. Larysa Sendich, Sebastian Campos, Lawrence and Jacqueline Palumbo, Barb Levin and Jim Axelrad, thank you for always being there when we need you most. To my mother-in-law, Christina R. Davis, thank you for your leadership in the community, and most especially for Allison. To my father-in-law, Richard R. Davis, thank you for all you have done for our family. Our mutual love of history allowed us to get to know one another. I only wish we could attend a lecture together on the women in the arena. To my father, Bill O'Keefe, I'll take every minute of every day we get together. To my mother, Heather Holmes O'Keefe, there is nothing a boy can't do when he has a mother like you. Jonathan, Landon, and Luke O'Keefe, my brother and nephews, thank you for your loving support. Auntie Gwen, thank you for reading all the way to the end! To Elsa and Alton, the future is yours, and I will always be in the arena for you. I will end where I began, with gratitude for the woman in the arena above and beyond them all: Allison, this is for you.

Sources

"About Mrs. Roosevelt." *Christian Advocate*, February 28, 1901.

Amos, James. *Theodore Roosevelt: Hero to His Valet*. New York: The John Day Company, 1927.

Adams, Henry. *Letters of Henry Adams, 1892–1918*, ed. Worthington Chauncey Ford, Boston: Houghton Mifflin Company, 1938.

Axelrod, Alan. "Lesson 17." *Theodore Roosevelt, CEO: 7 Principles to Guide and Inspire Modern Leaders*. New York: Union Square & Co., 2012.

Baier, Lowell E. "The Cradle of Conservation: Theodore Roosevelt's Elkhorn Ranch, an Icon of America's National Identity." *Theodore Roosevelt Association Journal* 28, no. 1 (2007): 15–22.

Bailey, Thomas, and Katherine Joslin. *Theodore Roosevelt: A Literary Life*. Lebanon, NH: ForeEdge/University Press of New England, 2018.

Berfield, Susan. *The Hour of Our Fate: Theodore Roosevelt, J.P. Morgan, and the Battle to Transform American Capitalism*. New York: Bloomsbury, 2020.

Beschloss, Michael. "When T.R. Saw Lincoln." *New York Times*, May 21, 2014.

Bird, Kai, and Martin J. Sherwin. *American Prometheus: The Triumph and Tragedy of J. Robert Oppenheimer*. New York: Random House, 2005.

Brands, H. W., ed. *The Selected Letters of Theodore Roosevelt*. New York: Cooper Square Press, 2001.

"A Brilliant Society Event." *New York Times*, December 9, 1880.

Brinkley, Douglas. *The Wilderness Warrior: Theodore Roosevelt and the Crusade for America*. New York: Harper Perennial, 2010.

"The Brownsville Incident." Theodore Roosevelt Digital Library, Dickinson State University, theodorerooseveltcenter.org/Learn-About-TR/TR-Encyclopedia/Race-Ethnicity-and-Gender/The-Brownsville-Incident#:~:text=The%20Brownsville%20Incident,-Subjects%3A%20Texas--&text=President%20Theodore%20Roosevelt%20discharged%20without,of%20the%20omelee%20in%20town.

Butt, Archie. *Letters of Archie Butt*. Garden City, NY: Doubleday Page & Co., 1924.

Butt, Major Archibald. *Taft and Roosevelt: The Intimate Letters of Archie Butt, Military Aide*, Vol 1. New York: Doubleday, Doran, 1930.

Caroli, Betty Boyd. *The Roosevelt Women.* New York: Basic Books, 1998.

Centers for Disease Control. "Achievements in Public Health, 1900–1999: Healthier Mothers and Babies." *Morbidity and Mortality Weekly Report*, October 1, 1999, https://www.cdc.gov/mmwr/preview/mmwrhtml/mm4838a2.htm.

Chan, A. W. "Alcoholism and Epilepsy." *Epilepsia* (July/August 1985): 323–33, doi: 10.1111/j.1528-1157.1985.tb05658.x.

Chanler, Margaret. *Roman Spring.* Boston: Little, Brown, and Company, 1934.

Churchwell, Sarah. "America's Original Identity Politics." *The New York Review*, February 7, 2019, https://www.nybooks.com/daily/2019/02/07/americas-original-identity-politics/.

Clark, Elizabeth B. "Matrimonial Bonds: Slavery and Divorce in Nineteenth-Century America." 8 *Law & History Review* 25 (1990).

Cole, Corinne Alsop. Interview with Hermann and Mary Hagedorn, Transcript, November 23, 1954. Theodore Roosevelt Collection, Houghton Library, Harvard College.

Congressional Medal of Honor Society. "Theodore Roosevelt Jr." https://www.cmohs.org/recipients/theodore-roosevelt-jr.

Connolly, Michael J. "'I Make Politics My Recreation': Vice President Garret A. Hobart and Nineteenth Century Republican Business Politics." Newark: New Jersey Historical Society. *New Jersey History* 125, no. 1 (2010): 20–39, doi:10.14713/njh.v125i1.1019.

Cordery, Stacy A. *Alice: Alice Roosevelt Longworth, from White House Princess to Washington Power Broker.* New York: Viking, 2007.

———. "Defining a Woman's Duty: The Effect of the Roosevelt Women on TR's Views About Women," September 21, 2018, Theodore Roosevelt Center Symposium, Dickinson State University.

———. "The Precious Minutes Before the Crowded Hour: Edith and Theodore Roosevelt in Tampa, 1898." *Theodore Roosevelt Association Journal* 31, no. 1–2 (2010): 22–31.

Cordery, Stacy A. Rozek. "'Princess Alice': The Life and Times of Alice Roosevelt Longworth." *Theodore Roosevelt Association Journal* 23, no. 4 (2000): 10–14, TRAJ023_4_D.pdf.

Cowan, Geoffrey. *Let the People Rule: Theodore Roosevelt and the Birth of the Presidential Primary System.* New York: W. W. Norton, 2016.

Cowles, Anna Roosevelt. *Letters from Theodore Roosevelt to Anna Roosevelt Cowles, 1870 to 1918.* New York: Charles Scribner's Sons, 1924.

———. Memoir. Theodore Roosevelt Collection, Houghton Library, Harvard University.

Crotty, Rob. "Teddy Roosevelt and Abraham Lincoln in the Same Photo." National Archives, "Pieces of History" blog.

Cullinane, Michael Patrick. *Remembering Theodore Roosevelt: Reminiscences of His Contemporaries.* New York: Palgrave Macmillan, 2021.

———. "Tasting the Bitter Cup: Theodore Roosevelt's Last Days." *Theodore Roosevelt Association Journal* 46, no. 3 (2023): 10–34.

Cutright, Paul Russell. "Twin Literary Rarities of TR," *Theodore Roosevelt Association Journal* 12 (1985): 2.

Dalton, Kathleen. *Theodore Roosevelt: A Strenuous Life.* New York: Vintage, 2004.

"Early History of the Badlands," *Theodore Roosevelt and the Dakota Badlands.* National Park Service, https://www.nps.gov/parkhistory/online_books/hh/thro/throb.htm.

The Editors. "Wilson and Roosevelt." *The New Republic,* November 4, 1916, https://newrepublic.com/article/92253/wilson-and-roosevelt.

"Elkhorn Ranch." *Atlas Obscura,* https://www.atlasobscura.com/places/elkhorn-ranch.

Falzone, Catherine. "Jonathan Edwards and the Flying Spiders." *From the Stacks* (September 29, 2015), https://blog.nyhistory.org/jonathan-edwards-and-the-flying-spiders/.

Fitch, Catherine A., and Steven Ruggles. "Historical Trends in Marriage Formation, United States, 1850–1990," Department of History, University of Minnesota, n.d., Fig. 1, p. 8; and Table 1, p. 26, chrome-extension://efaidnbmnnnibpcajpcglclefind mkaj/https://users.pop.umn.edu/~ruggles/Articles/Fitch_and_Ruggles.pdf.

"Ford Franchise Bill." *New York Times,* May 1, 1899, 3, https://www.nytimes .com/1899/05/01/archives/ford-franchise-tax-bill-no-assessment-can-be-made -until-fall-says.html.

Fuller, Jaime. "A Theodore Roosevelt Reading List." *Lapham's Quarterly* (December 17, 2018). https://www.laphamsquarterly.org/roundtable/theodore-roosevelt-reading-list.

Gable, John Allen. *The Bull Moose Years: Theodore Roosevelt and the Progressive Party.* Port Washington, NY: Kennikat Press, 1978.

Goldin, Claudia. "The Work and Wages of Single Women, 1870–1920," *Journal of Economic History* 40, no. 1 (March 1980): 81–88, https://www.jstor.org/stable/2120426.

"Good Night Lee, Hig," *Time,* August 26, 1966. https://content.time.com/time/subscriber/article/0,33009,842705,00.html.

Goodwin, Doris Kearns. *The Bully Pulpit: Theodore Roosevelt, William Howard Taft, and the Golden Age of Journalism.* New York: Simon & Schuster, 2013.

Gould, Lewis L. *Edith Kermit Roosevelt: Creating the Modern First Lady.* Lawrence: University Press of Kansas, 2013.

———. *Theodore Roosevelt.* New York: Oxford University Press, 2012.

Green-Wood Cemetery Archives. Lot 10268 (Roosevelt Lot). Vital Card, Elliott Roosevelt, 1894.

Hagedorn, Hermann. *The Roosevelt Family of Sagamore Hill.* New York: Macmillan, 1954.

———. Research Notes of Hermann Hagedorn. Hermann Hagedorn Papers, Houghton Library, Harvard College.

———. "Bad Lands Notes." Hermann Hagedorn Papers, Houghton Library, Harvard College.

———. "Rough Riders Notes." Hermann Hagedorn Papers, Houghton Library, Harvard College.

Hagner, Isabella. *Memoirs of Isabella Hagner 1901–1905*. www.whitehousehistory.org /memoirs-of-isabella-hagner-1901-1905.

Halberstam, David, "The Vantage Point," *The New York Times*, October 31, 1971, https://timesmachine.nytimes.com/timesmachine/1971/10/31/91310513.html ?pageNumber=131.

Halliday, E. M. "Theodore Roosevelt, Feminist." *American Heritage* 30, no. 1 (December 1978), https://www.americanheritage.com/theodore-roosevelt-feminist#1.

Hassett, William D. *Off the Record with FDR, 1942–1945*. New Brunswick: Rutgers University Press, 1958.

Hauptman, Lawrence M. "John E. Wool and the New York City Draft Riots of 1863: A Reassessment." *Civil War History* 49, no. 4 (December 2003): 370–87, 10.1353 /cwh.2003.0088.

Higginson, Henry Lee. "A Hint for the Rich." *The Atlantic Monthly*, March 1920.

Higham, John. *Strangers in the Land: Patterns of American Nativism, 1860–1925*. New Brunswick, NJ: Rutgers University Press, 1955.

Hofstadter, Richard. *The American Political Tradition: And the Men Who Made It*. 1948; reprint ed., New York: Vintage, 1989.

"Teddy Roosevelt and Abraham Lincoln in the Same Photo." Pieces of History: A Blog of the U.S. National Archives, https://prologue.blogs.archives.gov/2010/11/09 /teddy-roosevelt-and-abraham-lincoln-in-the-same-photo/.

"Hon. Leverett Saltonstall Dead," *The Boston Globe*, April 17, 1895.

Huddleston, Connie M., and Gwendolyn I. Koehler. *Divided Only by Distance & Allegiance: The Bulloch/Roosevelt Letters, 1861–1865*. Roswell, GA: Friends of Bulloch, 2016.

———. *Mittie and Thee: An 1853 Roosevelt Romance*. Roswell, GA: Friends of Bulloch, 2015.

Hunt, John Gabriel, ed. *The Essential Theodore Roosevelt*. New York: Gramercy Books, 1994.

"In His Memory, January 6, 1919." https://www.trgravesite.org/gravesite.html.

Jamison, Kay Redfield. *Exuberance: The Passion for Life*. New York: Vintage, 2005.

Jenkinson, Clay. "Twenty-Three Crossings at Breakneck Speed." September 22, 2018, Theodore Roosevelt Center Symposium, Dickinson State University.

John F. Schrank Municipal Court Records, Exhibit 3, Page 4: Police Interview, Milwaukee Public Library, https://content.mpl.org/digital/collection/SchrankMCR /id/87/rec/3.

Kantrowitz, Stephen. *Ben Tillman and the Reconstruction of White Supremacy*. Chapel Hill: The University of North Carolina Press, 2000.

Knutson, Lawrence L. "Alice Roosevelt Longworth, Wild Thing." *Salon* (June 7, 1999), https://web.archive.org/web/20060517181942/http://www.salon.com/people/fea ture/1999/06/07/longworth/.

Koehler, Gwendolyn I., and Connie M. Huddleston. *Between the Wedding and the War: The Bulloch/Roosevelt Letters, 1854–1860*. Roswell, GA: Friends of Bulloch, 2016.

Kohn, Edward P., ed. *A Most Glorious Ride: The Diaries of Theodore Roosevelt, 1877–1886*. Albany: State University of New York Press, 2015.

Lange, Katie. "Medal of Honor Monday: Army Lt. Col. Teddy Roosevelt." U.S. Department of Defense, February 18, 2019, https://www.defense.gov/News/Feature-Sto ries/story/Article/1756807/medal-of-honor-monday-army-lt-col-teddy-roosevelt/.

Lawrence, Ken. "You Furnish the Pictures and I'll Furnish the War." History News Network (November 24, 2019), https://historynewsnetwork.org/article/173692.

Leech, Margaret. *In the Days of McKinley*. New York: Harper, 1959.

Livingstone, David. *Missionary Travels*. London: John Murray, 1857.

Logevall, Fredrik. *JFK: Coming of Age in the American Century, 1917–1956*. New York: Random House, 2020.

"Louise Vierick." *Success Magazine* (October 1905).

Luker, Ralph E. *The Social Gospel in Black and White: American Racial Reform, 1885–1912*. Chapel Hill: University of North Carolina Press, 1991.

"The Lusitania Disaster." Library of Congress, https://www.loc.gov/collections/world -war-i-rotogravures/articles-and-essays/the-lusitania-disaster/#:~:text=On%20 May%207,%201915,%20the,1,195%20perished,%20including%20123%20Americans.

"Mary Ledwith." Theodore Roosevelt Center at Dickinson State University, https:// www.theodorerooseveltcenter.org/Research/Digital-Library/Record?libID=0282 006&from=https%3A%2F%2Fwww.theodorerooseveltcenter.org%2FAdvanced-Sea rch%3Fr%3D1%26st1%3D5%26t1%3D%2522Nannies%2522%26v%3Dexpanded.

McCullough, David. *Mornings on Horseback: The Story of an Extraordinary Family, a Vanished Way of Life, and the Unique Child Who Became Theodore Roosevelt*. New York: Simon & Schuster, 1981.

"McKinley and Roosevelt, Unanimously Nominated for President and Vice-President." *New York Tribune*, June 22, 1900, front page.

McKinley, Jesse. "Why N.Y.C. Mayors Have White House Dreams (and Voters Dash Them)." *New York Times*, November 11, 2019.

McPhee, John. *Giving Good Weight*. New York: Farrar, Straus & Giroux, 1979.

Mellon, Rachel Lambert. "President Kennedy's Rose Garden." White House Historical Association, www.whitehousehistory.org/president-kennedys-rose-garden.

Millard, Candice. *The River of Doubt: Theodore Roosevelt's Darkest Journey*. New York: Broadway Books, 2005.

Miller, Kristie. *Isabella Greenway: An Enterprising Woman*. Tucson: University of Arizona Press, 2004.

Morgan, H. Wayne. *William McKinley and His America*. Kent, OH: Kent State University Press, 2003.

Morison, Elting E., ed. *The Letters of Theodore Roosevelt: The Years of Preparation, 1868–1898.* Cambridge: Harvard University Press, 1951.

Morris, Edmund. *Colonel Roosevelt.* New York: Random House, 2010.

———. "The Cyclone Assemblyman." *American Heritage* (February/March 1979): 30, no. 2, https://www.americanheritage.com/cyclone-assemblyman.

———. *The Rise of Theodore Roosevelt.* 1979, updated ed., New York: Random House, 2010.

———. *Theodore Rex.* New York: Random House, 2001.

Morris, Sylvia Jukes. *Edith Kermit Roosevelt: Portrait of a First Lady.* New York: Random House, 2001.

"Mrs. Stuyvesant Fish Talks in Pungent Style." *New York Times*, September 27, 1903.

Muchowski, Keith. "100 Years Ago: The Death of Quentin Roosevelt," New York City College of Technology, City University of New York, 2018.

National Park Service, "Early History of the Badlands," *Theodore Roosevelt and the Dakota Badlands*, https://www.nps.gov/parkhistory/online_books/hh/thro/throb.htm.

National Park Service, "Theodore Roosevelt National Park," http://npshistory.com /publications/thro/index.htm.

Nietzsche, Friedrich. "Maxims and Arrows," aphorism 8. *Twilight of the Idols* (1888).

The Ohio State University, Department of History, "Roosevelt in Africa," ehistory.osu .edu/exhibitions/1912/content/RooseveltInAfrica.

Oxford English Dictionary. New York: Oxford University Press, 1971.

Parsons, Frances Theodora. *Perchance Some Day.* Privately printed, 1951.

"Persons of Interest." *Harper's Bazaar* 36 (June 1902): 532.

Pinchot, Gifford. *Breaking New Ground.* New York: Harcourt, Brace, 1947.

Pollin, Burton R. "Theodore Roosevelt to the Rescue of the Poe Cottage." *The Mississippi Quarterly* 34, no. 1 (Winter 1980–81): 51–59.

Popik, Barry. *The Big Apple*, Barry Popik website, https://www.barrypopik.com/index .php/new_york_city/entry/all_politics_is_local//.

Pringle, Henry. ". . . Especially Pretty Alice." *American Heritage* 9, no. 2 (1958), https:// www.americanheritage.com/especially-pretty-alice.

———. Research notes of Henry Pringle. Theodore Roosevelt Collection, Houghton Library, Harvard College.

Theodore Roosevelt: A Biography. New York: Harcourt, Brace, 1931.

Putnam, Carleton. *Theodore Roosevelt, Volume One: The Formative Years, 1858–1886.* New York: Charles Scribner's Sons, 1958.

Raab Collection. Theodore Roosevelt Victory Message, November 8, 1898. Original manuscript: https://www.raabcollection.com/presidential-autographs/tr-victory.

Randolph, Mary. *Presidents and First Ladies*, New York: D. Appleton-Century Company, Inc., 1936.

Richman, Jeffrey I. *Brooklyn's Green-Wood Cemetery: New York's Buried Treasure.* New York: The Green-Wood Historic Fund, 2008.

Rickenbacker, Capt. Edward V. *Fighting the Flying Circus.* New York: Frederick A. Stokes Company, 1919.

Riis, Jacob. "In the Roosevelt Home." New York *Sun*, January 1, 1899.

Risen, Clay. *The Crowded Hour: Theodore Roosevelt, The Rough Riders, and the Dawn of the American Century.* New York: Scribner, 2019.

Robinson, Corinne Roosevelt. *The Call of Brotherhood and Other Poems.* New York: Charles Scribner's Sons, 1912.

——. *My Brother Theodore Roosevelt.* New York: Charles Scribner's Sons, 1921.

——. *One Woman to Another and Other Poems.* New York: Charles Scribner's Sons, 1914.

Robinson, Monroe. "Mother Bore Her Part," Theodore Roosevelt Collection, Houghton Library, Harvard College.

Rockwell, A. D., MD. *Rambling Recollections.* New York: Paul B. Hoeber, 1920.

Roosevelt, Edith Kermit. Diary of Edith Kermit Roosevelt, September 14, 1901. Theodore Roosevelt Collection, Houghton Library, Harvard College.

——. "Speech to the Woman's Roosevelt Memorial Association," March 15, 1933. *Roosevelt House Bulletin* (Spring 1933).

Roosevelt, Edith Kermit, and Kermit Roosevelt. *American Backlogs: The Story of Gertrude Tyler and Her Family, 1660–1860.* New York: Charles Scribner's Sons, 1928.

Roosevelt, Theodore. "The Books That I Read and When and How I Do My Reading." Theodore Roosevelt Center, Dickinson State University, America collection, https://www.theodorerooseveltcenter.org/Research/Digital-Library/Record?libID=o292909.

——. "Citizenship in a Republic." Address at the Sorbonne in Paris, France. Gerhard Peters and John T. Woolley, eds., *The American Presidency Project*, https://www.presidency.ucsb.edu/documents/address-the-sorbonne-paris-france-citizenship-republic.

——. *The Foes of Our Own Household.* New York: George H. Doran, 1917; reprint ed., No publisher, 2010.

——. *Hunting Trips of a Ranchman.* New York: G. P. Putnam's Sons, 1885.

——. *In Memory of My Darling Wife Alice Hathaway Roosevelt and of My Beloved Mother Martha Bulloch Roosevelt Who Died in the Same House and on the Same Day on February 14, 1884.* New York: Press of G. P. Putnam's Sons, [1884].

——. Letter to the Editor. *Utica Morning Herald*, April 30, 1884.

——. "Municipal Administration: The New York Police Force." *The Atlantic Monthly* (September 1897), https://www.theatlantic.com/magazine/archive/1897/09/municipal-administration-the-new-york-police-force/519849/.

——. *The Naval War of 1812.* New York: Putnam, 1882.

——. *Presidential Addresses and State Papers of Theodore Roosevelt.* New York: Collier & Sons, 1914.

——. Progressive Party campaign speech, Madison Square Garden, New York, NY,

1912. Library of Congress, Theodore Roosevelt Papers: Series 16: Additions 1760–1993; Addition I, 1760–1930; Speeches and writings, https://www.loc.gov /resource/mss38299a.00208/?st=gallery.

———. *Ranch Life and the Hunting Trail*. 1888; reprint ed., New York: The Century Company, 1911.

———. *The Rough Riders*. New York: Charles Scribner's Sons, 1899.

———. Speech at Berkeley, California, March 23, 1911.

———. "Speech Before the National Convention of the Progressive Party," Chicago, August 6, 1912. In John Gabriel Hunt, ed. *The Essential Theodore Roosevelt*. New York: Gramercy Books, 1994, 282–306.

———. Speech ["It Takes More Than That to Kill a Bull Moose"] at Milwaukee, Wisconsin, October 14, 1912, https://www.theodoreroosevelt.org/content.aspx?page _id=22&club_id=991271&module_id=338394.

———. Speech ["The Strenuous Life"] Before the Hamilton Club, Chicago, April 10, 1899. https://theodoreroosevelt.org/content.aspx?page_id=22&club_id=991271&module _id=339361.

———. *Theodore Roosevelt: An Autobiography*. 1913; reprint ed., New York: Da Capo, 1985.

Roosevelt Sr., Mrs. Theodore, Mrs. Kermit Roosevelt, Richard Derby, and Kermit Roosevelt. *Cleared for Strange Ports*. New York: Charles Scribner's Sons, 1927.

Rove, Karl. *The Triumph of William McKinley: Why the Election of 1896 Still Matters*. New York: Simon & Schuster, 2015.

Sletten, Rolf. *Roosevelt's Ranches: The Maltese Cross & the Elkhorn*. Medora, ND: Theodore Roosevelt Medora Foundation, 2015.

"Social Gossip." *Washington Post*, April 1, 1907, 7.

Springer, Patrick. "Teddy Roosevelt Credited North Dakota for Gaining Office." *Fargo Forum*, September 4, 2010, https://www.inforum.com/newsmd/teddy-roosevelt -credited-north-dakota-for-gaining-office.

Stimson, Henry. *Recollections of Henry Stimson*, 1913. Henry L. Stimson Papers, Sterling Memorial Library, Yale University.

Strouse, Jean. *Morgan: American Financier*. New York: HarperCollins, 1999.

Sullivan, Mark. "Visit Recalls Past of Mrs. Roosevelt." *The Evening Star*, August 11, 1932.

"The Story of Archibald Butt, First-Class Passenger, *Titanic*." The National Archives (U.K.), https://www.nationalarchives.gov.uk/titanic/stories/archibald-butt.htm.

Styple, William B. ed. *Generals in Bronze: Interviewing the Commanders of the Civil War*. Kearny, NJ: Belle Grove Publishing Company, 2005.

Taft, William Howard. William Howard Taft Papers. Manuscript Division. Library of Congress.

Teague, Michael. *Mrs. L.: Conversations with Alice Roosevelt Longworth*. Garden City, NY: Doubleday, 1981.

———. "Theodore Roosevelt and Alice Hathaway Lee: A New Perspective." *Harvard*

Library Bulletin 33, no. 3 (Summer 1985): 225–38, http://nrs.harvard.edu/urn-3:HUL.InstRepos:42671437.

"The Texas Adventures of Elliott Roosevelt—Part 2." *Lubbock Avalanche-Journal*, June 29, 2019, https://www.lubbockonline.com/news/20190629/caprock-chron icles-texas-adventures-of-elliott-roosevelt---part-2/.

Thayer, William Roscoe. Research files for Theodore Roosevelt, Houghton Library, Harvard College.

———. *Theodore Roosevelt: An Intimate Biography.* Boston: Houghton Mifflin Company, 1919.

Troy, Leo. *Trade Union Membership, 1897–1962.* Cambridge, MA: National Bureau of Economic Research, 1965: 1, http://www.nber.org/books/troy65-1.

United States Department of State, Office of the Historian. "The Secretary of State to the Ambassador in Germany (Gerard)," telegram, April 18, 1916, https://history .state.gov/historicaldocuments/frus1916Supp/d308.

"An Update on Elliott Roosevelt." May 6, 2022, Vita Brevis, https://vitabrevis.ameri canancestors.org/2022/05/an-update-on-elliott-roosevelt/.

Vivian, James F. *The Romance of My Life: Theodore Roosevelt's Speeches in Dakota.* Fargo: Prairie House for the Theodore Roosevelt Medora Foundation, 1989.

Wagenknecht, Edward. *The Seven Worlds of Theodore Roosevelt.* New York: Longmans, Green, 1958.

Washburn, Charles G. *Theodore Roosevelt: The Logic of His Career.* Boston: Houghton Mifflin Company, 1916.

Wead, Doug. *All the Presidents' Children: Triumph and Tragedy in the Lives of America's First Families.* New York: Atria, 2003.

"The Weather," *New York Times*, February 13, 1884. https://timesmachine.nytimes.com /timesmachine/1884/02/13/issue.html

Weaver, John D. *The Brownsville Raid.* 1970; reprint ed., College Station: Texas A&M Press, 1992.

"When New York Wanted to Secede." *New York Divided*, New York-Historical Society. https://www.nyhistory.org/blogs/when-new-york-wanted-to-secede.

"White House Social Record." *New York Times*, June 8, 1902.

White, John H. *The Great Yellow Fleet.* San Marino, CA: Golden West Books, 1986.

Wilson, David Alec. *East and West.* London: Methuen & Co. Ltd., 1911.

Wister, Owen. *Roosevelt: The Story of a Friendship, 1880–1919.* New York: Macmillan, 1930.

Woolley, John, and Gerhard Peters. *The American Presidency Project.* UC Santa Barbara, https://www.presidency.ucsb.edu/statistics/elections/1912.

Wood, Frederick S. *Roosevelt As We Knew Him: Personal Recollections of 150 Friends and Associates.* Reprint ed., Whitefish, MT: Kessinger Publishing, 2010.

Wood, George. *Natural History.* London: G. Routledge, 1894.

"Yellow Journalism, Richard Harding Davis (1864–1916)." *Crucible of Empire: The Spanish-American War.* PBS, https://www.pbs.org/crucible/bio_davis.html.

Source Notes

PREFACE

1. Lowell E. Baier, "The Cradle of Conservation: Theodore Roosevelt's Elkhorn Ranch, an Icon of America's National Identity," *Theodore Roosevelt Association Journal* 28, no. 1 (2007): 15–22.

2. TR to Alice Hathaway Lee Roosevelt, November 5, 1881, Theodore Roosevelt Collection, Houghton Library, Harvard College.

3. Michael Teague, *Mrs. L: Conversations with Alice Roosevelt Longworth* (Garden City, NY: Doubleday, 1981), 22.

4. Michael Patrick Cullinane, *Remembering Theodore Roosevelt: Reminiscences of His Contemporaries* (New York: Palgrave Macmillan, 2021), 126.

5. Corinne Roosevelt Robinson, *My Brother Theodore Roosevelt* (New York: Charles Scribner's Sons, 1921), 194.

6. William D. Hassett, *Off the Record with FDR* (New Brunswick: Rutgers University Press, 1958), 40, and as cited in the epigraph of Sylvia Jukes Morris, *Edith Kermit Roosevelt: Portrait of a First Lady* (New York: Random House, 2001).

1: TEEDIE

1. Gwendolyn I. Koehler and Connie M. Huddleston, *Between the Wedding and the War: The Bulloch/Roosevelt Letters, 1854–1860* (Roswell, GA: Friends of Bulloch, 2016), 225.

2. Corinne Roosevelt Robinson, *My Brother Theodore Roosevelt* (New York: Charles Scribner's Sons, 1921), 1–2.

3. A. D. Rockwell, MD, *Rambling Recollections* (New York: Paul B. Hoeber, 1920), 261.

4. Michael Teague, *Mrs. L: Conversations with Alice Roosevelt Longworth* (Garden City, NY: Doubleday, 1981), 19.

5. Theodore Roosevelt, *Autobiography* (1913; reprint ed., New York: Da Capo, 1985), 11–12.

6. Edmund Morris, *The Rise of Theodore Roosevelt* (1979; updated ed., New York: Random House, 2010), 5.

7. Statistics on the number of slaves are found at Bullochhall.org, "Slave Quarters," https://bullochhall.org/exhibits.html.

8. Connie M. Huddleston and Gwendolyn I. Koehler, *Mittie and Thee: An 1853 Roosevelt Romance* (Roswell, GA: Friends of Bulloch, 2015), 12.

9. Betty Boyd Caroli, *The Roosevelt Women* (New York: Basic Books, 1998), 33.

10. Huddleston and Koehler, *Mittie and Thee*, 28–29.

11 Huddleston and Koehler, *Mittie and Thee*, 35.

12. Koehler and Huddleston, *Between the Wedding and the War*, 44–45.

13. David McCullough, *Mornings on Horseback: The Story of an Extraordinary Family, a Vanished Way of Life, and the Unique Child Who Became Theodore Roosevelt* (New York: Simon & Schuster, 1981), 67.

14. Caroli, 22; Huddleston and Koehler, *Mittie and Thee*, 156.

15. Caroli, 22.

16. Huddleston and Koehler, *Mittie and Thee*, 201.

17. Koehler and Huddleston, *Between the Wedding and the War*, 40–42.

18. Mittie Roosevelt to Anna Bulloch Gracie, July 28, 1872, Theodore Roosevelt Collection, Houghton Library, Harvard College.

19. Koehler and Huddleston, *Between the Wedding and the War*, 104.

20. Koehler and Huddleston, *Between the Wedding and the War*, 96, 75.

21. Koehler and Huddleston, *Between the Wedding and the War*, 104.

22. Theodore Roosevelt, *Autobiography*, 11.

23. Edmund Morris, *The Rise of Theodore Roosevelt*, 9.

24. "When New York Wanted to Secede," *New York Divided*, New York-Historical Society, https://www.nyhistory.org/blogs/when-new-york-wanted-to-secede.

25. Lawrence M. Hauptman, "John E. Wool and the New York City Draft Riots of 1863: A Reassessment," *Civil War History* 49, no. 4 (December 2003): 370–87, 10.1353/cwh.2003.0088.

26. Connie M. Huddleston and Gwendolyn I. Koehler, *Divided Only by Distance & Allegiance: The Bulloch/Roosevelt Letters, 1861–1865* (Roswell, GA: Friends of Bulloch, 2016), 118.

27. Huddleston and Koehler, *Divided Only by Distance & Allegiance*, 113.

28. Huddleston and Koehler, *Divided Only by Distance & Allegiance*, 104.

29. Huddleston and Koehler, *Divided Only by Distance & Allegiance*, 100–102.

30. Huddleston and Koehler, *Divided Only by Distance & Allegiance*, 170.

31. Huddleston and Koehler, *Divided Only by Distance & Allegiance*, 95, 98, 96.

32. Huddleston and Koehler, *Divided Only by Distance & Allegiance*, 62.

33. Huddleston and Koehler, *Divided Only by Distance & Allegiance*, 100–102.

34. Huddleston and Koehler, *Divided Only by Distance & Allegiance*, 124–25.

35. Huddleston and Koehler, *Divided Only by Distance & Allegiance*, 132, 142, 214–15.

36. Theodore Roosevelt, Sr., to Theodore Roosevelt, Jr., December 31, 1861, Theodore Roosevelt Collection, Houghton Library, Harvard College.

37. Edmund Morris, *The Rise of Theodore Roosevelt*, 10.

38. Huddleston and Koehler, *Divided Only by Distance & Allegiance*, 217.

39. Huddleston and Koehler, *Divided Only by Distance & Allegiance*, 219.

40. Huddleston and Koehler, *Divided Only by Distance & Allegiance*, 312.

41. Caroli, 74.

42. Edmund Morris, *The Rise of Theodore Roosevelt*, 19–20.

43. Michael Patrick Cullinane, *Remembering Theodore Roosevelt: Reminiscences of His Contemporaries* (New York: Palgrave Macmillan, 2021), 60–61.

44. Koehler and Huddleston, *Between the Wedding and the War*, 162.

45. Huddleston and Koehler, *Divided Only by Distance & Allegiance*, 335–36.

46. Interview with Danny Prebutt, Museum Curator of the Manhattan National Park Service sites including the Theodore Roosevelt Birthplace. Also see James Dunwoody Bulloch, Find a Grave, https://www.findagrave.com/memorial/10666674/james-dunwoody-bulloch.

47. Edmund Morris, *The Rise of Theodore Roosevelt*, 21.

48. Caroli, 140.

49. Corinne Roosevelt Robinson, *My Brother Theodore Roosevelt*, 44.

50. Edmund Morris, *The Rise of Theodore Roosevelt*, 22.

51. Corinne Roosevelt Robinson, *My Brother Theodore Roosevelt*, 43–44.

52. Corinne Roosevelt Robinson, *My Brother Theodore Roosevelt*, 44.

53. The keepsake bears a paper label: "Delforge, Rue de la Madeleine, 44, Bruxelles," and is in Box 8: items 198-252 220 of the Roosevelt-Derby-Williams papers (Hollis ID 990091328510203941) in the collections of the Houghton Library, Harvard College. TR diary entries, November 22 and 30, 1869, in Edmund Morris, *The Rise of Theodore Roosevelt* (New York: Random House, 2010), 27.

54. Corinne Roosevelt Robinson, *My Brother Theodore Roosevelt*, 48.

55. Corinne Roosevelt Robinson, *My Brother Theodore Roosevelt*, 49.

56. Huddleston and Koehler, *Divided Only by Distance & Allegiance*, 350; Corinne Roosevelt Robinson, *My Brother Theodore Roosevelt*, 36.

57. Huddleston and Koehler, *Divided Only by Distance & Allegiance*, 350.

58. Corinne Roosevelt Robinson, *My Brother Theodore Roosevelt*, 354.

59. Cullinane, 67.

60. Edmund Morris, *The Rise of Theodore Roosevelt*, 25.

61. David McCullough, *Mornings on Horseback: The Story of an Extraordinary Family, a Vanished Way of Life, and the Unique Child Who Became Theodore Roosevelt* (New York: Simon & Schuster, 1981), 105.

62. Johann Wolfgang von Goethe, "The Erl-King," https://www.poemhunter.com /poem/the-erl-king/.

63. Edmund Morris, *The Rise of Theodore Roosevelt*, 26.

64. Edmund Morris, *The Rise of Theodore Roosevelt*, 26–27.

65. Corinne Roosevelt Robinson, *My Brother Theodore Roosevelt*, 47.

66. David McCullough, *Mornings on Horseback*, 82.

67. Rockwell, 261.

68. Corinne Roosevelt Robinson, *My Brother Theodore Roosevelt*, 50.

69. Corinne Roosevelt Robinson, *My Brother Theodore Roosevelt*, 50.

70. Friedrich Nietzsche, "Maxims and Arrows," aphorism 8, *Twilight of the Idols* (1888).

71. Corinne Roosevelt Robinson, *My Brother Theodore Roosevelt*, 49–50.

2: EDIE

1. Edith Kermit Roosevelt and Kermit Roosevelt, *American Backlogs: The Story of Gertrude Tyler and Her Family, 1660–1860* (New York: Charles Scribner's Sons, 1928), 233.

2. Although some sources say that Isaac Carow and Eliza Mowatt had eight children, only seven are documented by name in genealogical records. One among these, John Carow, died young (perhaps before his first birthday), which meant that Isaac's estate was divided among the six (doubtfully seven) surviving children, of which Charles was the only male.

3. Edith Kermit Roosevelt and Kermit Roosevelt, *American Backlogs*.

4. Interview with Kermit Roosevelt Jr. (with gratitude to Priscilla Roosevelt and Kermit "Kim" Roosevelt III for first telling the author this remarkable story).

5. Alice Roosevelt Longworth to Hermann Hagedorn, November 9, 1954, cited in Sylvia Jukes Morris, *Edith Kermit Roosevelt: Portrait of a First Lady* (New York: Random House, 2001), 15.

6. "Mary Ledwith," Theodore Roosevelt Center at Dickinson State University, https://www.theodorerooseveltcenter.org/Research/Digital-Library/Record?libID=0282006&from=https%3A%2F%2Fwww.theodorerooseveltcenter.org%2FAdvanced-Search%3Fr%3D1%26st1%3D5%26t1%3D%2522Nannies%2522%26v%3Dexpanded.

7. Theodore Roosevelt quoted by Maurice Egan in a letter to Edith Roosevelt, November 30, 1907, and cited in Sylvia Jukes Morris, 16.

8. Lewis L. Gould, *Edith Kermit Roosevelt: Creating the Modern First Lady* (Lawrence: University Press of Kansas, 2013), 5, citing Edith Roosevelt, letter to Cecilia Beaux, December 12, 1930, Cecilia Beaux Papers, Archives of American Art, Washington, D.C.

9. Edith Williams to Sylvia Morris, April 1976, cited in Sylvia Jukes Morris, 16.

10. Edith Kermit Roosevelt Collection, Sagamore Hill National Historic Site, National Park Service.

11. Michael Beschloss, "When T.R. Saw Lincoln," *New York Times*, May 21, 2014, https://www.nytimes.com/2014/05/22/upshot/when-tr-saw-lincoln.html; Rob Crotty, "Teddy Roosevelt and Abraham Lincoln in the Same Photo," National Archives "Pieces of History" blog, https://prologue.blogs.archives.gov/2010/11/09/teddy-roosevelt-and-abraham-lincoln-in-the-same-photo.

12. Edith Roosevelt, "Speech to the Woman's Roosevelt Memorial Association March 15, 1933," *Roosevelt House Bulletin* (Spring 1933).

13. Anna Roosevelt Cowles (Bamie) to William S. Cowles, Jr., August 19, 1929, cited in Sylvia Jukes Morris, 17.

14. Michael Patrick Cullinane, *Remembering Theodore Roosevelt: Reminiscences of His Contemporaries* (New York: Palgrave Macmillan, 2021), 72.

15. Carleton Putnam, *Theodore Roosevelt, Volume One: The Formative Years, 1858–1886* (New York: Charles Scribner's Sons, 1958), 33.

16. Kathleen Dalton, *Theodore Roosevelt: A Strenuous Life* (New York: Vintage, 2004), 48.

17. Theodore Roosevelt, *Theodore Roosevelt: An Autobiography* (1913; reprint ed., New York: Da Capo, 1985), 16–17.

18. Thomas Bailey and Katherine Joslin, *Theodore Roosevelt: A Literary Life* (Lebanon, NH: ForeEdge/University Press of New England, 2018), 2–3; Jaime Fuller, "A Theodore Roosevelt Reading List," *Lapham's Quarterly* (December 17, 2018), https://www.laphamsquarterly.org/roundtable/theodore-roosevelt-reading-list; Theodore Roosevelt, *Theodore Roosevelt: An Autobiography* (1913; reprint ed., New York: Da Capo, 1985), 17.

19. Sylvia Jukes Morris, 19.

20. Edith Kermit Roosevelt to Kermit Roosevelt, April 28, 1912, cited in Sylvia Jukes Morris, 19; Betty Boyd Caroli, *The Roosevelt Women* (New York: Basic Books, 1998), 189; Michael Teague, Mrs. L.: *Conversations with Alice Roosevelt Longworth* (Garden City, NY: Doubleday, 1981), 36.

21. Sylvia Jukes Morris, 42.

22. Sylvia Jukes Morris, 44.

23. Sylvia Jukes Morris, 23, 80.

24. Sylvia Jukes Morris, 42.

25. Sylvia Jukes Morris, 51.

26. Sylvia Jukes Morris, 54.

27. Sylvia Jukes Morris, 44.

28. Sylvia Jukes Morris, 45.

29. Scrapbook of Edith Kermit Carow and Emily Tyler Carow, March 10, 1875– March 17, 1878, in the collection of Sagamore Hill National Historic Site, National Park Service.

30. Sylvia Jukes Morris, 47.

3: ON HIS OWN

1. Corinne Roosevelt Robinson, *My Brother Theodore Roosevelt* (New York: Charles Scribner's Sons, 1921), 89.
2. Corinne Roosevelt Robinson, *My Brother Theodore Roosevelt*, 90.
3. David McCullough, *Mornings on Horseback: The Story of an Extraordinary Family, a Vanished Way of Life, and the Unique Child Who Became Theodore Roosevelt* (New York: Simon & Schuster, 1981), 35. Corinne Roosevelt Robinson, *My Brother Theodore Roosevelt*, 1.
4. Betty Boyd Caroli, *The Roosevelt Women* (New York: Basic Books, 1998), 73.
5. Betty Boyd Caroli, *The Roosevelt Women*, 75.
6. Carleton Putnam, *Theodore Roosevelt, Volume One: The Formative Years, 1858–1886* (New York: Charles Scribner's Sons, 1958), 134.
7. Hermann Hagedorn Research Notes, Hermann Hagedorn Papers, Houghton Library, Harvard College; David McCullough, *Mornings on Horseback*, 160.
8. Kathleen Dalton, *Theodore Roosevelt: A Strenuous Life* (New York: Vintage, 2004), 64.
9. Henry Davis Minot to Dr. Charles Folsom, April 18, 1878, Minot Family Papers, Massachusetts Historical Society.
10. David McCullough, *Mornings on Horseback*, 168.
11. Sylvia Jukes Morris, *Edith Kermit Roosevelt: Portrait of a First Lady* (New York: Random House, 2001), 53.
12. Theodore Roosevelt to Anna Roosevelt (Bamie), January 22, 1877, in Elting E. Morison, ed., *The Letters of Theodore Roosevelt: The Years of Preparation, 1868–1898* (Cambridge: Harvard University Press, 1951), 22.
13. Theodore Roosevelt to Corinne Roosevelt (Conie), February 5, 1877, in Elting E. Morison, ed., *The Letters of Theodore Roosevelt*, 23.
14. Scrapbook of Edith Kermit Carow and Emily Tyler Carow, March 10, 1875–March 17, 1878, in the collection of Sagamore Hill National Historic Site, National Park Service.
15. Sylvia Jukes Morris, 55.
16. Sylvia Jukes Morris, 56.
17. Theodore Roosevelt to Corinne Roosevelt (Conie), June 3, 1877, in Elting E. Morison, ed., *The Letters of Theodore Roosevelt*, 28.
18. Ibid.
19. Clinton Hart Merriam review in *Nuttall Ornithological Society Bulletin* cited in Paul Russell Cutright, "Twin Literary Rarities of TR," *Theodore Roosevelt Association Journal* 12 (1985), 2.
20. Edmund Morris, *The Rise of Theodore Roosevelt* (1979; updated ed., New York: Random House, 2010), 69.
21. Theodore Roosevelt, *Ranch Life and the Hunting Trail* (1888; reprint ed., New York: The Century Company, 1911), 59.
22. Theodore Roosevelt, Diary, entries from January 23 to February 7, 1878, in Edward

P. Kohn, ed., *A Most Glorious Ride: The Diaries of Theodore Roosevelt, 1877–1886* (Albany: State University of New York Press, 2015), 18–19.

23. Edmund Morris, *The Rise of Theodore Roosevelt*, 70.

24. Theodore Roosevelt, Diary, February 12, 1878, in Kohn, ed., 19.

25. Theodore Roosevelt, Diary, February 12, 1878, in Kohn, ed., 19.

26. Theodore Roosevelt, Diary, February 12, 1878, in Kohn, ed., 19–20.

27. Corrine Roosevelt, undated autograph in Emily Tyler Carow's autograph album in the collection of Sagamore Hill National Historic Site, National Park Service.

28. Theodore Roosevelt, Diary, February 19–26, 1878, in Kohn, ed., 20–21.

29. Henry Davis Minot to Theodore Roosevelt, February 17, 1878, Theodore Roosevelt Collection, Houghton Library, Harvard College.

30. Theodore Roosevelt to Henry Davis Minot, January 11, 1879, Minot Family Papers, Massachusetts Historical Society.

31. Theodore Roosevelt, Diary, March 3, 1878, in Kohn, ed., 21.

32. Theodore Roosevelt, Diary, March 3–5, 1878, in Kohn, ed., 21–22.

33. Theodore Roosevelt, Diary, April 1, 1878, in Kohn, ed., 25.

34. Theodore Roosevelt, Diary, April 10–18, 1878, in Kohn, ed., 26–28.

35. Caroli, 74.

36. Sylvia Jukes Morris, 57.

37. Theodore Roosevelt, Diary, April 18–21, 1878, in Kohn, ed., 27–28.

38. Unlikely though it may seem, Theodore Roosevelt had a lifelong fascination with the works of Edgar Allan Poe. See Theodore Roosevelt, "The Books That I Read and When and How I Do My Reading," Theodore Roosevelt Digital Library, Dickinson State University, America collection, https://www.theodoreroosevelt center.org/Research/Digital-Library/Record?libID=0292909; Burton R. Pollin, "Theodore Roosevelt to the Rescue of the Poe Cottage," *The Mississippi Quarterly* 34, no. 1 (Winter 1980–81): 51–59; Theodore Roosevelt, *Hunting Trips of a Ranchman* (New York: G. P. Putnam's Sons, 1885), 11; Theodore Roosevelt, *Presidential Addresses and State Papers of Theodore Roosevelt* (New York: Collier & Sons, 1914), Part I, 456, and Part IV, 426; Archie Butt, *Letters of Archie Butt* (Garden City, NY: Doubleday Page & Co., 1924), 124; and Edward Wagenknecht, *The Seven Worlds of Theodore Roosevelt* (New York: Longmans, Green, 1958), 51.

39. Theodore Roosevelt, Diary, May 15, 1878, in Kohn, ed., 31.

40. Corinne Roosevelt Robinson, *My Brother Theodore Roosevelt* (New York: Charles Scribner's Sons, 1921), 111–13.

41. Theodore Roosevelt, Diary, June 9, 1878, in Kohn, ed., 34.

42. Theodore Roosevelt, Diary, August 6, 1878, in Kohn, ed., 44.

43. Theodore Roosevelt, Diary, August 22, 1878, in Kohn, ed., 46–47.

44. Carleton Putnam, *Theodore Roosevelt, Volume One: The Formative Years, 1858–1886* (New York: Charles Scribner's Sons, 1958), 170.

45. Sylvia Jukes Morris, 58–59.
46. Theodore Roosevelt, Diary, August 24, 1878, in Kohn, ed., 47.
47. Edmund Morris, *The Rise of Theodore Roosevelt*, 74.
48. Theodore Roosevelt to Anna Roosevelt Cowles (Bamie), September 20, 1886, Theodore Roosevelt Collection, Houghton Library, Harvard College.
49. Caroli, 140–41.
50. Theodore Roosevelt, Diary, October 9–10, 1878, in Kohn, ed., 54–55.
51. Theodore Roosevelt, Diary, October 18, 1878, in Kohn, ed., 56.

4: "A RARE AND RADIANT MAIDEN"

1. Theodore Roosevelt, Diary, October 19, 1878, in Edward P. Kohn, ed., *A Most Glorious Ride: The Diaries of Theodore Roosevelt, 1877–1886* (Albany: State University of New York Press, 2015), 56.
2. Theodore Roosevelt, Diary, October 19, 1878, in Kohn, ed., 56.
3. Theodore Roosevelt, Diary, October 20, 1878, in Kohn, ed., 56.
4. Theodore Roosevelt, Diary, October 27, 1878, in Kohn, ed., 57.
5. Theodore Roosevelt, Diary, November 2, 1878, in Kohn, ed., 58.
6. Theodore Roosevelt, Diary, November 3, 1878, in Kohn, ed., 58.
7. Theodore Roosevelt, Diary, November 10, 1878, in Kohn, ed., 60.
8. Theodore Roosevelt to Anna Roosevelt (Bamie), November 10, 1878, Theodore Roosevelt Collection, Houghton Library, Harvard College.
9. Theodore Roosevelt to Corinne Roosevelt (Conie), November 10, 1878, in Elting E. Morison, ed., *The Letters of Theodore Roosevelt: The Years of Preparation, 1868–1898* (Cambridge: Harvard University Press, 1951), 35–36.
10. Betty Boyd Caroli, *The Roosevelt Women* (New York: Basic Books, 1998), 74.
11. Theodore Roosevelt, Diary, November 27, 1878, in Kohn, ed., 61.
12. "Hon Leverett Saltonstall Dead," *The Boston Globe*, April 17, 1895.
13. "Good Night, Lee Hig," *Time*, August 26, 1966.
14. Henry Lee Higginson, "A Hint for the Rich," *The Atlantic Monthly*, March 1920.
15. John McPhee, *Giving Good Weight* (New York: Farrar, Straus & Giroux, 1979), 163.
16. "Knickerbocker," *Oxford English Dictionary* (New York: Oxford University Press), 1971.
17. "Brahmin," *Online Etymological Dictionary*, https://www.etymonline.com/search?q=Brahmin; Fredrik Logevall writes in his superb first volume on the life of John F. Kennedy: "Holmes describes a young Bostonian: 'He comes of the Brahmin caste of New England. The harmless, inoffensive, untitled aristocracy.'" Fredrik Logevall, *JFK: Coming of Age in the American Century, 1917–1956* (New York: Random House, 2020), 659.
18. Margaret Chanler, *Roman Spring* (Boston: Little, Brown, and Company, 1934), 234, 117.

19. Theodore Roosevelt, Diary, November 28, 1878, in Kohn, ed., 61.

20. Edmund Morris, *The Rise of Theodore Roosevelt* (1979; updated ed., New York: Random House, 2010), 85.

21. Edmund Morris, *The Rise of Theodore Roosevelt*, 85.

22. Theodore Roosevelt, Diary, December 11, 1878, in Kohn, ed., 62.

23. David McCullough, *Mornings on Horseback: The Story of an Extraordinary Family, a Vanished Way of Life, and the Unique Child Who Became Theodore Roosevelt* (New York: Simon & Schuster, 1981), 211–12.

24. Theodore Roosevelt, Diary, December 21, 1878, in Kohn, ed., 63.

25. Theodore Roosevelt, Diary, December 22, 1878, in Kohn, ed., 63.

26. Theodore Roosevelt, Diary, December 25, 1878, in Kohn, ed., 64.

27. Carleton Putnam, *Theodore Roosevelt, Volume One: The Formative Years, 1858–1886* (New York: Charles Scribner's Sons, 1958), 166.

28. Henry F. Pringle Research Notes, Theodore Roosevelt Collection, Houghton Library, Harvard College.

29. Theodore Roosevelt, Diary, January 5, 1879, in Kohn, ed., 72.

30. Theodore Roosevelt, Diary, January 6 and 8, 1879, in Kohn, ed., 73.

31. Theodore Roosevelt, Diary, January 11, 1878, in Kohn, ed., 73.

32. Theodore Roosevelt, Diary, January 15, 1879, in Kohn, ed., 73.

33. Theodore Roosevelt, Diary, January 25, 1879, in Kohn, ed., 74.

34. Theodore Roosevelt, Diary, January 26, in Kohn, ed., 74.

35. Theodore Roosevelt, Diary, March 29 and April 2, 1879, in Kohn, ed., 81.

36. Edmund Morris, *The Rise of Theodore Roosevelt*, 91; Theodore Roosevelt, Diary, April 3, 1879, in Kohn, ed., 81.

37. Theodore Roosevelt, Diary, April 18, 19, and 20, 1879, in Kohn, ed., 82, 83; Theodore Roosevelt to Anna Roosevelt (Bamie), April 20, 1879, in Morison, ed., 38.

38. Theodore Roosevelt, Diary, April 26, 1879, in Kohn, ed., 84.

39. Theodore Roosevelt, Diary, May 11 and 12, 1879, in Kohn, ed., 86.

40. Edmund Morris, *The Rise of Theodore Roosevelt*, 92; Theodore Roosevelt to Conie Roosevelt, May 5, 1879, Theodore Roosevelt Collection, Houghton Library, Harvard College; Theodore Roosevelt, Diary, May 8, 1879, in Kohn, ed., 85.

41. Theodore Roosevelt, Diary, May 13 and 14, 1879, in Kohn, ed., 86, 87.

42. See Merriam-Webster's definition of *jehu* at https://www.merriam-webster.com/dictionary/jehu#:~:text=In%20the%2017th%20century%2C%20English%20speakers%20began%20using%20%22jehu%22,%22%20is%20encountered%20occasionally%2C%20too. Students of the Bible may note that Jehu was actually the son of Jehoshaphat and the *grandson* of Nimshi, but he is nevertheless more commonly mentioned as the *son* of Nimshi.

43. Edmund Morris, *The Rise of Theodore Roosevelt*, 92.

44. Theodore Roosevelt, Diary, May 20, 1879, in Kohn, ed., 87.

45. Kohn, ed., 69.
46. Theodore Roosevelt, Diary, May 20, 1879, in Kohn, ed., 87.
47. Theodore Roosevelt, Diary, May 22 and 24, 1879, in Kohn, ed., 87.
48. Theodore Roosevelt, Diary, June 14, 1879, in Kohn, ed., 89.
49. Theodore Roosevelt, Diary, June 15, 1879, in Kohn, ed., 90.
50. Theodore Roosevelt, Diary, June 16, 1879, in Kohn, ed., 90.
51. Theodore Roosevelt, Diary, June 17, 1879, in Kohn, ed., 90.
52. Theodore Roosevelt, Diary, June 18, 1879, in Kohn, ed., 90.
53. Theodore Roosevelt, Diary, June 19, 1879, in Kohn, ed., 90.
54. Edmund Morris, *The Rise of Theodore Roosevelt*, 93.
55. Theodore Roosevelt, Diary, June 20, 1879, in Kohn, ed., 91.
56. Theodore Roosevelt, Diary, January 25, 1880, in Kohn, ed., 127. In this entry, TR writes: "It was nearly eight months since I had first proposed to her . . ." which would put the first possible proposal around Class Day on June 20, 1879.
57. Theodore Roosevelt, Diary, June 24, 1879, in Kohn, ed., 91–92.
58. David McCullough, *Mornings on Horseback: The Story of an Extraordinary Family, a Vanished Way of Life, and the Unique Child Who Became Theodore Roosevelt* (New York: Simon & Schuster, 1981), 204.
59. Corinne Roosevelt Robinson, *My Brother Theodore*, 113.
60. Theodore Roosevelt, Diary, June 26-28, 1879, in Kohn, ed., 92.
61. Kathleen Dalton, *Theodore Roosevelt: A Strenuous Life* (New York: Vintage, 2004), 72.

5: COURTING ALICE

1. Private Collection of Mary Kongsgaard and Dick Williams.
2. Theodore Roosevelt, Diary, August 16, 1879, in Edward P. Kohn, ed., *A Most Glorious Ride: The Diaries of Theodore Roosevelt, 1877–1886* (Albany: State University of New York Press, 2015), 98.
3. Theodore Roosevelt, Diary, September 25, 1879, in Kohn, ed., 105.
4. Theodore Roosevelt, Diary, September 26 and 27, 1879, in Kohn, ed., 106.
5. Richard Welling, "My Classmate Theodore Roosevelt," *The American Legion Monthly*, January 1929.
6. Edmund Morris, *The Rise of Theodore Roosevelt* (1979; updated ed., New York: Random House, 2010), 98.
7. Henry F. Pringle Research Notes, Theodore Roosevelt Collection, Houghton Library, Harvard College.
8. Theodore Roosevelt to Martha Bulloch Roosevelt (Mittie), October 20, 1879, Theodore Roosevelt Collection, Houghton Library, Harvard College.
9. Michael Patrick Cullinane, *Remembering Theodore Roosevelt: Reminiscences of His Contemporaries* (New York: Palgrave Macmillan, 2021), 128–30.
10. Cullinane, 69.

11. Cullinane, 89.

12. Betty Boyd Caroli, *The Roosevelt Women* (New York: Basic Books, 1998), 65.

13. Kay Redfield Jamison, *Exuberance: The Passion for Life* (New York: Vintage 2005), 3.

14. Theodore Roosevelt, Diary, October 27, 1879, in Kohn, ed., 109–10.

15. Theodore Roosevelt, Diary, November 2, 1879, in Kohn, ed., 111.

16. Ibid.

17. Edmund Morris, *The Rise of Theodore Roosevelt*, 100.

18. Henry F. Pringle, *Theodore Roosevelt: A Biography* (New York: Harcourt, Brace & World, Inc., 1931), 31.

19. Theodore Roosevelt, Diary, November 10, 1879, in Kohn, ed., 111; Edmund Morris, *The Rise of Theodore Roosevelt*, 100.

20. Theodore Roosevelt, Diary, November 16, 1879, in Kohn, ed., 112.

21. Theodore Roosevelt, Diary, November 18, 1879, in Kohn, ed., 112–13.

22. Theodore Roosevelt, Diary, November 22, 1879, in Kohn, ed., 113.

23. Theodore Roosevelt, Diary, November 26, 1879, in Kohn, ed., 114.

24. Theodore Roosevelt, Diary, November 28, 1879, in Kohn, ed., 114.

25. Theodore Roosevelt, Diary, November 30, 1879, in Kohn, ed., 114.

26. Theodore Roosevelt, Diary, December 2, 1879, in Kohn, ed., 115.

27. Henry F. Pringle Research Notes, Theodore Roosevelt Collection, Houghton Library, Harvard College.

28. Edmund Morris, *The Rise of Theodore Roosevelt*, 104.

29. Theodore Roosevelt, Diary, December 17, 1879, in Kohn, ed., 116.

30. Edmund Morris, *The Rise of Theodore Roosevelt*, 101.

31. Theodore Roosevelt, Diary, December 18, 1879, in Kohn, ed., 116.

32. Henry Davis Minot to Theodore Roosevelt, December 1879, Minot Family Papers, Massachusetts Historical Society.

33. Henry F. Pringle Research Notes, Theodore Roosevelt Collection, Houghton Library, Harvard College.

34. Theodore Roosevelt, Diary, December 25–26, 1879, in Kohn, ed., 117.

35. Theodore Roosevelt, Diary, December 28–29, 1879, in Kohn, ed., 118.

36. Theodore Roosevelt, Diary, December 31, 1879, in Kohn, ed., 118.

37. Ibid.

38. Theodore Roosevelt, Diary, January 1, 1880, in Kohn, ed., 124.

39. Theodore Roosevelt, Diary, January 2, 1879, in Kohn, ed., 124.

40. Henry F. Pringle, *Theodore Roosevelt: A Biography*, 31; also Henry F. Pringle, ". . . Especially Pretty Alice," *American Heritage* 9, no. 2 (1958), https://www.americanheritage.com/especially-pretty-alice.

41. David McCullough, *Mornings on Horseback: The Story of an Extraordinary Family, a Vanished Way of Life, and the Unique Child Who Became Theodore Roosevelt* (New York: Simon & Schuster, 1981), 220.

42. Theodore Roosevelt, Diary, November 6, 1880, in Kohn, ed., 164.

43. Corinne Roosevelt Robinson, *My Brother Theodore Roosevelt* (New York: Charles Scribner's Sons, 1921), 111.

44. Theodore Roosevelt to Martha Bulloch Roosevelt (Mittie), January 11, 1880. Theodore Roosevelt Collection. Houghton Library. Harvard University.

45. Theodore Roosevelt, Diary, January 25, 1880, in Kohn, ed., 127.

46. Ibid. For the Class Day entry see Theodore Roosevelt, Diary, June 20, 1879, in Kohn, ed., 91.

47. Theodore Roosevelt, Diary, January 25, 27, and 30, 1880, in Kohn, ed., 127–128.

48. Edmund Morris, *The Rise of Theodore Roosevelt*, 104. In his citation, Morris notes this letter is in a private collection. Having failed to encounter the original, the presumption is that it remains so.

49. Theodore Roosevelt, Diary, January 25, 1880, in Kohn, ed., 126–27.

50. Theodore Roosevelt, Diary, January 30, 1880, in Kohn, ed., 127–128.

51. Theodore Roosevelt, Diary, September 1, 1878, in Kohn, ed., 48.

52. Theodore Roosevelt to Anna Roosevelt (Bamie), January 28, 1880. Theodore Roosevelt Collection. Houghton Library. Harvard University.

53. Alice Hathaway Lee to Martha Bulloch Roosevelt (Mittie), February 3, 1880. Theodore Roosevelt Collection. Houghton Library. Harvard University.

54. Theodore Roosevelt to Martha Bulloch Roosevelt (Mittie), February 8, 1880, in Elting E. Morison, ed., *The Letters of Theodore Roosevelt: The Years of Preparation, 1868–1898* (Cambridge: Harvard University Press, 1951), 43.

55. Kathleen Dalton, *Theodore Roosevelt: A Strenuous Life* (New York: Vintage, 2004), 22.

56. David McCullough, *Mornings on Horseback: The Story of an Extraordinary Family, a Vanished Way of Life, and the Unique Child Who Became Theodore Roosevelt*, 220.

57. Theodore Roosevelt, Diary, February 3, 1880, in Kohn, ed., 128.

58. Theodore Roosevelt, Diary, February 10, 1880, in Kohn, ed., 129.

6: "*NOTHING WHATEVER* ELSE BUT YOU"

1. Theodore Roosevelt, Diary, February 23, 1880, in Edward P. Kohn, ed., *A Most Glorious Ride: The Diaries of Theodore Roosevelt, 1877–1886* (Albany: State University of New York Press, 2015), 131.

2. Theodore Roosevelt, Diary, March 26, 1880, in Kohn, ed., 135.

3. Quoted in Richard Hofstadter, *The American Political Tradition: And the Men Who Made It* (1948; reprint ed., New York: Vintage, 1989), 210.

4. E. M. Halliday, "Theodore Roosevelt, Feminist," *American Heritage* 30, no. 1 (December 1978), https://www.americanheritage.com/theodore-roosevelt-feminist#1.

5. Carleton Putnam, *Theodore Roosevelt, Volume One: The Formative Years, 1858–1886* (New York: Charles Scribner's Sons, 1958), 194.

6. Theodore Roosevelt to Henry Davis Minot, February 13, 1880, in Elting E.

Morison, ed., *The Letters of Theodore Roosevelt: The Years of Preparation, 1868–1898* (Cambridge: Harvard University Press, 1951), 43.

7. Edmund Morris, *The Rise of Theodore Roosevelt* (1979, updated ed., New York: Random House, 2010), 107; William Roscoe Thayer research files for Theodore Roosevelt, Houghton Library, Harvard College; Research Notes of Hermann Hagedorn. Hermann Hagedorn Papers, Houghton Library, Harvard College.

8. Theodore Roosevelt, Diary, July 24, 1880, in Kohn, ed., 148–49; Theodore Roosevelt to Corinne Roosevelt (Conie), July 24, 1880, in Elting Morison, ed., *The Letters of Theodore Roosevelt: The Years of Preparation, 1868–1898*, 45.

9. Sylvia Jukes Morris, *Edith Kermit Roosevelt: Portrait of a First Lady* (New York: Random House, 2001), 62.

10. Stacy Cordery, "Defining a Woman's Duty: The Effect of the Roosevelt Women on TR's Views About Women," September 21, 2018, Theodore Roosevelt Center Symposium, Dickinson State University; Dr. Stacy Cordery's lecture at the Theodore Roosevelt Center's 2018 Symposium at Dickinson State University advanced this "west/rest cure" idea, building upon Dr. Kathleen Dalton's career of profound research and the excellent single-volume biography, *Theodore Roosevelt: A Strenuous Life* (New York: Vintage, 2004).

11. Theodore Roosevelt to Alice Hathaway Lee, August 15, 1880, Theodore Roosevelt Collection, Houghton Library, Harvard College.

12. Theodore Roosevelt, Diary, September 9 and 10, 1880, in Kohn, ed., 155, 156.

13. Theodore Roosevelt, Diary, September 18, 1880, in Kohn, ed., 157.

14. Alice Lee Roosevelt to Theodore Roosevelt, August 30, 1880, Theodore Roosevelt Collection, Houghton Library, Harvard College.

15. Theodore Roosevelt to Corinne Roosevelt (Conie), September 12, 1880, in Elting E. Morison, ed., *The Letters of Theodore Roosevelt: The Years of Preparation, 1868–1898*, 46.

16. Theodore Roosevelt, Diary, September 20, 1880, in Kohn, ed., 157.

17. David McCullough, *Mornings on Horseback*, 317–18.

18. Theodore Roosevelt, Diary, October 3, 1880, in Kohn, ed., 160.

19. Alice Hathaway Lee to Theodore Roosevelt, October 6, 1880, Theodore Roosevelt Collection, Houghton Library, Harvard College.

20. Theodore Roosevelt to Alice Hathaway Lee, October 17, 1880, Theodore Roosevelt Collection, Houghton Library, Harvard College.

21. Fanny Smith diary, quoted in Sylvia Jukes Morris, 64.

22. Ibid.

23. Ibid.

24. Fanny Smith diary, quoted in Sylvia Jukes Morris, 65.

25. Kathleen Dalton, *Theodore Roosevelt: A Strenuous Life* (New York: Vintage, 2004), 78.

26. Fanny Smith diary, quoted in Sylvia Jukes Morris, 65.

27. Michael Patrick Cullinane, *Remembering Theodore Roosevelt: Reminiscences of His Contemporaries* (New York: Palgrave Macmillan, 2021), 128–30.

28. Sylvia Jukes Morris, 66–69.

29. Stacy A. Cordery, *Alice: Alice Roosevelt Longworth, from White House Princess to Washington Power Broker* (New York: Viking, 2007), 22.

30. "A Brilliant Society Event," *New York Times*, December 9, 1880.

31. Sylvia Jukes Morris, 68.

32. Transcript of Corinne Alsop Cole interview with Hermann and Mary Hagedorn, November 23, 1954, Theodore Roosevelt Collection, Houghton Library, Harvard College.

33. Dalton, 80.

34. Betty Boyd Caroli, *The Roosevelt Women* (New York: Basic Books, 1998), 142.

35. Letter from Corinne Roosevelt (Conie) to Douglas Robinson, March 21, 1881, Theodore Roosevelt Collection, Houghton Library, Harvard College.

36. Caroli, 143.

37. Monroe Robinson, "Mother Bore Her Part," Theodore Roosevelt Collection, Houghton Library, Harvard College.

38. Transcript of Corinne Alsop Cole interview with Hermann and Mary Hagedorn, November 23, 1954, Theodore Roosevelt Collection, Houghton Library, Harvard College.

39. Edith Kermit Roosevelt to Corinne Roosevelt (Conie), February 15, 1881, Theodore Roosevelt Collection, Houghton Library, Harvard College.

40. Theodore Roosevelt, Diary, November 4, 1880, in Kohn, ed., 164.

41. Theodore Roosevelt, Diary, November 6, 1881, in Kohn, ed., 164.

42. Theodore Roosevelt, Diary, March 18, 1881, in Kohn, ed., 186.

43. Theodore Roosevelt, Diary, December 4, 1880, in Kohn, ed., 167.

44. Edmund Morris, *The Rise of Theodore Roosevelt*, 119.

45. Cornell Law School Legal Information Institute, "caveat emptor," https://www.law.cornell.edu/wex/caveat_emptor/.

46. Theodore Roosevelt, Diary, March 24, 1881, in Kohn, ed., 186.

47. Theodore Roosevelt, Diary, May 2, 1881, in Kohn, ed., 189.

48. Alice is quoted in Owen Wister, *Roosevelt: The Story of a Friendship, 1880–1919* (New York: Macmillan, 1930), 24; Theodore Roosevelt to Alice Lee Roosevelt, March 29, 1881, Theodore Roosevelt Collection, Houghton Library, Harvard College.

49. Dalton, 79.

50. *Theodore Roosevelt: An Autobiography* (1913; reprint ed., New York: Da Capo, 1985), 57.

51. Corinne Roosevelt Robinson, *My Brother Theodore Roosevelt* (New York: Charles Scribner's Sons, 1921), 106.

52. Edmund Morris, *The Rise of Theodore Roosevelt*, 124–25.

53. Barry Popik, *The Big Apple*, Entry from June 13, 2009, Barry Popik website, https://www.barrypopik.com/index.php/new_york_city/entry/all_politics_is_local//.

54. Theodore Roosevelt, Diary, May 12, 1881, in Kohn, ed., 190.

55. Theodore Roosevelt, Diary, May 13, 14, 15, and 21, 1881, in Kohn, ed., 190.

56. Theodore Roosevelt, Diary, May 25, 1881, in Kohn, ed., 191.

57. Theodore Roosevelt, Diary, June 1, 1881, in Kohn, ed., 192.

58. Theodore Roosevelt, Diary, June 11, 1881, in Kohn, ed., 193.

59. Theodore Roosevelt, Diary, June 17, 18, 22, 23, and July 1, 1881, in Kohn, ed., 193–94.

60. Anna Roosevelt Cowles, *Letters from Theodore Roosevelt to Anna Roosevelt Cowles, 1870 to 1918* (New York: Charles Scribner's Sons, 1924), 44–45.

61. Zermatt Matterhorn, "Grave of the Unknown Climber," https://www.zermatt.ch/en/Media/Attractions/Grave-of-the-Unknown-Climber, accessed July 3, 2021.

62. Theodore Roosevelt, Diary, August 3 and 4, 1881, in Kohn, ed., 197–198.

63. Theodore Roosevelt to Anna Roosevelt (Bamie), August 5, 1881, in Elting E. Morison, ed., *The Letters of Theodore Roosevelt: The Years of Preparation, 1868–1898*, 49–50.

64. Theodore Roosevelt, Diary, October 17, 1881, in Kohn, ed., 201.

65. Theodore Roosevelt, Diary, October 28, 1881, in Kohn, ed., 201.

66. Theodore Roosevelt, Diary, November 4, 1881, in Kohn, ed., 202.

67. Edmund Morris, *The Rise of Theodore Roosevelt*, 133.

68. Theodore Roosevelt, Diary, November 1, 1881, in Kohn, ed., 202.

69. Theodore Roosevelt to Alice Hathaway Lee Roosevelt, November 5, 1881, Theodore Roosevelt Collection, Houghton Library, Harvard College.

70. Theodore Roosevelt, Diary, "Memoranda," following entry for December 26, 1881, in Kohn, ed., 203–4.

71. Theodore Roosevelt, Diary, November 8, 1881, in Kohn, ed., 202.

72. Theodore Roosevelt, Diary, November 16, 20, and December 3, 1881, in Kohn, ed., 202.

73. Theodore Roosevelt, *The Naval War of 1812* (New York: Putnam, 1882), 135–36.

7: NEVERMORE

1. Theodore Roosevelt, Diary, January 25, 1880, in Edward P. Kohn, ed., *A Most Glorious Ride: The Diaries of Theodore Roosevelt, 1877–1886* (Albany: State University of New York Press, 2015), 127.

2. Edmund Morris, "The Cyclone Assemblyman," *American Heritage* 30, no. 2 (February/March 1979), https://www.americanheritage.com/cyclone-assemblyman.

3. Edmund Morris, "The Cyclone Assemblyman."

4. Theodore Roosevelt to Martha Bulloch Roosevelt (Mittie), February 20, 1883, in Elting E. Morison, ed., *The Letters of Theodore Roosevelt: The Department of the Navy, continued 1898* (Cambridge: Harvard University Press, 1951), 60.

5. Theodore Roosevelt to Alice Hathaway Lee Roosevelt, April 6, 1882, Theodore Roosevelt Collection, Houghton Library, Harvard College.

6. Michael Teague, "Theodore Roosevelt and Alice Hathaway Lee: A New Perspective," *Harvard Library Bulletin* 33, no. 3 (Summer 1985): 225–38, http://nrs.harvard .edu/urn-3:HUL.InstRepos:42671437.

7. Theodore Roosevelt to Alice Hathaway Lee Roosevelt, November 5, 1881, Theodore Roosevelt Collection, Houghton Library, Harvard College.

8. Theodore Roosevelt to Alice Hathaway Lee Roosevelt, December 31, 1882, Theodore Roosevelt Collection, Houghton Library, Harvard College..

9. Theodore Roosevelt to Alice Hathaway Lee Roosevelt, April 6, 1882, Theodore Roosevelt Collection, Houghton Library, Harvard College.

10. Theodore Roosevelt to Alice Hathaway Lee Roosevelt, March 6, 1883, Theodore Roosevelt Collection, Houghton Library, Harvard College.

11. Theodore Roosevelt, "Citizenship in a Republic," Address at the Sorbonne in Paris, France, Gerhard Peters and John T. Woolley, eds., The American Presidency Project: https://www.presidency.ucsb.edu/documents/address-the-sor bonne-paris-france-citizenship-republic.

12. Theodore Roosevelt to Alice Hathaway Lee Roosevelt, April 28, 1883, Theodore Roosevelt Collection, Houghton Library, Harvard College.

13. Edmund Morris, *The Rise of Theodore Roosevelt* (1979; updated ed., New York: Random House, 2010), 184.

14. Teague, "Theodore Roosevelt and Alice Hathaway Lee," 236.

15. *Adventures of Huckleberry Finn* (New York: Charles L. Webster & Company, 1885), 366.

16. Centers for Disease Control, "Achievements in Public Health, 1900–1999: Healthier Mothers and Babies," *Morbidity and Mortality Weekly Report*, October 1, 1999, https://www.cdc.gov/mmwr/preview/mmwrhtml/mm4838a2.htm.

17. Theodore Roosevelt to Alice Hathaway Lee Roosevelt, September 2, 1883, Theodore Roosevelt Collection, Houghton Library, Harvard College.

18. Theodore Roosevelt to Martha Bulloch Roosevelt (Mittie), September 4, 1883, as quoted in Edmund Morris, *The Rise of Theodore Roosevelt*, 186.

19. Theodore Roosevelt to Alice Hathaway Lee Roosevelt, September 8, 1883, Theodore Roosevelt Collection, Houghton Library, Harvard College.

20. Theodore Roosevelt to Alice Hathaway Lee Roosevelt, September 14, 1883, Theodore Roosevelt Collection, Houghton Library, Harvard College.

21. Theodore Roosevelt to Alice Hathaway Lee Roosevelt, September 14, 1883, Theodore Roosevelt Collection, Houghton Library, Harvard College.

22. Theodore Roosevelt to Alice Hathaway Lee Roosevelt, September 17, 1883, Theodore Roosevelt Collection, Houghton Library, Harvard College.

23. Theodore Roosevelt to Alice Hathaway Lee Roosevelt, September 20, 1883, Theodore Roosevelt Collection, Houghton Library, Harvard College.

24. Theodore Roosevelt to Alice Hathaway Lee Roosevelt, September 23, 1883, Theodore Roosevelt Collection, Houghton Library, Harvard College.

25. Kathleen Dalton, *Theodore Roosevelt: A Strenuous Life* (New York: Vintage, 2004), 87.

26. Dalton, 87.

27. Alice Hathaway Lee Roosevelt to Theodore Roosevelt, February 11, 1884, Theodore Roosevelt Collection, Houghton Library, Harvard College.

28. Anna Bulloch Gracie to Alice Roosevelt, March 25, 1884, Theodore Roosevelt Collection, Houghton Library, Harvard College. This remarkable letter is more properly described as a firsthand account written by Aunt Anna to a one-month-old baby Alice because Anna feared she might not live long enough to tell Alice the story. "If I died before she is old enough to tell her just these few things," Anna wrote. Macabre, but perhaps reasonable considering Anna had just lost her beloved sister and Alice.

29. Anna Bulloch Gracie to Alice Roosevelt, March 25, 1884, Theodore Roosevelt Collection, Houghton Library, Harvard College.

30. Theodore Roosevelt to Dora Watkins, February 13, 1884, in Elting E. Morison, ed., *The Letters of Theodore Roosevelt: The Department of the Navy, continued 1898* (Cambridge: Harvard University Press, 1951), 65.

31. "The Weather," *New York Times*, February 13, 1884, https://timesmachine.nytimes.com/timesmachine/1884/02/13/issue.html.

32. Hermann Hagedorn, "Transcript of Interview with George Spinney and Isaac Hunt," Theodore Roosevelt Collection, Houghton Library, Harvard College. This dinner took place at the Harvard Club in 1920 and copies also exist in the records of the Theodore Roosevelt Association at Sagamore Hill. See also: Carleton Putnam, *Theodore Roosevelt, Volume One: The Formative Years, 1858–1886* (New York: Charles Scribner's Sons, 1958), 250.

33. Carleton Putnam, *Theodore Roosevelt, Volume One: The Formative Years, 1858–1886* (New York: Charles Scribner's Sons, 1958), 386. Edmund Morris disputes the veracity of this quote on p. 816 of his *Notes*: "Put. (p. 386) has Elliott saying this directly to Theodore; but he contradicts his only source, Pringle, who says the statement was made to Corinne Roosevelt Robinson." Yet, Morris asserts that Theodore later exclaimed, "There *is* a curse on this house!" which the author cites here. It would be strange, if not inconceivable, that Theodore would repeat the dramatic phrase without having heard it either from Elliott or Conie. Thus the author cites Putnam here and Morris next. Only Henry Pringle and Conie Roosevelt know who said the dramatic and memorable phrase to whom and in what order.

34. Edmund Morris, *The Rise of Theodore Roosevelt*, 230.

35. Theodore Roosevelt, Diary, February 14, 1884, in Kohn, ed., 228.

8: "HELL, WITH THE FIRES OUT"

1. Edmund Morris, *The Rise of Theodore Roosevelt* (1979; updated ed., New York: Random House, 2010), 231.

2. Edmund Morris, *The Rise of Theodore Roosevelt*, 231.

3. Grace Dodge to Anna Roosevelt (Bamie), February 15, 1884, Theodore Roosevelt Collection, Houghton Library, Harvard College.

4. Julia M. de Forest to Anna Roosevelt (Bamie), February 19, 1884, Theodore Roosevelt Collection, Houghton Library, Harvard College.

5. Irvine Bulloch to Anna Roosevelt (Bamie), February 16, 1884, Theodore Roosevelt Collection, Houghton Library, Harvard College.

6. Ella Bulloch to Anna Roosevelt (Bamie) and Corinne Roosevelt Robinson (Conie), February 16, 1884, Theodore Roosevelt Collection, Houghton Library, Harvard College.

7. Edmund Morris, *The Rise of Theodore Roosevelt*, 232.

8. Francis W. Lee to Anna Roosevelt (Bamie), February 20, 1884, Theodore Roosevelt Collection, Houghton Library, Harvard College.

9. Edmund Morris, *The Rise of Theodore Roosevelt*, 230–31.

10. Rev. John Hall, in Theodore Roosevelt, *In Memory of My Darling Wife Alice Hathaway Roosevelt and of My Beloved Mother Martha Bulloch Roosevelt Who Died in the Same House and on the Same Day on February 14, 1884* (New York: Press of G. P. Putnam's Sons [1884]), 7–15.

11. Quoted in Roosevelt, *In Memory of My Darling Wife Alice Hathaway Roosevelt and of My Beloved Mother Martha Bulloch Roosevelt*; the poetic quotation is from "Marco Bozzaris" by the American poet Fitz-Greene Halleck (1790–1867).

12. Edmund Morris, *The Rise of Theodore Roosevelt*, 231.

13. Edmund Morris, *The Rise of Theodore Roosevelt*, 232.

14. Roosevelt, *In Memory of My Darling Wife Alice Hathaway Roosevelt and of My Beloved Mother Martha Bulloch Roosevelt*, 3–4; According to Roosevelt historian Gregory Wynn's research, TR likely printed no more than a dozen copies of the memorial book. By 2024, only half that number are known to exist, one of which surfaced during the writing of this book. Remarkably, this copy is the only one with an inscription: "Rose Lee April 26th 1884." From the grave, Alice's older sister answers a previously unsolved mystery: TR wrote and published the memorial before, not while, he was in the Badlands. The rare artifact was acquired by Heather C. and William G. O'Keefe for public display at the Theodore Roosevelt Presidential Library in Medora, North Dakota.

15. Theodore Roosevelt, Diary, February 17, 1884, in Edward P. Kohn, ed., *A Most Glorious Ride: The Diaries of Theodore Roosevelt, 1877–1886* (Albany: State University of New York Press, 2015), 229.

16. Edmund Morris, *The Rise of Theodore Roosevelt*, 232.

17. Unidentified writer to Anna Roosevelt (Bamie), March 1, 1884, Theodore Roosevelt Collection, Houghton Library, Harvard College.

18. Stacy A. Cordery, *Alice: Alice Roosevelt Longworth, from White House Princess to Washington Power Broker* (New York: Viking, 2007), 17.

19. Edmund Morris, *The Rise of Theodore Roosevelt*, 232–34.

20. Michael Teague, "Theodore Roosevelt and Alice Hathaway Lee: A New Perspective," *Harvard Library Bulletin* 33, no. 3 (Summer 1985): 225–38.

21. Sagamore Hill National Historic Site Collection, Catalog numbers 8162–8166, National Park Service.

22. Theodore Roosevelt to Andrew White, February 18, 1884, in H. W. Brands, ed., *The Selected Letters of Theodore Roosevelt* (New York: Cooper Square Press, 2001), 30.

23. Edmund Morris, *The Rise of Theodore Roosevelt*, 270. Morris describes 422 Madison as Theodore's "pied-à-terre on visits to New York" though she was "not keen on the idea of brother and sister sharing the same town address." In 1886, Bamie purchases an additional row house at 689 Madison Avenue. Both homes were the setting for major events in the lives of the Roosevelts, with the home at 422 Madison Avenue playing a central role from 1884–1886 and again during Roosevelt's governorship. The historic events at 689 Madison are captured in *The New York Times*: https://timesmachine.nytimes.com/timesmachine/1998/03/01/750484 .html?pageNumber=237.

24. Anna Roosevelt Cowles Memoir, 2, Theodore Roosevelt Collection, Houghton Library, Harvard College.

25. Unidentified writer to Anna Roosevelt (Bamie), February 16, 1884, Theodore Roosevelt Collection, Houghton Library, Harvard College.

26. Edmund Morris, *The Rise of Theodore Roosevelt*, 247–48.

27. Theodore Roosevelt, Letter to the Editor, *Utica Morning Herald*, April 30, 1884, quoted in Edmund Morris, *The Rise of Theodore Roosevelt*, 248–49.

28. "Dressed Beef in the West. The Business Enterprise of the Marquis de Mores," *The New York Times*, February 25, 1884, https://timesmachine.nytimes.com/timesmachine/1884/02/25/106271765.html?pageNumber=8.

29. Theodore Roosevelt to Alice Hathaway Lee Roosevelt, September 23, 1883, Theodore Roosevelt Collection, Houghton Library, Harvard College.

30. Edmund Morris, *The Rise of Theodore Roosevelt*, 246–47.

31. Edmund Morris, *The Rise of Theodore Roosevelt*, 247.

32. Carleton Putnam, *Theodore Roosevelt, Volume One: The Formative Years, 1858–1886* (New York: Charles Scribner's Sons, 1958), 445.

33. Edmund Morris, *The Rise of Theodore Roosevelt*, 259.

34. Owen Wister, *Roosevelt: The Story of a Friendship, 1880–1919* (New York: Macmillan, 1930), 26–27.

35. Putnam, 467.

36. Theodore Roosevelt, Diary, entries from June 9 to June 27, 1884, in Kohn, ed., 229-230.

37. Edmund Morris, *The Rise of Theodore Roosevelt*, 262–63; Theodore Roosevelt, *Hunting Trips of a Ranchman* (New York: G. P. Putnam's Sons, 1885), 17.

38. Theodore Roosevelt to Anna Roosevelt (Bamie), September 20, 1884, in Anna Roosevelt Cowles, *Letters from Theodore Roosevelt to Anna Roosevelt Cowles, 1870 to 1918* (New York: Charles Scribner's Sons, 1924), 68. Alice quoted in Michael Teague, *Mrs. L: Conversations with Alice Roosevelt Longworth* (Garden City, NY: Doubleday, 1981), 10–11.

39. Theodore Roosevelt to Anna Roosevelt (Bamie), June 17, 1884, in Cowles, *Letters*, 57–58.

40. Theodore Roosevelt to Henry Cabot Lodge, June 18, 1884, Henry Cabot Lodge Papers, Massachusetts Historical Society.

41. Theodore Roosevelt to Anna Roosevelt (Bamie), August 17, 1884, in Cowles, *Letters*, 63.

42. National Park Service, "Early History of the Badlands," *Theodore Roosevelt and the Dakota Badlands*, https://www.nps.gov/parkhistory/online_books/hh/thro/throb.htm.

43. Edmund Morris, *The Rise of Theodore Roosevelt*, 75.

44. Edmund Morris, *The Rise of Theodore Roosevelt*, 75.

45. Hermann Hagedorn, "Bad Lands Notes," Hermann Hagedorn Papers, Houghton Library, Harvard College.

46. William Wingate Sewall, *Bill Sewall's Story of TR* (New York: Harper & Brothers Publishers, 1919), 47–48.

47. Hermann Hagedorn, "Bad Lands Notes," Theodore Roosevelt Collection, Houghton Library, Harvard College.

48. Theodore Roosevelt to Anna Roosevelt (Bamie), September 20, 1884, in Anna Roosevelt Cowles, *Letters from Theodore Roosevelt to Anna Roosevelt Cowles, 1870 to 1918* (New York: Charles Scribner's Sons, 1924), 66.

49. "Presidential Election of 1884: A Resource Guide," Library of Congress, https://www.loc.gov/rr/program//bib/elections/election1884.html.

50. Edgar Allan Poe, *The Narrative of Arthur Gordon Pym of Nantucket* (London: Wiley & Putnam, 1838), 248.

51. Lowell E. Baier, "The Cradle of Conservation: Theodore Roosevelt's Elkhorn Ranch, an Icon of America's National Identity," *Theodore Roosevelt Association Journal* 28, no. 1 (2007): 15–22. Also cited in Douglas Brinkley, *The Wilderness Warrior: Theodore Roosevelt and the Crusade for America* (New York: Harper Perennial, 2010), 194.

52. It is possible that the antlers are preserved in the collections of the National Museum of Natural History. Darrin Lunde, author of *The Naturalist: Theodore Roosevelt, A Lifetime of Exploration, and the Triumph of American Natural History* (New York: Crown,

2016), and Collections Manager, Division of Mammals at the National Museum of Natural History, discovered two locked skulls in the museum collection. Lunde offers an intriguing backstory: "These specimens [USNM 19234] were found in the Little Rocky Mountains north of Carroll, Montana, in February of 1882, and by August of 1883 they were in the hands of Clinton Levi Merriam, the U.S. congressman from New York. Some years later, Merriam sent the antlers to the United States National Museum by way of his son, the mammalogist Clinton Hart Merriam, and the specimen has remained a part of the Smithsonian collection ever since. While I found no 'smoking gun' specifically linking USNM 19234 to TR's naming of his Elkhorn Ranch, it certainly seems very plausible that he was at least aware of the specimen given the timing of his first arrival in the Badlands in September of 1883, and it may have influenced the naming of his ranch in the fall of 1884. Roosevelt was a New York State Assemblyman at this time, and he later became a frequent correspondent to the mammalogist C. Hart Merriam." Also see "Elkhorn Ranch," in *Atlas Obscura*, https://www.atlasobscura.com/places/elkhorn-ranch.

53. Rolf Sletten, *Roosevelt's Ranches: The Maltese Cross & The Elkhorn* (Medora, ND: Theodore Roosevelt Medora Foundation, 2015), 73.

54. William Wingate Sewall, *Bill Sewall's Story of TR*, 5.

55. Edmund Morris, *The Rise of Theodore Roosevelt*, 288.

56. Theodore Roosevelt to Anna Roosevelt (Bamie), April 29, 1885, Theodore Roosevelt Collection, Houghton Library, Harvard College.

57. National Park Service, "Theodore Roosevelt National Park," http://npshistory .com/publications/thro/index.htm; TR speech at ceremony laying the cornerstone for the Carnegie Library on the campus of Fargo College, September 5, 1910, in Patrick Springer, "Teddy Roosevelt Credited North Dakota for Gaining Office," *Fargo Forum* September 4, 2010, https://www.inforum.com/newsmd/ teddy-roosevelt-credited-north-dakota-for-gaining-office.

58. Theodore Roosevelt to Anna Roosevelt (Bamie), May 12, 1885, Theodore Roosevelt Collection, Houghton Library, Harvard College. This letter and several more cited by the author in this chapter came to light because of the good work of the Theodore Roosevelt Association and Lieutenant Colonel Gregory Wynn, USMC (Ret.), in particular. Wynn's remarkable discovery fills a deficit in correspondence between Bamie and TR, especially in the most critical year of 1885. https://archive .blogs.harvard.edu/houghton/new-pages-to-turn-recent-additions-to-houghtons -theodore-roosevelt-collection/ and see also: Gregory A. Wynn, "A Remarkable Cache of Newly Discovered TR Letters," and "A Remarkable Cache of Newly Discovered TR Letters, Group One: The Six TR-to-Bamie Letters from 1885," *Theodore Roosevelt Association Journal XL*, no. 1–2–3 (2019): 7–33.

59. Theodore Roosevelt to Anna Roosevelt (Bamie), May 12, May 17, 1885, Theodore Roosevelt Collection, Houghton Library, Harvard College.

60. Theodore Roosevelt to Anna Roosevelt (Bamie), June 5, 1885, Theodore Roosevelt Collection, Houghton Library, Harvard College.

61. Theodore Roosevelt to Anna Roosevelt (Bamie), August 30, 1885, Theodore Roosevelt Collection, Houghton Library, Harvard College.

62. Theodore Roosevelt to Anna Roosevelt (Bamie), September 1, 1885, Theodore Roosevelt Collection, Houghton Library, Harvard College.

63. Theodore Roosevelt to Anna Roosevelt (Bamie), September 7, 1885, Theodore Roosevelt Collection, Houghton Library, Harvard College.

64. Medora historical marker, "The Shooting of Riley Luffsey," https://www.hmdb.org/PhotoFullSize.asp?PhotoID=324326.

65. Edmund Morris, *The Rise of Theodore Roosevelt*, 301–2.

66. Edmund Morris, *The Rise of Theodore Roosevelt*, 303.

67. Edmund Morris, *The Rise of Theodore Roosevelt*, 304.

68. Edmund Morris, *The Rise of Theodore Roosevelt*, 307. The Marquis de Mores's grandiose dreams of a beef empire collapsed later in 1885, and he ultimately sold his ranchlands. He returned to France, took a commission in the French army, and became involved in a railroad scheme in Vietnam (then being colonized by France), became a leader in French anti-Semitic politics, and served in French colonial North Africa. He was assassinated in Algeria, possibly with the complicity of the French government, on June 9, 1896.

69. Sylvia Jukes Morris, *Edith Kermit Roosevelt: Portrait of a First Lady* (New York: Random House, 2001), 78–79.

9: REUNITED

1. Sylvia Jukes Morris, *Edith Kermit Roosevelt: Portrait of a First Lady* (New York: Random House, 2001), 65, 67.

2. Michael Teague, *Mrs. L.: Conversations with Alice Roosevelt Longworth* (Garden City, NY: Doubleday, 1981), 36.

3. Edmund Morris, *The Rise of Theodore Roosevelt* (1979; updated ed., New York: Random House, 2010), 308.

4. Edmund Morris, *The Rise of Theodore Roosevelt*, 308.

5. Sylvia Jukes Morris, 67.

6. Catherine A. Fitch and Steven Ruggles, "Historical Trends in Marriage Formation, United States, 1850–1990," Department of History, University of Minnesota, n.d., Fig. 1, p. 8; and Table 1, p. 26, chrome-extension://efaidnbmnnnibpcajpcglclefindmkaj/https://users.pop.umn.edu/~ruggles/Articles/Fitch_and_Ruggles.pdf.

7. Claudia Goldin, "The Work and Wages of Single Women, 1870–1920," *Journal of Economic History* 40, no. 1 (March 1980): 81–88, https://www.jstor.org/stable/2120426.

8. https://www.statista.com/statistics/1040079/life-expectancy-united-states-all
   -time/; Centers for Disease Control, "Achievements in Public Health, 1900–1999:
   Control of Infectious Diseases," *Morbidity and Mortality Weekly Report* 48, no. 29
   (July 30, 1999): 621–29, https://www.cdc.gov/mmwr/preview/mmwrhtml/mm482
   9a1.htm#:~:text=In%201900%2C%20the%20three%20leading,than%205%20years%20(1).

9. Theodore Roosevelt, Diary, February 16, 1884, in Edward P. Kohn, ed., *A Most
   Glorious Ride: The Diaries of Theodore Roosevelt, 1877–1886* (Albany: State University
   of New York Press, 2015), 228–29.

10. Edmund Morris, *The Rise of Theodore Roosevelt*, 270–71.

11. Edmund Morris, *The Rise of Theodore Roosevelt*, xxix.

12. Theodore Roosevelt to Anna Roosevelt (Bamie), September 20, 1886, Theodore
    Roosevelt Collection, Houghton Library, Harvard College.

13. Sylvia Jukes Morris, 70.

14. Kathleen Dalton, *Theodore Roosevelt: A Strenuous Life* (New York: Alfred A. Knopf,
    2002), 80.

15. Sylvia Jukes Morris, 15; 71–72.

16. Teague, *Mrs. L.: Conversations with Alice Roosevelt Longworth*, 36.

17. Theodore Roosevelt, Speech before the Hamilton Club, Chicago, April 10, 1899.

18. Theodore Roosevelt to Alice Hathaway Lee, June 8, 1880, Theodore Roosevelt
    Collection, Houghton Library, Harvard College.

19. Edmund Morris, *The Rise of Theodore Roosevelt*, 310–11.

20. Edmund Morris, *The Rise of Theodore Roosevelt*, 313.

21. Dalton, 105.

22. Edmund Morris, *The Rise of Theodore Roosevelt*, 316.

23. James F. Vivian, *The Romance of My Life: Theodore Roosevelt's Speeches in Dakota*
    (Fargo, ND: Prairie House for the Theodore Roosevelt Medora Foundation, 1989),
    9–10.

24. Vivian, 10.

25. Anna Roosevelt Cowles, *Letters from Theodore Roosevelt to Anna Roosevelt Cowles,
    1870 to 1918* (New York: Charles Scribner's Sons, 1924), 86.

26. Theodore Roosevelt to Anna Roosevelt (Bamie), August 11, 1886, Theodore Roo-
    sevelt Collection, Houghton Library, Harvard College.

27. Kristie Miller, *Isabella Greenway: An Enterprising Woman* (Tucson: University of
    Arizona Press, 2004), 8.

28. Rolf Sletten, *Roosevelt's Ranches: The Maltese Cross & the Elkhorn* (Medora, ND:
    Theodore Roosevelt Medora Foundation, 2015), 175.

29. Sletten, 175.

30. Sletten, 175.

31. Edmund Morris, *The Rise of Theodore Roosevelt*, 335.

32. Betty Boyd Caroli, *The Roosevelt Women* (New York: Basic Books, 1998), 81.

33. Sylvia Jukes Morris, 53.

34. Edmund Morris, *The Rise of Theodore Roosevelt*, 336–37; this letter, from TR to Bamie on September 20, 1886, is worth a read and is helpfully digitized by the Theodore Roosevelt Center: https://www.theodorerooseveltcenter.org/Research /Digital-Library/Record?libID=0280054.

35. Theodore Roosevelt to Anna Roosevelt (Bamie), September 20, 1886, cited in Sylvia Jukes Morris, 90–91.

36. Sylvia Jukes Morris, 91; Dalton, 106–7.

37. Edmund Morris, *The Rise of Theodore Roosevelt*, 358.

38. Edith Carow to Theodore Roosevelt, June 8, 1886, cited in Sylvia Jukes Morris, 85–88.

39. Anna Roosevelt (Bamie) to Edith Kermit Carow, October 23, 1886, Theodore Roosevelt Collection, Houghton Library, Harvard College; With appreciation to historian David Welky, who pointed out the significance of this letter to the author and comments: "We know that Edith wasn't crazy about the idea of TR pursuing a political career. Here, however, Bamie's not just preparing Edith for the fact that TR will stay in politics, but also making it clear that politics is where TR needs to be."

40. Anna Roosevelt (Bamie) to Edith Kermit Carow, October 23, 1886, Theodore Roosevelt Collection, Houghton Library, Harvard College.

41. Teague, *Mrs. L.*, 36.

42. Michael Patrick Cullinane, *Remembering Theodore Roosevelt: Reminiscences of His Contemporaries* (New York: Palgrave Macmillan, 2021), 130.

43. Sylvia Jukes Morris, 101.

44. Sylvia Jukes Morris, 101.

45. Teague, *Mrs. L.*, 12–13.

46. Theodore Roosevelt to Anna Roosevelt (Bamie), January 10, 1887, Theodore Roosevelt Collection, Houghton Library, Harvard College.

47. Michael Patrick Cullinane, *Remembering Theodore Roosevelt: Reminiscences of His Contemporaries*, 69.

48. Margaret Chanler, *Roman Spring* (Boston: Little, Brown, and Company, 1934), 203.

49. Anna Roosevelt Cowles, *Letters from Theodore Roosevelt to Anna Roosevelt Cowles, 1870 to 1918* (New York: Charles Scribner's Sons, 1924), 107.

50. Sylvia Jukes Morris, 102.

51. Dalton, 78.

52. "Most handshakes for a head of state," Guinness World Records, https://www .guinnessworldrecords.com/world-records/65487-most-handshakes-by-a-head -of-state.

53. Cullinane, 68–69.

54. Mark Sullivan, "Visit Recalls Past of Mrs. Roosevelt," *The Evening Star*, August 11, 1932.

55. Sylvia Jukes Morris, 103.

56. Sylvia Jukes Morris, 103.

57. Sylvia Jukes Morris, 103.

58. Sylvia Jukes Morris, 104.

59. Sylvia Jukes Morris, 105.

60. Robert Browning, "Two in the Campagna," https://www.poetryfoundation.org/poems/43778/two-in-the-campagna.

10: "TWENTY-THREE CROSSINGS AT BREAKNECK SPEED"

1. Betty Boyd Caroli, *The Roosevelt Women* (New York: Basic Books, 1998), 170–71.

2. Margaret Chanler, *Roman Spring* (Boston: Little, Brown, and Company, 1934), 255.

3. Chanler, *Roman Spring*, 254–55.

4. Sylvia Jukes Morris, *Edith Kermit Roosevelt: Portrait of a First Lady* (New York: Random House, 2001), 107.

5. Sylvia Jukes Morris, 112.

6. Sylvia Jukes Morris, 126.

7. Mark Sullivan, "Visit Recalls Past of Mrs. Roosevelt," *The Evening Star*, August 11, 1932.

8. Corrine Roosevelt Robinson (Conie) to Anna Roosevelt Cowles (Bamie), August 13, 1888, Theodore Roosevelt Collection, Houghton Library, Harvard College.

9. Caroli, 94.

10. Corinne Roosevelt Robinson, *My Brother Theodore Roosevelt* (New York: Charles Scribner's Sons, 1921), 139, 136.

11. Corinne Roosevelt Robinson, *My Brother Theodore Roosevelt*, 140.

12. Clay Jenkinson, "Twenty-Three Crossings at Breakneck Speed," September 22, 2018, Theodore Roosevelt Center Symposium, Dickinson State University.

13. Corinne Roosevelt Robinson, *My Brother Theodore Roosevelt*, 144.

14. Corinne Roosevelt Robinson, *My Brother Theodore Roosevelt*, 143.

15. Corinne Roosevelt Robinson, *My Brother Theodore Roosevelt*, 145.

16. Mary Randolph, *Presidents and First Ladies* (New York: D. Appleton-Century Company, Inc., 1936), 178; also quoted in Hermann Hagedorn, *Roosevelt Family of Sagamore Hill* (New York: Macmillan, 1954), 194.

17. Michael Patrick Cullinane, *Remembering Theodore Roosevelt: Reminiscences of His Contemporaries* (New York: Palgrave Macmillan, 2021), 126–27.

18. Cullinane, 126–27.

19. William D. Hassett, *Off the Record with FDR* (New Brunswick: Rutgers University Press, 1958), 40, and as cited in the epigraph of Sylvia Jukes Morris, *Edith Kermit Roosevelt: Portrait of a First Lady* (New York: Random House, 2001).

20. Edmund Morris, *The Rise of Theodore Roosevelt* (1979; updated ed., New York: Random House, 2010), 489.

21. Jesse McKinley, "Why N.Y.C. Mayors Have White House Dreams (and Voters Dash Them)," *New York Times*, November 11, 2019.

22. Theodore Roosevelt, "Municipal Administration: The New York Police Force," *The Atlantic Monthly* (September 1897), https://www.theatlantic.com/magazine/archive/1897/09/municipal-administration-the-new-york-police-force/519849/.

23. Theodore Roosevelt, "Municipal Administration."

24. Cullinane, 39. Also see A. W. Chan, "Alcoholism and Epilepsy, *Epilepsia* (July/August 1985): 323–33, doi: 10.1111/j.1528-1157.1985.tb05658.x.

25. Corinne Roosevelt Robinson (Conie) in conversation with Augusta Munn Tilney, transcript, Sagamore Hill National Park Service, New York, in Cullinane, 12.

26. Vita Brevis, "An Update on Elliott Roosevelt," May 6, 2022, https://vitabrevis.americanancestors.org/2022/05/an-update-on-elliott-roosevelt/; Corinne Roosevelt Robinson (Conie) to Anna Roosevelt (Bamie), August 15, 1894, Theodore Roosevelt Collection, Houghton Library, Harvard College; Green-Wood Cemetery Archives, Lot 10268 (Roosevelt Lot), Vital Card, Elliott Roosevelt, 1894.

27. Corinne Roosevelt Robinson (Conie) to Anna Roosevelt (Bamie), August 15, 1894, Theodore Roosevelt Collection, Houghton Library, Harvard College.

28. Henry Davis Minot also met a tragic end, though without addiction as the cause. On an overnight train, Minot was instantly killed in a violent derailment in 1890. Roosevelt's classmate, fellow naturalist, and coauthor was only thirty-one.

29. Theodore Roosevelt to Patty Selmes, April 26, 1896, Greenway Collection, Arizona Historical Society as cited in Kristie Miller, *Isabella Greenway: An Enterprising Woman* (Tucson: University of Arizona Press, 2004), 16.

30. Theodore Roosevelt to Patty Selmes, October 5, 1896, Greenway Collection, Arizona Historical Society as cited in Kristie Miller, *Isabella Greenway*, 17.

31. Theodore Roosevelt to Patty Selmes, August 8, 1897, Greenway Collection, Arizona Historical Society as cited in Kristie Miller, *Isabella Greenway*, 17.

32. Edmund Morris, *The Rise of Theodore Roosevelt*, 527.

33. Edmund Morris, *The Rise of Theodore Roosevelt*, 532.

34. Dalton, 137.

35. Caroli, 97.

36. Caroli, 97.

37. Caroli, 100.

38. Caroli, 102.

39. Memoir of Anna Roosevelt Cowles, Theodore Roosevelt Collection, Houghton Library, Harvard College.

40. Memoir of Anna Roosevelt Cowles.

41. Theodore Roosevelt to Anna Roosevelt (Bamie), August 5, 1895, Theodore Roosevelt Collection, Houghton Library, Harvard College.

42. Elizabeth B. Clark, "Matrimonial Bonds: Slavery and Divorce in Nineteenth-Century America," 8 *Law & History Review* 25 (1990).

43. Caroli, 107.

44. Caroli, 103.

45. Cullinane, 65, 69.

46. Edmund Morris, *The Rise of Theodore Roosevelt*, 560.

47. Anna Roosevelt Cowles, *Letters from Theodore Roosevelt to Anna Roosevelt Cowles, 1870 to 1918* (New York: Charles Scribner's Sons, 1924), 171.

48. Anna Roosevelt Cowles, *Letters from Theodore Roosevelt to Anna Roosevelt Cowles, 1870 to 1918*, 188.

49. Maria Longworth Storer, "How Theodore Roosevelt Was Appointed Assistant Secretary of the Navy," *Harper's Weekly*, 56, no. 2893 (July 1, 1912).

50. Karl Rove, *The Triumph of William McKinley: Why the Election of 1896 Still Matters* (New York: Simon & Schuster, 2015), 342.

51. Anna Roosevelt Cowles, *Letters from Theodore Roosevelt to Anna Roosevelt Cowles, 1870 to 1918*, 195.

52. Anna Roosevelt Cowles, *Letters from Theodore Roosevelt to Anna Roosevelt Cowles, 1870 to 1918*, 193.

53. Karl Rove, *The Triumph of William McKinley: Why the Election of 1896 Still Matters*, 343.

54. Karl Rove, *The Triumph of William McKinley: Why the Election of 1896 Still Matters*, 345.

55. Maria Longworth Storer, "How Theodore Roosevelt Was Appointed Assistant Secretary of the Navy," *Harper's Weekly*, 56, no. 2893 (July 1, 1912); Bellamy Storer, Maria's husband, was recalled by President Roosevelt from his post as ambassador to Austria-Hungary in 1906. The public recall split the Roosevelts and Storers, and Bellamy published several letters and articles in retaliation. The *New York Times* and many others delighted in the controversy: https://timesmachine.ny times.com/timesmachine/1912/06/01/100536433.pdf.

56. Cullinane, 64.

57. H. W. Brands, ed., *The Selected Letters of Theodore Roosevelt* (New York: Cooper Square Press, 2001), 157–58.

11: THE CROWDED HOUR

1. Clay Risen, *The Crowded Hour: Theodore Roosevelt, The Rough Riders, and the Dawn of the American Century* (New York: Scribner, 2019), 48. Interestingly, Risen notes on p. 296 of his *Notes*: "One could argue that the April 27, 1865, sinking of the *Sultana*, a paddlewheel steamer carrying former Union prisoners of war, killing 1,192, was a naval disaster. But the *Sultana* was a commercial vessel, and not all its passengers were military." The sinking of the *Sultana* was overshadowed by the assassination of President Abraham Lincoln, a defining event in the childhood of Theodore Roosevelt.

2. Risen, 15.

3. Stacy A. Cordery, "The Precious Minutes Before the Crowded Hour: Edith and Theodore Roosevelt in Tampa, 1898," *Theodore Roosevelt Association Journal* 31, no. 1–2 (2010): 22–31.

4. Sylvia Jukes Morris, *Edith Kermit Roosevelt: Portrait of a First Lady* (New York: Random House, 2001), 170.

5. Sylvia Jukes Morris, 171.

6. Sylvia Jukes Morris, 171.

7. Risen, 8.

8. Henry Adams, *Letters of Henry Adams, 1892–1918*, ed. Worthington Chauncey Ford (Boston: Houghton Mifflin Company, 1938), 172; Sylvia Jukes Morris, "The Historian and the Hostess," *The Washington Post*, December 25, 1983, https://www.washingtonpost.com/archive/entertainment/books/1983/12/25/the-historian-and-the-hostess/54dc2677-0641-4d52-be95-6b8943abf5b8/; Sylvia Morris, 126.

9. Margaret Chanler, *Roman Spring* (Boston: Little, Brown, 1934), 285.

10. Theodore Roosevelt to Dr. Alexander Lambert, April 1, 1898, in Elting E. Morison, ed., *The Letters of Theodore Roosevelt: The Department of the Navy, continued 1898* (Cambridge: Harvard University Press, 1951), 807–9.

11. Sylvia Jukes Morris, 174.

12. Risen, 180.

13. Michael Patrick Cullinane, *Remembering Theodore Roosevelt: Reminiscences of His Contemporaries* (New York: Palgrave Macmillan, 2021), 251; Risen, 76.

14. Risen, 62.

15. Kathleen Dalton, *Theodore Roosevelt: A Strenuous Life* (New York: Vintage, 2004), 173.

16. "Yellow Journalism, Richard Harding Davis (1864–1916)," PBS, *Crucible of Empire: The Spanish-American War*, https://www.pbs.org/crucible/bio_davis.html. For Hearst's role in fomenting the Spanish-American War, see Ken Lawrence, "You Furnish the Pictures and I'll Furnish the War," History News Network (November 24, 2019), https://historynewsnetwork.org/article/173692.

17. Cameron County, Pennsylvania, *Press* (June 30, 1898), cited in Risen, 9–10, 137.

18. Risen, 10.

19. Corinne Roosevelt Robinson, *My Brother Theodore Roosevelt* (New York: Charles Scribner's Sons, 1921), 163.

20. Cordery, "The Precious Minutes Before the Crowded Hour," 22–31.

21. Edmund Morris, *The Rise of Theodore Roosevelt* (1979, updated ed., New York: Random House, 2010), 658.

22. Dalton, 173.

23. Dalton, 177.

24. Corinne Roosevelt Robinson, *My Brother Theodore Roosevelt*, 166.

25. Risen, 171. Risen cites "Research Materials for the Rough Riders," Hermann

Hagedorn Collection, Theodore Roosevelt Collection, Houghton Library, Harvard College.

26. Risen, 194.

27. "The Spanish-American War, 1898," Office of the Historian, https://history.state
.gov/milestones/1866-1898/spanish-american-war.

28. Charles G. Washburn, *Theodore Roosevelt: The Logic of His Career* (Boston: Houghton Mifflin Company, 1916), 22.

29. Archie Butt, *Letters of Archie Butt* (Garden City, NY: Doubleday Page & Co., 1924), 146.

30. Theodore Roosevelt to Patty Selmes, July 31, 1898, Greenway Collection, Arizona Historical Society as cited in Kristie Miller, *Isabella Greenway: An Enterprising Woman* (Tucson: University of Arizona Press, 2004), 18.

31. Robert Ferguson to Edith Kermit Roosevelt, July 5, 1898, as cited in Edmund Morris, *The Rise of Theodore Roosevelt*, 687–88, and Corinne Roosevelt Robinson, *My Brother Theodore Roosevelt*, 173–74. Interestingly, the July 5 letter is addressed to Edith but Conie, TR's posthumous publicist, weaves it expertly into *My Brother*. Similar language is used in a letter from Robert Ferguson to Corinne Roosevelt Robinson (Conie), June 20, 1898, Greenway Collection, Arizona Historical Society as cited in Kristie Miller, *Isabella Greenway*, 18. The June 20 letter, however, is prior to both Las Guasimas and the Battle of San Juan Heights.

32. Edmund Morris, *The Rise of Theodore Roosevelt*, 693.

33. David Halberstam, "The Vantage Point," *The New York Times*, October 31, 1971. https://timesmachine.nytimes.com/timesmachine/1971/10/31/91310513.html?page
Number=131.

34. Prior to 2024, governors have pulled way ahead, twenty-seven of them having become president versus seventeen senators.

12: A RISING TIDE

1. Theodore Roosevelt, *The Rough Riders* (New York: Charles Scribner's Sons, 1899), 124.

2. Sylvia Jukes Morris, *Edith Kermit Roosevelt: Portrait of a First Lady* (New York: Random House, 2001), 183.

3. Sylvia Jukes Morris, 183–84.

4. Theodore Roosevelt to Henry Cabot Lodge, September 19, 1898, in Elting E. Morison, ed., *The Letters of Theodore Roosevelt: The Department of the Navy, continued 1898* (Cambridge: Harvard University Press, 1951), 876.

5. Jacob Riis, "In the Roosevelt Home," New York *Sun*, January 1, 1899.

6. Kathleen Dalton, *Theodore Roosevelt: A Strenuous Life* (New York: Alfred A. Knopf, 2002), 180.

7. Dalton, 179–80.

8. Theodore Roosevelt Victory Message, November 8, 1898. Original manuscript now

in the Raab Collection, https://www.raabcollection.com/presidential-autographs/tr-victory.

9. Dalton, 180; Lewis L. Gould, *Edith Kermit Roosevelt: Creating the Modern First Lady* (Lawrence: University Press of Kansas, 2013), 19.

10. Sylvia Jukes Morris, 193.

11. See Edmund Morris, *The Rise of Theodore Roosevelt* (1979; updated ed., New York: Random House, 2010), 731–34, 744–45; and "Ford Franchise Bill," *New York Times*, May 1, 1899, p. 3, https://www.nytimes.com/1899/05/01/archives/ford-franchise-tax-bill-no-assessment-can-be-made-until-fall-says.html.

12. Edmund Morris, *The Rise of Theodore Roosevelt*, 744.

13. Frances Theodora Parsons, *Perchance Some Day* (Privately printed, 1951), 124.

14. Dalton, 184–86.

15. Dalton, 189.

16. Corinne Roosevelt Robinson, *My Brother Theodore Roosevelt* (New York: Charles Scribner's Sons, 1921), 185. Conie explains the Roosevelt real estate: "During his incumbency as governor of New York State he always made his headquarters either at the house of my sister, Mrs. Cowles, or at my house, and many were the famous breakfast parties at 422 Madison Avenue in those strenuous days." As explained on p. 177, n. 23 (p. 441), Bamie first purchased 422 Madison in 1884 and then the row house at 689 Madison in 1886. Conie neglects to mention that she actually lived in New Jersey and hosted at the Roosevelt home when her brother was in the city. Roosevelt's residency was, for a moment, an issue in the gubernatorial campaign. He had signed an affidavit that his actual residence was in Washington, D.C., and had paid no resident taxes in either New York City or Oyster Bay for several years.

17. Corinne Roosevelt Robinson, *My Brother Theodore Roosevelt*, 186.

18. Corinne Roosevelt Robinson, *My Brother Theodore Roosevelt*, 191.

19. Corinne Roosevelt Robinson, *My Brother Theodore Roosevelt*, 194.

20. Dalton, 188.

21. Corinne Roosevelt Robinson, *My Brother Theodore Roosevelt*, 188–89.

22. Sylvia Jukes Morris, 539.

23. Sylvia Jukes Morris, 200.

24. Dalton, 188.

25. Gould, *Edith Kermit Roosevelt*, 19.

26. Sylvia Jukes Morris, 197.

27. Theodore Roosevelt, Speech ["The Strenuous Life"] before the Hamilton Club, Chicago, April 10, 1899, https://www.theodoreroosevelt.org/content.aspx?page_id=22&club_id=991271&module_id=339361.

28. Theodore Roosevelt to Henry Cabot Lodge, July 1, 1899, in Elting E. Morison, ed., *The Letters of Theodore Roosevelt: The Department of the Navy, continued 1898* (Cambridge: Harvard University Press, 1951), 1022–23.

29. Dalton, 191.

30. Michael J. Connolly, "'I Make Politics My Recreation': Vice President Garret A. Hobart and Nineteenth Century Republican Business Politics," *New Jersey History* (Newark: New Jersey Historical Society) 125, no. 1 (2010): 33.

31. Alice Roosevelt Longworth, *Crowded Hours: Reminiscences of Alice Roosevelt Longworth* (New York: Charles Scribner's Sons, 1933), 34.

32. Theodore Roosevelt to Henry Cabot Lodge, December 11, 1899, in Elting E. Morison, ed., *The Letters of Theodore Roosevelt: The Department of the Navy, continued 1898*, 1108.

33. Theodore Roosevelt to Henry Cabot Lodge, January 30, 1900, in Elting E. Morison, ed., *The Letters of Theodore Roosevelt: The Department of the Navy, continued 1898*, 1153.

34. Theodore Roosevelt to Henry Cabot Lodge, February 2, 1900, in Elting E. Morison, ed., *The Letters of Theodore Roosevelt: The Department of the Navy, continued 1898*, 1160.

35. Edith Kermit Roosevelt to Ethel Roosevelt, March 12, 1900, Theodore Roosevelt Collection, Houghton Library, Harvard College.

36. Corinne Roosevelt Robinson, *My Brother Theodore Roosevelt*, 196–97.

37. Dalton, 191.

38. Frederick S. Wood, *Roosevelt as We Knew Him: Personal Recollections of 150 Friends and Associates* (Reprint ed., Whitefish, MT: Kessinger Publishing, 2010), 72–75.

39. Doris Kearns Goodwin, *The Bully Pulpit: Theodore Roosevelt, William Howard Taft, and the Golden Age of Journalism* (New York: Simon & Schuster, 2013), 263.

40. "McKinley and Roosevelt, Unanimously Nominated for President and Vice-President," *New York Tribune*, June 22, 1900, front page.

41. Margaret Leech, *In the Days of McKinley* (New York: Harper, 1959), 542.

42. Nathan Miller, *Theodore Roosevelt: A Life* (New York: HarperCollins, 1992), 342.

43. Theodore Roosevelt to Henry Cabot Lodge, quoted in Edmund Morris, *The Rise of Theodore Roosevelt*, 741.

44. Edmund Morris, *The Rise of Theodore Roosevelt*, 767.

45. New York *World*, June 22, 1900, quoted in Sylvia Jukes Morris, 205.

46. Dalton, 195.

47. Sylvia Jukes Morris, 206.

48. Gould, *Edith Kermit Roosevelt*, 22.

49. Betty Boyd Caroli, *The Roosevelt Women* (New York: Basic Books, 1998), 116.

50. Caroli, 117.

51. Corinne Roosevelt Robinson, *My Brother Theodore Roosevelt*, 200.

52. Stacy A. Cordery, *Alice: Alice Roosevelt Longworth, from White House Princess to Washington Power Broker* (New York: Viking, 2007), 40.

53. Caroli, 85.

54. Michael Teague, *Mrs. L.: Conversations with Alice Roosevelt Longworth* (Garden City, NY: Doubleday, 1981), 112.

55. Sylvia Jukes Morris, 209.

56. Dalton, 197.

57. Dalton, 198.

58. Caroli, 117.

59. Sylvia Jukes Morris, 212.

60. Sylvia Jukes Morris, 212.

61. Sylvia Jukes Morris, 214.

62. Edmund Morris, *Theodore Rex* (New York: Random House, 2001), 11.

63. Corinne Roosevelt Robinson, *My Brother Theodore Roosevelt*, 204.

64. Diary of Edith Kermit Roosevelt, September 14, 1901, Theodore Roosevelt Collection, Houghton Library, Harvard College.

65. Nathan Miller, *Theodore Roosevelt: A Life*, 349.

66. Nathan Miller, *Theodore Roosevelt: A Life*, 342.

67. Nathan Miller, *Theodore Roosevelt: A Life*, 354–55. Miller notes on p. 355 that "there is some question about the accuracy of some of [H. H.] Kohlsaat's recollections." Kohlsaat was a Republican and the editor of the *Chicago Times-Herald*. The oft-repeated phrase "damned cowboy" has grown from lore to legend, and there is no question Hanna was deeply upset by the death of his good friend and the accidental rise of TR.

68. Corinne Roosevelt Robinson, *My Brother Theodore Roosevelt*, 206–7.

13: PARTNERS IN HISTORY

1. Michael Patrick Cullinane, *Remembering Theodore Roosevelt: Reminiscences of His Contemporaries* (New York: Palgrave Macmillan, 2021), 128.

2. Anna Roosevelt Cowles, *Letters from Theodore Roosevelt to Anna Roosevelt Cowles, 1870 to 1918* (New York: Charles Scribner's Sons, 1924), 252.

3. Kathleen Dalton, *Theodore Roosevelt: A Strenuous Life* (New York: Alfred A. Knopf, 2002), 207.

4. Corinne Roosevelt Robinson, *My Brother Theodore Roosevelt* (New York: Charles Scribner's Sons, 1921), 207.

5. Dalton, 203, 207.

6. Kai Bird and Martin J. Sherwin, *American Prometheus: The Triumph and Tragedy of J. Robert Oppenheimer* (New York: Random House, 2005), 293. Stimson is known to contemporary audiences as a result of Bird and Sherwin's Pulitzer Prize–winning masterpiece and the brilliant film adaptation by Christopher Nolan. In one particularly memorable scene, Secretary Stimson strikes Kyoto, Japan, from the list of possible targets for the atomic bomb. The line was ad-libbed (https://www.nytimes.com/2023/07/20/movies/christopher-nolan-oppenheimer.html), but it may have basis in fact: https://www.bbc.com/news/world-asia-33755182.amp. On the very first page of the first chapter in Sherwin and Bird's book, they note Oppenheimer was born when "Theodore Roosevelt was using the bully pulpit of the

White House to argue that good government in alliance with science and applied technology could forge an enlightened new Progressive Era" (p. 9).

7. Henry Stimson, *Recollections of Henry Stimson*, 1913, Henry L. Stimson Papers, Sterling Memorial Library, Yale University.

8. Gifford Pinchot, *Breaking New Ground* (New York: Harcourt, Brace, 1947), 314.

9. Margaret Chanler, *Roman Spring* (Boston: Little, Brown and Company, 1934), 203.

10. James Amos, *Theodore Roosevelt: Hero to His Valet* (New York: The John Day Company, 1927), 33; https://archives.fbi.gov/archives/news/stories/2005/february/amos022805. Amos, the last person to see TR alive, served as a special agent in the FBI for thirty-two years. He worked on the "Murder, Inc." and Duquesne Nazi spy ring cases, among others. He was so indispensable to the Bureau that FBI Director J. Edgar Hoover and President Franklin D. Roosevelt exempted him from retirement in 1944. https://newspapers.library.in.gov/cgi-bin/indiana?a=d&d=INR19440304-01.1.7&e=-------en-20--1--txt-txIN-------.

11. Amos, *Theodore Roosevelt: Hero to His Valet*, 33.

12. Amos, *Theodore Roosevelt: Hero to His Valet*, 9, 30.

13. Amos, *Theodore Roosevelt: Hero to His Valet*, 33.

14. Isabella Hagner, *Memoirs*, www.whitehousehistory.org/ whitehousehistory_26 hagner.pdf, 83.

15. Theodore Roosevelt to Anna Roosevelt (Bamie), February 11, 1894, in Cowles, *Letters*, 135.

16. Cowles, *Letters*, 252.

17. Dalton, 222.

18. Lewis L. Gould, *Edith Kermit Roosevelt: Creating the Modern First Lady* (Lawrence: University Press of Kansas, 2013), 28.

19. Lewis L. Gould, *Edith Kermit Roosevelt: Creating the Modern First Lady*, 30; Betty Boyd Caroli, *The Roosevelt Women* (New York: Basic Books, 1998), 197; Gould, *Edith Kermit Roosevelt*, 30, citing "Social Gossip," *Washington Post*, April 1, 1907, 7.

20. Caroli, 197; Gould, *Edith Kermit Roosevelt*, 31; "Persons of Interest," *Harper's Bazaar* 36 (June 1902): 532; "About Mrs. Roosevelt," *Christian Advocate*, February 28, 1901, quoting from *The Presbyterian*.

21. Amos, *Theodore Roosevelt: Hero to His Valet*, 33, 35.

22. Theodore Roosevelt to Anna Roosevelt (Bamie), October 13, 1889, in Cowles, *Letters*, 107; Caroli, 197; Helen Taft to William Howard Taft, February 1, 1902, William Howard Taft Papers, Manuscript, Library of Congress; "Mrs. Stuyvesant Fish Talks in Pungent Style," *New York Times*, September 27, 1903, cited in Gould, *Edith Kermit Roosevelt*, 31.

23. "White House Social Record," *New York Times*, June 8, 1902.

24. Kristie Miller, *Isabella Greenway: An Enterprising Woman* (Tucson: University of Arizona Press, 2004), 22.

25. Miller, *Isabella Greenway: An Enterprising Woman*, 33.

26. Michael Patrick Cullinane, *Remembering Theodore Roosevelt: Reminiscences of His Contemporaries*, 130.

27. Theodore Roosevelt to Booker T. Washington, September 14, 1901, https://www.whitehousehistory.org/photos/a-letter-from-president-theodore-roosevelt-to-booker-t-washington.

28. Caroli, 157.

29. Theodore Roosevelt to Joseph Bucklin Bishop, October 5, 1904, Theodore Roosevelt Collection, Houghton Library, Harvard College, and cited in Dalton, 216. A digital record of this letter can be found at the Theodore Roosevelt Center: https://www.theodorerooseveltcenter.org/Research/Digital-Library/Record/ImageViewer?libID=o281313&imageNo=1.

30. Stephen Kantrowitz, *Ben Tillman and the Reconstruction of White Supremacy* (Chapel Hill: The University of North Carolina Press, 2000), 259, and cited in Dalton, 216.

31. Dalton, 277.

32. Ralph E. Luker, *The Social Gospel in Black and White: American Racial Reform, 1885–1912* (Chapel Hill: University of North Carolina Press, 1991), 141.

33. Dalton, 216.

34. Gould, *Edith Kermit Roosevelt*, 94–96.

35. Dalton, 216.

36. Dalton, 216.

37. Gould, *Edith Kermit Roosevelt*, 2.

38. "The Brownsville Incident," Theodore Roosevelt Digital Library, Dickinson State University, theodorerooseveltcenter.org/Learn-About-TR/TR-Encyclopedia/Race-Ethnicity-and-Gender/The-Brownsville-Incident#:~:text=The%20Brownsville%20Incident,-Subjects%3A%20Texas--&text=President%20Theodore%20Roosevelt%20discharged%20without,of%20the%20melee%20in%20town. In *The Brownsville Raid* (1970; reprint ed., College Station: Texas A&M Press, 1992), journalist John D. Weaver concluded that the white citizens who accused Black soldiers in the incident lied. The book prompted Congress to investigate, and in 1972 Congress reversed Roosevelt's dismissal order, and President Richard M. Nixon pardoned the soldiers and issued honorable discharges. In all but one instance, these acts of restitution were posthumous. In 1973, Congressman Augustus F. Hawkins and Senator Hubert H. Humphrey won congressional enactment of a tax-free pension for the only surviving soldier, Dorsie Willis, who received $25,000.

39. Dalton, 509–10; 524.

40. Dalton, 523.

41. "Editorial: Theodore Roosevelt," *The Crisis* 17, no. 4 (February 1919), 163, in Dalton, 523–24.

42. Corinne Roosevelt Robinson, *My Brother Theodore Roosevelt*, 106.

43. Dalton, 225.

44. Susan Berfield, *The Hour of Our Fate: Theodore Roosevelt, J.P. Morgan, and the Battle to Transform American Capitalism* (New York: Bloomsbury, 2020), 9.

45. Morgan quoted in the New York *World*, May 11, 1901, and in Jean Strouse, *Morgan: American Financier* (New York: HarperCollins, 1999), xi–xii.

46. Dalton, 225–26.

47. Dalton, 226.

48. Caroli, 95.

49. Rachel Lambert Mellon, "President Kennedy's Rose Garden," White House Historical Association, www.whitehousehistory.org/president-kennedys-rose-garden.

50. The 1903 instrument was donated to the Smithsonian Institution in 1938, after Steinway presented its 300,000th piano to President and Mrs. Franklin D. Roosevelt, who accepted it on behalf of the nation. This "Roosevelt piano" from 1938 is now considered the White House "State" piano.

51. Gould, *Edith Kermit Roosevelt*, 49–50.

52. Gould, *Edith Kermit Roosevelt*, 45.

53. Amos, *Theodore Roosevelt: Hero to His Valet*, 37.

54. Dalton, 220. Dalton cites in particular a letter from Frederick M. Davenport to Hagedorn (December 31, 1948), which remarks on Edith's access to information.

55. Dalton, 233–35; Sylvia Jukes Morris, *Edith Kermit Roosevelt: Portrait of a First Lady* (New York: Random House, 2001), 240.

56. A. Maurice Low to Nelson W. Aldrich, September 5, 1902, Aldrich Papers, Manuscript Division, Library of Congress as cited by Gould, *Edith Kermit Roosevelt*, 44.

57. Gould, *Edith Kermit Roosevelt*, 44.

58. Sylvia Jukes Morris, 244–45.

59. Dalton, 234; Sylvia Jukes Morris, 240, 244.

60. Dalton, 234.

61. Cowles, *Letters*, 252–55.

62. Leo Troy, *Trade Union Membership, 1897–1962* (Cambridge, MA: National Bureau of Economic Research, 1965), 1, http://www.nber.org/books/troy65-1.

63. Dalton, 222.

64. Michael Patrick Cullinane, *Remembering Theodore Roosevelt: Reminiscences of His Contemporaries* (New York: Palgrave Macmillan, 2021), 128–30.

65. Cullinane, 128–30.

66. Dalton, 223.

67. Caroli, 194; Edward Wagenknecht, *The Seven Worlds of Theodore Roosevelt* (New York: Longmans, Green, 1958), 169.

68. Dalton, 212.

69. Dalton, 220.

70. Dalton, 232.

71. Caroli, 399.

72. Dalton, 239.

73. Caroli, 400.

74. Corinne Roosevelt Robinson, *My Brother Theodore Roosevelt*, 238.

75. Caroli, 405.

76. Michael Teague, *Mrs. L.: Conversations with Alice Roosevelt Longworth* (Garden City, NY: Doubleday, 1981), 36–37; Edmund Morris, *The Rise of Theodore Roosevelt* (1979; updated ed., New York: Random House, 2010), 233, citing interview with Alice Roosevelt Longworth (November 9, 1954, collection of the Theodore Roosevelt Birthplace), in which she reported this as Edith Roosevelt's snide conjecture. Teague was written after the publication of Morris and presents the quote with a slight difference and the same effect: "My stepmother added a typically caustic twist by telling my brother Ted, who naturally repeated it to me, that it was just as well that my mother had died when she did because my father would have been bored to death by staying married to her." Each version is from the same source, Alice Roosevelt Longworth, the interviews separated by thirty years.

77. Michael Teague, *Mrs. L.: Conversations with Alice Roosevelt Longworth*, 37.

78. Alice Roosevelt Longworth, *Crowded Hours: Reminiscences of Alice Roosevelt Longworth* (New York: Charles Scribner's Sons, 1933), 9.

79. Amos, *Theodore Roosevelt: Hero to His Valet*, 29.

80. Corinne Roosevelt Robinson, *My Brother Theodore Roosevelt*, 217.

81. Corinne Roosevelt Robinson, *My Brother Theodore Roosevelt*, 214; Cowles, *Letters*, 261.

82. Anna Roosevelt Cowles, *Letters from Theodore Roosevelt to Anna Roosevelt Cowles, 1870 to 1918* (New York: Charles Scribner's Sons, 1924), 261.

83. Corinne Roosevelt Robinson, *My Brother Theodore Roosevelt*, 217.

84. Corinne Roosevelt Robinson, *My Brother Theodore Roosevelt*, 217.

85. Cowles, *Letters*, 265.

14: TRIUMPH, REGRET, AND RELIEF

1. Kathleen Dalton, *Theodore Roosevelt: A Strenuous Life* (New York: Alfred A. Knopf, 2002), 264.

2. Owen Wister, *Roosevelt: The Story of a Friendship, 1880–1919* (New York: Macmillan, 1930), 244.

3. Sylvia Jukes Morris, *Edith Kermit Roosevelt: Portrait of a First Lady* (New York: Random House, 2001), 280.

4. Lewis L. Gould, *Edith Kermit Roosevelt: Creating the Modern First Lady* (Lawrence: University Press of Kansas, 2013), 98.

5. Dalton, 271.

6. Corinne Roosevelt Robinson, *My Brother Theodore Roosevelt* (New York: Charles Scribner's Sons, 1921), 223.

7. Corinne Roosevelt Robinson, *My Brother Theodore Roosevelt*, 146.

8. Dalton, 271.

9. Corinne Roosevelt Robinson (Conie) to Anna Roosevelt Cowles (Bamie), March 5, 1905, Theodore Roosevelt Collection, Houghton Library, Harvard College.

10. Betty Boyd Caroli, *The Roosevelt Women* (New York: Basic Books, 1998), 156.

11. Cullinane, Michael Patrick, *Remembering Theodore Roosevelt: Reminiscences of His Contemporaries* (New York: Palgrave Macmillan, 2021), 128.

12. William B. Styple, ed., *Generals in Bronze: Interviewing the Commanders of the Civil War* (Kearny, N.J.: Belle Grove Publishing Company, 2005), 250.

13. Corinne Roosevelt Robinson, *My Brother Theodore Roosevelt*, 220–21.

14. Dalton, 273.

15. Dalton, 243, 274, 208.

16. Kristie Miller, *Isabella Greenway: An Enterprising Woman* (Tucson: University of Arizona Press, 2004), 33–34, 38.

17. Caroli, 121–22; Dalton, 259.

18. Sylvia Jukes Morris, 80.

19. Theodore Roosevelt to Eleanor Brooks Saltonstall, May 23, 1907, Theodore Roosevelt Papers. Library of Congress Manuscript Division.

20. Lowell E. Baier, "The Cradle of Conservation: Theodore Roosevelt's Elkhorn Ranch, an Icon of America's National Identity," *Theodore Roosevelt Association Journal* 28, no. 1 (2007): 15–22; also cited in Douglas Brinkley, *The Wilderness Warrior: Theodore Roosevelt and the Crusade for America* (New York: Harper Perennial, 2010), 194.

21. Brinkley, 194.

22. Theodore Roosevelt, *Theodore Roosevelt: An Autobiography* (1913; reprint ed., New York: Da Capo, 1985), 372.

23. Theodore Roosevelt, speech at Berkeley, California, March 23, 1911.

24. Theodore Roosevelt, *Autobiography*, 572.

25. Major Archibald Butt, *Taft and Roosevelt*, 399.

26. Dalton, 388.

27. Mark Sullivan, "Visit Recalls Past of Mrs. Roosevelt," *The Evening Star*, August 11, 1932.

28. Stacy A. Cordery, *Alice: Alice Roosevelt Longworth, from White House Princess to Washington Power Broker* (New York: Viking, 2007), 472.

29. Dalton, 357.

30. Dalton, 277.

31. Corinne Roosevelt Robinson, *My Brother Theodore Roosevelt*, 250–51.

32. Corinne Roosevelt Robinson, *My Brother Theodore Roosevelt*, 251.

33. Corinne Roosevelt Robinson, *My Brother Theodore Roosevelt*, 251–53.

34. Caroli, 159.

35. Corinne Roosevelt Robinson, *My Brother Theodore Roosevelt*, 253.

36. Caroli, 159.

37. Dalton, 344.

38. Dalton, 342.

39. The Ohio State University, Department of History, "Roosevelt in Africa," ehis tory.osu.edu/exhibitions/1912/content/RooseveltInAfrica.

40. Edith Kermit Roosevelt to Henry Cabot Lodge, n.d. [November 11, 1908], Henry Cabot Lodge Papers, Massachusetts Historical Society, as cited in Dalton, 344.

15: LION IN WINTER

1. Corinne Roosevelt Robinson, *My Brother Theodore Roosevelt* (New York: Charles Scribner's Sons, 1921), 254.

2. Dalton, 357.

3. Theodore Roosevelt, "Citizenship in a Republic," Address at the Sorbonne in Paris, France, Gerhard Peters and John T. Woolley, eds., The American Presidency Project: https://www.presidency.ucsb.edu/documents/address-the-sorbonne-paris-france-citizenship-republic.

4. Dalton, 347.

5. Dalton, 365.

6. Geoffrey Cowan, *Let the People Rule: Theodore Roosevelt and the Birth of the Presidential Primary System* (New York: W. W. Norton, 2016), 18.

7. Dalton, 366.

8. Cowan, 19.

9. Dalton, 365.

10. Dalton, 369.

11. Dalton, 375.

12. Betty Boyd Caroli, *The Roosevelt Women* (New York: Basic Books, 1998), 163, 164.

13. Corinne Roosevelt Robinson, *The Call of Brotherhood and Other Poems* (New York: Charles Scribner's Sons, 1912), 3–4.

14. Corinne Roosevelt Robinson, *My Brother Theodore Roosevelt*, 266.

15. Corinne Roosevelt Robinson, *My Brother Theodore Roosevelt*, 267.

16. Cowan, *Let the People Rule*, 12.

17. Major Archibald Butt, *Taft and Roosevelt: The Intimate Letters of Archie Butt, Military Aide*, Vol. 1 (New York: Doubleday, Doran 1930), 166–67.

18. Dalton, 507.

19. Major Archibald Butt, *Taft and Roosevelt*, 580–81; quoted in part in Cowan, *Let the People Rule*, 24.

20. Ibid.

21. Ibid.

22. "The Story of Archibald Butt, First Class Passenger, *Titanic*," The National Archives (UK), https://www.nationalarchives.gov.uk/titanic/stories/ikipedia-butt.htm.

23. Cowan, 28.

24. Dalton, 379.

25. Cowan, 28–29.

26. Major Archibald Butt, *Taft and Roosevelt*, 122.

27. Sylvia Jukes Morris, *Edith Kermit Roosevelt: Portrait of a First Lady* (New York: Random House, 2001), 348.

28. Major Archibald Butt, *Taft and Roosevelt*, 168.

29. Major Archibald Butt, *Taft and Roosevelt*, 280.

30. Stacy A. Cordery, *Alice: Alice Roosevelt Longworth, from White House Princess to Washington Power Broker* (New York: Viking, 2007), 219.

31. Cordery, *Alice*, 219.

32. Owen Wister, *Roosevelt: The Story of a Friendship, 1880–1919* (New York: Macmillan, 1930), 26–27.

33. Cowan, 2.

34. Dalton, 388.

35. Cordery, *Alice*, 219.

36. Edmund Morris, *Colonel Roosevelt* (New York: Random House, 2010), 646.

37. Dalton, 400.

38. Dalton, 399.

39. Dalton, 400.

40. Dalton, 402.

41. Dalton, 387.

42. John F. Schrank Municipal Court Records, Exhibit 3, Page 4: Police Interview, Milwaukee Public Library, https://content.mpl.org/digital/collection/Schrank MCR/id/87/rec/3.

43. Doris Kearns Goodwin, *The Bully Pulpit: Theodore Roosevelt, William Howard Taft, and the Golden Age of Journalism* (New York: Simon & Schuster, 2013), 732.

44. Edmund Morris, *The Rise of Theodore Roosevelt* (1979; updated ed., New York: Random House, 2010), xxi. Some sources add "the baby at every christening," such as the authoritative Stacy Cordery, *Alice: Alice Roosevelt Longworth, from White House Princess to Washington Power Broker* (New York: Viking, 2007), 54.

45. "It Takes More Than That to Kill a Bull Moose," Speech by Theodore Roosevelt in Milwaukee, Wisconsin, October 14, 1912, from a stenographic report reprinted by the Theodore Roosevelt Association: https://www.theodoreroosevelt.org/con tent.aspx?page_id=22&club_id=991271&module_id=338394.

46. Alan Axelrod, "Lesson 17," *Theodore Roosevelt, CEO: 7 Principles to Guide and Inspire Modern Leaders* (New York: Union Square & Co., 2012), 16.

47. Sylvia Jukes Morris, 386.

48. Sylvia Jukes Morris, 387.

49. Sylvia Jukes Morris, 387; Dalton, 405.

50. Sylvia Jukes Morris, 387.

51. Sylvia Jukes Morris, 388.

52. Doris Kearns Goodwin, *The Bully Pulpit*, 734.

53. Theodore Roosevelt to Cecil Spring-Rice, December 31, 1912, quoted in Alan Axelrod, *Theodore Roosevelt, CEO*, 15.

54. Cordery, *Alice*, 234.

55. Dalton, 381.

56. Roosevelt spoke at the second Madison Square Garden "completed in 1890 . . . [and] was once again New York City's epicenter of cultural and large-scale events," https://madisonsquarepark.org/community/news/2021/04/history-of-madison-square-garden/.

57. Caroli, 161.

58. Corinne Roosevelt Robinson, *My Brother Theodore Roosevelt*, 275.

59. Library of Congress, Progressive Party campaign speech, Madison Square Garden, New York, N.Y., 1912; John Allen Gable, *The Bull Moose Years: Theodore Roosevelt and the Progressive Party* (Port Washington, NY: Kennikat Press, 1978), 128–29.

60. Edith Kermit Roosevelt to Kermit Roosevelt, November 6, 1912, in Sylvia Jukes Morris, 389.

61. John Woolley and Gerhard Peters, The American Presidency Project, UC Santa Barbara: https://www.presidency.ucsb.edu/statistics/elections/1912.

62. Dalton, 403.

63. Dalton, 406.

64. Corinne Roosevelt Robinson, *My Brother Theodore Roosevelt*, 264.

16: PUT OUT THE LIGHT

1. Corinne Roosevelt Robinson, *My Brother Theodore Roosevelt* (New York: Charles Scribner's Sons, 1921), 267.

2. Kathleen Dalton, *Theodore Roosevelt: A Strenuous Life* (New York: Alfred A. Knopf, 2002), 408–9.

3. Candice Millard, *The River of Doubt* (New York: Broadway Books, 2005), 45.

4. Millard, 45.

5. Dalton, 351.

6. Dalton, 427.

7. Millard, 46.

8. Even the *Vandyck* had bad luck: https://www.theodorerooseveltcenter.org/Blog/Item/A%20Story%20of%20A%20Ship.

9. Sylvia Jukes Morris, *Edith Kermit Roosevelt: Portrait of a First Lady* (New York: Random House, 2001), 399; Edith Kermit Roosevelt to Anna Roosevelt Cowles,

October 15, 1913, Theodore Roosevelt Collection, Houghton Library, Harvard College.

10. Dalton, 430, 433.

11. Dalton, 436.

12. Corinne Roosevelt Robinson, *My Brother Theodore Roosevelt*, 428.

13. Betty Boyd Caroli, *The Roosevelt Women* (New York: Basic Books, 1998), 171.

14. Corinne Roosevelt Robinson, *One Woman to Another and Other Poems* (New York: Charles Scribner's Sons, 1914), 1–6.

15. Theodore Roosevelt to William Sewall, April 7, 1916, https://www.shapell.org /manuscript/theodore-roosevelt-criticizes-president-woodrow-wilson-cow ardice/#transcripts.

16. Corinne Roosevelt Robinson, *My Brother Theodore Roosevelt*, 278–79.

17. Library of Congress, "The Lusitania Disaster," https://www.loc.gov/collections /world-war-i-rotogravures/articles-and-essays/the-lusitania-disaster/#:~:text =On%20May%207,%201915,%20the,1,195%20perished,%20including%20123%20 Americans.

18. United States Department of State, Office of the Historian, "The Secretary of State to the Ambassador in Germany (Gerard)," telegram, April 18, 1916, https:// history.state.gov/historicaldocuments/frus1916Supp/d308.

19. The Editors, "Wilson and Roosevelt," *The New Republic* (November 4, 1916), https://newrepublic.com/article/92253/wilson-and-roosevelt.

20. Corinne Roosevelt Robinson, *My Brother Theodore Roosevelt*, 297.

21. Corinne Roosevelt Robinson, *My Brother Theodore Roosevelt*, 298.

22. Corinne Roosevelt Robinson, *My Brother Theodore Roosevelt*, 303.

23. The National Constitution Center celebrated "The remarkable career of Charles Evan Hughes" on April 11, 2023, noting he was perhaps "the man most qualified to be president who wasn't." Hughes lost the 1916 race by losing California by just 4,000 votes. The state's governor, Hiram Johnson, did not support Hughes. Johnson was TR's vice presidential candidate on the Progressive Party ticket in 1912.

24. Dalton, 454

25. Dalton, 450

26. Dalton, 462–63.

27. James Amos, *Theodore Roosevelt: Hero to His Valet* (New York: The John Day Company, 1927), 32–33.

28. See Sarah Churchwell, "America's Original Identity Politics," *The New York Review* (February 7, 2019), https://www.nybooks.com/daily/2019/02/07/americas-original -identity-politics/; John Higham, *Strangers in the Land: Patterns of American Nativism, 1860–1925* (New Brunswick, NJ: Rutgers University Press, 1955), 198, https:// archive.org/details/strangersinlandpoohigh_0/page/198.

29. Dalton, 476.

30. Corinne Roosevelt Robinson, *My Brother Theodore Roosevelt*, 330.

31. Dalton, 476.

32. Edith Kermit Roosevelt to Ruth Lee, November 29, 1916, Theodore Roosevelt Collection, Houghton Library, Harvard College.

33. Dalton, 477.

34. Dalton, 368.

35. Dalton, 481.

36. Corinne Roosevelt Robinson, *My Brother Theodore Roosevelt*, 337.

37. Between the two world wars, Ted became a cofounder of the American Legion and, while pursuing a successful business career, served in the U.S. Army Reserve and attended the elite General Staff College. In World War II, he rose to the rank of brigadier general. He led the 26th Infantry during Operation Torch, the invasion of North Africa. For his service in that theater, the Free French commander, General Alphonse Juin, decorated him with the Croix de Guerre. By the approach of D-Day, the Allied invasion of France, Ted was in rapidly failing health, afflicted with a bad heart and debilitating arthritis. Nevertheless, he beseeched the division-level commanding officer, Major General Raymond "Tubby" Barton, to allow him to accompany his men on the initial D-Day assault. After repeatedly turning him down, Barton finally gave in, telling Roosevelt that he did not expect him to return alive. In this way, Brigadier General Theodore Roosevelt Jr. became the only U.S. general officer to make the D-Day landing. On July 12, 1944, a month after his triumph on Utah Beach, Ted died, in France, of a heart attack.

38. Capt. Edward V. Rickenbacker, *Fighting the Flying Circus* (New York: Frederick A. Stokes Company, 1919), 193.

39. Keith Muchowski, "100 Years Ago: The Death of Quentin Roosevelt," New York City College of Technology, City University of New York, 2018. See also https://academicworks.cuny.edu/cgi/viewcontent.cgi?article=1317&context=ny_pubs.

40. Dalton, 503.

41. Sylvia Jukes Morris, 423.

42. Corinne Roosevelt Robinson, *My Brother Theodore Roosevelt*, 345.

43. Corinne Roosevelt Robinson, *My Brother Theodore Roosevelt*, 346.

44. Corinne Roosevelt Robinson, *My Brother Theodore Roosevelt*, 346.

45. Corinne Roosevelt Robinson, *My Brother Theodore Roosevelt*, 347.

46. Dalton, 505.

47. Owen Wister, *Roosevelt: The Story of a Friendship, 1880–1919* (New York: Macmillan, 1930), 371.

48. Dalton, 509.

49. Corinne Roosevelt Robinson, *My Brother Theodore Roosevelt*, 359–60.

50. Dalton, 519.

51. Nathan Miller, *Theodore Roosevelt: A Life* (New York: HarperCollins, 1992), 559.

52. James Amos, *Theodore Roosevelt: Hero to His Valet*, 147.

53. Corinne Roosevelt Robinson, *My Brother Theodore Roosevelt*, 352.

54. Corinne Roosevelt Robinson, *My Brother Theodore Roosevelt*, 362.

55. Wister, 371.

56. James Amos, *Theodore Roosevelt: Hero to His Valet*, 154.

57. Margaret Chanler, *Roman Spring* (Boston: Little, Brown, and Company, 1934), 202.

58. Dalton, 513; Ethel Roosevelt Derby to Richard Derby, January 8, 1919, Theodore Roosevelt Collection, Houghton Library, Harvard College.

59. James Amos, *Theodore Roosevelt: Hero to His Valet*, 156; Corinne Roosevelt Robinson, *My Brother Theodore Roosevelt*, 364.

60. James Amos, *Theodore Roosevelt: Hero to His Valet*, 157.

AFTERWORD: CLEARED FOR STRANGE PORTS

1. Corinne Roosevelt Robinson, *My Brother Theodore Roosevelt* (New York: Charles Scribner's Sons, 1921), 365.

2. Quoted in "In His Memory, January 6, 1919," https://www.trgravesite.org/gravesite.html.

3. Kathleen Dalton, *Theodore Roosevelt: A Strenuous Life* (New York: Alfred A. Knopf, 2002), 517.

4. Michael Patrick Cullinane, "Tasting the Bitter Cup: Theodore Roosevelt's Last Days," *Theodore Roosevelt Association Journal* 44, no. 3 (2023): 16.

5. Dalton, 517.

6. *The New York Times*, June 12, 1920, 2, as quoted in Betty Boyd Caroli, *The Roosevelt Women* (New York: Basic Books, 1998), 135.

7. Corinne Roosevelt Robinson (Conie) to Corinne Roosevelt Alsop (Corinney), November 3, 1921, Theodore Roosevelt Collection, Houghton Library, Harvard College.

8. Dalton, 515.

9. Michael Patrick Cullinane, *Remembering Theodore Roosevelt: Reminiscences of His Contemporaries* (New York: Palgrave Macmillan, 2021), 128.

10. Michael Patrick Cullinane, *Remembering Theodore Roosevelt: Reminiscences of His Contemporaries*, 129.

11. Margaret Chanler, *Roman Spring* (Boston: Little, Brown and Company, 1934), 255.

12. Anna Roosevelt Cowles, *Letters from Theodore Roosevelt to Anna Roosevelt Cowles, 1870–1918* (New York: Charles Scribner's Sons, 1924).

13. Anna Roosevelt Cowles (Bamie) to Corinne Roosevelt Robinson (Conie), March 10, 1926, Theodore Roosevelt Collection, Houghton Library, Harvard College.

14. Corinne Roosevelt Robinson, *My Brother Theodore Roosevelt*, 354.

15. Michael Patrick Cullinane, *Remembering Theodore Roosevelt: Reminiscences of His Contemporaries*, 67.

16. Caroli, 179.

17. Sara Delano Roosevelt to Corinne Roosevelt Robinson (Conie), November 17, 1928, Theodore Roosevelt Collection, Houghton Library, Harvard College.

18. Caroli, 117.

19. Caroli, 128.

20. Corinne Roosevelt Robinson (Conie) to Henry Pringle, September 22, 1930, Theodore Roosevelt Collection, Houghton Library, Harvard College.

21. Research notes of Henry Pringle, Theodore Roosevelt Collection Houghton Library, Harvard College.

22. Edith Kermit Roosevelt to Ethel Roosevelt Derby, November 8, 1931, Theodore Roosevelt Collection, Houghton Library, Harvard College.

23. Dalton, 517.

24. Michael Teague, *Mrs. L.: Conversations with Alice Roosevelt Longworth* (Garden City, NY: Doubleday, 1981), 36–37.

25. Chanler, *Roman Spring*, 203.

26. Caroli, 199.

27. Major Archibald Butt, *Taft and Roosevelt: The Intimate Letters of Archie Butt, Military Aide*, Vol. 1 (Garden City, NY: Doubleday, Doran, 1930), 181.

28. Dalton, 507.

29. Mrs. Theodore Roosevelt Sr., Mrs. Kermit Roosevelt, Richard Derby, and Kermit Roosevelt, *Cleared for Strange Ports* (New York: Charles Scribner's Sons, 1927), 5.

30. Sylvia Jukes Morris, *Edith Kermit Roosevelt: Portrait of a First Lady* (New York: Random House, 2010), 542.

31. *60 Minutes*, CBS News Broadcast Archives, "'Princess' Alice is 90," February 17, 1974, Introduction by Morley Safer and interview by Eric Sevareid.

32. Stacy A. Cordery, *Alice: Alice Roosevelt Longworth, from White House Princess to Washington Power Broker* (New York: Viking, 2007), 472.

33. Ibid.

34. Stacy A. Rozek Cordery, "'Princess Alice': The Life and Times of Alice Roosevelt Longworth," *Theodore Roosevelt Association Journal* 23, no. 4 (2000): 10–14, TRAJ023_4_D.pdf; Stacy Cordery, "Defining a Woman's Duty: The Effect of the Roosevelt Women on TR's Views About Women," September 21, 2018, Theodore Roosevelt Symposium, Dickinson State University.

35. Theodore Roosevelt, "Rural Life," *Outlook Magazine*, August 27, 1910.

36. Theodore Roosevelt to Theodore Douglas Robinson, September 26, 1902, Private Collection.

37. Theodore Roosevelt, Diary, January 5, 1879, in Edward P. Kohn, ed., *A Most Glorious Ride: The Diaries of Theodore Roosevelt, 1877–1886* (Albany: State University of New York Press, 2015), 72.

Index

Image Credits

1. Courtesy of Sagamore Hill National Historic Site, National Park Service, Oyster Bay, NY.
2. Special Collections, Fine Arts Library, Harvard College.
3. Theodore Roosevelt Collection Photographs, Houghton Library, Harvard College.
4. E. H. T. Anthony. *The Funeral of President Lincoln, New-York, April 25th.* Broadway New York, ca. 1865. Courtesy Library of Congress, Prints & Photographs Division.
5. Courtesy of Sagamore Hill National Historic Site, National Park Service, Oyster Bay, NY.
6. Photograph by Allison Davis O'Keefe, Sagamore Hill National Historic Site, National Park Service, Oyster Bay, NY.
7. Photograph by Allison Davis O'Keefe, Sagamore Hill National Historic Site, National Park Service, Oyster Bay, NY.
8. Courtesy of Sagamore Hill National Historic Site, National Park Service, Oyster Bay, NY.
9. Courtesy of Sagamore Hill National Historic Site, National Park Service, Oyster Bay, NY.
10. Photograph by Allison Davis O'Keefe, Sagamore Hill National Historic Site, National Park Service, Oyster Bay, NY.
11. Photograph by Allison Davis O'Keefe, Sagamore Hill National Historic Site, National Park Service, Oyster Bay, NY.
12. Theodore Roosevelt Collection Photographs, Houghton Library, Harvard College.
13. Theodore Roosevelt Collection Photographs, Houghton Library, Harvard College.
14. Photograph by Julius Ludovici, ca. 1883. Theodore Roosevelt Collection Photographs, Houghton Library, Harvard College.
15. Photograph by Allen & Rowell, Boston, Massachusetts. Theodore Roosevelt Collection Photographs, Houghton Library, Harvard College.
16. Photographs by Allen & Rowell, Boston, Massachusetts, May 10, 1879. Theodore Roosevelt Collection Photographs, Houghton Library, Harvard College.

17. Photographs by Allen & Rowell, Boston, Massachusetts, May 10, 1879. Theodore Roosevelt Collection Photographs, Houghton Library, Harvard College.
18. Theodore Roosevelt Collection Photographs, Houghton Library, Harvard College.
19. Theodore Roosevelt Collection Photographs, Houghton Library, Harvard College.
20. Photograph by Allison Davis O'Keefe, Sagamore Hill National Historic Site, National Park Service, Oyster Bay, NY.
21. Roosevelt, Theodore. *Theodore Roosevelt Papers: Series 8: Personal Diaries, -1884; Vol. 7, 1884, Feb. 14–Dec. 17. -Dec. 17, 1884.* Courtesy Library of Congress, Manuscripts Division, Theodore Roosevelt Papers.
22. Courtesy of Sagamore Hill National Historic Site, National Park Service, Oyster Bay, NY.
23. Bain, George Grantham, Photographer. *Theodore Roosevelt in.*, 1885. Courtesy Library of Congress, Prints & Photographs Division.
24. Theodore Roosevelt Collection Photographs, Houghton Library, Harvard College.
25. Theodore Roosevelt Collection Photographs, Houghton Library, Harvard College.
26. Theodore Roosevelt Collection Photographs, Houghton Library, Harvard College.
27. Photograph by Pirie MacDonald, February 17, 1900. Theodore Roosevelt Collection Photographs, Houghton Library, Harvard College.
28. Courtesy Library of Congress, Prints & Photographs Division.
29. Courtesy of Eleanor Roosevelt National Historic Site, National Park Service.
30. *Mrs. Theodore Roosevelt / Henry, Washington, D.C.*, None [between 1901–1909] Photograph. Courtesy Library of Congress, Prints & Photographs Division.
31. Theodore Roosevelt Collection Photographs, Houghton Library, Harvard College.
32. Personal collection of the author.
33. Edward Windsor Kemble, *Harper's Weekly*, February 17, 1912.
34. Courtesy of Sagamore Hill National Historic Site, National Park Service, Oyster Bay, NY.

About the Author

EDWARD F. O'KEEFE is the CEO of the Theodore Roosevelt Presidential Library Foundation. He previously spent two decades in broadcast and digital media, during which time he received a Primetime Emmy Award for his work with Anthony Bourdain, two Webby Awards, the Edward R. Murrow Award, and a George Foster Peabody Award for ABC News coverage of 9/11. A former fellow at the Harvard Kennedy School, he graduated with honors from Georgetown University. He was born in North Dakota and lives in New York with his wife, daughter, and son.